CHANGING STATES, CHANGING NATIONS

This book presents the remarkable constitutional reforms undertaken by the Blair and Brown governments in the UK. The reforms are remarkable in that they had the potential to change the way Britons understood the national identity of the UK. The book illuminates the ambitions of the key players in Whitehall and Westminster and is enriched through a study of comparable constitutional reforms in Canada and Australia: the Charter of Rights and Freedoms pioneered by Pierre Trudeau and the attempt by Paul Keating to make Australia a Republic. The Canadian and Australian chapters are a contribution to the political history of those nations and a device for understanding the changes in Britain.

The author is an expert in the use of Freedom of Information and was a senior policy maker in Whitehall working primarily on constitutional reform. Readers will benefit from the author's unrivalled access to interviewees and documentary sources in the three countries covered in the book.

Changing States, Changing Nations

Constitutional Reform and National Identity in the Late Twentieth Century

Andrew McDonald

•HART•
OXFORD • LONDON • NEW YORK • NEW DELHI • SYDNEY

HART PUBLISHING
Bloomsbury Publishing Plc
Kemp House, Chawley Park, Cumnor Hill, Oxford, OX2 9PH, UK
1385 Broadway, New York, NY 10018, USA
29 Earlsfort Terrace, Dublin 2, Ireland

HART PUBLISHING, the Hart/Stag logo, BLOOMSBURY and the Diana logo are trademarks of Bloomsbury Publishing Plc

First published in Great Britain 2020

A catalogue record for this book is available from the British Library.

Library of Congress Cataloging-in-Publication data

Names: McDonald, Andrew, author.

Title: Changing states, changing nations : constitutional reform and national identity in the late twentieth century / Andrew McDonald.

Description: Oxford, UK ; New York, NY : Hart Publishing, an imprint of Bloomsbury Publishing, 2020. | Includes bibliographical references and index.

Identifiers: LCCN 2020035986 (print) | LCCN 2020035987 (ebook) | ISBN 9781509928729 (hardback) | ISBN 9781509943494 (paperback) | ISBN 9781509928736 (Epub) | ISBN 9781509928743 (pdf)

Subjects: LCSH: Constitutional history—Great Britain. | Constitutional history—United States. | Constitutional history—Canada. | Constitutional history—Australia. | Law reform—History. | Constitutional law. | National characteristics. | Citizenship.

Classification: LCC K3161 .M373 2020 (print) | LCC K3161 (ebook) | DDC 342.03—dc23

LC record available at https://lccn.loc.gov/2020035986

LC ebook record available at https://lccn.loc.gov/2020035987

ISBN: HB: 978-1-50992-872-9
ePDF: 978-1-50992-874-3
ePub: 978-1-50992-873-6

Typeset by Compuscript Ltd, Shannon

In memory of my parents, to whom I owe everything.

AJW (Mac) McDonald (1920–1986)

Eileen McDonald (née Sharkey) (1922–2013)

‘Change is the nature of life, and its hope.’

Gore Vidal, *Washington DC*

FOREWORD

In August 1977, I sat watching Steve Ovett in the 1500 metres final in the World Cup. He was fast and stylish. The best miler that Britain or, quite likely, the world had ever produced. Having watched him glide to victory with characteristic ease, I remarked to my father that that would help 'our' points total. He looked at me as though I had taken leave of my senses. He had cheered Ovett home alongside me. But he could not see why his son should refer to the team as 'ours'. Neither Britain nor England was represented in the World Cup: Ovett was running for Europe. My father – politically radical but socially conservative – could take no pleasure in the success of a European team. A reluctant supporter of Britain's political ambitions in Europe he could not relate to it instinctively as his – or ours. Britain was his country. He had fought for it in the war. He had raised his family there. He respected its traditions, even if its politics frustrated him. He had no time for its monarchy but he would stand for the national anthem and for its flag and he would pause for the Act of Remembrance. He hated British snobbery but he lauded Britain's commitment to fair play. He was, by most measures, a patriot. This was not a reasoned choice; it was an unarticulated instinct.

In his account of the way that nationalism is woven into our consciousness, Michael Billig pauses to make a confession. When a British sportsman succeeds, he cheers. If he or she beats off international opponents he takes delight in their superiority. For a moment, We are better than Them. Billig – who dissects modern nationalism with a critical and disapproving mien – cannot help himself. He is clearly as puzzled by his reactions as he is disappointed. But the next victory will still bring him pleasure.[1]

Loyalty to the nation is persistent and pervasive. Commonly the product of ethnic identity, of attachment to place, of commitment to common ideals, of faith in a future destiny and of pride in a shared past – it can be all these things, or none of them. And our own experience of national identity is not constant over time: my sense of Britishness is different from my father's. Mine is not the product of wartime, nor of a sense of struggle from impoverished origins. Mine has been shaped by a more affluent, safer life – and a life in a country whose social and ethnic composition has changed out of all recognition since my father's youth. The outward expression of my patriotism might have much in common with my father's – the flag, the anthem, the Act of Remembrance – but I am honouring a quite different country.

[1] Michael Billig, *Banal Nationalism* (London, Sage, 1995) 125.

Perspectives

I state this at the outset because it seems fair, in a book about the nation and national identity, to be clear about my starting points – not least because the book is particularly concerned with *my* nation. I am, by most measures, a patriot. There is, in addition, a personal dimension to my interest in reform of the state: I worked on constitutional reform as an official in the UK civil service and so I am practitioner as well as observer. But this is not a memoir. My involvement came after the British reforms which are the primary subject of chapter two and before those which are the subject of chapter five. I served as Constitution Director from 2003–05. Later, I was the first CEO of the Independent Parliamentary Standards Authority (2009–14), a constitutional novelty in that it involved external regulation of Parliament, but not an innovation that is relevant to the main theme of this book.

I have not used my status as a former official to seek privileged access to official papers.

My perspective on this topic has been shaped in part by my time as a policy-maker. The preoccupations of modern public policy are converging. Across the world, administrations are trying to lever up the quality of public services while minimising the burden on the taxpayer. They are searching for solutions which bring together public, private and third sector resources. They are focussing on meeting the particular needs of local communities and of individual citizens.

Consider one example. When Britain brought its Freedom of Information (FOI) legislation into effect in January 2005, it was following a course which some 50 states had already travelled. Each had to address local concerns in framing their legislation, but if (as many do) we concentrate on those differences we are holding the wrong end of the telescope to our eye. FOI is a presumptive right to official information, qualified by exemptions and overseen by an independent adjudicator (typically, a court or ombudsman). The balance between access and secrecy can be struck in many different ways, but those designing and running FOI systems are essentially tackling a common problem, with similar solutions. The potential for learning from one another is enormous, but these opportunities are taken rarely. All too often we choose to focus on what it is that makes our own problem distinct or more difficult – meriting bespoke treatment. And we ignore the insights and experience of others.

Last, but not least, I am an historian by training and my methods are those of an historian.

ACKNOWLEDGEMENTS

I have incurred many debts in the preparation of this manuscript and I happily acknowledge them here. The research was made possible by support from a number of institutions and individuals. Notable among those are the Fulbright Commission, which granted me a fellowship; the Institute of Governmental Studies at the University of California, Berkeley which provided a congenial and stimulating academic home during the fellowship; and Sir Alex Allan, then my permanent secretary at the Department for Constitutional Affairs, who granted me a sabbatical from my official duties when others would not have done so. Further support was provided by the Department of Canadian Heritage and by the Australian National University, who generously made me a visiting fellow. It has been a pleasure to work with the editorial team at Hart Publishing. Scores of interviewees have given of their time and insights and I am grateful to each of them and to all those individuals who have contributed ideas and who have commented on the draft. I particularly thank Belinda Brown, Jack Citrin, Philip Coppel, Mary Dawson, Ian Gambles, Robert Hazell, Louise London, Joseph McDonald, Juliet McDonald, Ross McKibbin, Giles Mandelbrote, Emran Mian, Warren Newman, Dennis Pearce, Sir Hayden Phillips, Michael Piggott, the late Nelson Polsby, Peter Riddell, Martin Sixsmith, Susan Sterett, Jack Straw, Greg Terrill and Michael Wills. I owe a special debt of gratitude to Juliet, my daughter, for her forbearance with this book during its long gestation.

London, May 2020

CONTENTS

Foreword ... *ix*
Acknowledgements ... *xi*
Archives and Manuscript Collections Consulted, with Abbreviations Used in Notes ... *xvii*
Publisher's Note ... *xix*

1. Constitutional Reform and National Identity ... 1
I. Constitutional Reform in Britain under Blair and Brown ... 2
II. Comparative Studies of Constitutional Reform ... 3
III. Rationale for Selection of Case Studies ... 5
IV. Definitions: Nation and Nation State ... 9
V. National Myths and Symbols ... 11
VI. National Identity ... 13
VII. Changes in National Identity ... 14
VIII. National Identity and Constitutional Reform ... 15
IX. Comparative Case Studies ... 21
X. Changing States, Changing Nations ... 22

2. 'Doing Good By Stealth': Tony Blair and Reform of the British Constitution ... 24
I. Labour and Constitutional Reform ... 25
II. Labour and the Maximalists: The 1987 Parliament ... 28
III. Labour Policy-making in the Wake of the 1992 Defeat ... 32
IV. Labour and the Nation ... 34
V. New Labour and the Constitution ... 35
VI. Shuffling the Pack: Preparing for Government ... 41
VII. New Labour, No Britain ... 48
VIII. Cook-Maclennan ... 49
IX. From the Manifesto to the Polls ... 56
X. The Election ... 58
XI. Into Government ... 59
XII. The First Session: May 1997–November 1998 ... 62
XIII. The Second Session: November 1998–November 1999 ... 68
XIV. The End of the Affair: New Labour and the Liberal Democrats ... 73
XV. The Third and Fourth Sessions: November 1999–June 2001 ... 75
XVI. The First Term: Constitutional Reform Delivered? ... 76
XVII. The 2001 Manifesto ... 78

XVIII. The Constitution in the Second Term: 2001–05 79
XIX. The Constitution in the Third Term: Blair's Final Years 84
XX. Britain's Quiet Constitutional Revolution 86

3. 'Just Watch Me': Pierre Trudeau and the Canadian Constitution 88
I. Canada at the Centenary 89
II. Enter Trudeau 92
III. From the Centenary to Victoria 101
IV. Stasis 104
V. From PQ Victory to Liberal Defeat 105
VI. A Final Chance 111
VII. Quebec Votes 113
VIII. Constitutional Reform in the Wake of the No Vote 115
IX. Going it Alone 120
X. One Last Try 129
XI. Aftermath 139
XII. Consequences 142
XIII. The Sesquicentenary of Confederation 148

4. 'A Small But Significant Step': Australia and the Republic 150
I. The Combatants 150
II. Enter Paul Keating 156
III. Mapping the Course: The Republic Advisory Committee 160
IV. Becalmed 162
V. John Howard and the Republic 166
VI. The Convention 169
VII. Australia Votes No 173
VIII. Why the Republic was Lost 177
IX. Where Next for Republican Australia? 187
X. Constitutional Change and National Identity 191

5. 'Power to The People'?: The UK Constitution After Blair 194
I. Brown Arrives 194
II. Britishness 196
III. Governance of Britain 198
IV. The Coalition and Constitutional Reform 200
V. Brexit 203
VI. What Next for the British Constitution? 205
VII. Public Engagement 208
VIII. Public Reaction to the Reforms 211
IX. The Future of Britain 212
X. Brown and the Constitution 215

6. Changing States, Changing Nations 216
I. Three Stories: One Pattern? 216
II. Lessons for Reformers? 221
III. Re-engineering National Identity 226
IV. Changing States, Changing Nations 229

Note On Sources 233
Select Bibliography 234
Index 239

ARCHIVES AND MANUSCRIPT COLLECTIONS CONSULTED, WITH ABBREVIATIONS USED IN NOTES

Alberta, Lougheed	Papers of Peter Lougheed, Provincial Archives of Alberta
BL CU	British Library, London: Constitution Unit Papers (De Res 165)
FCO, FOI	Foreign & Commonwealth Office, London: Freedom of Information release on Canada, 1980–82
Justice	Records of the Department of Justice, Ottawa
LAC, John.	Library and Archives Canada, Ottawa: Ted Johnson Papers Library and Archives
LAC, Trud.	Library and Archives Canada, Ottawa: Pierre Elliott Trudeau Papers
NAA, Con. Con.	Papers of the Constitutional Convention, National Archives of Australia, Canberra
NAA, Keating	Papers of Paul Keating, National Archives of Australia, Sydney
NLA, CCF	National Library of Australia, Papers of the Constitutional Centenary Foundation
PCO, ATI	Privy Council Office, Ottawa, Canada: Access to Information release
PM&C, Canberra	Records of the Department of the Prime Minister and Cabinet, Canberra
RAC	Records of the Republic Advisory Committee in the possession of Prof. George Winterton, University of Sydney
State Lib. NSW, ARM	Papers of the Australian Republican Movement, State Library of New South Wales, Sydney

State Lib. NSW, Collins	Papers of Peter Collins, State Library of New South Wales, Sydney
Syd, ARM	Records of the Australian Republican Movement (ARM) in the possession of the ARM at its headquarters in Sydney

PUBLISHER'S NOTE

1

Constitutional Reform and National Identity

A browse through new non-fiction titles over the last 20 years would serve as testimony to the growing interest in identity politics and, in particular, to the burgeoning work on national identity. Nationalism of one sort or another has long commanded the interest of scholars, but in recent years the methodology used by sociologists and political scientists studying nationalism has become more complex. As liberals become ever more fearful of nativism and populism, so the reader browsing new works has become used to doom-laden titles such as *How Democracy Ends*.[1] Trump's reckless nationalism in the US has done much to encourage this mood. The same may be said for the authoritarianism of Putin's Russia. Plenty of ink has been spilt on the Russification of the former Soviet Union.[2] Others have chosen to document the growth of more assertive national identities in the former Soviet Republics.[3] Leaving aside these studies, which are inspired by fear of actual or potential conflicts, there has been a comparable increase in scholarly work on the national identity – and, or nationalisms – of otherwise peaceable Western democracies. The imagining of the Spanish nation has attracted significant attention, notably from Kamen, from Balfour and Quiroga and now from JH Elliott.[4] This has clearly been encouraged by the possibility that the Basque country or Catalonia might secede. The agonies of Britain have aroused the interest of historians and political scientists who want to understand Brexit or to determine whether the UK will remain united.

The Left has always had an ambiguous relationship with the nation state, tempted by it as the most effective vehicle for collective enterprise and sacrifice but fearing its ability to mobilise ethnic nationalism, which has cast its deep shadow over the twentieth century. In recent years there has been an attempt to recover

[1] David Runciman, *How Democracy Ends* (London, Profile Books, 2018); or if you prefer your doom in the plural, see Steven Levitsky and Daniel Ziblatt, *How Democracies Die* (Viking, London, 2018).

[2] See, eg, Arkady Ostrovsky, *The Invention of Russia* (London, Atlantic Books, 2015).

[3] Timothy Snyder, *The Reconstruction of Nations* (New Haven and London, Yale University Press, 2003).

[4] Henry Kamen, *Imagining Spain* (New Haven and London, Yale University Press, 2008); Sebastian Balfour and Alejandro Quiroga, *The Reinvention of Spain* (Oxford, Oxford University Press, 2007); JH Elliott, *Scots and Catalans* (New Haven and London, Yale University Press, 2018).

the nation state for benign purposes. This exercise has often been clouded with controversy, as the efforts of Goodhart, Tamir and Judis show.[5]

The involvement of historians in the debates over national identity was predictable. If politicians are tempted to dream up new futures for their nations and to base them on the historic development of their countries, it is inevitable that historians will feel the need to engage with these amateur interlopers. This tension has been played out in episodes of the 'history wars' where historians in the US, the UK, Canada and Australia have felt it necessary to fight off what they have seen as the corrupting influence of politicians on historical scholarship.[6]

Turning more specifically to the topic of this book, constitutions have attracted some interest from lawyers and political scientists exploring whether national identity can subsist in fundamental law. This is particularly evident in work on the post-Soviet constitutions in Eastern Europe and on some studies of comparative constitutions but it is fair to say that the theme has not commanded the attention of many scholars.

This introductory chapter has three purposes. First, it sets out the narrow and, then, the broader objectives of the book. Second, it explains the selection of three episodes of constitutional reform for particular study. And third, it acknowledges that the territory on which we are about to embark is fraught with methodological and definitional difficulties and so I offer a navigational guide to the perils ahead. In doing so I explain what the book is *not* as much as what it *is*.

I. Constitutional Reform in Britain under Blair and Brown

At its narrowest, this is a book about constitutional reforms undertaken in Britain by the first Blair administration. It seeks to trace the origins of those reforms and to explain how they came about. There is a particular explanatory need here because the reforms were not accompanied by a public narrative setting out their objectives. And these were not trivial reforms. Under the Blair Governments of 1997–2007 – and especially in their first term (1997–2001) – the British constitution underwent radical, transformative change. In quick succession, the Blair administrations devolved power to Scotland, Wales and London; and gave Britons a Human Rights Act. Subsequently, the Blair Government legislated for a new Supreme Court; introduced new methods of voting; provided new rights of access

[5] David Goodhart, *The British Dream* (London, Atlantic Books, 2013); Yael Tamir, *Why Nationalism* (Princeton and London, Princeton University Press, 2019); John B Judis, *The Nationalist Revival* (Columbia Global Reports, New York, 2018).

[6] This topic is discussed through the book but the best primer on the topic, from an Australian viewpoint, is Stuart Macintyre and Anna Clark, *The History Wars* (Carlton, Victoria, Melbourne University Press, 2004).

to official information; and redefined the relationship between the executive and the judiciary. There were setbacks: reform of the House of Lords never got further than the early compromise to eject most of the hereditary peers; English regional assemblies proved to be a diversion; and the bid to reform the office of Lord Chancellor ended in a last minute reprieve for the title, if not the substance, of the post. But taken together the reforms represent the most dramatic changes the British state has experienced since the introduction of universal suffrage in 1918–28.

This, then, is change of symbolic *and* substantive significance. Devolution of power most obviously raised questions of national identity – not just for Wales and Scotland, but for England and for the union as a whole. Asymmetric devolution – in which power is devolved differentially to subsidiary nations and regions – is technically feasible but it begs a number of questions. Why should I regard the devolution settlement as final if I know that my neighbour has been given greater powers of self-determination than I have? And why, if I am English, should I tolerate the absence of a parliament devoted to the consideration of English issues?

We will explore the way in which the Blair reforms were conceived and the manner of their execution. They had the potential to reshape the British state and to change our understanding of what it was to be a British citizen. Why, then, the public modesty about such radicalism? The Blair Government was not known for its modesty on other aspects of its record.

II. Comparative Studies of Constitutional Reform

Having explored the British origins of these reforms, we will then look elsewhere for other examples of constitutional reforms which had a bearing on the state and on citizens' sense of the nation. In looking for parallels, we will restrict ourselves to fundamental reforms (or attempted reforms) in two other major common law jurisdictions at or about the turn of the twentieth/twenty-first century. We do so in the hope they will shed light on the British experience; that they will contribute to the constitutional history of those nations; and that they will serve the broader purpose of this book.

Our criteria lead us to two stories of reform in other Commonwealth countries in the latter part of the twentieth century: the introduction of the Charter of Rights and Freedoms in Canada and the attempt to make Australia a Republic. I will describe each briefly here before returning to them in chapters three and four.

A. Canada's Charter of Rights and Freedoms

In 1980 Canada came close, not for the first time and not for the last, to splitting apart. The people of Quebec voted on whether to secede. The national Prime Minister, Pierre Trudeau, led a successful campaign against secession and responded to the vote by bringing forward sweeping reforms: a constitution exclusively under Canadian control and a new bill of rights (the Charter) defining and protecting the core values shared by all Canadians. Trudeau, in his last term in office, set out to entrench liberal rights *and* to strengthen Canadians' sense of common purpose.

In closely choreographed moves, the Westminster and Ottawa Parliaments passed the Trudeau reforms into law in 1982. Their passage marked a turning point in Canada's constitutional development. The Charter has propelled the Supreme Court into a central role in Canadian public life. The Court has not hesitated to strike down federal and state laws nor has it shied away from a dialogue with the legislature on the constitutionality of proposed legislation and from resolving controversial policy issues. Justices have learned to become public figures and to write judgments which are meant for a non-specialist audience. Ministers, for their part, have learned to accept the Court as a new player in Canadian politics. Aside from anything else, they have referred policy issues to it in the hope that a Court decision might shield them from criticism.

If 1982 revolutionised the country's constitutional order, it also gave Canadians a statement of what it was to be Canadian. Opinion poll evidence shows strong support for the Charter both as a symbol of the country and as an expression of national identity. Even in Quebec, the Charter has enjoyed consistent popularity.

The Charter has its critics. Some see it as divisive. Others point to judicial activism and claim that the Charter has made Canada more like the US (in other words, a move in the wrong direction). Canadian unity, the same critics maintain, is no more secure than it was in 1982: another referendum on Quebec succession (the third) remains possible once the political and economic circumstances in the province are more favourable.

But none of this can gainsay the Charter's success in ushering in a rights-based culture and its remarkable hold on the public imagination. This is constitutional change which spoke to its popular audience, rapidly securing a prominent place in the public consciousness. Trudeau's ambitions as a nation-builder remain contentious to this day, and his record contested. We will explain how the changes were brought about and will consider the report card some four decades on.

B. An Australian Republic

Popular support for an Australian republic had been increasing steadily, but unspectacularly, since the 1950s. The cause took on a new urgency with the appointment of Paul Keating as Prime Minister in 1991. In the following year he set out a new vision for Australia – as a multicultural country, a country which would make good its obligations to the Indigenous Peoples, an Asian country and a regional power integrated ever more closely with the economies of East Asia. There was no place in his vision for Australia's British legacy – and certainly no place for the Queen as head of state.

Keating's aggressive prosecution of his agenda put the opposition Liberal-National coalition on the defensive. Even after Keating's Australian Labor Party (ALP) lost the 1996 general election the Republic question did not go away. The incoming coalition had already committed itself to call a constitutional convention to consider the question. The convention held in 1998 led in turn to a referendum the following year – a referendum to decide whether the Australian head of state should be a president nominated by the Prime Minister and appointed by Parliament. Despite 65 per cent popular support for the general proposition that Australia should become a Republic, the referendum was decisively rejected. The issue has not gone away – it remains part of the ALP policy slate – but it is no longer a first-order question.

And so this is a story of a failed project. Or, at best, a project which has stalled. It is unquestionably a story of an attempt to capture a nation's imagination with a new vision of what might be. A story of an attempt to enlist support for a new direction and a rejection of its former course. The new vision was not, at its core, about constitutional change but the constitutional proposition came to symbolise Keating's broader agenda. Under most circumstances, the Australian head of state has few powers: the office is insignificant unless imbued with symbolic importance. This story is all about symbolism. It is no less important for that, but we should be clear that we are not discussing changes to substantive constitutional powers. Symbolic change depends, critically, on the way the issue is communicated to the people and the way in which support for the proposition is sought.

III. Rationale for Selection of Case Studies

The selection of the Australian and Canadian stories is open to challenge and it is worth exploring some of those challenges here. First, we should tidy out of the way some of the objections which are most readily dismissed. The UK, as we all know, does not have a codified constitution. But no constitution is fully codified and even the British have taken some cautious steps towards codification and the introduction of higher law. And so we are dealing with questions of degree here, not differences between absolutes. The mechanisms of change we are studying here also differ: in our chosen cases we have two examples of statutory reform and one attempt at change of an embedded constitution (Australia). But our interest in all three is in the motivation of the political actors, their engagement with their people and their impact on the nation. And in those matters, these parliamentary jurisdictions have much in common. Moreover, they are three common law jurisdictions with a strong sense of legal community between them. Their judges trade precedents across jurisdictional boundaries and the Australian and Canadian judiciary more or less cheerfully acknowledge their debt to the British common law. In matters of constitutional law, British precedent continues to inform practice in Canada and Australia, even after the patriation of their constitutions. The judicialisation of politics provides the backdrop for each of our case studies. In each of the three jurisdictions studied here there are vigorous debates about the power of the judiciary vis à vis other branches of government.

If the constitutional diversity of the three countries does not threaten our approach, what of the way in which the three national communities think of themselves? Is the idea of 'the nation' seen from such radically different perspectives as to invalidate the present exercise?

One way of thinking about those questions might be to consider the structure of the nation states. Two are federal; one is not. But the distinction does not take us far. It reminds us that in Canada and Australia there are state and provincial identities which compete with the nation for affection and loyalty. But the same is true of Britain. Wales and Scotland have long had national identities of their own and the new, quasi-federal structure of the union provides greater opportunity to articulate those identities – internally and externally. Equally, we are beginning to see that it has the flexibility to allow the expression of English identity.

But this gives rise to a more important distinction amongst our sample. Britain and Canada are both multi-national states: they have within them communities which meet our definition of what it is to be national. Even if we put Northern Ireland to one side, we are still left with the Welsh, Scots and Québécois. All three now have national political leaders and legislatures of their own. This, as we will see, gives national identity a particular dynamic – especially in Canada, where the prospect that the nation may break up has been a persistent theme in national politics ever since federation.

If only two of our countries are multi-national, all three of them are multi-racial and multi-ethnic. We cannot attempt here to explore how racial and ethnic identity has a differential impact on individuals' understanding of nationhood – but we should be cognisant of this diversity in reaching any conclusions about popular reactions to the nation. And we should pause to note the radical differences in response offered by each country to the challenges of racial and ethnic diversity. Each has sought to resolve the tension between the unity of the nation on the one hand and the tug of racial and ethnic identity on the other. Canada and Britain have embraced a liberal multiculturalism; whereas Australia has come to espouse a strain of multiculturalism which urges minorities to respect their obligations to the nation, and to resist a descent into 'tribalism'.

Continue to work away at this theme, and we might note that two of these countries were settled by Europeans (many of them from the third). And that those two struggle with mixed success to locate their Indigenous Peoples within their nations' self-image. Pursue this theme further and we might wonder whether the antiquity of one of our countries might set it apart from the others. But before we embrace this as yet further evidence of diversity amongst our sample, we should enter a word of caution. After all the UK did not assume its present territorial limits until 1922, with the creation of the Irish Free State, and its departure from the European Union shows a continued appetite for radical change. The long history of each of the component parts of the UK is, of course, relevant to our notion of Britishness, but the relationship is neither simple nor direct. Indeed, Linda Colley has shown us that British national identity was forged no earlier than the eighteenth century.[7]

What are we to make of these contrasting routes to nationhood and of the diversity of the populations of our three countries? First, this discussion should serve as a caution against any simplistic conclusions about what the nation 'means' to its people. Our perception of the nation may be refracted through our attachment to our social class, our locality, our ethnic community and our race. These attachments may supplement one another or co-exist in tension. One resident of Montreal will be proud to be Québécois and Canadian; his neighbour may reject this duality. And so any conclusions about the impact of public policy on the personal experience of national identity must necessarily be cautious.

Would we be better off with a sample of three states, each constituted by a single nation whose composition is ethnically and racially uniform? We would have fewer variables – but then we would not have a sample at all: modern states are poly-ethnic and often multi-national. The nation state is not, and never has been, a harmonious unit in which all communities respond to the nation as one. The nation state has always been contested and challenged from within. Mass migration and increasing ethnic diversity ask new and difficult questions of the nation state, but we would do well to recall that the nation has always been in question and national identity is best understood as dynamic, not static.

That said, we should also note that each of our countries has a distinct starting point in its approach to its policy on the nation. Each is trying to resolve peculiar national and ethnic tensions, and is doing so within the limits of a public discourse which may be more or less comfortable about diversity and immigration. But in the last 40 years each of our countries has wrestled with two questions. The first is the larger and more elusive. In the face of increasing and persistent diversity, how can we fashion a sense of national identity which speaks to the nation as a whole? The second is consequential. In conjuring up a new (or old) vision of the nation, how are we to resolve the tension between an individual's attachment to the particular (a class, ethnicity or race, for example) and his/her bond to the general (the nation)?

We can see these questions running through recent debates. Samuel Huntington's controversial 2004 study of American national identity asks simply, Who are we? His answer celebrates the virtues of America's Anglo-Protestant culture and argues that its distinctive qualities should be nurtured if the country is not to lose its way.[8] In a series of speeches in 2004–06, Britain's Prime Minister-in-waiting, Gordon Brown, set out to define Britishness. His conclusion focused on three values which, he maintained, are emblematic of what is best about the British: liberty, responsibility and fairness. In Canada, the Conservative Party leader Stephen Harper

[7] Linda Colley, *Britons. Forging the Nation, 1707–1837* (New Haven, Yale University Press, 1992) *passim*.

[8] Samuel P Huntington, *Who are We? The Challenges to America's Identity* (New York, Simon and Schuster Paperbacks, 2004).

used his successful 2006 general election campaign to delineate Canadian national character. And in Australia the most recent engagement in the so-called History Wars was provoked by the opening of the National Museum of Australia. In this partisan bout, politicians and academics argued over whose story should be told in the new museum: the history of the European settlers who 'discovered' the continent or the history of the Indigenous Peoples; the history of the British dominion that became a sovereign state or the history of an immigrant country, of a country of minorities?

Before we place too much emphasis on the diversity of our three countries, it is worth dwelling on the challenges they share. At or about the turn of the century, each of them was experiencing strains common to liberal democracy at that time. Each was searching for a policy response to high net immigration;[9] each showed a lack of trust in public institutions and in their elected representatives, and voters in each were more volatile, willing to weaken the position of hitherto dominant political parties. In part because of these tensions, political leaders in each were questioning the course set by their predecessors and seeking to determine a new national purpose or project.[10]

I should be clear at the outset that this is not a conventional work of comparative political analysis. I have not selected a number of case studies and subjected them to uniform scrutiny. Nor have I cast my net wide in the hope of distilling some universal patterns or explanations. The primary purpose of the book, as stated, is to understand the British reforms. The Canadian and Australian examples have been selected both because I think they will help us to do that and because they merit study in their own right. Nor do I argue that their stories are unique. The book might have been written with different case studies or, indeed, with different case studies from Australia and Canada. The constitutional status of the Indigenous Peoples in both countries might, for example, have been candidates. Ultimately, I have alighted on these two stories because I think they help us to understand Britain and to understand broader questions of constitutional reform and national identity. The three countries studied here are, of course, quite different in structure and heritage: one is experimenting with asymmetric devolution; two are federal; and one is bicultural. We need to respect these differences but they

[9] Whether measured in absolute or proportionate terms, Canada, Australia and the UK were in the top ten countries for highest immigration in 2015: Gilles Pison, 'Which countries have the most immigrants' (10 March 2019) *The Conversation*.

[10] For evidence of declining trust, see Hansard Society, *Audit of Political Engagement* (2019) esp. 8–9; Australian Election Study (2019) esp. 98, 99; Angus Reid Institute, 'Trust in Government: Canadians wary of politicians and their intentions' (2019); for voter volatility see Edward Fieldhouse et al, *Electoral Shocks* (Oxford, Oxford University Press, 2020) *passim;* Australian Election Study (2019) esp. 21; Richard Johnston, *Canada's Baffling Party System* (IRRP, 2017); and for political disengagement, see Hansard Society, *Audit* (2019) esp. 13–14; Simon Tormey, *The Contemporary Crisis of Contemporary Representative Democracy* (Papers on Parliament, nr 66); and for turnout in Canadian elections see www.elections.ca/content.aspx?section=ele&dir=turn&document=index&lang=e (last accessed on 21 May 2020).

need not distract from our study of reform. We might have widened our sample to include one or more civil law jurisdictions but ultimately, the reform story and the political context within which they were played out are more important for our purposes than the legal framework within which they occurred.

Here, then, is our broader purpose. I am interested in a particular species of constitutional reform in liberal democracies. That is to say, I want to understand better the way reforms have been executed (or attempted) with a view to reshaping the nation's sense of itself. I do not aspire to distil universal truths from these three stories and I recognise that the choice of the stories is limiting in this regard. But I do want to reflect on what they tell us about the state, the nation and citizens' sense of themselves at the turn of the twentieth and twenty-first centuries. And I am particularly interested in how attempts to change the first of these elements (the state) can impact on the second and third. Can reform of institutions change the way we think about ourselves and the way we relate to one another?

If it was not immediately clear at the opening of this chapter that I need to define my terms then references to the state, the nation and national identity should have established that as my next task.

IV. Definitions: Nation and Nation State

The definition of the core concepts we will be using has been the subject of vigorous debate over some 200 years. I want simply to identify the meanings I will attribute to them while sketching in some of the conceptual controversies.

The easiest place to start is the nation state. This is the political vehicle and administrative apparatus of the nation. So far, so straightforward. But enquire further and two questions arise. First, is the nation state in its purest form a common occurrence? And second, what exactly is the nation?

At every turn, we are told that the nation is enfeebled and under threat. Globalisation calls into question the power of national government to influence the economic destiny of the country. Mass migrations – especially mass migrations towards the more economically developed nations – challenge the ability of states to manage their immigration policies, or even their borders, in a coherent fashion. And from within, the state struggles to respond successfully to the tensions caused by competing sub-national identities.

None of these challenges should be lightly dismissed. But before we address them it is as well to be clear that they challenge the *nation state* as much as the *nation* itself, and that the two are not coterminous. The nation has often sought and found its political expression in the nation state. But there are many nations without a state (the Catalans, for example) and a state may embrace more than one nation (Canada, Britain) or, even more commonly, may embrace many ethnicities. And in extreme cases, the creation of the state may precede the creation of a nation: d'Azeglio famously observed at the time of Italian unification: 'We have created Italy, now we must create Italians'. This book is concerned with how the sense of nationhood can be changed within the context of nation states *and* multinational states. And so the challenges we have enumerated are germane, but they bear differentially on the nation and on the nation state.

If the nation and the nation state are under pressure, why choose this moment to write a study which explores their recent past and speculates on their future development? The first reason is simple and practical: the nation state is persistent and powerful. The British trauma over Brexit provides perhaps the most remarkable, but not the only, example of this. Across the developed world, the nation state continues to have a monopoly on the use of legitimate force, to conduct foreign policy, to command the allocation of a large slice of national wealth and to shape welfare, educational and cultural policy for its citizens. In many Western countries the state may have chosen to deliver public services through private or third sector partners, but this does not mean that public policy is any less ambitious, nor that the state is any less influential in the lives of its citizens.

The second reason relates to what nation states may yet achieve. The existence of the nation state and the continued loyalty of citizens to the concept or reality of nationhood provide the opportunity for the creation of public goods. I subscribe to the view of nations put forward by David Miller: if citizens identify with the nation and feel solidarity with their compatriots then they are likely to engage in obligations towards them. The nation is, or has the potential to be, an ethical union amongst mutually supportive citizens.[11] It was John Stuart Mill who first argued that representative government could be fostered by nationality because the former could draw on the reserves of mutual sympathy associated with the latter.

Miller would not mount his philosophical defence of the nation if the national idea did not continue to command popular support. The nation state's utility would disappear if nobody wanted to identity with the nation itself. His is an instrumental view of nationhood – but it is none the worse for that.

What, then is this sense of nationhood that has shaped and re-shaped our political geography over the last five centuries? I will not add to the burgeoning list of definitions of the nation, but will adopt Anthony Smith's: 'a named human community occupying a homeland and having common myths and a shared history, a common public culture, a single economy and common rights and duties for all members'.[12] There are two dimensions to this account: the tangible (place, economic transactions and social obligations) and the intangible (a sense of community, of a past, of a cultural life). Smith rightly gives equal weight to both and argues that each is essential for nationhood. One consequence of the intangible dimension is that the nation does not exist unless its members believe that it does. Unless they recognise that they have a common history and that

[11] David Miller, *Citizenship and National Identity* (Cambridge, Polity, 2000) Ch 2.
[12] Anthony D Smith, *Nationalism. Theory, Ideology, History* (Cambridge, Polity, 2001) 13.

they are party to a common culture the nation cannot live and breathe. As Renan wrote more than 100 years ago, the nation's very existence is subject to a 'daily plebiscite':[13] if its adherents cease to believe in it, it withers and dies. It is Benedict Anderson's envisioning of the nation as 'an imagined community' that will primarily preoccupy us in this book.[14]

V. National Myths and Symbols

The nation is continually creating and re-creating the symbolic expressions of what it aspires to be. We can see that most readily in the evolution of our national myths. As David Miller has observed, 'it is precisely because of the mythical or imaginary elements in national identity that it can be reshaped to meet new challenges and new needs'. But we can see the same process of reinvention in the architecture of our national buildings, in the reform of our constitutions, in the drafting of our national histories and in the design of national crests or, more modishly, of national logos. At times unconscious; at times purposeful and deliberate. At times defensive; at times aggressive. At times a desire to reach back into a nation's past; at times an attempt to reach beyond past or present difficulties to imagine a new future.

And at every turn we are surrounded by symbols of the nation: on our coinage; on our flag poles; on our stamps; and on the chests of our athletes. They are the visual representation – the daily reminders – of the national community of which we are members.

The constancy of those national symbols is significant. Even if a country invests them with new meanings and reinterprets them, it strives for continuity in the symbols themselves. The annual gathering at the Cenotaph in Whitehall has now passed its centenary. It honours the fallen in wars unimagined at its inauguration; and it now reflects a broader spectrum of faiths – but its overall form and ritual have been slow to change. National symbols acquire recognition and affection over time, through continuity rather than change.

These national symbols are no more than visual cue cards, prompting us to acknowledge the nation. They may be invested with a simple message: a head on a coin a reminder that we are in a monarchy; a flag that tells us that our country was born from the union of its predecessors. But for more subtle messages about our national identity we have to look to our national myths or to the way in which are national institutions are ordered and the way in which they represent themselves to us as citizens.

[13] Ernest Renan, *Qu'est ce qu'une nation* (1882) cited in Timothy Baycroft and Mark Hewitson (eds), *What is a Nation? Europe 1789–1914* (Oxford, Oxford University Press, 2006) 1.

[14] See Benedict Anderson, *Imagined Communities. Reflections on the Origin and Spread of Nationalism*, 2nd edn (London, Verso, 1991).

Let us take one further example. Australia, like most countries, chose to place its national war memorial in its capital. That much is unremarkable, but the design for the new national capital, Canberra, drove home the significance of the nation's debt to those who had fallen in World War I. The whole street plan of the city and its sightlines were designed as an act of obeisance to the memorial. Parliamentarians cannot escape the reminder of their fallen compatriots as they look out from their hilltop legislature. And every step of the way along Anzac Drive visitors are reminded in statuary of the campaigns in which Australians have fought and died.

This is remembrance on a grand scale. But it is more than that. As one enters the war memorial itself, it is clear that one is honouring both death and birth. The death of those whose names are inscribed on the walls; and the birth of a nation and of its new symbols. The birth of a nation said to have 'come of age' (curious phrase) during the carnage at Gallipoli and on the Western Front. The birth of the myth of the Digger – the tough, hard-working, long-suffering Australian solider whose idealised form towers above the pilgrim come to this secular shrine.

But as with all national symbols, the memorialising of Australia's 'birth' in World War I is reinterpreted by each generation. Consider, for example, Paul Keating's speech at the interment of the unknown soldier in 1993. His tone was anti-war but pro-soldier. He dwelt on the waste of life but captured a new, more hopeful message for a more egalitarian age. An elegy for lost generations, but a hymn to a democratic Australia, triumphing against the odds. A new perspective on Australian loss – one that drew on the myths that went before it, but which invested them with new meaning for a different age.

I should offer an immediate word of reassurance to those of you who are queasy about my apparent comfort with myths and national storytelling, with what may be (and often is) bad history or with instrumental, distorted accounts of who we are and who we might be in future. I do not propose that we should set aside historical criticism or normative judgements when confronted with a nation's own self-image. To take just one example, Britain's official efforts to document the Great War should be seen as a defensive reaction by the state to its record in that war. Historians helped to craft the state's view of the past, using sources denied to others. The resulting publications are not without value, but the whole enterprise is questionable, whether seen from the perspective of an historian's ethics or as an essay in public policy.[15]

I do not subscribe uncritically to national myth-making. I accept that national myths may rely on a crude, partial retelling of a nation's past. Or on an optimistic, idealised foretelling of its future. But what matters here is the potency of myths. For good or ill, we are surrounded by national myths and symbols. Whether we

[15] Keith Wilson, 'Introduction: Governments, Historians, and "Historical Engineering"' and 'The Imbalance in *British Documents on the Origins of the War, 1898–1914:* Gooch, Temperley, and the India Office' in Keith Wilson (ed), *Forging the Collective Memory. Government and International Historians through Two World Wars* (Providence, RI, Berghahn Books, 1996) 1–27 and 230–64.

are aware of it or not, they pervade our sense of who we are as a people. They help shape our sense of connection with our fellow citizens, with our communities and with our national institutions.

Given their potency, these myths have a social utility which has not escaped those who govern us. Depending on one's point of view, national myths are either an instrument used to maintain the hegemony of our national elites or they are evocations of the traditional values that we hold in common. Either way, they have the potential to buttress an existing social and political order or to foster change: they are no more than artefacts, whose influence – positive or negative – is for us to shape. We should not expect them to be subtle – indeed they may lose some of their utility if they are too subtle. In some ways I wish that the stories that my own country, Britain, told itself – and especially its young – about its national past would be less subtle and more readily engaging. This is not a call for a return to a history of Boudica and Britannia. But as a nation we are now so uncertain of our own narrative that we have lost the ability to tell ourselves a coherent story about who we are and where we have come from. The creation of a new narrative – and of new symbols – for Britain in the twenty-first century can be made to serve the needs of a multicultural society. Indeed it must be made to serve that purpose. As we will see, nation-building either brings the builders into conflict with historians already engaged in crafting their own stories of the nation or they enlist historians in the enterprise to tell new national stories.

VI. National Identity

Kwame Anthony Appiah has reminded us recently that national identity is just one of the 'lies that bind', that is to say it is one aspect of our identity, taking its part alongside race, creed, culture, class and, one might add, language.[16] Accepting Appiah's stricture and keeping Smith as our terminological guide, we may take national identity to be 'the continuous reproduction and reinterpretation of the pattern of values, symbols, memories, myths and traditions that compose the distinctive heritage of nations, and the identification of individuals with that pattern and heritage and with its cultural elements'.[17] Note here the sense of evolution over time. Our sense of the nation can flex and grow *and* it can be influenced by external agency, most obviously by a threat to the nation's security. When that threat is posed by another nation it often serves as a catalyst for change to national identity.[18] The nation has to feel some sense of continuity through time if it is to maintain its sense of identity. But the appearance of continuity customarily

[16] Kwame Anthony Appiah, *The Lies That Bind. Rethinking Identity* (London, Profile Books, 2018) *passim*.

[17] Anthony D Smith, *Nationalism. Theory, Ideology, History* (Cambridge, Polity, 2001) 18.

[18] Eric Hosbawm, *Nations and Nationalism since 1780* (Cambridge, Cambridge University Press, 1990) 91.

masks a continual reinvention of what it is to be national. Indeed if this is not happening the prospects for the nation may well be bleak: it will cease to capture the imagination of new generations and of new arrivals.

Seen in this context, we should be prompted to pay greater attention to the slow, rumbling debate over the nature of Britishness. When first initiated by Gordon Brown as Prime Minister, the debate – and the concept – were derided by many, cited as evidence of a sign of a country that had lost its way. Brexit has caused some to reconsider this critique. Threats to the integrity of the Union have given others pause. And if this were not troubling enough, the discovery in July 2005 that the London suicide bombers were born and raised in immigrant communities in the north of England posed an uncomfortable question for liberal opinion. Is the British model of multiculturalism failing? For the last 30 years we have known that for all our disagreements we do, at least, value diversity. But do we need a stronger sense of what it is to be British to bind us together – believer and non-believer, native-born and immigrant?

This is an important, difficult debate. But surely it is a debate that should be welcomed as the sign of a nation seeking to renew itself. A nation searching for ways of having a conversation about its future. Far better the awkward conversation than the painful silence in which questions hang unanswered. As with families, communities may nurse resentments quietly, enmities growing all the while. Think about British national identity and it is not long before you have to think about Europe, about immigration, about multiculturalism. Treacherous territory for the politician. But we cannot afford to leave this territory unexplored. Baulk at the debate over national identity and you are running a greater risk: over time Britain's self-image may become quaint, out-of-date – and irrelevant to the young and to new immigrants.

VII. Changes in National Identity

For political leaders who address the theme of national identity, there is one commonplace: our nation has changed out of all recognition from the one we inherited from our forefathers – and yet we share much with them. Witness Paul Keating at the interment of the unknown soldier from the Great War: 'This Australia and the Australia he knew are like foreign countries.'[19] This device serves an important purpose: it creates the rhetorical space in which to conjure up a new national vision while reaching back to honour our common past. But is it any more than a device? Many would object that the real purpose of such speeches is simply to enlist emotional support for the new project, the new vision. Appeals to the past, they might continue, are often bad history, distortions of the noble myths

[19] Paul Keating, Speech at the Funeral Service of the Unknown Australian Soldier (Canberra, 11 November 1993).

of our inheritance, attempts to strike a resonant note with the audience or electorate. Respond to such appeals and we are ignoring the real challenge: the nations of the developed world have undergone transformative social and economic change through the last century and the pace of change is increasing. The real project, the critics conclude, is to derive benefit from those changes; appeals to the past are no more than rhetorical soft soaping.

An acceptance of the nation as an imagined community is not an argument for bad history. But once one has accepted the premise of the imagined community, the terms of the debate change. I might argue that Britain is not, in any meaningful sense, the same country as the land which had the same name a century ago. Its population has grown from 38 to 66 million, it has become more ethnically diverse, its industries have been transformed, its agriculture has declined, its people have lost their faith in God, it has lost an Empire, it has joined the EU (and left again). But if you believe that Britain is still the country that it was, that the continuities are more important than the discontinuities, I cannot prove you wrong by marshalling my empirical evidence. Your sense of nation is as valid as mine – and if you find a politician's appeal to a version of our past to be emotionally resonant I should not find that troubling. Rather, I should offer one challenge to you – and a piece of advice to those who invoke the past in support of some present purpose. The challenge to you is that you should reject any appeal to national identity which is inimical to communities within the nation or beyond our borders. I accept the proposition that national sentiment can be mobilised in support of benign purposes, encouraging citizens to support projects which benefit them or their fellow citizens. But I am not blind to the ethnic nationalism which has spilt so much blood in the last two centuries. However distant it may seem from current discourse, we should remain watchful for it. The distortion of national history carries with it particular risk: it may render a myth more attractive to fellow nationals, but it may also blind them to that which is regrettable and shameful in the national past, leaving them resistant to the lessons to be drawn from those episodes.

VIII. National Identity and Constitutional Reform

And so at its broadest our topic may be described as the attempt to use constitutional change to re-imagine who we are as a nation and who we might be in future. We are choosing to focus primarily on one episode in Britain but we are hoping to gain insights which might be of broader application. But it is important to be clear that we are imposing further restrictions to our topic. We are only looking at national identity when it is a function of *formal changes to the constitution*.

It would have been possible to have written a study of attempts to bring about changes in national identity as brought about through immigration policy, to take just one example. Or we could have elected to examine policy domains that resonate particularly with a nation's self-image: healthcare in Canada or sport in Australia. These, and other options, may be viable – and so why alight upon formal constitutional reform?

Three reasons. First, the link between national identity and constitutions is readily made – and has repeatedly been made by those promoting constitutional change. Constitutions typically describe our mode of government, mandate our national institutions and define our national emblems. Each of these prescriptions is pregnant with potential meaning for the advocate of the nation. And the symbolic potential is not restricted to the constitution's subject matter: in the US, to take an extreme example, the constitutional text itself attracts reverence. It is the ark of the covenant in a national secular religion. In discussing the American story, Ackerman has noted that, 'the narrative we tell ourselves about our Constitution's roots is a deeply significant act of collective self-definition: its continual re-telling plays a critical role in the ongoing construction of a national identity'.[20]

Second, constitutions matter. They establish the rules which determine how political power is allocated and used. They concentrate power – or disperse it. They require us to coalesce and cooperate. Or they pit us in competition one with another. They protect minorities. Or they entrench the right of the majority to claim the spoils.

We care about how we are governed. We care about whether our governments are effective and trustworthy. But beyond that, we care about whether we have the opportunity to participate in decision making and whether we can hold public authorities to account. These assertions have long been made by democratic theorists, but now we have data which suggests that the quality of governance has a bearing on our quality of life. Using self-reported measures of life satisfaction from across the world, Helliwell and Huang conclude that 'the effects of good government remain as the single most important variable explaining international differences in life satisfaction'.[21]

Third, the choices nations make about their constitutions are revealing about the nations themselves. The process is two-way: constitutions help shape our sense of identity – by framing our debates – and they can come to reflect our sense of ourselves. The point can be readily illustrated if we consider the constitutional reforms in Eastern Europe after the collapse of the Soviet empire. There, renascent nationalism found its constitutional expression in quite different ways: Bulgaria banned parties organised on ethnic lines and established Bulgarian as the official language, both provisions to the detriment of the Turkish-speaking minority. God found His way into the Polish constitution. The Hungarians extended citizenship rights to their compatriots living abroad (of significance particularly to the

[20] Bruce Ackerman, *We the People* (Cambridge, Mass, Belknap Press, 1991) 36.

[21] John F Helliwell and Haifang Huang, 'How's your Government? International Evidence linking Good Government and Well-Being' *British Journal of Political Science* 2008, Vol 38, 617.

Hungarian minorities in Slovakia and Romania). And the Latvians took another route to national self-expression, by reverting to the inter-war constitution whose writ had been so rudely interrupted by the Soviet interlude from 1940–89. These decisions should all be seen as expressions of national identity, even if they were arrived at through different routes. They are important not just for what they show about the political mood in each country at a time of profound change, but for the way in which each has helped structure the politics and political discourse of the post-Soviet period.[22]

The inclusion of the qualifying adjective *formal* before *constitutional reform* is significant. I have chosen to exclude constitutional reform which is the result of reinterpretations of the law arising from judicial rulings. This is not to deny their significance but I am keen to examine the actions of a wider cast of reformers.

It is worth pausing here to ask whether constitutional change is a particular species of politics, whose practice is distinct from policy debates over, for example, healthcare or transport. Constitutional reform might invite participants to more grandiose rhetoric, but are there any distinctions in the process by which change is realised?

In most jurisdictions the answer to this question may appear obvious. By their very nature, most constitutions are inherently conservative: they prevent political actors from making hasty or unilateral changes to the rules governing the distribution of power. The mechanisms used to achieve this vary: in some systems, a super-majority in the legislature is needed to secure a change; in others a measure must be sanctioned by successive legislatures; in yet others popular approval must be sought in a referendum. Federal systems customarily require evidence of assent at both state and national level. And so the common conception is that constitutional change is unlike politics as usual, not least because it is so difficult to realise. As with many such commonsensical propositions, this is neither wholly foolish nor entirely satisfactory. It is important to understand why.

The formal barriers to constitutional change are not always high. In Hungary, for example, an amendment requires a two-thirds majority in Parliament as do many other legislative acts. Consequently constitutional politics in the post-Soviet period have come to resemble day-to-day politics. The UK offers a contrast. Constitutional reform in Britain does not have a distinct process beyond some relatively insignificant requirements concerning the way in which Parliament debates measures of constitutional importance. This, you might object, is so extreme an example as to be irrelevant. Britain is one of just three states without a formally codified constitution and so it is no surprise that the British lack special rules for constitutional reform. After all, they cannot even agree what is and what is not constitutional: if somebody brands a proposal 'unconstitutional' the objector

[22] The standard text on the constitutional reforms in Eastern Europe in the 1990s is Jon Elster, Claus Offe and Ulrich K Preuss, *Institutional Design in Post-Communist Societies. Rebuilding the Ship at Sea* (New York, Cambridge University Press, 1998) *passim* but especially 89–90.

should be understood to be saying simply 'I disagree'. It is certainly true that the British are not rigorous when it comes to identifying matters as constitutional, but the distinction between codified and uncodified constitutions is overstated. We will use the term 'constitution' to embrace the most important rules governing the distribution and use of power. These may not all be written down and they are never written down in one place. What is distinctive about the British constitution is not so much that it is (as is often claimed) unwritten. Rather, it has been written down over many years, in an infuriatingly large number of places. It cannot even claim to be entirely uncodified any more. Inch by inch, it has been codified through the import of higher law from the European Union – now to be undone – and by the UK's adherence to binding international treaties.

There is a declaratory value in being able to pick up the German Fundamental Law or the US Constitution and to assert that these are the principles that guide these nations and protect their citizens. But it is important that we understand that the value of this assertion is declaratory – it is about public illustration or demonstration. In civic education it is undoubtedly helpful to have one text which can be labelled 'the constitution', but that does not make the assertion any more accurate. The German Fundamental Law cannot be understood adequately without reference to countless statutes and to rulings of the Constitutional Court. The US Constitution needs to be read with the nation's other founding documents and, *inter alia*, with more than 200 years of Supreme Court jurisprudence.

Anthony King illustrates the point in another way. He notes that the rules governing elections to legislatures are unquestionably of constitutional importance. The selection of a proportional or majoritarian voting system fundamentally determines the way that political parties seek and use power. But in many jurisdictions the constitution is silent on the design of the electoral system, leaving the choice to legislators.[23]

If we accept that codified constitutions catalogue only a sub-set of the principles to be found in a national constitution, what implications does this have for our question about the nature of constitutional change? If constitutional rules are to be found in statute and not exclusively in a protected species of higher law, then the British example ceases to be exceptional: some categories of constitutional reform can be achieved by simple majorities in national legislatures. And by recognising the importance of rulings by the supreme or constitutional court, we broaden still further the means by which the constitution may change. This can be illustrated most simply by reference to the US.

The US Constitution puts a stern challenge in front of anyone seeking a formal amendment: a two-thirds majority in both houses of Congress and endorsement by the legislature in three-quarters of the states. Has that slowed down constitutional change in the US, a country which is fond of trumpeting the longevity of

[23] Anthony King, *Does the United Kingdom still have a Constitution?* (London, Sweet and Maxwell, 2001) 1–5.

its constitution? No. Rather it has diverted reformist energy into other channels. Change has come through the reinterpretation of the existing text by the Justices of the Supreme Court.

There have been instances when the elected branch of government has got the Court to change its mind through the crude exercise of brute force. The most celebrated instance was the threat by President Roosevelt in 1937, in the wake of his landslide re-election, to pack the Court with Justices more favourable to his New Deal legislation. The nine Justices saw that their cause was hopeless and in their 'stitch in time to save nine' they began to overturn their earlier jurisprudence on the New Deal.

But this episode has been the exception rather than the rule. More commonly, reformers have focussed their energy on securing the appointment of Justices favourable to their cause. The nomination process is now a choreographed ritual: Senators probe the nominee's record and views; and the nominee fences and blocks, anxious to avoid making any comment that might be damaging to his or her chances of approval in the Senate vote and determined not to say how he or she might determine cases which might come before the Court in future. Consequently the nomination hearings are rarely revealing of anything other than the deftness of the nominee's footwork. But behind the choreography the Senators' calculations are easy to discern: will this nominee advance an interpretation of the constitution which will be helpful to my policy objectives? To accept this is not to accept the reductionist view that all judicial activity is politics by another name. But it is to concede that courts are part of the political process, if that is understood to mean the process by which public policy is determined.

Constitutional change is best seen as political change like any other. That is not to deny constitutional reform a distinctive character. Reformers may have to surmount procedural obstacles which are particularly onerous. And they will be dealing with arguments of principle which may define the foundations of our politics. The very notion of constitutional renewal is one which divides constitutionalists: Jefferson, for example, argued that each nation should cast off the constitutional burden of its forefathers, but Madison warned that this would destabilise republican self-government.[24] It is true that these particular arguments are peculiar to constitutional change, but the *process* by which reformers and conservatives contest their case is best understood as a partisan battle between competing interests struggling for supremacy.

For politicians, some constitutional changes have a particular allure because they hold out the prospect of enduring reform. Witness, for example, the long-running campaign to change the Italian voting system. This was not an argument about the merits of the competing systems: it was in essence about who would form subsequent administrations. If politicians can mobilise support for a reform

[24] See the discussion in Cass R Sunstein, *Designing Democracy. What Constitutions Do* (New York, Oxford University Press, 2001) 96.

which is then enshrined in higher law, they have secured an outcome which is less transitory than a simple legislative success and, while it survives, it can create the space and opportunity for the reformers to pursue their policy objectives.

If constitutional politics concerns itself with the mechanics of power, rather than the purposes for which power is exercised, we should not be surprised that political parties are inconsistent and instrumental when it comes to constitutional reform. Examples from either side of Atlantic illustrate the point. The British Labour Party began its life before World War I as a supporter of a proportional voting system. As a minor player in a first-past-the-post electoral system it was obvious that greater proportionality would increase its parliamentary representation. But by the 1920s, after the Liberal Party had split and the system began to magnify Labour's growing support, the party lost interest in changing the voting system. The American example is of similar date. Before the advent of the New Deal Court, progressives favoured policy reform through formal constitutional amendment – and duly secured provision for a federal income tax and for the popular election of senators. But once the Democrats had a grip on both the Court and the Presidency, their enthusiasm for constitutional reform waned: it had served its purpose.[25]

Certain constitutional changes do not fit my general characterisation. Some may be technical refinements commanding bipartisan support. Others may not even be recognised as constitutional change by those debating the merits of a reform. For example, Sweden is unusual in regarding Freedom of Information as a right of fundamental constitutional importance. Access laws in other countries may be equally significant in making the state accountable to its citizens, but for the moment, at least, they are denied the dignity afforded to constitutional law.

We should set these exceptions to one side. Our concern is with constitutional reform which promotes or defends a political interest by whichever means is expedient. We will focus on the actions taken by political elites – and specifically on their attempts to secure constitutional reform as a means of influencing a nation's sense of itself. This does not mean that formal constitutional change is the preserve of elites or that reform is initiated and executed by them without outside agency or restraint. Consider, for example, the circumstances that gave rise to constitutional reform in Britain at the end of the twentieth century. The case for change was not new: the campaign for home rule for Scotland, for example, was as old as the century itself. But after the suffrage reforms of 1918 and 1928, the appetite for constitutional reform had apparently been sated. The forces which revived interest late in the century had little to do with the constitution. By the 1970s Britain was seen by many to be in terminal decline: trapped by its oppositional, class-based politics and consistently outperformed by its principal European competitors. West Germany was the most common (and least flattering) economic reference point.

[25] For a fuller discussion, see Clement E Vose, *Constitutional Change: Amendment Politics and Supreme Court Litigation since 1900* (Lexington, Lexington Books, 1972) 342–45.

Advocates for systemic change in Britain pointed up the differences in the two political systems: the Germans stressed social partnership, coalition-building and the sharing of power. All very different from trench warfare in Westminster. But if reformers began to win the argument in the 1970s, the key political change did not come until 1993 when Labour, a party long in opposition, adopted constitutional reform in its quest for policy propositions which would make it electable. In chapter two we will examine that story more fully, but this quick outline serves to show that the constitutional reform in Britain was not, or was not exclusively, an initiative of the elite. It was a product of economic decline and of the functioning of the British party system: Labour needed a new policy platform. That does not gainsay the role of elites in interpreting the cause of the decline or in advocating change, but it does provide context for their contribution.

A 'constitutional moment' is the notion that constitutions in flux can be particularly revealing about the fundamental choices made by a polity about how it wants to organise its future.[26] And, for the purposes of this book, constitutional moments may be especially revealing because they give national leaders the space and opportunity to influence a nation's self-image. This is seen most obviously at a time of constitution-making. New constitutions are preponderantly the product of war, liberation, conquest or revolution. Moments which, by their very nature, expose decisions about a nation's destiny. The constitutional changes described in this book are of a less dramatic, more incremental character. But the general proposition holds good: moments of significant constitutional change are commonly associated with attempts to imprint a new vision on a nation's imagination. If one is attempting to re-order the fundamental rules governing the exercise of power, one has to offer some explanation to citizens as to why this should be necessary. And those explanations, whether self-serving or otherwise, commonly appeal to a nation's sense of self and its future. We will examine why and how those appeals have been made – and we will gauge their consequences.

IX. Comparative Case Studies

This book does not comply with all of the methodological requirements a political scientist may impose on a comparative study. But in general terms we are unquestionably engaged in a work of comparison.

Policy studies that use a strict comparative methodology often disappoint. Their enthusiasm for the comparative enterprise takes them through the departure lounge but then they lapse into administrative tourism. So keen are they to demonstrate their new understanding of the countries they are visiting that they

[26] The concept was first used by Bruce Ackerman; my use of it here differs somewhat from his, but my debt to him remains.

are drawn, ineluctably towards relativism. Case study is heaped upon case study – each is dutifully understood in its own terms – and the reader is left wondering why, if the differences in culture, practice or politics are so great, the writer did not choose to stay at home and spare us the journey.

Studies of comparative constitutions illustrate the problem.[27] Some are essentially exercises in taxonomy, classifying the different species to be found in the world's constitutional menagerie. The author tours the exhibits and concludes that the world is a diverse and wondrous place. Others do not even aspire to classification and they content themselves with a description of the distinguishing features of the wildlife they have encountered. Faced with this approach, it is almost possible – almost – to sympathise with those who dismiss comparativism as a waste of time, encouraging us (and especially those of us who are British) to focus on understanding what is particular (and noble) about our own constitutional arrangements.

Mercifully, a number of scholars have shown us that it is possible to understand what is distinctive about individual constitutions *and* to use their contrasting experience to explore a common theme. The examples I have in mind here include the work of Peter Oliver and Charles Epps. Oliver has charted the process through which former British dominions came to cut their final constitutional links to Westminster. Epps' work has looked at the emergence of a rights culture, showing the different courses followed by each of his case studies, but drawing out the importance in each of the legal and financial resources needed to bring causes to court. Through comparative methodology, Oliver and Epps succeed in showing us each of their chosen jurisdictions in a new light.[28] They reach the objective which Robert Kagan has described as 'to reveal roads not taken, unconsciously maintained patterns, and sources of resistance to change'.[29]

X. Changing States, Changing Nations

The challenge to a coherent national identity from diversity is made greater by the erosion of popular engagement in democratic politics. Political parties in each of our countries are losing members and are struggling to maintain local activities as volunteers fall away. Trends in voter turnout in national elections in Canada and

[27] Two of the better works of constitutional comparativism are edited collections of essays. See Keith G Banting and Richard Simeon (eds), *The Politics of Constitutional Change in Industrial Nations* (London and Basingstoke, Macmillan, 1985); Dawn Oliver and Carlo Fusaro (eds), *How Constitutions Change. A Comparative Study* (Oxford, Hart Publishing, 2013). But in each case, the strength of the contributions rests on the individual country studies rather than the overarching comparative approach.

[28] Peter C Oliver, *The Constitution of Independence. The Development of Constitutional Theory in Australia, Canada, and New Zealand* (Oxford, Oxford University Press, 2005). Charles R Epp, *The Rights Revolution: Lawyers, Activists, and Supreme Courts in Comparative Perspective* (Chicago, University of Chicago Press, 1998).

[29] Robert Kagan, *Adversarial Legalism* (Cambridge, Mass, Harvard University Press, 2001) 5–6.

the UK are all heading in the wrong direction; Australia is spared this pattern only by the legal obligation on voters to come to the polling booths. Robert Puttnam showed us, in his pioneering study, *Bowling Alone*, that civic paricipation was in decline in the US. But now we know from similar studies in the UK, Canada and Australia that their associational cultures are also in decay. Our electorates are becoming increasingly passive and disengaged from national political life. Politicians are competing for their attention against ever more pervasive electronic media – and they are losing.

With this as the context, what hope for a serious national conversation about the values we hold in common or the future which we might shape together? The space and opportunity for such debates is limited and only the most skilful will succeed in capturing the public's imagination.

For those who believe in the continuing potential of the nation to bring us to recognise our obligations to one another, these are urgent and difficult problems. Debates about Britishness or Canadianness may not be easy on the ear, but nor are they philosophical sideshows.

This book asks whether constitutional change be used to help us re-imagine ourselves and, if so, how? We will explore the conception, communication and execution of the change – and will weigh the factors which contributed to success or failure. This chapter has established the reference points for our discussion and has drawn out some of the distinctive features of our case studies; the four which follow immediately will examine those constitutional moments themselves.

The next chapter tackles those reforms which are at the heart of this book: those undertaken when Tony Blair was Prime Minister. In chapters three and four we then turn to Canada and Australia for comparative insight. And in chapter five we return to the British story with the reforms undertaken during the Brown Government and its successors.

2

'Doing Good By Stealth': Tony Blair and Reform of the British Constitution

In the summer of 1996, John Major launched repeated attacks on the Labour Party's constitutional reform programme. He told an audience in Glasgow in May that the opposition was, 'ready to play with the very survival of our United Kingdom for party political advantage'. The nation was in danger: it was imperilled by Labour's plans for devolution to Scotland and Wales. This was 'the most cynical policy of modern times'.[1] With less than a year to go to the general election, now was the moment to save the Union. Warming to a campaign theme which he judged to have been productive in the 1992 poll, Major developed a more wide-ranging critique of Labour's plans in London in June. His assault was to be followed by a series of speeches by his Cabinet colleagues, each of them pointing up the dangers posed by Labour's radical plans for the constitution. The Prime Minister promised 'the most thorough debate on the constitution for a generation'.[2]

The speeches were delivered. But the debate did not come to life. The public showed few signs of interest in Labour's plans for the constitution. The moment passed. The following May, Labour was elected on a manifesto promising radical change to Britain's constitution, a theme which attracted little attention in the election campaign. Over the next four years, the Government refashioned the institutions of the state and the relationship between the governed and the governing. Depending on one's taste in historical comparison, it was the most fundamental reform of the country's uncodified constitution since 1928, or 1911 – or even 1832.

This is the story of Labour's constitutional reforms: how and why the party came to champion them and what it did during its first term in office under Tony Blair. We will explore public attitudes to constitutional change and will ask what it meant for the British nation. Was the reform programme intended as an instrument of national renewal? The creation of new legislatures in Scotland, Wales and

[1] BL CU LXXVI file 204–5, Speech by John Major in Glasgow (12 May 1995).
[2] ibid. Speech by John Major at Centre for Policy Studies, London (26 June 1996).

Northern Ireland prompted the citizens of those parts of the UK to think afresh about what it meant to be Scottish, Welsh or Northern Irish. But what of British identity? Did the Human Rights Act prompt a reconsideration of the relationship between the citizen and the British state?

We will focus primarily on the story of New Labour's first term from 1997 to 2001, discussing its subsequent reforms more briefly. As we shall see, the tale of this remarkable period of change is as much a story of what did not happen as what did.

I. Labour and Constitutional Reform

A Labour veteran of the 1970s might have been bemused by the manifesto of 1997. The party which had been so scarred by the failed devolution project of the Callaghan Government was now committed to a much more comprehensive renewal of the constitution. This was not Labour territory – or, more accurately, it had not been Labour territory since the party had lost its enthusiasm for proportional representation (PR) soon after World War I. It had retained a commitment to Lords reform – further restricting the upper chamber's power of delay in 1949 and making an abortive attempt at change in Wilson's second government. But for much of the century Labour was preoccupied by securing control of the state, rather than transforming its constitutional order. A strong, centralised state was desirable: in the right hands it could become an instrument for economic and social reform and for the redistribution of wealth and opportunity between classes and across the country.

In the wake of the Kilbrandon Commission on the Constitution, which had been established by Wilson but did not report until 1973, the party committed itself to devolution to Scotland and Wales. The immediate incentive was the emergence of a nationalist threat north of the border, and the prospect of one in Wales. The political calculation was made by Labour leaders in London in the face of reluctance within the Scottish party and divisions among Welsh colleagues. Labour returned to power in 1974 with a pledge to devolve power, but the party remained sceptical about the benefits of constitutional reform, and opposed to any moves which would have empowered the judiciary at the expense of Parliament. Labour had regarded the judiciary with mistrust: ever since the 1901 Taff Vale ruling, judges had been the deemed inimical to the interests of collective labour. A parliamentary majority offered the best hope of protecting the party's traditional supporters.

Labour's reappraisal of constitutional reform owes much to the lessons it learned during the Thatcher administrations of 1979 to 1990. But the awakening of interest in the reform agenda predates Margaret Thatcher's arrival in Downing Street. The country's economic troubles in the 1960s and 1970s had begun to encourage the thought that Britain would only be able to compete more effectively with its European rivals if it breathed new life into its moribund constitution.[3] The inconclusive February 1974 election result had prompted renewed interest in the country's electoral system: Labour won four more seats than the Conservatives on a smaller share of the vote. When the Social Democratic Party was established in 1981, it immediately lent its voice to the Liberal Party's call for proportional representation. And the two parties campaigned through the 1980s for a broader programme of constitutional reform.

Within this context – of a developing critique of the country's economic ills and of the emergence of a third force in electoral politics – Labour's constitutional conversion began. Tony Wright, who was to become a Labour MP in 1997 and later chaired the Public Administration Select Committee, is clear who deserves most of the credit: 'In this sense it is Mrs Thatcher who perhaps has the best claim to be regarded as the real architect of constitutional reform in Britain. She provided an object-lesson in the nature of power in Britain's "flexible" constitution and, at the same time, a crash course of constitutional education for the Labour party'.[4] If there was a totemic moment in this constitutional education it was the abolition of the Greater London Council in 1986. Whatever their reservations about the course steered by the Labour group on the council, Labour supporters were quick to grasp the significance of this essay in the power of a government with a large parliamentary majority. Of equal significance was the result of the 1987 general election in Scotland. The Conservatives lost all but 10 of their seats there; and yet Scotland was to be ruled by a Conservative administration with a commanding majority in Westminster. The early trial of the poll tax north of the border served only to strengthen the nationalist cause; Scottish Labour, once a reluctant supporter of devolution, now argued the case with conviction, clear that it was both an electoral asset and a necessity if it were to head off the nationalists.

Over the course of the 1980s, constitutional reformers developed a standard critique of the Thatcher governments: they were over overcentralised, majoritarian, unaccountable and determined to remove whatever checks and balances remained in their way. Mrs Thatcher was their most effective recruiting sergeant and her 11 years in power created a public mood that was more sceptical and more willing to question established truths.[5] Constitutional reformers were, over time, able to exploit that mood for their advantage.

The principal, but not the first, cross-party movement for constitutional reform was Charter 88.[6] Established in the wake of the Conservatives' third successive electoral victory, it championed a maximalist position. I will use the term maximalism

[3] Anthony King, *Does the United Kingdom Still Have a Constitution?* (London, Sweet & Maxwell, 2001) 52–53.

[4] John Morrison, *Reforming Britain. New Labour, New Constitution?* (Edinburgh, Pearson Education, 2001) 26.

[5] Anthony King, *Does the United Kingdom Still Have a Constitution?* (London, Sweet & Maxwell, 2001) 74–76.

[6] Charter 88 was founded, unsurprisingly, in 1988 with a written constitution as its ultimate aim. Its moving spirit was, for many years, Anthony Barnett. See John Morrison, *Reforming Britain. New Labour, New Constitution?* (Edinburgh, Pearson Education, 2001) 28–29.

here to define a loose coalition on the centre-left who believed in thorough-going constitutional reform culminating in full codification. The key to Britain's renewal was to be found in the comprehensive renewal of the institutions of the state and of the systems through which citizens held their representatives to account. It was not concerned with grubby calculations of electoral arithmetic; nor was it interested in questions of national identity. Root and branch reform was to be secured through a codified constitution which was to be entrenched to protect it from the passing whim of temporary parliamentary majorities. Constitutional sovereignty was to take the place of parliamentary sovereignty. And to show that all of this was feasible, the IPPR, the centre-left think tank, sponsored a project to draw up a codified constitution. It was first published in 1991 when it seemed conceivable that the subsequent election would yield a hung parliament and substantive constitutional reform might be the price a Labour Government would have to pay for Liberal Democrat support.[7] This prospect was to come to naught, but the IPPR constitution was a signal of intent by the maximalists, who judged that their moment was at hand. Their cause had modest support in Parliament, but it began to command growing support amongst intellectuals, political commentators and lawyers. Most were at pains to distinguish their position from the incremental steps Labour had taken towards political reform. James Cornford, a leading figure amongst reformers, argued the case for a coherent, planned approach to decentralisation rather than an ad hoc response to centrifugal forces: 'the best way to avoid the late-Victorian nightmare of piecemeal disintegration is to think in advance of the general settlement to which individual decisions may impel you'.[8]

The maximalist approach was not best calculated to win over Labour doubters; and many in the party were unpersuaded. Neil Kinnock, leader when Charter 88 was launched, declined to endorse it, reputedly dismissing its advocates as, 'whiners, whingers and wankers'.[9] Kinnock's view of Charter 88 mellowed over time. However more determined resistance came from Roy Hattersley, the Shadow Home Secretary in the 1987 Parliament and so Labour's principal spokesman on much of this agenda.[10] He was intellectually committed to the defence of parliamentary sovereignty:

> True liberty requires action from the government. At best, a written constitution diminishes the importance of positive freedom – government action to enable more and more people to do and enjoy those things worth doing and enjoying. At worst, it actually prevents or inhibits that action from being taken.[11]

[7] Institute for Public Policy Research, *A Written Constitution for the United Kingdom* (London, Mansell, 1995).

[8] James Cornford, 'Towards a Constitutional Equation?' in Bernard Crick (ed), *National Identities. The Constitution of the United Kingdom* (Oxford, Blackwell, 1991) 165.

[9] The phrase has been cited by many. See, eg, Stuart Weir on 1 January 2010 on OpenDemocracyUK: www.opendemocracy.net/en/opendemocracyuk/success-of-charter-88/ (last accessed on 11 May 2020).

[10] Anthony Barnett, interview with the author, 2 August 2007.

[11] Roy Hattersley cited in John Morrison, *Reforming Britain. New Labour, New Constitution?* (Edinburgh, Pearson Education, 2001) 28.

Labour's hierarchy had some way to travel if it was to embrace the maximalists' new orthodoxy. But the emergence of Charter 88 and the intellectual debate around a codified constitution created a space in which supporters of Labour and of the newly formed Liberal Democrats could begin to explore cooperation on constitutional reform. The process was not easy – and the partisan enmities of the two parties were not readily set aside – but a dialogue was begun which would have been inconceivable in the early 1980s, in the wake of the SDP split from Labour.

II. Labour and the Maximalists: The 1987 Parliament

In the wake of Labour's defeat at the 1987 election, Kinnock launched a renewed effort to modernise the party. To that end, the party established a comprehensive policy review. Its final report in 1989 would have given constitutional reformers little reason for encouragement.

It opened its discussion of political renewal with a ritualised denunciation of Conservative rule:

> The government has defined freedom as liberation from public expenditure and collective obligation – a policy which often reduces the choices available to millions of men and women. In fact no government this century has been more authoritarian or concentrated more power in the hands of a central autocratic bureaucracy.[12]

It then proceeded to restate a number of Labour's existing policies. Commitments to an elected upper house and to Freedom of Information were reaffirmed. Labour's enthusiasm for judicial reform was once more expressed: it wanted to strip the Lord Chancellor of political responsibilities and to create a justice ministry. And when it came to Northern Ireland, Labour's preference remained unity by consent.[13] This policy was to change in the 1990s, but Northern Ireland was always tackled as a discrete policy issue, divorced from the broader constitutional reform agenda.

The Policy Review briskly rejected the notion of a Bill of Rights, sticking instead to a routine defence of parliamentary sovereignty. Its sole excursion into novelty on this front was to suggest that the second chamber would

> in effect, entrench our fundamental rights legislation. In the British system of government there is only one way of preventing a government with a substantial majority and supine backbenchers from transforming Parliament into an elective dictatorship. That is the creation of at least one House of Parliament which, because of its composition and construction, will not automatically accept Cabinet directives.[14]

[12] Labour Party, *Meet the Challenge. Make the Change. A New Agenda for Britain. Final Report of Labour's Policy Review for the 1990s* (Labour Party, 1989) 55.

[13] This policy was to remain until the 1992 election. Thereafter it was replaced by a commitment to the peace process and to respect for both traditions within Northern Ireland.

[14] Labour Party, *Meet the Challenge. Make the Change. A New Agenda for Britain. Final Report of Labour's Policy Review for the 1990s* (Labour Party, 1989) 56.

The upper chamber would be given the right to delay repeal of legislation affecting fundamental rights for the lifetime of a Parliament. Labour, it seemed, had reflected on the experience of Mrs Thatcher's decade in power – and had chosen to draw conclusions quite unlike those of the maximalists in Charter 88.[15]

But Labour's policy on the protection of fundamental rights was to evolve by the time of the 1992 election. Its manifesto promised a 'Charter of Rights' backed by a Bill of Rights. This was an awkward compromise between two strands of thought. The Charter arose from Labour's longstanding commitment to fight discrimination and to promote minorities. The Bill of Rights, a new arrival in Labour's policy portfolio, was a sign that the maximalists were beginning to make progress in shaping Labour's programme. Preparatory work had been done by Liberty, the pressure group, which had published a consultation document on the subject in 1991.[16] This canvassed support for a Bill of Rights that would be broad in scope. It would have some measure of protection from parliamentary revision while denying the judiciary the right to strike down legislation passed after the Bill of Rights.[17] The proposal serves as a reminder that maximalism sprang from diverse origins. The Liberty document was an example of constitutional reform as practised by the Left. It was concerned with addressing a perceived imbalance in the distribution of social power and so this Bill of Rights was to be accompanied by radical reform of the judiciary to make it more representative of society. Constitutional reformers on the Left typically had different objectives from liberal constitutionalists, who were preoccupied by the rights and liberties of the individual. But reformers from both traditions were to be found in tactical alliance, urging the maximalist cause on Labour policy-makers.[18] Liberal constitutionalists were more likely to show an interest in a reformulation of British citizenship – a concept which, as we will see, appears fleetingly along Labour's constitutional journey.

The concept of a Bill of Rights was ultimately smuggled into Labour's 1992 manifesto in a last minute manoeuvre by Patricia Hewitt, who had been Kinnock's policy coordinator until 1989 and had earlier been general secretary of the National Council for Civil Liberties (subsequently renamed Liberty).[19] But the manifesto left unclear the relationship between the Charter and the 'complementary' Bill. Equally, readers were left to guess at whether the Bill of Rights was to be entrenched and at its relationship to the European Convention on Human Rights. Shortly before the poll, Gordon Brown, a committed reformer who was then Shadow Chief Secretary, speculated that there might be a new European Bill

[15] For the anxiety about the ease with which reforms could be reversed, see JM Ross, 'The Road to the Constitution' in Bernard Crick (ed), *National Identities. The Constitution of the United Kingdom* (Oxford, Blackwell, 1991) 153.

[16] Liberty was known as the National Council for Civil Liberties until 1989.

[17] Liberty, *A People's Charter. Liberty's Bill of Rights. A Consultation Document* (London, Liberty, 1991).

[18] Francesca Klug, interview with the author, July 2007.

[19] ibid.

of Rights and that some, but not all, fundamental rights might be entrenched.[20] Labour had begun to revise its thinking on fundamental rights, but the process was still in train when the election intervened.

By contrast, Labour's thinking on the decentralisation of power had moved further, faster during the 1987 Parliament. The principal agent of change here was not the maximalism of Charter 88 but the response of the opposition parties in Scotland to the 1987 election result. In July 1988 the Campaign for a Scottish Assembly published an assertion of popular sovereignty and an appeal to all Scots to support a constitutional convention to determine their future. The Scottish National Party subsequently withdrew from the process but by March 1989 the other opposition parties and a broad coalition of churches, trades unions and community groups had established the Scottish Constitutional Convention (SCC). It was committed to proceed by consensus and, aside from agreeing a prospectus for devolution, it undertook to mobilise opinion in favour of a Scottish legislature. By 1990 it had agreed that Scotland should have a Parliament with the power to pass primary legislation and to vary taxes. It would be elected by proportional representation. Scottish Labour did not find it easy to accept some of the compromises which were needed to secure agreement in the Convention, but it was clear that the process might create a formidable alliance for change. And the party in London was sensitive to the shifting mood north of the border: more than a fifth of Labour's MPs represented Scottish seats. In 1992 the party's manifesto endorsed the Convention's model for a Scottish Parliament.

The story in Wales was altogether more difficult for Labour. Popular support for devolution had always been weaker than in Scotland and the 1979 referendum had produced an overwhelming defeat for the Yes cause. The Wales Labour Party had been divided on the issue during the Wilson and Callaghan Governments and the Gang of Six MPs, including Neil Kinnock, had campaigned for a No vote in 1979. Kinnock subsequently changed his view but the party remained ambivalent about devolution in Wales and concerned that it would lead to a reduction in the number of Welsh MPs at Westminster. In November 1989 the Campaign for a Welsh Parliament was revived, but it never developed the momentum of its Scottish counterpart. The Wales Labour Party wanted to determine its own policy on devolution and it would not be drawn into a cross-party convention to hammer out a consensus view. Labour's policy documents could not disguise the party's discomfort. In 1989 the Policy Review sidestepped the issue, focussing instead on local government. By the time of the 1992 poll, the party was again advocating an Assembly, but whereas the Scots were promised a Parliament within a year of the election, the priority in Wales was seen to be a Welsh Language Act.

The constitutional reforms Labour put before the voters in the 1992 election were discrete measures each calculated to achieve a particular objective or to

[20] Gordon Brown, Charter 88 Sovereignty Lecture (9 March 1992).

neutralise a specific threat. The party accepted the maximalists' diagnosis of the country's ills, but it was sceptical about the prescribed cure. And on some fronts, the party had stepped back even from its endorsement of particular remedies. In 1989, for example, the Policy Review had endorsed a uniform structure of elected regional government for England; by 1991 elected assemblies were to be the second of three steps towards regional government with tax-varying powers; but by 1992 regional elections were simply deferred until 'later'.

Labour's most uncomfortable compromise in 1992 concerned proportional representation. This had been rejected by the Policy Review in 1989 but the leadership had subsequently agreed to establish a working party to consider the issue. Its discomfort was evident in the scope and timing of the study: it would not consider Westminster elections and it would not report until after the next general election. But if this was calculated to neutralise the issue it failed to do so. First, the party conference voted, against the leadership's wishes, to expand the working party's remit to include elections to Westminster. Second, the members of the working party began to develop more enthusiasm for proportional representation than had originally been expected. And third, Labour's election campaign ran into difficulties over proportional representation. Charter 88 had dubbed 2 April Democracy Day and was marking the event with events across the country. At his morning press conference, Neil Kinnock was pressed to explain how he viewed a possible coalition and what he might do if the Liberal Democrats demanded proportional representation as the price for their support. Kinnock, acutely aware that the polls were suggesting the race was tight, gave the impression that he was open to cooperation. He went on to trial the possibility that the Liberal Democrats might join Labour's working party on the voting system. This did not play well with Liberal Democrats who were seeking to persuade Conservative supporters to vote for them: they feared that the prospect of a common front against the Major Government would help to shore up the Conservative vote.[21] Kinnock did not help himself by subsequently avoiding questions on PR. For his part, John Major did his best to exploit the opposition's discomfort, warning of the dangers posed by their constitutional radicalism.

In the inquest that followed Labour's unexpected defeat Roy Hattersley was among those who argued that Labour had brought some of its problems on itself by getting drawn into an event staged and controlled by Charter 88.[22] Whether or not this observation was well-founded, the memory of Democracy Day was to stay with Labour. The tangle over proportional representation in 1992 was to stick in New Labour's collective consciousness, influencing its handling of constitutional reform in the run-in to the subsequent election. Matthew Taylor, director of policy

[21] David Butler and Dennis Kavanagh, *The British General Election of 1992* (Basingstoke, Palgrave Macmillan, 1992) 128–30.

[22] John Morrison, *Reforming Britain. New Labour, New Constitution?* (Edinburgh, Pearson Education, 2001) 29.

from 1995, recalls that the conclusion drawn by New Labour was that constitutional policy was 'more dangerous than it was productive'.[23]

It is worth noting what was absent from Labour's recalibration of its constitutional policies. The reformulation of its policy slate was the product of many and various considerations – under Kinnock and, subsequently, under Smith – but at no stage was it motivated by a new vision for Britain.

III. Labour Policy-making in the Wake of the 1992 Defeat

In the immediate aftermath of the 1992 election, Labour's fourth straight defeat, there was a sense of grief in the party. If Labour could not win under such relatively propitious circumstances, could it ever again expect to secure a majority? And if its prospects under the current system were bleak, should it begin to campaign for a more pluralist democracy, in which power was more widely distributed and citizens had greater protection for their fundamental rights? Democracy Day may have been a tactical error, but was the maximalist agenda perhaps worth re-examination?

The first evidence that Labour was willing to make fundamental changes to its constitutional programme came in a lecture by John Smith, the party's new leader, in March 1993.[24] He took two steps towards the agenda favoured by his hosts, Charter 88. The first was one of emphasis: constitutional reform was now to be front and central in Labour's offer to the public. Smith sought to persuade the audience beyond the lecture hall that change to the way Britain was governed was essential if the country were to make its way in the coming century. Constitutional reform was no longer the preserve of the chattering classes. The second change was one of substance: it came in his advocacy of fundamental rights protection. He committed Labour to incorporating the European Convention on Human Rights (ECHR) into UK law.[25] The party which had historically been so suspicious of the judiciary was now embracing a rights instrument whose interpretation would become a matter for British judges to determine. And Smith did not rest his case on the contingent argument that British citizens would now be spared the cost and time of taking their cases all through the British courts before securing their Convention rights in Strasbourg.[26] Instead, he emphasised that it was right in principle that British citizens should have access to a charter of fundamental

[23] Matthew Taylor, interview with the author, 8 June 2007.

[24] John Smith, 'A Citizens' Democracy', Charter 88 Lecture (1 March 1993, press release text).

[25] The ECHR was ushered into existence by the Council of Europe in 1950. The UK took the lead in ratifying it (in 1951) but for many years it took the view that it was for others to incorporate it into their domestic law: as an exemplar of freedom and democracy the UK did not need to incorporate it into its own domestic law.

[26] Britain was the first signatory of the ECHR in 1949 and it gave its citizens the right of petition to the Strasbourg court in 1966.

rights which guaranteed them protection from the state. It was an emphatic renunciation of the position by Roy Hattersley during the previous Parliament. Smith's Charter 88 audience could not have hoped for more.

Smith's next move met with mixed reactions from maximalists. In May 1993 he said that Labour would hold a referendum on the voting system. Optimists welcomed this as opening the door to electoral reform and evidence of a willingness to embrace direct democracy. Pessimists warned that Labour had not shaken off its pick-and-mix approach to the constitution: this was no more than a canny political move to prevent division in its ranks over the findings of its own working party on electoral reform. The two interpretations were not incompatible and the issue soon passed from the headlines.

Smith's two interventions were the most eye-catching developments in Labour's constitutional journey in 1993 but in parallel, the party undertook a review of its whole constitutional programme, presenting the results to the party conference in October. Tony Blair, now the party's home affairs spokesman, promised a 'constitutional revolution of democratic accountability and control, to redistribute power from government to people'.[27] Blair's principal priority at the time was to reinvent the party as tough on crime and tough on the causes of crime and so development of constitutional policy was largely in the hands of Graham Allen, one of the junior home affairs spokesmen.

Allen's influence was apparent in the language of *A New Agenda for Democracy*, which was published in advance of the party conference. In tone as much as substance, this was Labour at its most pluralist.[28] Much of the policy agenda set out in 1992 was restated. The commitment to ECHR incorporation now became yet more ambitious. This was to be the first step to a British Bill of Rights, which might secure citizens' economic and social rights. Reformers of a nervous disposition might have been alarmed that the policy on regional devolution in England was under review. Or they might have raised an eyebrow at the reference to undertaking Lords reform in two stages. But they had plenty of reason to be pleased, not least that the party seemed to be open to rethinking the meaning of citizenship. Hitherto, Labour had seen citizenship through the lens of immigration policy.[29] But there were sufficient hints in *A New Agenda* to give encouragement to the Citizenship Foundation and its allies that their efforts to rethink modern citizenship were beginning to attract attention.[30]

Peter Riddell has rightly described *A New Agenda* as 'the high point of Labour's constitutional ambitions and of its commitment to pluralism and to an explicit

[27] John Morrison, *Reforming Britain. New Labour, New Constitution?* (Edinburgh, Pearson Education, 2001) 35.

[28] Labour Party, *A New Agenda for Democracy. Labour's Proposals for Constitutional Reform* (Labour Party, September 1993).

[29] See, eg, Labour Party, *Meet the Challenge. Make the Change. A New Agenda for Britain. Final Report of Labour's Policy Review for the 1990s* (Labour Party, 1989) 62.

[30] The Citizenship Foundation had been established in 1989 to promote understanding of the meaning of citizenship within a modern democracy. Smith's Charter 88 lecture had spoken of a citizen's democracy, without fully developing the theme.

system of checks and balances'.[31] Its acceptance by the party conference in October 1993 was also the highpoint for Charter 88's influence over Labour's programme. The party had travelled a long way from its more modest constitutional agenda in 1987 but, critically, it had not abandoned its piecemeal approach to reform: discrete constitutional solutions were endorsed as the solution to specific problems.

IV. Labour and the Nation

When John Smith spoke about British identity in his Charter 88 lecture he emphasised its plurality. Devolution of power would allow the distinct identities within Britain greater scope to express themselves. Scotland, Wales and the English regions would each find their voice within a decentralised European Union, alongside the Länder of Germany or the provinces of Spain. He did not address the future of Britain: he was giving an address on constitutional reform and he saw no reason to agonise about the future of the nation state. Viewed through the reformers' lens, the nation state was not fragile; on the contrary, its executive had become over-mighty during the Thatcher years and those powers were now to be redistributed. Smith was in no sense hostile to the nation state. A confirmed European, he nevertheless was at pains to stress that Labour would defend Britain's interests in Europe. But when it came to constitutional reform, Britain was not the challenge to be resolved. The problems to be solved were how best to respond to Scottish nationalism, what to do about Wales and how best to fashion a politically attractive response to over-centralisation. Nor did Labour's exploration of citizenship indicate a new found fascination with what it meant to be British. On the contrary, this arose from its emerging interest in the balance to be struck between a citizen's rights and responsibilities, a theme which was later to return as a reference point in New Labour thinking.

Insofar as Labour had a political need to engage with the nature of Britain and Britishness, that need was defensive. It had to rebut the charges that devolution would endanger the Union and that closer engagement with the European Union would entail a loss of British sovereignty.

A wider debate about Britishness was stirring during Smith's leadership. When Linda Colley's study of the origins of British national identity was published in 1992, she judged that Britain and Britishness were both contested concepts. Great Britain

> as it exists today must be seen both as one relatively new nation, and as three much older nations – with the precise relationship between these old and new alignments still changing and becoming more fiercely debated even as I write.[32]

[31] Peter Riddell, 'Labour's Conversion to Constitutional Reform' in Andrew McDonald (ed), *Reinventing Britain. Constitutional Change under New Labour* (London, Methuen, 2007) 44.

[32] Linda Colley, *Britons. Forging the Nation, 1707–1837* (New Haven, Yale University Press, 1992) 374.

But the debate had not yet forced itself onto the political agenda. Some of its earlier manifestations were dismissed as the polemical expression of Scottish nationalism.[33] The Scots and the Welsh were becoming more reluctant to describe themselves as 'British' but this development had not yet attracted much attention. Hugh Kearney's assessment in 1991 would have commanded general assent:

> All but a small proportion of the inhabitants of the United Kingdom accept the term 'British' when applied to them even if they do not apply it to themselves without some thought.[34]

In the early 1990s there was no obvious imperative driving Labour to answer 'the British question', still less was there any reason to make the bridge between Britishness and constitutional reform. This was the territory of maximalists like James Cornford; Labour remained unpersuaded of the virtues of symmetry and coherence in its constitutional plans. Insofar as it addressed the issue of national identity, it conceived of it as a Scottish, not a British, question.

V. New Labour and the Constitution

When Tony Blair became Labour leader in July 1994, after the death of Smith, he focussed the party's efforts determinedly on victory at the next election. Labour under his leadership became a formidable campaigning vehicle, relentless in its pursuit of Conservative weaknesses. Guided by regular private polls and focus groups convened by Philip Gould, the party identified the most effective points of attack on the Government and sought to shield or eliminate its own vulnerabilities.[35] Policies were refashioned or dropped if they were judged a liability. Blair was conscious that the election might come as early as 1996 and he was determined to make early progress in crafting a programme which would command popular support. Mindful of the charges of betrayal which had been levelled at the Wilson and Callaghan Governments, he wanted to assemble a package that could be delivered in its entirety within the lifetime of one Parliament.

What did all of this mean for Labour's constitutional agenda? Labour's own polls suggested that constitutional reform was not a salient issue. In the words of Matthew Taylor, it was a 'no votes area'.[36] Reformers could point to public polling that showed consistent support for Freedom of Information, a Bill of Rights and even a codified constitution. But there was little in these polls to convince the

[33] For a striking early example of a sustained polemic, see Tom Nairn, *The Break-up of Britain. Crisis and New Nationalism* (London, NLB, 1977).

[34] Hugh Kearney, 'Four Nations or One?' in Bernard Crick (ed), *National Identities. The Constitution of the United Kingdom* (Oxford, Blackwell, 1991) 3.

[35] David Butler and Dennis Kavanagh, *The British General Election of 1997* (Basingstoke, Macmillan, 1997) 129.

[36] Matthew Taylor, interview with the author, 8 June 2007.

sceptical. The respondents were not asked to make a balancing judgement between conflicting options: confronted with an invitation to acquire more rights, they typically agreed to the proposition. Enquire further and it became apparent that respondents favoured a Bill of Rights which guaranteed timely hospital treatment and a right to public information, neither of which were to be delivered by the ECHR. Other Labour commitments – including devolution to the English regions, a referendum on the voting system and an elected second chamber – could not even muster majority support. The public seemed to be open to some change, but there was a prevailing mood of confusion: in 1995, 69 per cent of those polled said that they knew 'hardly anything' or 'just a little' about the constitution.[37] New Labour protested to constitutional reform audiences that their ambitions were central to the party's ambitions, but there was a presentational risk here: if the party appeared to spend too much time on issues low on voters' list of expressed concerns, it could appear remote or irrelevant.[38] As Matthew Taylor put it, there was a general desire within New Labour's ranks 'to say we are not [going to be] a Government that is obsessed with things that the liberal intelligentsia is obsessed by but we are obsessed by the things that Middle England is obsessed by. People washing their Ford Mondeo are not talking about Lords reform.'[39]

Whereas the polls failed to convince New Labour that there was much to be gained from a progressive constitutional programme, there was plenty of evidence that the Major Government was vulnerable to the charge that it was sleazy and untrustworthy.[40] Polling in 1995 showed that there had been a sharp decline in public confidence in government, in parliament and in official advice. The proportion of those thinking the system of government could be improved 'quite a lot' or 'a great deal' had risen from 63 per cent in 1991 to 75 per cent in 1995. In 1973 just 49 per cent had expressed the same view.[41] Encouraged by the Government's difficulties, Tony Blair and Jack Straw, now Shadow Home Secretary, pursued the issue of trust relentlessly. And they repackaged Labour's work on accountability as a Governance of Britain Act, which they presented in evidence to the Committee on Standards in Public Life. The measure did not survive to find its way into the manifesto, but it had served its purpose: it allowed New Labour to remind the public of Conservative scandals while setting out proposals to tighten the accountability of ministers, officials and quangos.[42] Labour's attacks on the Government's conduct increased in ferocity as the poll approached. Encouraged by each of the personal

[37] State of the Nation, JRRT-MORI poll, April-May 1995.

[38] For protestations of the importance of reform, see Tony Blair, John Smith Memorial Lecture, London, 7 February 1996 (press release text) and Tony Blair, 'Democracy's Second Age' *Economist* (14 September 1996).

[39] Matthew Taylor, interview with the author, 8 June 2007.

[40] Ed Owen, interview with the author, 31 May 2007.

[41] Patrick Dunleavy, Helen Margetts, Trevor Smith and Stuart Weir, *Voices of the People. Popular Attitudes to Democratic Renewal in Britain* (London, Methuen, 2005) 71.

[42] Derek Foster, speech on accountability, 15 January 1996. Jack Straw, Charter 88 lecture, 26 June 1996 (press release text).

difficulties that beset Conservative Ministers, New Labour worked and reworked a line of attack that portrayed the Government as remote, out of touch, overcentralised, unaccountable – and untrustworthy.[43] It was, of course, a line first developed in the 1980s, but it was now trained on a weakened Government, and it had been developed to include the final, sulphurous suggestion – that the Government was dishonest. Speaking in June 1996, Jack Straw left his audience in no doubt as to the historical dimensions of the crisis brought about by his opponents, 'For the first time since the great reforms of the nineteenth century the probity of British public service is widely questioned.'[44]

The Government's difficulties presented New Labour with a tempting, and productive target. The opposition could have driven home its advantage without committing to an extensive programme of constitutional reform. And the party's commanding lead in the opinion polls was not obviously attributable to its reform proposals. Notwithstanding this, one electoral calculation did suggest that New Labour needed constitutional reform. Tony Blair and those around him did not regard victory at the next election as certain. The Major Government may have been beset by difficulties over tax, Europe and sleaze but Blair had had an uncomfortably close view of Labour's failure in 1992. He had drawn the lesson that New Labour had to attract supporters from across the political spectrum and that the Party had to be ready to work in government with the Liberal Democrats. Even if New Labour could secure one majority on its own, history taught that it would struggle to repeat the trick. If Blair's project was to be completed over two or three Parliaments, it was probable that Liberal Democrat support would be needed.[45] And from the outset, it was clear that Paddy Ashdown's party would not contemplate entry into Blair's Big Tent without securing a commitment to constitutional reform. The courtship of Ashdown was well under way in 1995 and the private talks between the two parties took on new impetus early in the following year in the face of uncertainty over the timing of the next general election.[46] Blair gave public expression to this through his promise of a new, less adversarial politics, allowing more scope for cross-party collaboration.[47]

Seen through the lens of New Labour's electoral calculations, constitutional reform was of some tactical value in seducing the Liberal Democrat leader – and some of his potential supporters. Did it have any greater hold on the New Labour imagination? A maximalist would probably have said not after reading Peter Mandelson

[43] See, eg, Peter Mandelson, *The Blair Revolution Revisited* (London, Politico's, 2002 edition) 186–88. Labour Party, *New Labour, New Life for Britain. Policy Pocket Guide* (Labour Party, October 1996) 37.

[44] Jack Straw, Charter 88 lecture, 26 June 1996 (press release text). Later that year the Labour Party announced a major campaign 'to restore trust in the way we are governed' (Labour Party press release, 5 September 1996).

[45] Peter Mandelson, *The Blair Revolution Revisited* (London, Politico's, 2002 edition) 206–207.

[46] Paddy Ashdown, *The Ashdown Diaries. Volume I: 1988–1997* (London, Penguin, 2000) 313–14, 325, 347, 353–54, 359, 404.

[47] Tony Blair, John Smith Memorial Lecture, London, 7 February 1996 (press release text). Labour Party, *New Labour, New Life for Britain* 36.

and Roger Liddle's 1996 primer on the Party's plans. The authors did not turn to constitutional reform until chapter eight – of eleven – and then they issued a tart warning to enthusiasts:

> The first priority should be to reflect the public's anxieties about the way we are governed. The reform agenda must spring from the voters' concerns and not follow the master plan of constitutional theorists or be dictated by the interests of the chattering classes.[48]

But theirs was an argument about tactics and priorities. There was no suggestion here of any ideological tension between the New Labour creed and constitutional reform. New Labour believed in social aspiration, in meritocracy, in choice, in rights – and in responsibilities. It asserted the importance of the community not for its own sake but out of a conviction that the community was uniquely valuable in nurturing individuals and in giving them access to opportunity. All of this was perfectly compatible with a reformist agenda built around constitutional safeguards for the individual. But that is not to say that constitutional reform was an indispensable component of New Labour thought. It is not obvious that Freedom of Information or the incorporation of the ECHR, to take just two examples, were necessary to the Blairite project to 'modernise' Britain. This was, above all, a pragmatic political movement bent on securing power and using it to bring about change that would benefit – and be seen to benefit – the many, not the few. It would have been possible to have excised any mention of constitutional reform from the party's programme without offending New Labour's core beliefs. But nobody would have contemplated doing so. Constitutional reform pre-dated New Labour. Its presence in the programme was secured by the mood of the party (John Smith's legacy), by political obligations (Scottish devolution) and by electoral ambition (the courtship of the Liberal Democrats). And in any event, two of the most senior Labour front benchers – Gordon Brown and Robin Cook – were personally committed to constitutional reform. It was never in doubt that New Labour would retain a commitment to a constitutional reform programme. But the new opposition leader soon formed the view that the content and timing of the programme were in play and that they would need to be reviewed as the party prepared for the coming election.

Any discomfort New Labour may have felt about the reform agenda was masked in the public presentation of its policies. Indeed, constitutional reform had a quite specific utility for New Labour. The weighty constitutional agenda served as ballast for two of New Labour's favourite, but more elusive themes: modernity and national renewal.

New Labour presented itself as the party of the new, of optimism, of the future. The contrast with the tottering Conservative Government, long in power, was made clear for all to see. Commitments to reform the House of Lords, to update procedure in the Commons and to change the format of Prime Minister's

[48] Peter Mandelson, *The Blair Revolution Revisited* (London, Politico's, 2002 edition) 209–10.

Questions all served as evidence that the modernisation rhetoric was backed by substantive policies.

The commitment to national renewal went beyond the commonplace offer of a party seeking electoral support in return for a promise to change the country for the better. In pledging itself to renew Britain, New Labour was pursuing a complex, and changing, rhetorical agenda. This was apparent in Tony Blair's party conference speech in 1995. In an arresting phrase he expressed the desire that Britain should be a 'young country again'. His peroration brought together the renewal of the party and of the country:

> The prize is immense. It is new Britain. One Britain: the people united by shared values and shared aims, a government governing for all the people, the party founded by the people back, truly as the people's party. New Labour. New Britain. The Party renewed, the country reborn.[49]

A number of ideas were jostling for attention here and in other speeches and statements in Blair's first couple of years as leader. There was the unmistakable sound of a page turning – simultaneously on old Labour and on Tory Britain. There was the repositioning of the party: the people's concerns were its concerns, their aspirations were its aspirations. There was the identification of party and country: New Labour would stand up for Britain and for Britons. There was the argument that Labour was now the patriotic party, married with an audacious bid to win back the Union Jack from the Conservatives. And there was the assertion that New Labour and Britain had a shared moral purpose: the renewal of Britain would give expression to the solidarity and generosity of its citizens, stifled for so long during the Tory years.[50]

Not all of these ideas secured sustained attention from New Labour, but the core concept of national renewal was a constant in the run-up to the 1997 election. Constitutional reform was grist to the rhetorical mill. What better evidence could there have been of the party's ambitions for the country than its plans to reinvigorate fusty national institutions, opening them up to public scrutiny and handing power to citizens?

New Labour smoothly absorbed constitutional reform into its political critique of the Major administration as over-centralised, out of touch, moribund and marked by the scent of corruption. Equally smoothly, it absorbed constitutional reform into its millennial appeal to the voters: constitutional reform would be one symbol of the rebirth of the country. Enquire after the intellectual underpinnings of New Labour's support for constitutional reform and the edifice immediately appears less secure. Jack Straw would argue for a new social contract in which the

[49] Tony Blair, speech at 1995 Labour Party Conference in Paul Richards (ed), *Tony Blair in his own Words* (London, Politico's, 2004) 135.

[50] Tony Blair, 1995 pamphlet on anniversary of 1945 election victory in Richards (ed), *Tony Blair* 104, 108; and 1995 conference speech, ibid, 135–36. Tony Blair, 'Democracy's Second Age' *Economist* (14 September 1996).

rights *and responsibilities* of state and citizen were articulated.[51] Gordon Brown would also use a communitarian rationale for reform, echoing Straw's approach. But Brown was at heart a Scottish radical, committed to the sovereignty of the people. Nobody attending to his 1992 Charter 88 lecture was left in any doubt on that point:

> the current movement for constitutional reform ... signals the demand for a decisive shift in the balance of power in Britain, a long overdue transfer of sovereignty from those who govern to those who are governed, from an ancient and indefensible Crown sovereignty to a modern popular sovereignty, not just tidying up our constitution but transforming it.[52]

For Brown, there were three actors: individual, community and state. In his two Charter 88 lectures, in 1992 and 1997, he all but eschews reference to the 'nation' other than to make clear his contempt for the narrow nationalism practised by the SNP.[53] Rhetoric about national renewal had no place at this stage in his reformist rationale. Insofar as there was a dominant intellectual influence on New Labour thinking, it was the communitarian doctrine of Amitai Etzioni.[54] Brown was particularly sympathetic to communitarianism and insofar as he looked overseas for inspiration, he looked to the US.

Differences in New Labour argumentation attracted little public attention at the time. The party was on the front foot. On the constitution, as on so much else, it had the political critique it needed to keep the Government on the defensive. Nor did the party itself see much reason for agonising over different arguments for supporting the same policies. As Matthew Taylor simply notes, 'we weren't really a very theoretical bunch'.[55] Indeed the party was under no particular pressure to give any serious thought to its constitutional reform programme. Individual elements of the programme periodically came under pressure, but it was not until the summer of 1996 that the Government tried to mount a sustained counter-attack on the constitutional reform agenda, and that attempt soon faltered. There was no pressing need to consider the programme, or even to work through the links between the separate strands. It seems possible that the Shadow Cabinet and the Joint Policy Committee did not even consider the programme as a whole until 1996, when the draft manifesto was being prepared. To all intents and purposes New Labour had a number of discrete constitutional policy commitments. Links between those policies would be made only if the responsible frontbenchers saw a need to make them. And the policies themselves would only be developed further

[51] Jack Straw, Charter 88 Lecture, 26 June 1996 (press release text).

[52] Gordon Brown, Charter 88 Sovereignty Lecture, 9 March 1992.

[53] ibid. Gordon Brown, Charter 88 speech, 12 July 1997.

[54] Etzioni was an American-Israeli sociologist, who attracted particular attention amongst advocates of the Third Way in politics in the 1990s. He emphasised the role and value of the community in society and politics. His influence on New Labour has, on occasions, been exaggerated: he does not appear in the autobiographies of either Tony Blair or Gordon Brown.

[55] Matthew Taylor, interview with the author, 8 June 2007.

if the same frontbenchers applied themselves to the task. If an issue was generating enough heat, or if it posed a long-term risk to New Labour's fortunes, the leader and his office would intervene. But otherwise frontbenchers were given their heads. The results were variable.

VI. Shuffling the Pack: Preparing for Government

Before we consider how New Labour modified its stance on individual elements of the reform programme, it is worth pausing briefly to consider the principal players. Robin Cook and Gordon Brown, the two most committed reformers in the Shadow Cabinet, were preoccupied with, respectively, the foreign affairs and Treasury portfolios. The Shadow Cabinet itself did not afford them the opportunity to engage in lengthy collective examination of policies beyond their own patch. Responsibility for individual constitutional policies was scattered amongst frontbenchers, the result either of arguments over turf or, more simply, of lack of thought. John Prescott led on regional development in England; Jack Straw took regional government. Freedom of Information was in Derek Foster's portfolio, but Jonathan Powell, Blair's chief of staff, was of the view that it was Jack Straw's brief.[56] There was also confusion surrounding Lords reform: did Straw lead on it or was it Derry Irvine, the Shadow Lord Chancellor?[57] Irvine, who was to lead the constitutional agenda in Labour's first term was not yet a dominant figure. He was still working full-time at the bar and so was not in a position to make anything other than fleeting interventions in party business. No single frontbencher had been assigned oversight of the programme but at least one of them hoped for the role. Robert Hazell, director of the newly established Constitution Unit, saw Jack Straw in July 1995 and pointed up the absence. Hazell noted at the time, '[Straw] liked the idea of a senior minister being constitutional reform supremo, and said it should be him.'[58] This was of a piece with the way Straw conducted himself as spokesman on home affairs: he was genuinely interested in policy, he was determined to prepare seriously for government and he would, given a chance, 'snaffle' additional responsibilities.[59] His ambition was made clear in September 1996 in *New Life for Government*, one of the few attempts the party made to set out its constitutional programme as a whole. Straw was the moving force behind it but he was denied formal recognition as the lead spokesman on the programme.[60]

[56] For the view that FOI was Straw's, see BL CU LXXII, Robert Hazell, note of a meeting on 10 November 1995 with Jonathan Powell, David Miliband and Pat McFadden.

[57] Powell and Straw thought the latter had Lords reform: ibid and BL CU LXXIII, file 201(b), Robert Hazell, note of a meeting with Jack Straw, 10 July 1995.

[58] BL CU LXXIII, file 201(b), Robert Hazell, note of a meeting with Jack Straw, 10 July 1995.

[59] The phrase is Straw's. Jack Straw, interview with the author, 7 January 2007.

[60] The pamphlet also carried the name of Straw's deputy, Doug Henderson and Derek Foster, Shadow Chancellor of the Duchy of Lancaster.

It is telling that Blair saw no need to impose greater order on the distribution of constitutional responsibilities in opposition and that he did not appoint a lead spokesman. If the programme had been at the core of New Labour's project it seems hard to believe that these arrangements would have persisted.

The party's central machine, such as it was, focussed its energies on pursuing the Government: it invested little in policy development. Matthew Taylor recalls that his job on appointment as policy director was 'to rid the policy directorate of its final pretensions to be an actual source of policy and instead to focus the policy team much more explicitly on things like rebuttal, campaign materials [etc]'.[61] The resources at the centre were meagre: in this period there was just one researcher on the home affairs brief and he was fully occupied generating attack lines. Frontbenchers had just one or two policy aides and in most cases their time horizon stretched no further than tonight's speech or this week's ministerial questions.

It was within this context that we should understand the changes made to Labour's constitutional ambitions from Tony Blair's election as leader through to the summer of 1996. Some policies were trimmed; others were reinvented; a handful of new ones were introduced. Others were simply neglected: witness Freedom of Information, which remained in the portfolio, little noticed and under-developed.[62] One or two were dropped altogether. State funding for political parties, a commitment in 1992, was quietly shelved in favour of a less risky attack on Tory sleaze. And unnoticed by all but a few, the party stifled its earlier enthusiasm for a Ministry of Justice and for a Judicial Appointments and Training Commission. We will focus here on the core of the programme, to understand what changed and why.

On human rights, Jack Straw inherited a clear commitment – by Smith and Blair – to the incorporation of the ECHR into domestic law and a residual aspiration to a British Bill of Rights. Straw, who had once opposed incorporation, chose not to renounce a policy so recently championed by his new leader. But he opted to let the Bill of Rights die of neglect. The proposition, which had not been fully articulated, was never quite put out of its misery, but it no longer had official sanction. Straw himself floated the notion of a Bill of Rights *and Responsibilities* in June 1996.[63] The idea would periodically flicker into life again, but it would not return as a serious proposition for another 11 years, by which time Straw was Justice Secretary and Brown Prime Minister.[64]

The ECHR itself seems never to have been at serious risk, but nor could New Labour muster much enthusiasm for it. It seemed altogether too remote from the

[61] Matthew Taylor, interview with the author, 8 June 2007.

[62] But there were some hints of the battles yet to come over FOI: Peter Mandelson, *The Blair Revolution Revisited* (London, Politico's, 2002 edition) 204–205.

[63] Jack Straw, Charter 88 Lecture, 26 June 1996 (press release text).

[64] For a reminder of Straw's continued interest in the idea see, BL CU LXIX, file 950(2), Robert Hazell, note of JCCR 7th meeting, 4 February 1997. For Straw's subsequent return to the theme once Justice Secretary see, eg, his lecture 'Modernising the Magna Carta', 13 February 2008, George Washington University.

concerns of Mondeo Man and Worcester Woman and no serious attempt seems to have been made to connect it to their preoccupations.[65] If anything, Straw repositioned ECHR incorporation so that it became an even more recondite affair. It was no longer promoted as the renewal of citizens' rights. Rather, it was defended as a prudent reform which would spare litigants the cost and trouble of taking their case on from the British courts to the European Court of Human Rights in Strasbourg.[66] When Straw and Paul Boateng published Labour's detailed policy in December 1996 it was a thoughtful, careful proposal. Heavily influenced by the Constitution Unit's analysis of incorporation a few months earlier, it selected the party's preferred mode of incorporation and it trimmed some flourishes judged by Straw to be unnecessary. To the dismay of some reformers in Labour and Liberal Democrat ranks, he softened Labour's commitment to establish a Human Rights Commission to champion the cause: it was now simply stated as an option on which views were invited. The proposition as a whole was now technocratic: its modest ambition captured precisely by the leaden slogan *Bringing Rights Home*. This policy might have been feared by hoteliers in Strasbourg, but nobody else need have been alarmed – or excited.[67]

On English regional government, Straw recognised that the party could not abandon its earlier commitments: at its simplest, it would need Labour MPs from London and the North of England to back Scottish and Welsh devolution – and they would expect something in return.[68] But again he showed himself to be cautious. As we have seen, Labour had already tempered its earlier enthusiasm for a tier of elected regional government. Straw continued the process, inching back even from the 1992 policy. By September 1996, the party's support for regional assemblies had been made subject to three conditions: they would only be introduced in areas which already had unitary local authorities; they would need approval by local referendums; and they would have to be established without adding to the overall cost of local government.[69] A similar approach was taken in London: elected city-wide government would be restored only if it could be done without additional expense and only after Londoners had voted for it in a referendum.

On Lords reform, Blair made a decisive intervention, redefining party policy in his conference speech in 1994. He focussed the party's commitment on a one or two clause bill to deny hereditary peers the right to sit and vote in the Lords. The following summer Jack Straw explained privately that he had no interest in moving beyond this bill, questioning if there was any appetite to introduce elections to the upper chamber.[70] By February 1996 Blair had alighted on a new formulation: first

[65] Matthew Taylor, interview with the author, 8 June 2007.

[66] See, eg, Jack Straw, Charter 88 Lecture, 26 June 1996 (press release text).

[67] For an example of minimalism in the presentation of ECHR incorporation, see Labour Party, *New Labour, New Life for Britain* (Labour Party, July 1996) 31.

[68] BL CU LXXIII, file 201(b), Robert Hazell note of a meeting with Jack Straw, 23 August 1995.

[69] Labour Party, *A New Voice for England's Regions. Labour's Proposals for English Regional Government* (Labour Party, September 1996) 12–13.

[70] BL CU LXXIII, file 201(b), Robert Hazell, note of a meeting with Jack Straw, 10 July 1995.

the hereditaries would be removed and then there would be a debate over how best to introduce democratic accountability into the upper house.[71] He wanted to focus on an objective which was eye-catching and readily achievable; he feared that the reconstitution of the upper house would be a time-consuming diversion.

On PR and Scottish devolution much of Blair's work had been done for him by his predecessors. Smith's commitment to a referendum on PR had calmed the party's fears. Memories of the Democracy Day debacle were still strong and so few wanted to risk reopening the question. The timing of a referendum was left obscure, but this was not a first order issue until the Liberal Democrats made it so in the winter of 1996–97.[72] As for Scottish devolution, the key decision had apparently come under Kinnock, when Labour had committed itself to the Scottish Constitutional Convention. This delivered its final report in November 1995.[73] The process of arriving at a cross-party consensus had been painful and even after the Convention was dissolved some worried that the compromises might come unstuck.[74] But few had any reason to doubt that New Labour had a settled policy, rendered inviolable by the death of Smith.

The same could not be said of the party's policy on Welsh devolution. The Welsh Labour Party remained bitterly divided. After the uneasy compromise in the 1992 manifesto, the whole question was referred to a policy commission. By 1995, the party in Wales had a new policy.[75] In the first year of the next Labour Government legislation would be passed establishing a Welsh Assembly. There would be no prior referendum. The Assembly would be elected on a First Past the Post ballot. There would be no Cabinet and the Assembly would not have the authority to pass primary legislation. The policy was more clearly delineated than it had been in 1992 and it received the endorsement of the national party conference in October 1995. But only the most optimistic believed that the matter had been resolved. Ron Davies, the energetic party spokesman on Wales, was clear that First Past the Post was untenable: it was plain for all to see that it had been selected to entrench Labour's control of the Assembly. Urged on by Blair, Davies fought a long internal battle, which was not won until March 1997, when the party in Wales finally accepted a proportional system. In London, the party regarded the Welsh proposals with disquiet. Would they amount to anything more than a talking shop? What would the English make of them?[76] How could the Assembly secure its legitimacy without a referendum? This last question, championed in

[71] Tony Blair, John Smith Memorial Lecture, 7 February 1996.

[72] BL CU LXXII, Robert Hazell note of a meeting with Pat McFadden, 7 June 1996.

[73] Scottish Constitutional Convention, *Scotland's Parliament. Scotland's Right,* (Edinburgh, 30 November 1995).

[74] BL CU LXXII Robert Hazell note of a meeting with Donald Dewar, 23 November 1996.

[75] Wales Labour Party, *Shaping the Vision. A Report on the Powers and Structures of the Welsh Assembly* (Cardiff, Wales Labour Party, May 1995).

[76] See, eg, the scepticism of Jack Straw: BL CU LXXIII, file 201(b), Robert Hazell note of a meeting with Jack Straw 23 August 1995. BL CU LXXIV, file 200B, Robert Hazell note of a meeting with Jack Straw, Kim Howells and Ben Lucas.

Wales by the *Western Mail*, was picked up in London by Jack Straw. How, he asked, could the party argue for referendums in the English regions but deny them to the Welsh – and the Scots?[77]

The referendum conundrum had begun to preoccupy the party's Devolution Committee, which Blair had quietly established in the winter of 1995–96. Derry Irvine, confidant of Blair and one of the sharpest minds on Labour's team, was in the chair. Its brief was to conduct a rigorous, private review of the whole devolution agenda. Above all, this was an exercise in risk avoidance. Having fumbled the ball so disastrously in 1992, the party wanted to eliminate any possibility of a reprise. Within the constitutional programme only devolution was thought to carry any significant risk: it was technically ambitious and it might, if mishandled, invite the charge that the party was risking the break-up of Britain.[78]

The Devolution Committee reported on time, by 14 June 1996. Shortly thereafter Blair decided to rewrite the party's policy on devolution in Scotland and Wales. Parliament would legislate for an Edinburgh Parliament and a Cardiff Assembly only if referendums had first been won in Scotland and Wales. Events now moved fast. Independently, the Constitution Unit had been preparing its own report on devolution, reaching the conclusion that victories in pre-legislative referendums were needed to generate the momentum needed to push the devolution statutes through Parliament. The Unit had shared the draft report privately with Labour and so the party was able to prepare its response ahead of time. The Unit published the report on 25 June. Two days later George Robertson, the party's Scotland spokesman, had the unenviable task of announcing that it was his 'personal recommendation' that there should be two referendums in Scotland – one on the establishment of a Parliament, the other on whether it should have tax-varying powers. They should be held simultaneously and in the first year of a new Parliament. A parallel announcement was made in Wales.

There was outrage at this dramatic reversal of policy. In Scotland, John McAllion, the party's constitutional spokesman, resigned in protest, having been kept in the dark. Some of New Labour's partners in the Constitutional Convention spoke of betrayal. And Liberal Democrat critics of Paddy Ashdown were given new reason to distrust their party's collaboration with New Labour.[79] In Wales, the announcement opened up the real prospect that devolution would founder again: the 1979 referendum had been lost decisively and this time round the polls did not make reassuring reading. The hurt done to Blair's relations with his own party in Scotland and Wales took a long time to heal: some suspected that the manoeuvre proved that the leader had never been sincere in his support for devolution. But this charge is wide of the mark: the announcements in June 1996 were

[77] BL CU LXXIII, file 201(b), Robert Hazell note of a meeting with Jack Straw, 10 July 1995.

[78] Matthew Taylor, interview with the author, 8 June 2007.

[79] For Liberal Democrat reaction, see Paddy Ashdown, *The Ashdown Diaries. Volume I: 1988–1997* (London, Penguin, 2000) 441–42.

prompted by the desire to avoid unnecessary risk. There was no intention of abandoning devolution.[80]

From 1994 to 1996 New Labour trimmed its sails and tossed unwanted baggage over the side. But it did not change course. By the summer of 1996 the party's constitutional programme was still recognisable as the one set out in *A New Agenda for Democracy* three years earlier. The language had changed: it was now more guarded and the mood more reticent. Relations with Charter 88 were more distant and New Labour would express disappointment at reformers' failure to connect democratic change with the mainstream political agenda. Grassroots campaigns on PR or constitutional renewal attracted little attention in the party's Millbank headquarters.[81] Freedom of Information (FOI) or Lords reform was good for a clap line in a conference speech but they were irrelevant to the battle for votes at the next election. Wax lyrical about the renewal of the constitution and Blair risked seeming out of touch with voters' concerns.[82] And the more that New Labour's planners looked beyond the election, the more that they urged caution on the constitutional agenda. Peter Mandelson, in particular, sought to manage reformers' expectations while privately expressing his fear that a New Labour Government might get bogged down in constitutional reform.[83]

New Labour may not have welcomed all of their constitutional inheritance, but it would be wrong to suggest that their contribution was simply to chip away at it. In the years after Blair became leader the party added three new themes to its constitutional programme.

In 1996 the party committed itself to a renewal of local government. This was far from novel: opposition parties invariably commit themselves to renewals of local government. What was striking in this episode was the willingness to experiment with new forms of local democracy. There were to be trials of elected mayors and each year a percentage of local councillors would be subject to election in an attempt to spark new interest among apathetic voters.

The second theme was altogether more tentative. Blair and Straw both hinted at an interest in active citizenship.[84] The Conservatives had conceptualised Britons as consumers of public services. New Labour did not directly challenge this, but it suggested that citizens might engage in a fuller relationship with the state. They could expect the state to protect their rights. But they could also be expected to discharge their responsibilities to their fellow citizens and to the community as a whole. As we have seen, Straw hinted that there might ultimately be a new charter enumerating civic rights and responsibilities. But this excursion into citizenship policy was not primarily an exercise in constitutional reform. The real energy behind it came from New Labour's determination that the party should never

[80] See Peter Riddell, 'Labour's Conversion to Constitutional Reform' in Andrew McDonald (ed), *Reinventing Britain. Constitutional Change under New Labour* (London, Methuen, 2007) 46.
[81] Matthew Taylor, interview with the author, 8 June 2007.
[82] Paddy Ashdown, *The Ashdown Diaries. Volume I: 1988–1997* (London, Penguin, 2000) 515.
[83] ibid. Peter Mandelson, *The Blair Revolution Revisited* (London, Politico's, 2002 edition) 209.
[84] See, eg, Tony Blair, John Smith Memorial Lecture (London, 7 February 1996).

again be seen as the champion of the feckless poor.[85] Interest in innovation in citizenship policy petered out over time: by the time the party went to the polls its approach to citizenship was focussed on support for firm but fair immigration controls, the promotion of civil rights and the fight against discrimination.

The third theme emerged more by accident than design. Blair and Brown both showed some signs of enthusiasm for widening access to decision-making and for strengthening popular engagement in the democratic process.[86] But until 1996 there was little to show for this enthusiasm. Over the course of that year New Labour emerged, to its own surprise, as the champion of direct democracy. It committed itself piecemeal to referendums for Scotland, for Wales, for the English regions and for London. For good measure it opened up the possibility of citizen-initiative referendums to determine whether there should be elected mayors. And finally, in the run-up to the 1997 poll it promised the electorate a vote before Britain adopted the Euro. A commitment to direct democracy did no harm to the party's modernising credentials but in truth this was a retrospective rationalisation of unrelated policy shifts, each driven by tactical calculations.

The same observation could be made of most of New Labour's reworking of its constitutional portfolio. Its focus was on electoral victory; it had no time for grand visions of democratic renewal and it would not hesitate to recast specific policies if they were proving problematic. Some in New Labour's ranks were reluctant reformers, but few found Smith's legacy objectionable.[87] In January 1995 Graham Allen wrote a pamphlet charting an internal party struggle between pluralists and centralisers.[88] Allen, who had been removed from the home affairs team by Blair, wrote of his fear that the centralisers would triumph in Smith's absence. But the story of these years was more prosaic. There was no major ideological feud. The pluralists had never had a secure grip on the party. New Labour did not see itself in a contest with them, nor did they accept that they were centralisers. Blair and his team had other priorities, notably Labour's economic credibility and its plans to reform public services. Constitutional reform simply did not matter.

The preparation of the draft manifesto in the summer of 1996 did nothing to disturb this pattern. As with so much of New Labour's work in this period it was essentially a political manoeuvre, not an exercise in policy-making.[89] The brief to Robin Cook and David Miliband was to craft a programme which would not endanger New Labour's electoral prospects and which could then be delivered. The painful tactical modifications to the constitutional programme had already been

[85] Matthew Taylor, interview with the author, 8 June 2007.

[86] See, eg, Tony Blair, 'Democracy's Second Age' *Economist* (14 September 1996). Gordon Brown, Charter 88 Speech, 12 July 1997.

[87] For the balance of opinion within New Labour's ranks, see CU BL LXXIII, file 201(b), Robert Hazell note of a meeting with Paul Boateng, 9 September 1996. See John Morrison, *Reforming Britain. New Labour, New Constitution?* (Edinburgh, Pearson Education, 2001) 264–65.

[88] Peter Riddell, 'Labour's Conversion to Constitutional Reform' in Andrew McDonald (ed), *Reinventing Britain. Constitutional Change under New Labour* (London, Methuen, 2007) 46.

[89] Matthew Taylor, interview with the author, 8 June 2007.

made and so Cook and Miliband had little to do. The commitments were strung together fluently enough, but the programme remained a piecemeal assembly of discrete commitments in search of an overriding theme. Not that this seemed to disturb the party faithful: 95 per cent of them endorsed it as the party's programme for government.

VII. New Labour, No Britain

John Major's counter-attack on the constitution got under way in a speech delivered on 12 May in Glasgow – six weeks or so before New Labour's announcement of pre-legislative referendums in Scotland and Wales. He was quick to seize on the opposition's discomfort on the issue, but this was no more than one illustration of the Prime Minister's broader charge: New Labour's proposals were dangerous and ill-thought out. Major had decided as early as the summer of 1995 to take the constitution as one of his principal campaign themes. His party would defend the nation state by rallying to the constitution at home and by standing up for British interests in Europe. The Conservatives did not expect to do much damage to New Labour by targeting their constitutional reforms, but they did hope to prevent the opposition from making the running on the issue. And in any event, they had to mount a defence against nationalists in Wales and Scotland and, more threateningly, against the Referendum Party in England. Major could, and did, speak passionately about the constitution. He was an instinctive Unionist and a committed parliamentarian.[90] He believed, even if the polls gave little support to the notion, that he had made an impact on the constitution in the 1992 election. Be that as it may, he saw Labour's plans, especially those for devolution as acts of vandalism which had to be stopped, if at all possible. He was to maintain those views long after devolution had been accepted by his own party.[91]

The Conservative campaign in the summer of 1996 was just that – conservative. It was embellished with some minor policy initiatives, but above all it was an essay in Burkean conservatism. This was a hymn to the historic evolution of the British constitution, a reminder of one of the country's abiding virtues – and a rallying call to the party's demoralised supporters. The Union was in danger. New Labour could not be trusted with the country's future. A poster campaign punched home the message for those slow on the up-take: images of a white flag appeared under the slogan 'New Labour, No Britain'.

Michael Forsyth, the Scottish Secretary, was one of those sent to the barricades by the Prime Minister. Not one to understate his case, he warned darkly of New Labour's plans for the break-up of the UK. This, he claimed, 'was the hour for patriotism'. Warming to his theme he tried to define the character of his own

[90] Norman Blackwell, interview with the author, June 2007.
[91] John Major, 'Labour's deadly legacy puts the Union at risk' *The Times* (10 September 2014).

patriotism but succeeded only in demonstrating that it was not easy for a Scot to address a London audience about the future of Britain:

> My country is Britain; and Scotland. The two identities are complementary and enriching. So are the dual identities of those who are British and English; or Welsh; or Northern Irish. All those ancient birthrights are enhanced by the shared legacy of our British Constitution. Let us hand it down to the coming generations – entire and whole and perfect – the inalienable heritage of our united destiny.[92]

It was clear that in the coming battle Forsyth would yield to no man in his admiration for Britain's constitution.

For a time, a debate over the future of Britain looked as though it might splutter into life. The Conservative predicted a Tartan Tax north of the border, warned of the costs of the Welsh Assembly and urged repeatedly that the country was at a crossroads. New Labour chose not to join the battle. It did what it needed to do in announcing the devolution referendums, it explained its reform plans when questioned – but it had no desire to join a national debate on whether their plans put Britain's survival at risk. In their stead, Paddy Ashdown did choose to take on the Conservative charge, arguing that devolution would strengthen the Union and exhorting his followers to challenge the Government's appeal to the flag:

> I believe the Tories can be beaten on patriotism – because their patriotism is not true patriotism, but false patriotism, tinged with an ugly English nationalism.[93]

Some Conservative partisans continued to hope that a toe-to-toe fight might be joined on the constitution and that it offered Major's Government their best hope of survival.[94] But they were to be disappointed. Ministers' own proposals failed to capture the public's imagination: modifications to arrangements for consulting on Scottish legislation rarely do. A lengthy poster campaign warned of New Labour, New Danger. But voters were unmoved.[95]

VIII. Cook-Maclennan

In the course of their campaign in the summer of 1996, the Conservatives were at pains to insist that the constitution was under threat from the combined forces of New Labour and their witless allies in the Liberal Democrats. It is true that the opposition parties had been in informal talks for a couple of years, but they had yet to settle down to a serious attempt to hammer out a joint constitutional programme.

[92] Michael Forsyth, devolution speech, London 8 July 1996.
[93] Paddy Ashdown, speech, 26 June 1996.
[94] For a late – and extreme – example, see the *Daily Mail*, 6 January 1997.
[95] David Butler and Dennis Kavanagh, *The British General Election of 1997* (Basingstoke, Palgrave Macmillan, 1997) 38.

Indeed, in the summer of 1996 the Liberal Democrats went to some lengths to distinguish their reform plans from those of New Labour. Bob Maclennan, who led for them on constitutional reform, was determined to show that it was possible to think of reform as one, integrated whole. With this in mind, the party published its Constitutional Declaration in August.[96] It set out the case for a codified constitution and promised that one of the first acts of a Liberal Democrat Government would be to bring forward a measure modestly entitled the Great Reform Bill. This provided, *inter alia*, for a Bill of Rights, for fixed term Parliaments and for a referendum on PR. Not even the most optimistic Liberal Democrat envisaged that this would come to pass. But this exercise in maximalism was more than a theoretical workout for the Liberal Democrats' constitutional team. It had a serious tactical purpose: Maclennan wanted to use it as a benchmark in any future negotiations with New Labour.[97]

Those talks finally got under way in earnest in October. New Labour would host a meeting at London's St Ermin's Hotel; and a few weeks later there would be a return match at the National Liberal Club. The sequence continued until a report of their eventual agreement was published in March. Maclennan led for the Liberal Democrats, Robin Cook for New Labour. Their supporting teams would change from one meeting to the next, but both sides were at pains to demonstrate that they were taking the process seriously, fielding senior spokesmen on all occasions. Robert Hazell of the Constitution Unit provided most of the papers.

These were private talks. Private talks which were heralded and accompanied by feverish discussion in the media, encouraged by Ministers who urged the electorate to wake from its slumbers and to witness the plot to dismember the UK.[98] The two parties themselves did little to maintain their own privacy, regularly briefing the press on progress and, in January, encouraging speculation that the Tory MP Hugh Dykes would defect and immediately join the talks. (He did the first, but not the second.) Backbenchers in both parties, especially those in Labour-Liberal Democrat marginals, expressed their unease at what might come of the process. But the liberal press saw the sense of collaboration and gave the talks their blessing.

It is worth pausing on the talks because they give us a unique perspective on New Labour's thinking on the eve of power. The party's contribution to the discussion should not be taken at face value – this was a negotiation, not a seminar – but the records of the meetings show us the party's tactics in the months before the election. More than that, they show the party being forced to attend to the policies to which it was committed but which it had neglected to think through.[99]

[96] Liberal Democrats, *A People's Britain. Constitutional Reform. The Liberal Democrat Agenda. A Statement of Aims and Principles* (July 1996).

[97] BL CU LXXVII, files 202, 203, 209, Robert Hazell, note of a telephone conversation with Bob Maclennan, 9 October 1996. Robert Maclennan, interview with the author, June 2007.

[98] See, eg, Stephen Dorrell quoted in *Western Mail* (30 October 1996).

[99] Jack Straw, interview with the author, 7 January 2007.

The two parties entered the talks with quite different objectives. Robin Cook saw his job as establishing common ground with the Liberal Democrats, common ground that might be marked out in a joint statement. He did not want to have a painful examination of difficult questions: his colleagues would not tolerate it.[100] More than once, Hazell tried the patience of the New Labour team by tabling papers which posed just those questions which the party wanted to ignore. More than once he was brushed aside, most often by Pat McFadden, the New Labour secretary to the talks and member of Blair's inner circle.[101] Jack Straw, who cheerfully recalls that he won his place in the team because he was a 'backmarker', more sceptical than his colleagues, left the Liberal Democrats in no doubts as to the limits of the process. New Labour was not about to start trading its policies in the talks. If Maclennan's team did not accept Labour's approach to an issue there would simply be no agreement on it.[102]

In November, Maclennan confided in Hazell that he had limited expectations of the talks. But he went on to express hopes which went far beyond anything Cook had in mind. His first objective was one the maximalists held dear: he wanted agreement on the contents of a White Paper articulating the shape of the programme. If they got beyond that stage he would want to agree the contents of individual bills.[103] But he also wanted to educate New Labour. The traditional champions of constitutional reform hoped to bring the arrivistes in the Labour Party to an understanding of what they had taken on. And if the doubters in the Liberal Democrats were to be persuaded Maclennan needed to get a clear commitment from New Labour on PR for Westminster or for the European Parliament – and preferably both. Maclennan consistently focussed on the need for principles, for coherence and for a governing framework. And he wanted this underpinned by detailed discussion of policy, an approach encouraged by Hazell.[104] This was not an agenda calculated to curry favour with the New Labour team, some of whom still puzzled over their own leader's enthusiasm for collaboration with the Liberal Democrats. In some ways it was a surprise that the talks lasted beyond Christmas.

The initial meetings focussed on parliamentary tactics. Some of the participants could recall the bloody trench warfare which had characterised the devolution legislation of the 1970s. If this was to be avoided, there had to be a clear, realistic timetable. New Labour pragmatists feared that constitutional agenda could crowd out the core of the party's programme. Reform enthusiasts knew that their chance

[100] BL CU LXVIII, file 950(1), Robert Hazell, note of a telephone conversation with Robin Cook, 28 November 1996.

[101] See, eg, BL CU, LXIX, file 950(2), Pat McFadden to Robert Hazell, 23 December 1996.

[102] Jack Straw, interview with the author, 7 January 2007. BL CU, LXIX, file 950(2), Robert Hazell note of JCCR meeting on 14 January 1997.

[103] BL CU LXVIII, file 950(1), Robert Hazell, note of a telephone conversation with Bob Maclennan, 14 November 1996.

[104] BL CU LXVIII, file 950(2), Robert Hazell to Robert Maclennan, 14 February 1997.

to bring about radical change might disappear if the legislative tactics were wrong. And nobody allowed themselves to assume that an incoming government might have a commanding majority in the Commons. The advice they received from Hazell was cautious: they should not attempt more than one or two constitutional bills a session.[105] Both parties wanted to move on Lords reform first, to remove the hereditary peers who might prove an obstacle to the rest of the programme.[106] Cook's initial instinct was to take through the devolution legislation within the same session. But the more the talks wore on, the more cautious New Labour became. By February, Cook was talking of just one constitutional bill a session, a move encouraged by Blair's office but resisted by Maclennan.[107]

Some of the discussions of individual policies were relatively straightforward. On Lords reform Straw and Roy Jenkins readily agreed to an early move against the hereditary peers, to be followed – in the subsequent Parliament – by the second stage of reform.[108] Cook sided with the Liberal Democrats in wanting an explicit commitment to an elected second chamber. But it was Straw, not for the first time, who held firm. The draft manifesto had included the phrase a 'more democratic and representative second chamber', a formulation purposely designed to allow for indirect elections and for the retention of a number of appointed members. Straw, who acted throughout as though he held the Lords brief, insisted that this formula be retained for fear of starting hares running.[109] The final agreement argued for the establishment of a joint parliamentary committee to bring forward proposals for a 'democratic and representative second chamber'.[110]

On devolution and human rights, Cook and his colleagues left the Liberal Democrats in no doubt as to which of them was the junior partner in the talks. Maclennan argued, as he did throughout, for a coherent, structured approach. If devolution to Scotland was given priority, what would happen to the English regions? Surely it would be better to pass an early framework bill for devolution, taking in the whole of the UK? Cook brushed this aside, giving Maclennan a tutorial in Realpolitik. New Labour was committed to legislation on a Scottish Parliament in the first year: retreat from this position was out of the question. Welsh devolution was more problematic – because of divisions in the Welsh Labour Party – and England was more difficult still.[111] The final text was candid about the parties' differences over a referendum in Scotland but it proceeded to set out New Labour's preferred game plan: early referendums in Scotland and then Wales; legislation to

[105] BL CU LXVIII, file 950(1), draft paper JCCR (96)2 (by Robert Hazell, but unsigned).
[106] BL CU LXVIII, file 950(2), Liberal Democrat aide memoire on Lords reform, tabled at JCCR by Lord Harris, 8 January 1997.
[107] BL CU LXVIII, file 950(2), Robert Hazell note of telephone conversation with Pat McFadden, 22 January 1997. Robert Hazell note of JCCR meeting on 11 February 1997.
[108] BL CU LXVIII, file 950(1), Robert Hazell note of JCCR meeting on 19 November 1997.
[109] BL CU LXVIII, file 950(2), Robert Hazell note of JCCR meeting on 8 January 1997. ibid. Robert Hazell note of JCCR meeting on 28 January 1997.
[110] Report of the Joint Consultative Committee on Constitutional Reform, para 82.
[111] BL CU LXVIII, file 950(1), Robert Hazell note of JCCR meeting on 3 December 1996.

follow on both within the first session; and action on the English regions to bring up the rear, on a timetable yet to be determined.[112]

On human rights, New Labour was equally brusque. Cook made clear that it was not a political priority: it did not resonate with voters. Straw, who had recently mapped out Labour's policy in public, was not minded to make a public retreat at the behest of the Liberal Democrats. In particular, he was not about to fall in love with the Liberal Democrats' Bill of Rights, having spent the last couple of years quietly stifling Labour's earlier dalliance with the same idea. The meeting on 7 February took the bold decision of referring the dispute to Straw and Anthony Lester to resolve. To the surprise of some, the talks survived this experiment.[113] To the surprise of none, Straw got his own way, subject only to the observation that the ECHR itself would need to be updated 'over time'.[114]

The most bruising encounters were reserved, inevitably, for the consideration of PR. Cook, who was personally sympathetic to PR, was conciliatory; Straw was brutal.[115] The arguments ran throughout January and the future of the talks was clearly in the balance.[116] The Liberal Democrats wanted a commitment to an early – and rapid – commission to recommend an alternative voting system for Westminster elections; the commission's preferred system should then be put to a referendum before the end of the first Parliament. For good measure, they wanted New Labour to accept that the 1999 European Parliament elections should make use of a regional list PR system. After some testy exchanges it took an intervention by Tony Blair to clear the way to an agreement: he issued a statement saying that the referendum would be held within the first Parliament.[117] The final tally sheet showed that the Liberal Democrats had made good progress: the commission was to be established early in the Parliament; within 12 months it would recommend an alternative system; and the voters would have a choice – during the first Parliament – between that system and First Past the Post. The joint statement also endorsed the regional list system for European elections, although it did not commit to make this reform in time for the 1999 poll.[118] New Labour had chosen to give ground on the issue which mattered most to the Liberal Democrats. Over more than two years Ashdown had made it clear to Blair that progress on PR was essential if there was to be any broader accommodation between the parties. Blair had, reluctantly and belatedly, found a way of keeping the Liberal Democrats in play without putting his own party's unity in jeopardy.

[112] Report of the Joint Consultative Committee on Constitutional Reform, paras 38–40, 44–46, 49.
[113] BL CU LXVIII, file 950(2), Robert Hazell note of JCCR meeting on 4 February 1997.
[114] Report of the Joint Consultative Committee on Constitutional Reform, para 23. Straw also had to accept the return of a Human Rights Commission, a commitment which New Labour had dropped. The party's manifesto, to be published a few weeks later, was silent on the modernisation of the ECHR and on the desirability of a Commission.
[115] BL CU LXVIII, file 950(2), Robert Hazell note of JCCR meeting on 14 January 1997.
[116] ibid. Robert Hazell note of JCCR meeting on 28 January 1997.
[117] BL CU LXVIII, file 950(2), Robert Hazell note of JCCR meeting on 11 February 1997.
[118] Report of the Joint Consultative Committee on Constitutional Reform, paras 54–63.

The tone of the Cook-Maclennan report was a fusion of New Labour pragmatism with the Liberal Democrats' aspiration that the reforms be seen as one integrated whole. Enquire closely and you can almost see the joins between rival drafts:

> [This] is a programme which offers Britain a constitution for the future, not the past. It will share power for the many, not preserve it in the hands of the few …
>
> The proposals set out in our report are presented as distinct measures yet they are closely related. Through them runs the common thread of empowering the people. To make this clear the new Government should make an early declaration setting out the principles behind its programme of constitutional reform and outlining the more open and modern democracy it seeks to create.[119]

The Liberal Democrats had succeeded in infusing the text with a pluralist tone and they had, briefly, won the battle for a public narrative, explaining the programme to the people. This was ground readily ceded by New Labour. Its priorities were of a different order. It had wanted, and it had now secured, a deal which did not disturb its own compromises over individual policies, while keeping open the possibility of support from the Liberal Democrats. And it knew that it would soon be able to finesse the policy positions adopted by Cook-Maclennan when it came to finalise its own manifesto.

One theme was notable for its absence from the final report. The text had much to say about Scotland, Wales and even England. It was upbeat about the empowerment of citizens, whose rights were to be secured. But it was all but silent on the future of Britain. This, after all, was seen as Conservative territory: why encourage the thought that Britain's future was in question? And so the report simply fended off the issue with the assertion that devolution would strengthen the Union. Neither Liberal Democrat theory nor New Labour calculation argued for anything more.

Looking back on the committee's work eight years later, Robin Cook argued that it had been right for New Labour to seek consensus on constitutional reform. He judged this to have had a beneficial effect on the programme as a whole, but he noted sadly that it had not drawn the public into the endeavour. That was the big issue which remained to be addressed.[120] But negotiations over wording conducted in semi-private were never going to drive up popular enthusiasm for the reform agenda. Attempts were afoot to focus public attention on the historic opportunity for change, but these were conducted in parallel, in a hermetically sealed process. Maximalists hoped that New Labour pragmatists would be forced to pay attention to their noisy carnival of conferences and campaigns. Charter 88's long-running Citizens' Enquiry was timed to culminate in early 1997, with a constitutional convention to be held after New Labour's expected victory.

[119] ibid, paras 14 and 86.

[120] Robin Cook and Robert Maclennan, *Looking Back, Looking Forward. The Cook-Maclennan Agreement Eight Years On* (London, New Politics Network, 2005) 4.

As the Parliament entered its final lap, Charter 88 cranked a new venture into life: its Democracy Campaign called for FOI, for a Bill of Rights, for PR and for decentralisation. But New Labour was not moved; it had never been moved by these displays. And on the eve of an election it was not about to signal a reversion to the 1980s, when interest groups could secure a place for their pet projects in the party's manifesto.

Only one constitutional choice continued to trouble New Labour's planners. How best to get their programme through the Lords, where their own troops were heavily outnumbered and far from battle-ready? Ivor Richard, Labour leader in the Lords, noted that just 111 of more than 1,200 Lords took the Labour whip. Their average age was 73 and 15 of them were too ill for active service.[121] Ranged against them were the Conservatives, by far the largest party but without an overall majority in the Lords. They were marshalled by Viscount Cranborne, whose reputation was already well established on the opposition benches. One senior Labour peer confided in the *Guardian*, 'Cranborne will be an absolute swine. He smiles a lot but he's a reactionary.'[122] Richard and others took the lesson that the early removal of the hereditaries was essential if the new Government was to make headway in the Lords. This was, of course, New Labour policy – endorsed by Cook-Maclennan in March. But doubts persisted as to whether it was prudent. Donald Dewar, the Shadow Chief Whip, was one of those who feared that the early removal of the hereditary peers might give a sense of added legitimacy to the second chamber.[123] A New Labour majority in the Commons might find itself ranged against a more assertive Lords in which the governing party would still be in a minority. Cook-Maclennan took this point and argued for reform of the 'transitional House' – that is, the Lords after the removal of the hereditaries and before what became known to the tone-deaf as the final solution. During the course of the next Parliament steps would be taken so that the party balance in the Lords 'more accurately reflect[s] the proportion of votes received by each party in the previous general election'.[124] Both parties had an interest in securing this outcome, but both were chary about talk of 'flooding' the Lords with their supporters. Some in New Labour ranks hankered after an alternative approach: the new Government should speak threateningly *and* carry a big stick: they should hold over the unreformed House the prospect of removal of the hereditary peers and the appointment of more peers to the New Labour and Liberal Democrat benches. The Lords, cowed by this prospect and by the mandate of the new Government, would be quiescent. If they still saw fit to resist the New Labour programme, they would be reminded of the terms of the Parliament Act and of the Salisbury Convention.[125]

[121] BL CU LXVIII, file 950(1), Robert Hazell note of JCCR meeting on 19 November 1997.

[122] 'Blair to scrap Lords reform' *Guardian* (9 November 1996).

[123] BL CU LXVIII, file 950(2), Robert Hazell note of JCCR meeting on 28 January 1997.

[124] Report of the Joint Consultative Committee on Constitutional Reform, para 81.

[125] 'Blair to scrap Lords reform' *Guardian* (9 November 1996). The Parliament Act 1949 limits the power of the Lords to delay legislation passed by the Commons. The Salisbury Convention is an understanding that the Lords will not frustrate bills foreshadowed in the governing party's election manifesto.

By the time David Miliband and Derry Irvine settled down to draft the party manifesto in March 1997 it was inevitable that they should include a commitment to root out the hereditary peers at the first opportunity. But that by itself did not resolve the thorny question of how best to secure New Labour's programme in the Lords. As it put the final touches to its constitutional programme the party continued to agonise as much about the tactics as the substance of its reforms.

IX. From the Manifesto to the Polls

And so it fell to Irvine and Miliband to conduct yet another audit of New Labour's programme. One, final search for hostages to fortune. From the 'mass of awful paper' they inherited they had to conjure a campaigning document, a coherent rationale for supporting the party and a template for New Labour's first term.[126]

In the final text they got round to the constitution in the penultimate chapter. Their route into the subject was sleaze: their proposals were introduced by means of a commitment to clean up British politics.[127] There were few policy surprises, but the reworking of Cook-Maclennan commitments showed that the larger party would not readily accept concessions to its smaller partner. On Lords reform the text of the draft manifesto was restored: the party was committed to 'a *more* democratic and representative' upper house.[128] The commitment to change the balance of party affiliation in the interim house was softened: the objective remained to reflect more accurately the votes cast at the previous general election, but it was left unclear when this goal would be attained.

The wording of the passage on PR must have attracted even more tooth grinding in the Liberal Democrat headquarters in Cowley Street. Readers were told that New Labour was committed to a referendum on the voting system for Westminster, that there would be an 'early' commission to consider alternatives and that the party had 'long supported' PR for Europe. But no guidance was offered on the timing of the referendum nor on whether PR would be introduced in time for the 1999 European elections.

Human rights were dealt with summarily: in three lines the party committed itself to bring rights home. Devolution plans had finally been settled and so they were simply reiterated. The party confirmed its intention to move quickly: referendums for Scotland and Wales were to be held by the autumn and, if the electorates gave their blessing, the devolution legislation would be taken through within the first year. The remainder of the programme was set out with brisk efficiency, the

[126] The phrase is Irvine's: Derry Irvine, interview with the author, 27 October 2006.

[127] The maximalists in the Liberal Democrats adopted the same approach: see Liberal Democrats, *Make the Difference. The Liberal Democrat Manifesto* (Liberal Democrats, 1997).

[128] The author's emphasis. Labour Party, *New Labour because Britain Deserves Better. Britain will be Better with New Labour* (Labour Party, 1997).

prose all the brisker in passages where the drafters recognised that the underlying policy was incomplete.[129]

The manifesto was served up to the voters in a cover emblazoned with the Union Jack. Familiar New Labour themes were paraded. This was the moment for national renewal; New Labour was the party of the whole nation; the choice, it was made clear, was between depravity and decay on the one hand and moral purpose on the other. The New Labour vision was of a modern efficient economy and of an inclusive community in which individuals could aspire to better their lot.

These themes did not readily embrace constitutional reform. The bridge between the reform agenda and national renewal remained unbuilt. The link to moral purpose was constructed by taking a circuitous route via sleaze. Irvine, whose job it was to impose order on the whole, later conceded that the constitutional chapter did not fit easily with the rest of the programme. It kept its place, he maintained, because of New Labour's uncertainty about its prospects at the polls and the consequent need to reach out to the liberal middle classes in general and to the Liberal Democrats in particular. Irvine's implication is clear. The programme was something of a fluke: if New Labour had had more confidence in the opinion polls it might have curbed its constitutional commitments. Reformers might give credit to the manifesto's principal draftsman, who took the historic opportunity offered to him.[130]

Asked to explain the 1997 constitutional programme Charlie Falconer – who was to succeed Irvine as Lord Chancellor in 2003 – offered a contrasting explanation in 2006. He chose to attach less importance to the agency of the manifesto draftsman. Instead he argued that the manifesto was an expression of the national mood. The Tory years had come to be seen as complacent and elitist. New Labour embodied the rejection of those elites, wherever they were to be found. The constitutional agenda resonated with this egalitarian impulse. FOI, Lords reform and ECHR incorporation were all remedies for a country which had lost trust in its in ruling elite – whether that elite was in the civil service, the House of Lords or in Cabinet. And devolution, certainly as far as the Scots were concerned, was about throwing off English dominion. It was not about bringing power to the people, it was about protecting the Scots from rule by the English.[131]

Falconer acknowledged that these themes were – and were to remain – implicit rather than explicit. The party was not under serious attack on its constitutional programme, an advantage it continued to enjoy once in power. Jack Straw, who was to become New Labour's third Lord Chancellor in 2007, concurs: '[we] weren't challenged sufficiently … the Tories [were] so much on their backs'. In 1997 the country was not in the throes of an identity crisis; there was no need for New Labour to refashion the nation's sense of itself. Voters wanted rid of the Tories.

[129] eg, FOI, which merited just eight words. Irvine later acknowledged that the reference to it was brief because the policy was incomplete: Derry Irvine, interview with the author, 27 October 2006.

[130] Derry Irvine, interview with the author, 27 October 2006.

[131] Charles Falconer, interview with the author, 21 September 2006.

New Labour captured the popular mood. Constitutional reform was simply a sideshow in a larger political drama.[132]

Unchallenged, inconsistent in its development and largely unnoticed: the party's constitutional programme was all of these things. It was also the most radical prospectus for institutional change put to voters by one of the two principal parties in a generation. And it had the potential to reshape the way Britain thought about itself.

X. The Election

The prospect of the coming election had not brought the Government's trials to an end. In early 1997 it was still beset by internal feuds. The long-running scandal over cash-for-questions briefly ceded its place on the front pages to news that Piers Merchant, MP for Beckenham, had been kissing a 17-year old nightclub hostess. It cannot have been an interlude which did much for the Prime Minister's humour.

His party went into the campaign 22 per cent behind in the polls. In the first two weeks New Labour's lead remained solid. Thereafter the race tightened somewhat, but shortly before the election on 1 May there was still a gap of 16 per cent between the parties. The Conservatives were dogged by differences over the Euro. And they could not shake off the taint of sleaze. Unable to dislodge Neil Hamilton MP as its candidate for Tatton, the party had to watch as New Labour and the Liberal Democrats withdrew their own candidates in favour of Martin Bell, the former BBC journalist. Bell ran a high profile campaign focussing on sleaze in general and, in particular, on Hamilton's alleged involvement in accepting cash for placing parliamentary questions.

The constitution barely featured as an issue. John Major returned to his 1992 charge that Britain was in danger. But his best efforts, and those of his Scottish lieutenant Michael Forsyth, were to no avail. An ill-advised comparison between the Scottish Parliament and a parish council was to cause Blair discomfort at a press conference in Edinburgh on 4 April. But it was no more than a temporary distraction.

The swing to New Labour on 1 May was more than 10 per cent. The party had won 44.4 per cent of the vote and a majority of 179. The New Labour tacticians had secured their prize: the party had made gains throughout middle England while retaining its grip on the north, Scotland and Wales. For the first time ever, the Conservatives had lost all of their seats in Scotland; and they were without an MP in Wales for the first time since 1906. Across the country, voters had weighed up the most effective means of unseating the Conservatives. And they had voted tactically, with devastating effect.

[132] Jack Straw, interview with the author, 7 January 2007.

Asked to give their reasons for choosing as they did, voters made clear the political salience of constitutional reform. It came sixteenth out of the sixteen issues they were given to rank.[133]

XI. Into Government

As Tony Blair began to appoint his Cabinet on 2 May, his colleagues surveyed the new political landscape with a sense of wonder. Many asked themselves if their luck could possibly hold. They had won once but they would surely struggle to pull off a second victory, let alone one on this scale. This was their moment and it had to be seized.

It was clear from the parliamentary arithmetic that they would encounter little resistance from the Conservatives in the Commons. John Major announced his resignation and the dispirited rump of his party was soon preoccupied by a leadership election. It was equally clear that New Labour had no need of the Liberal Democrats: Blair called Ashdown on 2 May to confirm that there would be no coalition, but he left open the prospect of future cooperation.[134] It seemed probable that the Government's toughest challenge might come in maintaining discipline over its massed ranks of backbenchers – and in the House of Lords.

Blair's first Cabinet contained few surprises. Donald Dewar was switched to the Scotland portfolio to oversee devolution; Nick Brown took his place as chief whip. Derry Irvine duly became Lord Chancellor and Jack Straw the Home Secretary. But neither was anointed to lead the Government's constitutional programme. Robert Hazell had continued to press the case for this role, repeatedly urging Blair's team to accept that the programme was big enough and complex enough to merit coordination by a senior non-departmental Minister based in the Commons.[135] His pleas fell on deaf ears, but it was made clear (not least by Irvine) that the Lord Chancellor would apply his mind to the complex inter-relationships within the programme.[136]

Cabinet committees were to be the mechanism through which coordination was to be effected. But the main constitutional committee, CRP, met for just one substantive meeting.[137] The Prime Minister saw no particular need for CRP: it was Irvine's job to work through the detail, to ensure the policies hung together

[133] Vernon Bogdanor, 'Constitutional Reform' in Anthony Seldon (ed), *The Blair Effect. The Blair Government 1997–2001* (London, Little, Brown, 2001) 144.

[134] John Rentoul, *Tony Blair. Prime Minister* (London, Time Warner Paperbacks, 2002) 325–26.

[135] BL CU LXXII, Robert Hazell to Jonathan Powell, 10 February 1997. BL CU LXXII, Robert Hazell to Jonathan Powell, 14 February 1997. BL CU LXXII, Robert Hazell to Jonathan Powell, 22 April 1997.

[136] Lord Irvine, 'My pivotal role in the constitutional revolution' *Times* (12 July 1997).

[137] There was one further, informal meeting before the summer recess to resolve a disagreement over the Scottish white paper. This was retrospectively dignified as a formal session of the committee.

and to resolve any disputes. This approach gave maximum scope to the Lord Chancellor, who chaired no fewer than eight subsidiary committees, including those on devolution, human rights and Lords reform. He worked the system hard, cross-examining Ministerial colleagues on the quality of their proposals, keeping officials up to the mark and driving the whole programme forward.[138] In doing so, he soon won the respect of the Cabinet Secretary, Robin Butler. By contrast, Butler was alarmed by Ministers' overall approach to the programme. Their inattention to detail and their lack of forward planning subsequently prompted him to say that their approach had been 'frivolous'.[139] No such charge could be laid at the door of the Irvine. He soon acquired an altogether different reputation: there was soon talk that he might overreach himself. Most of the Cabinet's big beasts – including the Chancellor and the Deputy Prime Minister – steered clear of constitutional reform. On the issues that mattered to them, Irvine was at pains to consult them out of committee. Accordingly they saw no need to attend the meetings. But Jack Straw was an exception to the rule, attending diligently and sedulously testing proposals for coherence. It was a continuation of the role he had played in opposition and by the autumn the tension between the sceptical Straw and the enthusiastic Irvine was beginning to draw media comment.

The most pressing choice facing the new Government was the shape of its legislative programme. The first parliamentary session was to be unusually long, running from May until the autumn of the following year. After the lengthy ruminations of Cook-Maclennan and of New Labour's own planners, the time had come for Blair to decide how many of the constitutional reforms would be taken through in the first session. In the week before the election he had warned Butler that he did not want to be bogged down by the constitution: he wanted the devolution bills through by the summer. Butler had protested that this was impossible: the referendum bill would be required first. The conversation had ended 'grouchily' with Blair conceding that the devolution legislation was to be through by the end of the first session. Butler recalls that the exchange was 'rather nervous-making': Blair simply wanted the reforms out of the way.[140]

But for all of the Prime Minister's impatience with constitutional reform, his Government's first Queen's Speech showed extraordinary ambition to remodel the British state. The manifesto commitment to hold the devolution referendums by the autumn dictated the overall shape of the first session and it ultimately resolved the timing of Lords reform. The upper chamber would be asked to approve the Government's devolution plans – for Scotland, Wales and London – before their tolerance (and tempers) were tested by the removal of the hereditary peers. That would wait for the second session. But even the prospect of devolution and ECHR

[138] Tony Blair later gave fulsome praise to his former pupil-master for his leadership of the constitutional programme, implicitly acknowledging that he (Blair) had delegated all but Northern Ireland (which was different) to his Lord Chancellor. See, Peter Hennessy and Robert Sheppard, *Reflections. Conversations with Politicians, Volume II* (London, Haus Publishing, 2019), 159–160.

[139] Robin Butler, interview with the author, June 2007.

[140] Robin Butler, interview with the author, June 2007.

incorporation within the first session was not enough for some. Within days of the election some newspapers and some in the Liberal Democrats were bemoaning the Government's failure to bring forward early legislation on FOI. The maximalists remained suspicious of New Labour: they did not believe it was faithful to the reformist cause even as it brought forward the most radical constitutional legislative programme for generations.

Why did Blair choose to invest so much legislative time so early in his Government on a theme which was always of secondary importance for him? The answer is disarmingly simple: early action on the constitution offered the prospect of radical reform without great expense. Whereas there was a long lag between the introduction of new social policies and the realisation of their objectives, constitutional reform apparently offered instant gratification: the act of passing a new law could be seen to have brought change about. This was all the more valuable in the first two years of New Labour's term, when its backbenchers wanted the Government to get ahead, but its room for manoeuvre was limited by its own commitment to abide by the Conservatives' spending limits. Kenneth MacKenzie, the official who led the team coordinating the reform programme, captures Ministers' intentions:

> [they] were anxious to discharge their manifesto obligations, especially the Scottish and Welsh referendums before their (at that time) unbelievable luck at the polls ran out. Moreover, on the face of it, these were all measures which could be credibly (if in some cases mistakenly) assumed to be delivered within the Chancellor of the Exchequer's strict policy of absorption of policy initiatives within the frozen existing budgets of those doing the initiating.[141]

At the meeting of CRP on the afternoon of 6 May officials felt obliged to raise the question of how Ministers wanted to present the programme to the public. MacKenzie and his colleagues were expecting to be asked to prepare a White Paper setting out the Government's ambitions and explaining its rationale. In opposition New Labour had shown itself to be exceptionally deft in its public presentation of its policies and earlier on 6 May it had given the most spectacular proof that it would continue to shape the news agenda: to universal surprise, it had announced that the Bank of England was to be granted operational independence. But when it came to constitutional reform the Government showed itself to be altogether more tentative. Contrary to the Cook-Maclennan agreement, there would be no statement of principles; there would be no White Paper. Ministers feared that its preparation would set the programme back, to little advantage. Irvine was particularly impatient with the idea: the manifesto (which he had drafted) had said all that needed to be said. Why did anyone need a second blueprint?[142]

[141] Kenneth MacKenzie, '"Tears Before Bedtime". A Look Back at the Constitutional Reform Programme since 1997' (2005) 20(1) *Public Policy and Administration* 12.

[142] Robin Butler, interview with the author, June 2007. Kenneth MacKenzie, interview with the author, July 2007.

But to Irvine's evident irritation, some commentators continued to press for the Government to explain its programme as one integrated whole. By July he was writing in self-exculpatory terms in *The Times*. Stung by Peter Riddell's argument that the reforms were a piecemeal assemblage, he protested that this was wide of the mark. Cook-Maclennan, the manifesto and the work of the Cabinet committees demonstrated that this was an integrated whole. And he went on to essay a short summary of the Government's intentions: it was 'delivering power to the people, balancing rights and responsibilities, and restoring confidence in our constitution'.[143] This was at least a richer commentary than the one offered in the same month by the Prime Minister in his preface to the Scottish devolution White Paper: 'the Government are pledged to clean up and modernise British politics'.[144] Irvine felt obliged to return to the question in the following year, when delivering the Constitution Unit's annual lecture. His text offers a number of nuanced rationales for the reform programme, but then he stiffens his sinews and offers up a soundbite, albeit a rather grand one, 'in a sentence: our objective is to put in place an integrated programme of measures to decentralise power in the United Kingdom; and to enhance the rights of individuals within a more open society'. Lest they take too much encouragement from this pithy summary, he at once undercut it with his repeated insistence that the programme did not spring from a single master plan and many of its strands were not interdependent. These were principled reforms but they were also pragmatic, infused with the hallowed New Labour maxim that 'what matters is what works'.[145]

It was to remain one of the puzzles of New Labour's first term that this administration, so adroit at public presentation, never sought or found a consistent and effective way of communicating its reform programme.

XII. The First Session: May 1997–November 1998

On 11 July Donald Dewar commented on the Government's early pace on devolution: 'we have been trying to do in several weeks what took several years in the 1970s'.[146] This was no idle boast. The Government had got off to a flying start on arrival: the Scottish Office had prepared referendum legislation in advance of the election and it was introduced into the Commons in June. Each of the subsequent milestones was reached. The Government's plans for an Edinburgh Parliament and a Cardiff Assembly were published in July; the referendums were held – and won – in September; the devolution bills were introduced before Christmas; and both had received royal assent by November 1998. And on top of all of this, the

[143] Lord Irvine, 'My Pivotal Role' *Times* (12 July 1997).
[144] *Scotland's Parliament* (Cm 3658, July 1997).
[145] Lord Irvine, *Government's Programme of Constitutional Reform* (London, Constitution Unit, 1998) 4, 8, 12–13.
[146] Donald Dewar, speech at Economist/Charter 88 Constitutional Convention, London, 11 July 1997.

Government consulted on its proposals for devolution to London, won approval in a referendum in May 1998 and had passed the necessary legislation before the close of the second session.

The parliamentary passage of the devolution legislation caused the Government few alarms. Much hard pounding on the fine detail of legislation had taken place within the Cabinet committee on devolution. Donald Dewar was on the front foot, determined to take his chance and enjoying the support of a Scottish Office team on top of its game. Ron Davies had an altogether trickier brief not least because his colleagues in Wales were, at best, ambivalent about devolution and through the summer of 1997 it seemed perfectly possible that the referendum would be lost. He and Dewar became accustomed to the stern scrutiny of Irvine and Straw. Dewar overcame his past difficulties with Irvine and the two forged an effective working relationship. Straw recalls that Dewar skilfully pushed 'the envelope to obtain more power for the Scottish Executive and Parliament than many of us wished'.[147]

Devolution in Wales remained more problematic, for reasons both predictable and unexpected. The referendum in September 1997 was decided by just 7,000 votes; on a turnout of 50.1 per cent, the Yes vote secured just 50.3 per cent. The Government of Wales Bill was to present fewer hazards for the Government, securing its place on the statute books by July 1998. Having cleared these hurdles, the Government was to stumble again when Ron Davies, who was expected to become the First Secretary in the Assembly, suddenly resigned in October. He refused to say how it was that his car had been stolen after a nocturnal walk on Clapham Common and so the Prime Minister's spokesman helpfully explained to the press that Davies's departure had been occasioned by 'a moment of madness'.

The preparation and passage of the Human Rights Bill was an altogether duller affair. The Government had the wind in its sails and faced little parliamentary resistance. It stuck closely to the policy Straw and Boateng had set out shortly before the election. Parliamentary sovereignty would not be seen to be threatened. Judges would not be able to strike down legislation but they would be able to issue declarations of incompatibility, prompting Parliament to decide what should become of the errant law. The Cook-Maclennan report had breathed new life into the idea of a Human Rights Commission to champion the law and to support litigants. But it did not win a place in the bill, to the fury of its advocates. When the bill came to be published, the Government again put the accent on saving litigants' time and money. The accompanying commentary – inevitably called *Rights Brought Home* – was silent about what the bill would mean for citizenship in Britain. But the text did hint briefly at broader ambitions, suggesting that it might enhance awareness of human rights.

Irvine mostly stuck to the script, giving a prosaic account of the measure's practical benefits when introducing the second reading debate in the Lords. But in lectures, particularly to legal audiences, he raised his sights to broader horizons.

[147] Jack Straw, interview with the author, 7 January 2007.

Britain was leaving behind the traditional common law protection of individual liberties; incorporation constituted a positive assertion of the citizen's rights against their depredation by the state. Once British judges could draw directly on ECHR principles, we would begin to see the Convention driving the development of jurisprudence within the UK. The bill should be understood as one expression of an international move to protect fundamental rights. In the British case, that move speeded up the constitutionalisation of the judiciary: British judges would become ever more accustomed to checking the action of other branches of government.[148] This was not language likely to play well with conservative critics suspicious of the long-term implications of the bill and those who stood ready – in the face of all the facts – to condemn the measure as yet another import from Brussels. Straw himself eschewed such rhetoric. At times, he would position incorporation within a broader dialogue about rights and responsibilities but he customarily stuck to a more familiar beat: this would help British litigants secure their rights in British courts. Only the most attentive or most expert listener would puzzle out that the Human Rights Act, as it became in 1998, might come to be regarded as a turning point in British legal history. And only the most perceptive of tabloid journalists realised that they had just acquired a new whipping boy. The White Paper which accompanied the bill had been agreed bilaterally between Straw and Irvine. It was only presented to their colleagues on the Cabinet Human Rights Committee on the day they were to approve it. There was no substantive examination in committee of the political or legal consequences of the measure: most Ministers understood it to be a modest reform.[149]

Even though Lords reform had been deferred until the second session, the question of what to do about the Lords loomed large during New Labour's first year. Just as Donald Dewar, chief whip in opposition, had worried about how the party would secure its business in the Lords now it fell to his successor, Nick Brown, to agonise over the Government's fortunes in the Other Place.[150] His mood was not helped when the Lords inflicted an early defeat on the referendum bill. William Hague, the new Conservative Party leader, was keen that his party in the Lords should take on the Government, but Viscount Cranborne was more cautious. He favoured a more selective approach, inflicting just enough defeats on the Government to bring it to see that it needed to strike a deal on the future of the hereditary peers.[151] The most spectacular assertion of Conservative power in the Lords came at the end of the first session. Cranborne, encouraged by Hague,

[148] Lord Irvine, *Human Rights, Constitutional Law and the Development of the English Legal System: Selected Essays* (Oxford, Hart Publishing, 2003) 52.

[149] Kenneth MacKenzie, interview with the author, July 2007.

[150] Janet Jones, *Labour of Love. The 'Partly-Political' Diary of a Cabinet Minister's Wife* (London, Politico's, 1999) 83.

[151] John Morrison, *Reforming Britain. New Labour, New Constitution?* (Edinburgh, Pearson Education, 2001) 161.

and supported by Liberal Democrats and cross-benchers, inflicted five successive defeats on the Government's legislation for a closed list PR system for the European elections. In the end, the Government only got its way by bringing the legislation back at the start of the second session.

Irvine began to turn his mind to Lords reform in the summer of 1997, even though legislation would wait until the second session. He sounded out the Prime Minister in August and was encouraged to work things up quietly. This immediately prompted the question as to who led for the Government on Lords reform. The future of the Lords could not easily be given to a Commons minister and so Straw had to stand aside. Irvine had strong views on the issue, but even he could not comfortably lead on the policy *and* chair the relevant committee. In the end, Richard, who thought it was his brief, did the legwork with his special adviser. But Irvine drove the policy from the chair.[152]

In January 1998 Richard was given clearance to open secret talks with his Conservative counterpart or, as he put it: 'they've agreed I can "tickle" Cranborne'.[153] In the opening exchange, it seemed that it might be possible to craft a deal in which the second chamber was two-thirds elected and one-third nominated. The talks continued intermittently. They survived exposure in the press in March, but Labour peers became restive at the secrecy. There was talk of a Green Paper on the future of the Lords and Richard himself trailed the idea of a Royal Commission to determine the future composition of the upper house. But an accommodation with the Conservatives remained elusive and the Government seemed not to have made up its own mind on the best course of action by the summer of 1998.[154] Richard himself was deemed not to be part of the solution: he was sacked in Blair's first ministerial reshuffle in July.

Lords reform was one of the topics discussed periodically in the Joint Consultative Committee on Constitutional Reform (JCCCR). This latest manifestation of Lib-Labbery looked a bit like a Cabinet committee – it was chaired by the Prime Minister and serviced by Cabinet Office officials – but it did not decide anything and it did not report to Cabinet. The idea had arisen in a conversation between Blair and Ashdown as they returned from the ceremony to mark Hong Kong's independence in July 1997. Andrew Rawnsley later called it 'a decorative addition, a presentational token of [Blair's] often voiced desire to embrace a more inclusive, more pluralistic style of politics'.[155] But its establishment also confirmed that both Blair and Ashdown wanted to keep alive their parties' collaboration in

[152] Ed Owen, interview with the author, 31 May 2007. Kenneth MacKenzie, interview with the author, July 2007. Janet Jones, *Labour of Love. The 'Partly-Political' Diary of a Cabinet Minister's Wife* (London, Politico's, 1999) 130.

[153] Janet Jones, *Labour of Love. The 'Partly-Political' Diary of a Cabinet Minister's Wife* (London, Politico's, 1999) 161.

[154] ibid, 210, 217, 221, 250, 265.

[155] Andrew Rawnsley, *Servants of the People. The Inside Story of New Labour* (London, Penguin, 2001) 193–94.

the hope that it might yet grow into something more substantive. Throughout 1997 they prowled around a possible deal which might have included PR for Europe, a commission on PR for Westminster and the eventual delivery of PR for Westminster elections, possibly in two stages. And even though the electoral arithmetic did not argue for it, a coalition continued to be an option taken seriously by both leaders. In November Ashdown thought he was close to an historic deal on PR. But Blair stepped back. He deferred any talk of a coalition until the following May, conscious of the price he would have to pay within his own party. The Deputy Prime Minister John Prescott was amongst those he risked losing if the Liberal Democrats were to come into government.[156]

Maclennan characterises the Liberal Democrats' status on the JCCCR as that of 'privileged petitioners'. They may have encouraged Ministers to attend more thoroughly to the reform agenda, but he hesitates to claim the committee achieved much. In truth, both sides found it frustrating.[157] Those Ministers who did bother to attend questioned its value and the Liberal Democrats hankered after more substantive involvement, particularly on Lords reform, FOI and PR. At times the relationship helped smooth the passage of constitutional legislation, but many would have considered this a modest return on the investment of time and energy.[158]

Through the first half of 1998 Ashdown continued to search for a deal on PR and an agreement on coalition government. But the Prime Minister remained elusive. By June the two leaders felt the need to breathe new life into their cooperation, issuing a Constitutional Declaration after a meeting of the JCCCR. Once more, it took Liberal Democrat intervention to persuade New Labour to endorse a statement of the principles that should animate constitutional reform. The two parties pledged to bring power closer to the people; to strengthen citizens' rights; to render government more accountable; and to make British institutions more representative. The declaration addressed the need for FOI, for regional development agencies, for regional chambers and for the removal of hereditary peers. But tellingly, it had little to say about the future composition of the upper chamber or about PR for Westminster.[159]

Voting reform was most immediately a matter for Roy Jenkins and his colleagues on the independent commission the Government had established in December 1997. As Ashdown waited anxiously for its report, he continued to press the Prime Minister for a deal. But the Prime Minister pointed up the difficulties he faced: New Labour might split over PR and, in any event, an early referendum on the subject might easily be lost. And he reminded Ashdown that New Labour continued to harbour doubts about the reform agenda: '[they] believe the public

[156] ibid, 197.

[157] Robert Maclennan, interview with the author, June 2007.

[158] See, eg, Ashdown's intervention on the London bill; Paddy Ashdown, *The Ashdown Diaries. Volume II: 1997–1999* (London, Allen Lane, 2002) 161.

[159] Michael White report on the constitutional declaration, *Guardian* (12 June 1998).

are constitutionally satiated and could suffer from constitutional indigestion if another big change was put to them now'.[160]

It was not hard to understand why Blair might have been sensitive to the charge that New Labour was now obsessed by the constitution. Only months before coming to power it had contemplated taking through just one constitutional reform bill in each session: in its first parliamentary year (albeit a long one) it had taken through 11. Some of the reforms were not of its choosing: the EU prompted legislation on the Treaty of Amsterdam and on data protection. But these were exceptions to the rule: for the most part the Government had chosen to put its legislative energies into the modernisation (as it would term it) of the constitution. Devolution and human rights were only part of the story. For the first time, political parties were made subject to registration, a measure which would facilitate the subsequent introduction of PR – whether for European elections or for Westminster. Regional Development Agencies were to be established in England, a first tentative step towards regional government.[161] But most remarkable of all was the Good Friday Agreement in Northern Ireland. Blair chose to invest considerable political capital in the multi-party talks in the province, putting new energy into a process which had got under way during the Major Government. He was rewarded with a cross-community accord which was emphatically endorsed by referendums north and south of the border in May 1998. Elections to the new Northern Ireland Assembly followed in June and power was eventually transferred to the power-sharing executive in December 1999. For all the subsequent trials of devolution, the Good Friday Agreement remains one of the most remarkable achievements of Blair's premiership. It is the one constitutional reform which owes most to his personal intervention. It is also the one constitutional reform which sat outside the main reform programme, handled by a distinct team of ministers and officials. British policy-makers of all parties had long conceived of Northern Ireland as a special case, deserving of particular treatment. Northern Ireland was, quite simply, different and the resolution of its plight took place in a distinct political space, far removed from talk of Lords reform, PR or, even, devolution to Scotland and Wales.

The Government's first session initiatives were not restricted to statutory reforms. The modernisation of Commons procedures got off to a bright start: a cross-party committee set out an agenda for reform as early as July 1997. But the opportunity was lost: the Government's own whips resisted the proposals and No 10 saw no reason to insist on them.[162] Some also detected the hand of Downing Street in the strange tale of FOI. After the early howls of protest that FOI would not be in the first Queen's Speech, campaigners took some comfort from the Government's willingness to press on with an early White Paper. They could hardly

[160] Paddy Ashdown, *The Ashdown Diaries. Volume II: 1997–1999* (London, Allen Lane, 2002) 259.

[161] But of the eight established, none was made answerable to the Regional Chambers (the indirectly elected bodies which were intended to be the precursor of elected regional government). No progress was made towards regional elections in the first term.

[162] Robert Hazell, 'Reforming the Constitution' (2001) 72(1) *Political Quarterly* 43–44.

believe their luck when *Your Right to Know* was published in December 1997. If its proposals had been translated into statutory form Britain would have acquired the most liberal access regime in the world. But the Government showed no great enthusiasm for effecting that translation and critics again predicted the worst when David Clarke, the Minister who sponsored the White Paper, was sacked in the July 1998 reshuffle. Responsibility was passed to Jack Straw.

But as the first session drew towards its close, only the most sceptical of reformers found it in their hearts to cavil over New Labour's peregrinations on FOI or Commons modernisation. The pace had been relentless. And almost all of the immediate objectives had been reached. Power was to be devolved to Scotland and Wales. The nightmare experience of the Callaghan Government had been avoided. Blair's insistence on pre-legislative referendums had been vindicated. Turnout had been disappointing, but the votes had drawn attention to the historic choice facing the people of Scotland and Wales. And the Yes votes not only eased the subsequent passage of the legislation through Parliament but they also served to entrench the devolution settlement. No subsequent government would attempt to retrieve power from Edinburgh and Cardiff without first holding a referendum. Whether or not that was the Prime Minister's intention when he changed his party's policy in June 1996, his manoeuvre has subsequently won grudging respect from advocates of devolution.

Predictably, the incorporation of the ECHR had attracted even less attention from the public. There had been no concerted opposition and the Government had done nothing to stir up potential opponents. There had been nothing covert about New Labour's approach, but nor had ministers striven officiously to capture the public's imagination.

The first session was to prove to be New Labour's high watermark. It retained a commanding lead in the polls over a dispirited opposition. Its management of the news agenda attracted admiration from the commentariat. Not until the end of 1997 did it first encounter choppy water. Rows over party funding and lone parent benefit briefly disturbed the Government's composure. But for the rest of the session it continued to carry all before it. And constitutional reform was carried on the tide. Skilfully, briskly, manifesto commitments were honoured. Britain's quiet constitutional revolution was well under way, but with little discussion of what it all might mean for Britain.

XIII. The Second Session: November 1998–November 1999

Writing on 13 November 1998, Michael White, the *Guardian's* political editor, remarked on the 'near-completed constitutional agenda'.[163] The Queen's Speech

[163] Michael White report on the constitutional declaration, *Guardian* (12 June 1998).

later the same month seemed to confirm his calculation: just four constitutional bills were planned. But this tally does not tell the full story. The Government was now faced with a series of tough political choices on big issues. Lords reform could be deferred no longer. The European elections bill, cause of repeated defeats for the Government in the Lords, had now to be reintroduced or shelved. The Jenkins commission had just delivered its report on PR. The Neill committee had recommended sweeping changes to the funding of political parties. And the Government had to decide how best to make good its promise to publish a draft FOI bill. For Jack Straw, in particular, there was to be no let-up: elections, party funding and FOI were all now in his portfolio.

And it was in the second session that business as usual seemed to return to British political life. The opposition staged a modest revival. And the Government encountered problems of its own. Peter Mandelson and Geoffrey Robinson had to resign as ministers in December. The following May it endured a backbench rebellion over incapacity benefit. And in June it could muster no more than 28 per cent of the vote in the European elections. It was against this backdrop that it sought to do the heavy lifting on constitutional reform.

Lords reform was first up. By the summer of 1998 it had fallen to Irvine rather than Richard to tickle Cranborne. In an interlude more suited to the eighteenth century than New Britain, their lordships began an inelegant bout of horsetrading over the future of the hereditary peers. Irvine suggested that 10 of their number might survive. Cranborne had 150 in mind. The gap was too wide. Cranborne felt moved to remind Irvine of the weakness of New Labour's position in the unreformed house: 'Right then. Then it's the battle of the Somme and Passchendaele. It's the complete buggerisation of your legislative timetable.'[164]

By November a deal had been struck. In all, 92 hereditary peers were to survive in the transitional House, their fate to be reconsidered when the second stage of reform was completed at a date yet to be fixed. Irvine saw the deal as an exercise in pragmatism. Cranborne had pulled off a deft manoeuvre – but had neglected to tell his own party leader of his dealings with the Government. Hague sacked him for his subterfuge but chose not to renounce the deal. In December the Government brought forward its bill to remove all hereditaries from the Lords, knowing that it would be amended to allow 92 of their number to survive. The parliamentary dance went on its way – and by November 1999 the Irvine-Cranborne horsetrade had taken on statutory form.

The bill to eject the hereditaries had been published on the same day as a White Paper intended to set the scene for stage two of reform. The primacy of the Commons was asserted. An appointments commission was promised, to curb the Prime Minister's powers in choosing members of the transitional House. And there was now another reworking of the party's policy on the final composition

[164] Andrew Rawnsley, *Servants of the People. The Inside Story of New Labour* (London, Penguin, 2001) 202.

of the Lords: it was to be 'a chamber which is more representative of the country as a whole'.[165] Quite what this might mean was a matter to be considered by a royal commission to be chaired by Lord Wakeham, whose long experience of Conservative Cabinets included time as Leader of the Commons and of the Lords. He was to report by December 1999.

In the meantime, the death throes of the unreformed House were to prove uncomfortable for the Government. In November 1998 it reintroduced its bill for a closed list PR system for European elections, threatening their Lordships with the appointment of 50 New Labour and Liberal Democrat peers *and* a sitting on Boxing Day to push the bill through. In the end, neither expedient proved necessary. The Government got its way but the Conservatives announced a policy of 'zero tolerance' for bad legislation, inviting question as to what their previous approach had been.[166] The Government continued to suffer defeats for the remainder of the session. And the ejection of the hereditaries was to provide it with little relief. Just 182 of the 666 peers left in the House took the Labour whip. And the transitional House was soon to demonstrate that it regarded itself as more legitimate than its predecessor, defeating the Government 15 times before the summer recess in 2000. Some of these reverses were rendered all the more galling for the Government because the defeats might have been avoided if all hereditary peers had been expelled. To compound the Government's frustration, it found its legislation backing up in the Lords: it had neither the procedural authority nor the votes to timetable bills in the upper house. It was not difficult to understand why many in New Labour came to see Lords reform less as an essay in democratisation and more as exercise in how best to secure the Government's business.

PR was to prove no easier for the Prime Minister, but some of his colleagues remained mystified as to why their leader had chosen to trouble himself with the issue. The October 1998 party conference gave vent to these sceptical voices. When the Jenkins report was published later that month, Blair gave it a cool reception, to Ashdown's evident dismay.[167] Jenkins and his colleagues had recommended a hybrid solution. They dismissed the Alternative Vote as unlikely to deliver parliamentary results proportional to votes cast. The Single Transferable Vote would provide proportionality at the expense of single member constituencies. The compromise was AV Plus: 80–85 per cent of MPs would be elected by the Alternative Vote in single member constituencies. The remainder would be chosen from top-up lists linked to county-sized constituencies. The outcome would not be precisely proportional, but it would be much closer to the ideal than First Past the Post and it would preserve the constituency link. Modelling of the 1997 election result showed that under AV Plus New Labour's majority would have shrunk from 179 to 77; the Conservatives would have fared little better than under First Past the Post; and the Liberal Democrats would have almost doubled their representation

[165] *Modernising Parliament. Reforming the House of Lords* (Cm 4183, 1998).
[166] *Guardian* (28 November 1998).
[167] Paddy Ashdown, *The Ashdown Diaries. Volume II: 1997–1999* (London, Allen Lane, 2002) 314.

to 89. It was not a formula likely to woo the Conservatives, who remained the most committed supporters of the status quo. But the more salient question was whether Jenkins had managed to craft a formula which would be sufficiently modest to attract the Prime Minister without frightening off the Liberal Democrats, who were still partisans of STV.

The early signs were not promising. In his Commons statement on 5 November Jack Straw reminded his listeners, if reminder were needed, that he had long been an advocate of First Past the Post. There was no need to rush consideration of Jenkins; no change could be introduced until the general election after next; it would be appropriate to learn from the experience of PR in Scotland, in Wales and at the European elections; and it would be prudent to have a clearer sense of what was to become of Lords reform.[168] As far as the Liberal Democrats were concerned, Straw might as well have completed his list by deferring consideration until frost had been detected on the upper reaches of Hell.

Over the coming months Liberal Democrats had little reason for renewed optimism. The Prime Minister showed no sign of countermanding Straw. And New Labour's disastrous showing in the June 1999 European polls made it even less likely that he would do so. It was one thing for the Prime Minister in a position of strength to contemplate a system which would have trimmed his majority. It was quite another for him to recommend to his party a switch which might have secured their return to the opposition benches. He knew that discontent in his own party was growing and it was as much as Blair could do to keep alive any commitment to voting reform, however modest. By July 2000 the leadership was fighting a rearguard action to retain the party's pledge to hold a referendum on the voting system. In the National Policy Forum that month, the commitment was reworked: change would not happen without a referendum. In October, the party conference gave full voice to its scepticism: consultation had revealed serious doubts about AV Plus; there was strong support for single member constituencies; and it would be wise to learn from Britain's new experiments in PR.[169] It was already clear that there would be no referendum in New Labour's first term but it now seemed unlikely that even a second term administration would contemplate a vote – unless parliamentary arithmetic forced it to do so.

But this is to run ahead of our examination of the Government's second session. Lords reform and PR may have been the principal preoccupations but the lesser items in the constitutional in-tray proved equally tricky. The Neill Committee had recommended statutory regulation of political parties, to be policed by an independent Electoral Commission. Donations above £5,000 were to be declared, but they were not to be subject to any limit on their size. There was to be a modest restraint on the spending arms race: no one party could spend more than £20m in a general election campaign. In July of the following year the

[168] John Morrison, *Reforming Britain. New Labour, New Constitution?* (Edinburgh, Pearson Education, 2001) 252.

[169] Labour Party, *Democracy and Citizenship* (2000) 159–60.

Government signalled that it would accept most of Neill's recommendations. But it baulked at Neill's strictures on government publicity in advance of referendums, trimming the period of neutrality to the 28 days before the poll. And Treasury scepticism caused it to reject Neill's proposal that donations to political parties should attract tax relief. The political message behind the Government's response was clear: we will honour our commitment to clean-up politics, but we want to do so with cross-party support. Hence there was no appetite to reopen the question of capping party donations. Any proposal to curb large donations inevitably put the two largest parties into contention, a point which was to be demonstrated in the Government's third term when inter-party agreement on comprehensive funding reform foundered on this issue. But for the moment this was a dog that did not bark – and the Government saw no cause to provoke it.

Publication of the draft FOI bill in May 1999 was greeted with dismay by campaigners. They protested that New Labour had been seduced by its experience of government: the early radicalism of *Your Right to Know* had given way to a puny bill which would not tackle Whitehall's culture of secrecy. The pre-legislative scrutiny of the bill proved to be an uncomfortable experience: the Government was on the back foot, mounting a lonely defence of the case for confidentiality. It was not a cause likely to win many friends. The Government was not obviously penitent for having led campaigners up to the top of the hill and down again, but it was left with plenty on which to reflect before introducing the bill in the following session.

Beyond Westminster, the party had preoccupations of a different order. It came under serious pressure in the campaigns to elect the Scottish Parliament and the Welsh Assembly. The SNP mounted a spirited challenge and at one stage it seemed possible that the nationalists would beat Labour into second place in Scotland. Labour chose to focus on health and education, steering clear of constitutional issues. But Gordon Brown judged it necessary to respond to the nationalists' surge in the polls by warning of the perils of independence. He mounted a defence of the Union. Britain was diverse, not uniform. But it was bound together by the benefits that flowed from unity and by the values it held in common:

> I understand Britishness as being outward-looking, open and internationalist, a commitment to democracy and tolerance, to creativity and enterprise and to public service, and to justice or, as we often put it, to fair play.[170]

This was a theme to which he would often return in the years to come.

Labour recovered in the polls and emerged on 6 May with 56 seats to the SNP's 35. Lacking an overall majority, it sought support from the Liberal Democrats. Coalition-building was not an art much needed by recent generations of British politicians and it did not come easily to everyone, not least to New Labour in London, who mistakenly thought of themselves as participants. But a deal was

[170] Andrew Rawnsley, *Servants of the People. The Inside Story of New Labour* (London, Penguin, 2001) 252.

struck and Donald Dewar duly came into his inheritance as Scotland's *first* First Minister.

Labour's experience in the Welsh elections was no easier. The installation as leader of Alun Michael, London's preferred candidate, had done nothing for the humour of the party in Wales. Again Labour faced a strong challenge from the nationalists and in the vote on 6 May it was denied an overall majority, an outcome which would once have been unthinkable. Michael opted to form a minority administration rather than seek support from one or more of the smaller parties. His reign was to last just nine months.

By the close of the second session, the Government had (more or less) attained its primary goal on Lords reform; it had calmed backbench fears of the early introduction of PR; and it had found a way forward on party funding which would command cross-party support. None of this was comfortable and significant political capital had been expended in securing progress. This investment might have been easier to accept if the fruits of the Government's labours were immediately obvious. But it had had to endure criticism for its tergiversations on FOI, PR and Lords reform. The electorate had shown precious little gratitude in the May elections for Scotland and Wales. And the new administrations in Edinburgh and Cardiff soon showed signs of steering an independent course. None of this was likely to persuade New Labour doubters to warm to their constitutional toils. Britain was being reshaped – but at a cost to the party. It fell to the Prime Minister himself to argue for the long view. In an address to the Scottish Parliament in March 2000, he defended the reforms:

> When people point to differences in devolved policy and ask me, 'Isn't it a problem?' my response is that it is devolution. Not an accident, but the intention. Other people say it represents the end of Britain. The truth is quite the opposite. Our identity as Britain is a matter of our values and our interests. It is not about fossilizing institutions and refusing to change them. Indeed it would be failure to modernise that would lead to the end of Britain. That is why we are bringing our constitution up to date. To make sure that it does give effect to our continuing values in fast-changing circumstances.[171]

XIV. The End of the Affair: New Labour and the Liberal Democrats

The second session was to mark the turning point in New Labour's relations with the Liberal Democrats. In the summer and autumn of 1998, Ashdown had sought movement from Blair on FOI, Lords reform and, of course, PR. The Prime Minister continued to explore options with the Liberal Democrat leader, even floating the idea of a Big Bang referendum to be held in the second term: voters might be

[171] John Morrison, *Reforming Britain. New Labour, New Constitution?* (Edinburgh, Pearson Education, 2001) 73.

asked to decide simultaneously on PR and the future composition of the Lords. But Ashdown would have been forgiven for thinking that the emphasis was on jam tomorrow. Substantive changes to policy were few and far between. There was even an unseemly squabble at the JCCCR as to whether the Liberal Democrats could be trusted to see the Lords White Paper before publication.[172]

In November 1998 the two leaders tried again, announcing that they were to broaden their parties' cooperation beyond constitutional reform. Each was taken to task by critics on their backbenches. Neither was repentant, talking of their shared commitment to a new style of politics, rejecting the tribalism of the past.[173] But by January Ashdown had announced that he was to resign. In his final months as leader he finally accepted that Blair would not yield on PR for Westminster. But he encouraged the Prime Minister to offer concessions to his successor, in the hope that the parties' cooperation might survive his own departure. Blair seemed ready to consider a move on PR for local government or a softer line on FOI.[174] But nothing was forthcoming. And in August 1999 Charles Kennedy was elected leader of the Liberal Democrats. He wanted his party to be 'equidistant' between its Conservative and New Labour foes. Collaboration with the Government was off the agenda.

Looking back on the JCCCR, Robert Maclennan acknowledged that it did secure one modest change of Government policy. When Irvine finally did part with the draft White Paper on Lords reform the Liberal Democrats insisted that the text be amended to reflect one of the agreements reached in March 1997. The final text included the aspiration that the transitional House should reflect the balance of votes cast at the previous election. Cook-Maclennan had not been entirely forgotten.[175]

At a pinch, Liberal Democrats might also have claimed the credit for the introduction of PR in European elections, but this may well have happened in any case, even if not in time for the 1999 poll. But for the Prime Minister, constitutional reform had only ever provided the context in which he and Ashdown had explored the prospect of a more substantive collaboration. Maclennan, who had always opposed a coalition with New Labour, was clear on Blair's priorities:

> Once it became clear that the JCC was not attractive to the Liberal Democrats as a forecourt to Labour's 'big tent' it rather lost its appeal to the Prime Minister.[176]

Ashdown was more generous. For all the frustrations of his dealings with Blair – whether on constitutional reform or on a coalition – he did not question the Prime Minister's sincerity. He maintained that Blair was serious about reshaping British politics. Encouraged by Roy Jenkins, Blair was tempted by the prospect of making

[172] Paddy Ashdown, *The Ashdown Diaries. Volume II: 1997–1999* (London, Allen Lane, 2002) 384.
[173] Michael White report, *Guardian* (13 November 1998).
[174] Paddy Ashdown, *The Ashdown Diaries. Volume II: 1997–1999* (London, Allen Lane, 2002) 473.
[175] Robert Maclennan, interview with the author, June 2007.
[176] Robin Cook and Robert Maclennan, *Looking Back, Looking Forward. The Cook-Maclennan Agreement Eight Years On* (London, New Politics Network, 2005) 17.

the twenty-first century the progressive century, dominated by the centre-left, just as the twentieth century had been dominated by the Conservatives. The vision could not have been realised without PR for Westminster. Why was it not delivered? In Ashdown's view the Prime Minister was simply unable to overcome the formidable obstacles from within his own party.[177]

XV. The Third and Fourth Sessions: November 1999–June 2001

Michael White's verdict on the constitutional reform programme had been premature. In November 1998 the Government still had plenty of ground to cover. But the Queen's Speech 12 months later made it clear that the Government's constitutional ambitions for the remainder of the Parliament were all but exhausted.

FOI finally made it onto the statute books in 2000, but only after a bruising parliamentary passage in which Ministers again found themselves fighting an unpopular rearguard action. The regulation of party funding had an altogether easier ride: the uneasy truce between the major parties held firm. More controversial was the modification in electoral law to allow for experiments with new forms of voting, a venture which was to cause the Government much angst in its second term. And New Labour's own enthusiasm for novelty in local government found its way onto the statute books, with legislation to provide for elected mayors and for cabinets with executive authority.

With PR shelved – at least until the next election – the trickiest issue left to tackle was Lords reform. The Government took a vow of silence on the subject while Wakeham and colleagues were deliberating, not even offering evidence to the commission itself. Some on the government benches began to fear that New Labour would soon be outflanked on the issue. But the Conservatives' policy commission fought shy of radicalism, proposing two alternative models for a part-elected, part-nominated House.[178]

Radical was not an adjective that many felt tempted to attach to the Wakeham report when it was published in December 1999. The primacy of the Commons was asserted; nominated members should be selected by a new statutory appointments commission; at least 20 per cent of the House should be without party affiliation; existing life peers should remain; and efforts should be made to increase the representation of women and of ethnic minorities. As for elections, Wakeham offered a menu with three options: the elected proportion of the House should neither be

[177] John Morrison, *Reforming Britain. New Labour, New Constitution?* (Edinburgh, Pearson Education, 2001) 257.

[178] By June 2000 the Conservatives were outflanking New Labour: Sir George Young pledged that the Conservatives felt that even the boldest of the Wakeham options (a 35% elected House) did not go far enough.

less than 12 per cent nor more than 35 per cent. The press was not generous in its reception of the report, which many interpreted as a fix, calculated to cause the Government minimum discomfort.

The parliamentary debates on the report added little to public understanding of the Government's intentions. The Commons, which did not stir itself to consider Wakeham until June 2000, heard Margaret Beckett say that the Government was 'minded to accept the broad outlines' of the report'.[179] But she would not be drawn on the detail, nor on timing. The Government did act to establish an appointments commission but it did not adhere to Wakeham's prescription: the commission would not have statutory authority and its brief would be confined to vetting new peers for propriety and to recommending crossbenchers.[180]

In September the commission advertised for nominations for crossbenchers. No 10 heralded a new era of 'people's peers'. But reformers were unimpressed, predicting that the commission would ultimately put forward candidates drawn from the Great and the Good. The commission's first list confirmed the prediction and the phrase 'people's peers' was quietly dropped.

By September, if not before, it was clear that Lords reform would not be further advanced in New Labour's first term. What mattered now – on Lords reform and on the rest of the constitutional agenda – was what the party would say in its manifesto, and what the voters would say in the coming general election.

XVI. The First Term: Constitutional Reform Delivered?

In his survey of New Labour's constitutional achievements in its first term Robert Hazell detects just two blemishes. Nothing had been done about elected regional government in England and there had not been a referendum on PR. But close textual analysis of the 1997 manifesto text – and this was a text prepared to withstand just such analysis – suggests than even these blemishes are imaginary. Neither regional government nor the referendum were explicit first term pledges. The party had honoured each of its many manifesto commitments.[181]

What should we make of the record as it stood on the eve of the June 2001 general election? Few were willing to question the Government's industry, nor the

[179] John Morrison, *Reforming Britain. New Labour, New Constitution?* (Edinburgh, Pearson Education, 2001) 184.

[180] In other words, the commission's brief was in line with the Government's own preference as expressed in its White Paper.

[181] Robert Hazell, 'Reforming the Constitution' (2001) *Political Quarterly* 46. See also, Andrew McDonald and Robert Hazell, 'What happened next. Constitutional Reform under New Labour' in Andrew McDonald (ed), *Reinventing Britain. Constitutional Change under New Labour* (London, Methuen, 2007) 10–15.

scale of what had been achieved. The Scots had a Parliament for the first time in almost 300 years; the Welsh had their first elected assembly; citizens could mount human rights cases in British courts; and the referendum, so long a novelty in Britain, now seemed to be commonplace. The British constitution, always a malleable construct, seemed as though it had been changed for good. No sooner were the new institutions established than they appeared to be permanent fixtures: only the Welsh Assembly seemed vulnerable. This development tempted spectators and participants from across the political spectrum to offer conclusive judgements on the Government's reforms. From the Right, Peter Hitchens uttered a lament for the country he had once known. All he held dear was now at risk: Britain had been transformed in readiness for its absorption into a European superstate. Peter Mandelson offered a contrasting view, but he was no less definitive. Devolution had seen off the nationalists, civic rights had been secured. He conceded that there was more to do, not least to modernise local government and to engage citizens in their democracy, but Britain's constitutional reforms were the most radical since the Great Reform Act of 1832.[182]

Whether one celebrated the reforms or was dismayed by them, it was tempting to brigade them together and to conceive of them as a new constitutional settlement. But wiser heads warned that it was too early to speak in such terms. Writing in 2001, Anthony King accepted that most of the changes were irreversible, but he reminded his readers that questions remained about the future of Northern Ireland, the role of local government, the use of the referendum and (even) the party system itself. And New Labour's original agenda had not been exhausted, even if the terms of its 1997 manifesto had been fulfilled. What of Lords reform? What of PR? What of British membership of the Euro?[183]

During the Government's first term Britain began an experiment in complex, dynamic change. By June 2001 its new institutions were just that – new. The judiciary had only just begun to make use of human rights principles. Citizens did not yet have access to all of the rights for which Parliament had legislated. The country had not yet experienced a head-on clash between Westminster and Edinburgh – or Cardiff. Constitutional reform *begins* with Royal Assent, it is not delivered by the stroke of the monarch's pen. What matters is how the institutions perform in practice; what people make of their new rights; and how the state – in its multiple manifestations – interacts with citizens. Those questions were particularly pressing when the reforms were motivated by such disparate forces as those which lay behind the 1997 manifesto.

[182] Peter Hitchens, 'A Slow Motion Revolution' in Keith Sutherland, *The Rape of the Constitution?* (Thorverton, Imprint Academic, 2000) 157–67. Peter Mandelson, *The Blair Revolution Revisited* (London, Politico's, 2002 edition) xxii–xxiii.

[183] Anthony King, *Does the United Kingdom Still Have a Constitution?* (London, Sweet & Maxwell, 2001) 80–97.

XVII. The 2001 Manifesto

It was inevitable that the 2001 manifesto should have a more defensive tone than its 1997 counterpart: at its simplest, New Labour now had a record to defend. But the passage on political renewal (as it was now called) leant particularly heavily on what had been done rather than on what might be done. Devolution to Scotland, Wales and Northern Ireland was defended. Modernisation of the Commons was celebrated. Readers were reminded of those changes which *had* been made to voting systems. And, should anybody have been troubling over New Labour's use of special advisers, reassurance was given that the party would uphold the civil service's impartiality. The forward agenda was sketched in more tentatively, the party's discomfort all too plain to see. Jack Straw's now familiar formula on Jenkins was given another airing: the report would be reviewed in the light of experience of the new PR systems. There was no commitment to a referendum, simply an acknowledgement that any change would require approval at a referendum. On Lords reform, drafters fell back on the security offered by the 1997 draft: the party still wanted the House to be 'more representative and democratic'. Support for Wakeham was confirmed and the party would 'seek to implement it in the most effective way possible'. The appointments commission would be put on a statutory footing. An English Parliament, which had begun to attract some support among Conservatives, was not, we were told, part of New Labour's plans.[184]

New Labour had always been ambivalent about PR for Westminster and about stage two of Lords reform. By 2001 the party knew how tiresome each could prove and it had all but lost sight of the benefits that might accrue from pressing on. Its residual interest in the policies had dissipated. This much is easy to understand, but the difficulties over these two policies do not entirely explain the tone of 2001 manifesto. Why were the architects of Britain's constitutional revolution so unhappily rooted on the back foot?

Nothing that had happened over the course of the first term had persuaded New Labour that voters cared much about constitutional reform. This was an agenda which offered the party little prospect of gain and much scope for pain. The Government's first serious reverse, back in the autumn of 1997, had come over party funding, when Bernie Ecclestone's £1m donation to New Labour had been revealed. Later, Blair had had to watch, impotent, as Rhodri Morgan replaced Alun Michael as First Secretary in Cardiff. Worse still, he had to watch, again powerless, as Ken Livingstone – the embodiment of the Labour Left in the 1980s – was elected as Mayor of London. And all the while, Blair had to endure criticism that he was careless about the proprieties of Cabinet government and that his No 10 team

[184] The Conservatives had begun to make some progress on the issue of English votes for English laws after a speech on the issue by their leader, William Hague, in July 1999. See Hugo Young, *The Hugo Young Papers* (Allen Lane, London, 2008) 609.

manipulated the news agenda for party advantage. Matthew Taylor sums up the cumulative effect:

> Labour went off track in its first term because of Wales and London, because of the allegations of spin and sofa politics ... and it meant that [democratic renewal] no longer felt like a space that Labour politicians could talk about with a great deal of pride.[185]

Insofar as there was fresh energy in the party's plans for political renewal, it was expressed in an enthusiasm for active, engaged local government. Indeed, it seemed to signal that it was leaving old-style constitutional reform behind, declaring boldly, 'Change comes from the bottom up as much as the top down. For the last 50 years, governments have failed to respond to this basic truth.'[186] This chimed with the party's burgeoning interest in active citizenship and in local engagement.[187] But the manifesto had a more managerial focus: it wanted to drive up the quality of local services, to deliver best value and to change the financial incentives for local authorities, giving greater discretion to the best. It had little to say about the involvement of citizens in taking decisions which affected their lives and their neighbourhoods. The manifesto was equally elusive when it came to English regional government. Awkwardly, it simply repeated the policy as first stated in 1997: some regions may seek their own political voice. John Prescott's vision had not been abandoned, but the party could not bring itself to express enthusiasm for the cause. Nor did it have anything to offer on the future of England as a nation or a political entity, a theme which prompted it to be nervous throughout Tony Blair's time in office.

New Labour's judgement about the political salience of the constitution was confirmed during the election campaign. It attracted no greater interest than it had done in 1997 and voters told pollsters that it was a marginal issue for them.[188] Indeed much of the electorate failed to summon up any interest at all in the election. New Labour was returned with a majority of 165, but turnout fell to just 59 per cent, the lowest since 1918.

XVIII. The Constitution in the Second Term: 2001–05

Even the most ardent New Labour loyalist would be hard pressed to argue that the Government's second term did much to resolve its two most intractable constitutional dilemmas. Its work on PR took place out of public view. Government began

[185] Matthew Taylor, interview with the author, 8 June 2007.

[186] Labour Party, *Ambitions for Britain* (Labour Party, 2001) 34.

[187] See, eg, Labour Party, *Democracy and Citizenship. Consultation Paper* (Labour Party, 1999) and *Democracy and Citizenship* (Labour Party, 2000).

[188] Vernon Bogdanor, 'Our New Constitution' (2004) 120 *Law Quarterly Review*.

a review of the country's new PR systems, but nothing had been published by the time of the 2005 election. The party went to the country offering – a review.

By contrast, the Government's attempts to wrestle with Lords reform were all too public. It published its own proposals in 2001, reworking Wakeham and selecting an option his commission had not offered: the Government favoured a House which was 80 per cent nominated and 20 per cent elected. But it soon became clear that this was not a settled view shared by all ministers. Irvine, who was now unquestionably in the lead on Lords reform, let it be known that he was opposed to a hybrid house, part-elected and part-nominated. His preference was for a nominated house whereas Robin Cook, now leader of the Commons, favoured a predominantly elected chamber. Having given a commitment to a free vote on the issue, the Prime Minister finally stated his own view: he, like Irvine, was opposed to hybridity, a new term in the political lexicon. The free vote – or, more accurately, votes – did nothing to resolve the matter. On 4 February 2003, the Commons voted down all seven options put before it, rejecting everything from a wholly nominated house to one which was wholly elected. All it did agree on was that the Lords should not be abolished. In parallel votes, Lords voted down all options which included elections. But they, at least, did have a favoured solution: they voted overwhelmingly in favour of a wholly nominated house. Lords reform, which had long sat in the Difficult tray, now seemed bound for the Too Difficult tray.

But the Government tried again. Lord Falconer, Irvine's successor as Lord Chancellor, proposed making progress on those issues where progress seemed possible: the appointments commission should be put on a statutory footing and the remaining hereditary peers should be removed. This provoked a furious row over whether the Government was breaking faith with an undertaking Irvine had given to the house during the stage one reforms. Opposition peers maintained that the Government could not, in good faith, drive out the 92 until the long-term composition of the house had been determined. Irvine protested that the new proposals were consistent with his earlier pledge. Elaborate textual exegesis followed. But by March 2004 the Government had concluded that the game was not worth the candle: Falconer announced that there would be no further action on Lords reform for the remainder of the Parliament. Commentators were left to wait for the terms of the manifesto commitment to see whether the party would break the logjam by identifying a solution with sufficient precision in its manifesto to be able to face down the opposition in the Lords in the next Parliament.

The third item of unfinished business, first trailed in the 1997 manifesto, proved no more comfortable for the Government. John Prescott indicated that England's appetite for regional assemblies would finally be tested with polls in the north-east, the north-west and Yorkshire and the Humber. When it seemed probable that the Government was riding for a fall, plans for the north-west and Yorkshire and the Humber were put on hold. In November 2004, voters in the north-east were asked for their views on a regional assembly, a proposal characterised by opponents as a white elephant. An all-postal ballot was used to improve turnout, but less than half the electorate bothered to vote. The proposition was lost by 78 per cent to 22 per cent suffering rejection in every district in the region. Elected regional government in England had been killed off for the foreseeable future.

New Labour's interest in local government reform was to prove more rewarding. Having driven local authorities hard during the first term with a regime of central targets and inspections, the character of central-local relations was now reworked. Government showed itself willing to grant 'earned autonomy' to the most effective authorities. And, more broadly, there was an interest in alternative governance arrangements which did not conform to conventional notions of local democracy. NHS Trusts were established, granting hospitals greater control over their resources. And schools were offered the chance to secure new financial and management freedoms.

There was much debate about whether this New Localism amounted to a coherent strategy or to a loose association of policies pursued by different departments at different times. Geoff Mulgan, the New Labour strategist, captured this:

> The emphasis now is on devolution, fewer targets and more local accountability. But the debate about what 'New Localism' actually means is far from settled. One reason is the uneven capacity and legitimacy of local government ... A second is the fact that public demands for guaranteed minimum standards are if anything becoming even more intense. A third is the inherent difficulty of reconciling equity and diversity.[189]

Subsequently, New Localism began to morph into Micro Localism, an enthusiasm to empower neighbourhoods and parish councils. As the second term came to a close, New Labour continued to search for new ways of driving up civic engagement – whether through the ballot box or through more active participation in running local communities.

David Blunkett, now at the Home Office, addressed the same problem from a different perspective, briefly reviving New Labour's interest in citizenship. To be fully free, citizens had to engage in community life. They could not be expected to do that, nor could civic life flourish, unless they had an understanding of what it meant to be a citizen.[190] Hence civics returned to the school curriculum and for the first time new citizens were invited to attend citizenship ceremonies, to mark their acceptance of their new rights and responsibilities. Britain was following in the footsteps of Canada, Australia and the US in recognising that unless the state demonstrated that it valued citizenship, it was improbable that citizens – new or old – would do so. Unless Britain's constitution – ancient or modern – was explained, what hope could there be for a more engaged and empowered citizenry?

The party – indeed all parties – were preoccupied by the question of engagement during the second term. The sharp fall in turnout at the general election had been a shock. Optimists reasoned that it was no more than a rational response to a poll whose outcome was never in doubt. Pessimists constructed a nightmarish

[189] Anthony Seldon and Dennis Kavanagh, *The Blair Effect 2001–5* (Cambridge, Cambridge University Press, 2005) 72.

[190] David Blunkett, *Civil Renewal: a New Agenda. The CSV Edith Kahn Memorial Lecture, 11th June 2003* (Home Office and CSV, nd) 12.

vision of atomised communities and of individuals isolated from their neighbours, distrustful of public authorities and remote from the political process. Britain was bowling alone, its associational culture atrophied, its social capital in ruins. Sales of the works of Robert Putnam soared, not least among New Labour policy-makers.[191] But diagnosis proved easier than treatment and all parties went into the 2005 election nervous as to whether voters would return to the polling booths.

Human rights presented the Government with a number of challenges in the second term, some predictable and others out of the blue. The Human Rights Act had been brought into force in 2000 and the Government initially found cause for modest self-congratulation: the courts did not seize up under the weight of spurious human rights claims; the judiciary began to make cautious use of ECHR principles; and declarations of incompatibility were few and far between. So far, so good. Having struck a careful balance in the Human Rights Act, the Government was loath to have it upset by external events. The EU's Charter of Fundamental Rights and Freedoms had just that potential. The Charter had begun life as a political declaration issued at the Inter-Governmental Conference in Nice in December 2000. But it began to take on a more threatening aspect when the EU's Constitutional Convention began to explore its incorporation into a future Constitutional Treaty for the Union. The last thing the Government wanted was for the Treaty to establish new justiciable rights in economic and social matters. And so Britain fought a defensive battle in the negotiations over the draft treaty, seeking to preserve its labour market flexibility and to protect the public purse from claims to new entitlements to public services. The battle was sufficiently successful for the Government to feel able to agree to the final text at a summit in June 2004. But the treaty was subsequently to founder when Dutch and French voters rejected it in referendums.

The terrorist attacks on 9/11 were to present the Government with an altogether sterner test of its commitment to the Human Rights Act. It felt obliged to derogate from Article 5 of the Convention (the right to liberty and security) to give it scope to extend its powers of detention of terrorist suspects. But otherwise it wrestled with the new threat from international terrorism within the constraints imposed by the Act. Falconer later contrasted what happened after 9/11 with the response to IRA bombings in 1974. The Wilson Government took through tough anti-terrorist legislation and the courts made robust use of it. It was expected that Parliament alone should determine what was acceptable. But the Human Rights Act changed the role and authority of the judiciary: it was expected that judges would have a say in determining what constituted an acceptable response to terrorism after 9/11. It is far better, Falconer concluded, that society should reach

[191] Robert D Putnam, an American political scientist, won acclaim for his monograph *Bowling Alone* (New York, Simon & Schuster, 2000) which traced the decline of civic and political participation in the US. For his influence on New Labour, see eg: Labour Party, *Democracy, Political Engagement, Citizenship and Equalities. National Policy Forum Consultation Document* (Labour Party, 2003) 4.

its conclusions on the balance between security and freedom by reference to a set of principles – the ECHR.[192]

But those principles chafed and frustrated the executive. Most obviously they frustrated the Home Secretary who railed at interventions by the judiciary in matters he felt should remain the province of Parliament. For a time he conducted an angry public spat with the Lord Chief Justice, provoked by unpopular judicial rulings on criminal justice or terrorist cases. This was uncharted territory for the British and in the short-term, at least, the arguments did nothing for the popularity of the new human rights legislation. The tabloid press would protest that it ran in the face of common sense, a subversion of the British way of doing things. Louis Blom-Cooper offered a more measured assessment:

> The contemporary ructions between minister and judiciary occur in the context of increased resort to judicial review and the enhanced powers of the courts under the Human Rights Act. The Blair administration could hardly complain of the activism of the top judiciary; their enactment positively invited the test of its legislative programme for its compatibility with the provisions of the European Convention on Human Rights.[193]

The second term included one constitutional novelty. In June 2003, No 10 surprised everybody by announcing that the office of Lord Chancellor was to be abolished, the UK was to have a Supreme Court and in future a Judicial Appointments Commission would handle the selection of the judiciary in England and Wales. It was as though Downing Street had suddenly been overcome by an enthusiasm for Labour's constitutional policies of the early 1990s. Reformers who had long since despaired of the Government's radicalism expressed shock – and approval. But more significant was the reaction from those who felt that they might have been involved in the development of the proposals before decisions were announced. Consultation documents followed some weeks later, but goodwill had already been lost. Falconer, the new Lord Chancellor, had the unenviable task of piloting the Constitutional Reform Bill – embracing all three reforms – through an angry House of Lords. The Act found its way onto the statute books shortly before the 2005 general election – heavily amended, but consistent with the Government's principal policy objectives. It was far and away the most surprising constitutional reform of New Labour's second term.

The creation of a Supreme Court and the associated reforms were self-evidently significant reforms but they will not be receiving extensive analysis here. This is for two reasons. They were not part of any broader agenda. They were consistent with the devolution settlement but did not enhance it. They potentially left the judiciary in a stronger position to articulate Human Rights principles, but that was not the intention: indeed, the measures were significantly modified in negotiation with the

[192] Charles Falconer, interview with the author, 21 September 2006.

[193] Louis Blom-Cooper, 'Government and Judiciary' in Anthony Seldon and Dennis Kavanagh, *The Blair Effect 2001–5* (Cambridge, Cambridge University Press, 2005) 251.

judiciary and in their passage through Parliament. The proposals do not play any significant part in the discussion of the nation or national identity because they were conceived as part of a political stratagem which was almost wholly divorced from constitutional principles or policy.

The best account of the genesis of these reforms is by Andrew Le Sueur. He reminds us that reform of this sort had surfaced from time to time in Labour's thinking over the previous 20 years or so. But the political energy had been injected into the process by the manoeuvring of aides in No 10. They wanted rid of the constitutional embarrassment of the Lord Chancellor (at once a member of the executive, the judiciary and the legislature) and of its overmighty office-holder, former pupil-master to the Prime Minister and opponent to change. They stitched into the 'plan' the creation of a Supreme Court and of a judicial appointments commission. The rickety structure was prematurely brought into the open as the consequence of an unrelated reshuffle which was deemed to be the moment to sack Irvine. A press release was drafted and the word was out, all without a moment's Cabinet scrutiny or consultation with the judiciary. It was an object lesson in how not to mount fundamental reform and it presented an insuperable problem for any who cared to argue that the measures were part of a coherent New Labour strategy on constitutional renewal.[194]

XIX. The Constitution in the Third Term: Blair's Final Years

The 2005 manifesto spoke of voice and choice: local communities would be given greater say in determining what was right for them. Parish councils would be given new powers and communities would be given access to new resources. Disengagement, and its ugly sister mistrust, remained the party's primary preoccupations.

There were few surprises in the manifesto's constitutional commitments. PR was, of course, to be subject to a review; a referendum remained necessary before any change could be approved. There was a new urgency in the passage on the House of Lords. Its reform would be completed; the hereditaries would be removed. But the emphasis was now as much on the powers of the upper chamber as on its composition: the reformed Lords had to be '*effective*, legitimate and more representative without challenging the primacy of the House of Commons'.[195]

[194] Andrew Le Sueur, 'From Appellate Committee to Supreme Court: a Narrative' in Louis Blom-Cooper, Brice Dickson and Gavin Drewry (eds), *The Judicial House of Lords* (Oxford. Oxford University Press, 2009).

[195] Labour Party, *Britain forward not back. The Labour Party Manifesto 2005* (Labour Party, 2005) 110. Emphasis added by author.

It was hoped that by taking a fresh look at the role of the upper house it might be possible to unlock the question of composition. But the party would not prescribe a solution. Despite the experience of the inconclusive votes in February 2003, the question would be left to a free vote.

The party gave tacit confirmation to the nostrum that devolution was a process, not an event. It pledged to review the powers of the London Mayor and to enhance the powers of the Welsh Assembly. But it remained tight-lipped on exactly what it would do in response to the Richard commission's recommendation that the Assembly be granted primary legislative powers. When it came to Northern Ireland it was difficult to miss the note of exasperation; but it was equally clear that New Labour would do all it could to salvage the Good Friday Agreement.

In the two years until Tony Blair left office in June 2007, the devolution landscape was redrawn. The London Mayor was given new powers. The Welsh Assembly was put on a new footing, even if the full ambition of the Richard commission was not realised: the Assembly's legislative authority was increased, but it was denied the power to create primary legislation. The Government conceded that this might happen in time, but only after approval in a referendum. Devolution was finally restored to Northern Ireland and Blair's legacy was left, improbably, in the hands of Ian Paisley and Martin McGuiness. But an even greater shock came in Scotland, just weeks before Blair's departure. The SNP emerged as the largest party in the May 2007 elections. For the first time, Westminster and Whitehall had to hunker down in the face of a nationalist administration committed to independence. Devolution was to face its sternest test.

The final Blair Government continued to toil in other parts of the constitutional vineyard but none of its efforts was as eye-catching as the reshaping of devolution. Lords reform continued to frustrate all concerned. PR, if reviewed, was reviewed quietly. The Judicial Appointments Commission opened its doors for business. And legislation was taken through to provide for an Equality and Human Rights Commission. The new body was to have a broad remit to promote equality and to fight discrimination, but central to its purpose was the protection of human rights. Long after the Liberal Democrats inserted a commitment to a Human Rights Commission in the Cook-Maclennan deal, Britain had a champion for the cause. New Labour's change of heart is revealing. By the third term it was more receptive to the argument that constitutional change depended on cultural and attitudinal change. The Government, which at times had fought shy of a battle with the tabloids over human rights, was now willing to sanction an independent commission to improve understanding and to join the public debate.

This shift is indicative of the last period of Blair's constitutional reforms. In the third term there were few institutional reforms, no grand plans to extend new rights to citizens. But there was a new understanding of just how difficult it was to change the relationships between citizen and state. And there was a new commitment to work for the long-term renewal of those relationships. This was apparent in the extension of citizenship education – for schoolchildren and new citizens – to include democratic participation. The same commitment was clear in the Government's attempts to find innovative ways of involving citizens in policy-making, building on a major consultation on health policy in 2005.

XX. Britain's Quiet Constitutional Revolution

From time to time Britain's small band of constitution-watchers have felt moved to ask, nervously, 'Are New Labour's reforms working?' The question inevitably prompts much discussion about the purpose of the reforms and the outcomes sought by their authors. This chapter has shown that New Labour put before the country a piecemeal programme. It was not shaped in accordance with some master plan: contrary to what some have claimed, there never was a master plan. During its years in opposition the party accumulated a catalogue of reform commitments, each accepted as a remedy to a particular ill. And those were domestic solutions to domestic problems: the party rarely looked overseas for inspiration in its policy-making. Over time, those commitments were reworked according to political need, but the party rarely felt the need to think through the inter-relationships within the programme, let alone present the programme as one, coherent whole. They were not animated by a new vision for Britain. In truth, the reforms were a second order question for New Labour under Tony Blair. In chapter five, we will see whether Gordon Brown, for whom they had always been a first order issue, was able to impose coherence on the reform programme.

But one question was left unanswered by reformers during the Blair administrations.[196] What did all of this mean for the nation? If one is reformulating the Union through devolution and renewing the nature of citizenship through the Human Rights Act, one might have expected the British question to have forced itself onto the agenda. But the Blair Labour Party, with its dependence on Scottish votes and the prominence of Scots on its front bench, chose to look the other way. Insofar as it tackled the question, it did so from a quite different perspective. Net immigration to Britain was 48,000 in 1997; in the following year it rose to 140,000. By 2005 it was averaging almost 500,000 a year. This was the consequence of conscious policy, not least the decision to open the labour market to immigrants from the new EU accession states. And the Treasury was clear that Britain's economic health depended on an expansion of the workforce.

By the time Tony Blair left office, it was accepted that the sharp increase in net immigration was causing problems with what became known as social cohesion. Racism was again a subject of active concern, even if its targets were different from those who had faced it in the 1960s. The discovery that the 7/7 bombers were British-born Muslims only added to the tension and to the pressure on the Government to respond. The response, when it came, took many forms.

[196] This paragraph and the two that follow are influenced by David Goodhart, *The British Dream* (Atlantic Books, London, 2013).

The Government was at pains to show solidarity with Muslim Britons; to combat Muslim radicalisation; to toughen the asylum regime; and to make more of the award of British citizenship. (But the link from citizenship to the broader constitutional reform programme was still a rickety affair.)

Multiculturalism, a feature of British social policy since the 1960s, was retained but its tone was re-set. Tony Blair himself reformulated it as 'the right to be different, the duty to integrate'. But the challenge posed to multiculturalism by rapid immigration was not fully accepted. Still less was it acknowledged that increased diversity might ultimately threaten the nation state itself.[197] The 'British question' was infrequently voiced under Blair, let alone answered.

The Government exposed itself to ridicule when it flirted with the 'Cool Britannia' brand shortly after its election in 1997. It invited celebrities from the worlds of design and pop music to a reception at No.10 to thank them for their support in the campaign. It was a callow PR stunt which soon faded from the headlines. It did not pretend to address the character of the British nation, but it was to remain one of the Government's few initiatives which voters remember as having anything to do with the nation. It is fair to say that Tony Blair had left plenty of scope to his successor to shape the future of the Union and the nations within it. We will return to the way Gordon Brown went about that task in chapter five, but before that we will examine the way in which two liberal democracies – Canada and Australia – were using constitutional reform in a conscious attempt to re-engineer national identity in the late twentieth century.

[197] Paul Collier, *Exodus* (Allen Lane, London, 2013) 244.

3

'Just Watch Me': Pierre Trudeau and the Canadian Constitution

Pierre Trudeau's speech did not leave anybody in any doubts as to the significance of the moment. Canada had come of age:

> Today, at long last, Canada is acquiring full and complete sovereignty. The Constitution of Canada has come home … It is my deepest hope that Canada will match its new legal maturity with that degree of political maturity which will allow us all to make a total commitment to the Canadian ideal.[1]

The setting was quintessentially Canadian. The stage had been set up on Parliament Hill, framed by the gothic excesses of Ottawa's Parliament buildings. The crowd held maple leaf flags. 'O Canada' was sung. It rained. The Queen presided. Prime Minister Trudeau and Justice Minister Chrétien signed the proclamation of the Constitution Act, attended by the two officials who had laboured for so long to secure this prize. And the premiers of all but one of the provinces were on display, their differences with Ottawa set aside and the day celebrated as the fruit of Canadian compromise and comity. René Lévesque, premier of Quebec, stayed away. Listening to the Prime Minister's speech was one of his oldest political allies from Quebec. Seated among the guests of honour, he turned to his neighbour and whispered, 'the words of a traitor'.[2] It was all thoroughly Canadian.

This chapter tells the story of how it was that Canada's 'new constitution', as the Queen and others described it, came to be proclaimed that day, 17 April 1982; how it was that Canada finally took control of its own constitutional destiny, enshrining a charter of rights in its fundamental law, protecting the language rights for French and English-speaking communities, recognising the treaty rights of Canada's Indigenous Peoples, and committing the country to measures to equalise wealth between provinces.[3] There are many possible starting points for this story: some would begin in 1763, when Louis XV ceded Canada to George III, others in 1867, when the British North America Act, Canada's first constitution, was passed by the Westminster Parliament. But this chapter will take up the story at the centenary

[1] LAC Trud. MG 26.013, vol 52, Speech at the proclamation of the constitution (17 April 1982).
[2] Joe Clark, interview with the author, May 2006. Original in French.
[3] The Canada Act 1982 (UK) was not in fact a new constitution, but an important addition to the existing one. The British North America Act 1867, which was subsequently to be known as the Constitution Act 1867, remains in force.

of that Act, when Canadians were prompted – not for the first time – to consider who they were and what was the nature of their federation. In the 15 years that followed they – or their leaders – wrestled with those questions and in April 1982 they arrived at an answer. It was an answer that was to transform the country and its sense of itself: the Charter of Rights and Freedoms would become a symbol of the nation, celebrated in each of the provinces; its entrenchment would draw the judiciary into questions of social policy and public administration, shifting the balance between legislatures and the courts; and the isolation of Quebec would stiffen the resolve of separatists, while inciting federalists to conjure up ever more elaborate solutions for the country's constitutional ills.

I. Canada at the Centenary

John Robarts, the Conservative premier of Ontario, took the view that the nation should mark the centenary of the British North America Act in that most Canadian of ways – by seeking agreement on the reform of the constitution. He invited his fellow provincial premiers to a conference billed as *A Confederation of Tomorrow*. And in doing so he helped spark a renewed bout of anxious introspection and a flurry of new constitutional prescriptions for the federation. In the months that followed, tensions between the Liberal Government in Ottawa and the premiers soon came to the surface, many of them provoked by Ottawa's abrasive Justice Minister, Pierre Elliott Trudeau. Federalists might have differed over the distribution of powers between the federal government and the provinces, or over the wisdom of Senate reform, but they were agreed that Canada was still a young country which had the chance – the need – to bind its diverse communities together while respecting their differences. More than a century after the British North America Act, federalists still faced the challenge of nation-building.

As this debate got under way, even the most redoubtable federalist might have endorsed Robertson Davies' maxim that Canada is 'not a country you love, it is a country you worry about'. Their celebration of Canadian diversity masked genuine fears about the sustainability of the nation. This was a country torn by centrifugal forces. The influence of Britain was fading but was still potent in some parts of English Canada. More powerful was the inexorable lure of the US. Canada's vast land mass stretched east-west across a continent, but people's lives were organised around the north-south axis. Their cities, their factories, their jobs all clustered along the border; they watched American television, listened to American music; and they sheltered under the American nuclear umbrella. Twelve years after the centenary, the Pepin-Robarts Taskforce on Canadian Unity identified a 'multiplicity of solitudes': it agonised over the isolation of urban communities from the dwindling rural population; it pointed up the growing disparity in wealth among the provinces – exacerbated by the oil-boom in Alberta; it emphasised the growing ethnic diversity of the cities, fuelled by increased immigration; and it appealed to the nation to embrace the cause of its Indigenous Peoples – who had yet to find their voice in 1967. It is little wonder that Anglo-Tories like George Grant feared for the very survival of the country, predicting that it would come apart in the face of modernity and the market economy.

By the mid-1960s, when Grant was writing his celebrated *Lament for a Nation*, there was added reason to worry about the nation. Quebec, long under the authoritarian rule of Maurice Duplessis's Union Nationale party, was experiencing a cultural and economic resurgence under the Liberals of Jean Lesage. Denied opportunity for so long by the Anglo-Quebec elites, the ethnic majority now seized its moment: Franco-Quebec identity was vigorously asserted in the arts, in language and in journalism. And the Quiet Revolution soon expressed itself in a search for self-determination. Lesage spoke of the Quebec desire to become '*maîtres chez nous*'. For some this meant greater autonomy, but for others the logic of Canada's dualism led, inevitably, to separation. Either way, there was pressure for constitutional change. All parties in Quebec came to see the state as the engine which would drive the province's renewal. To create the space in which the provincial government could operate, Quebec began to press for the transfer of powers from Ottawa. The constitution was to become the arena in which identity politics were to be played out.

Writing before the Quiet Revolution, Maurice Lamontagne, a Quebec academic who was to advise two federal Prime Ministers, foresaw the choice that was to come into focus in the course of the 1960s:

> The way in which Quebec currently participates in the life of the Canadian federation is that of a province submitting to the drawbacks of the federation without benefiting from all its advantages, while the rest of Canada is in a hurry to attain new objectives ... The province of Quebec must therefore become conscious of this reality and make a choice.[4]

In 1967 General de Gaulle visited Montreal and fanned the flames of separatism by declaring to the crowds '*Vive le Québec libre!*' Ottawa invited him to leave the country and the moment captured international headlines. But de Gaulle was doing no more than shining a light on a separatist movement which already had momentum and energy. In 1968 the Parti Québécois (PQ) was formed from dissident Liberals and independent sovereigntists; René Lévesque became its first leader; and its first article of association committed it to separation from Canada.

In searching for a common purpose for the nation, it was not immediately obvious what a federalist might use to light the way. Canada did not have a founding myth. Its constitution had not been forged in the crucible of a popular revolution, nor had it ever been endorsed by an expression of popular support. Canada's

[4] Maurice Lamontagne, *Le Fédéralisme Canadien. Evolution et problèmes* (Sainte-Foy, Presses de l'Université Laval, 1954) 284 and 286 cited in Guy LaForest, 'One never knows ... Sait-on jamais?' in Michael Murphy (ed), *Canada: the State of the Federation 2005. Quebec and Canada in the New Century: New Dynamics, New Opportunities* (Montreal and Kingston, McGill – Queen's University Press, 2007). Translation by LaForest.

founding charter, the British North America Act, was aptly described as 'a colonial piece of legislation, written in the pedestrian language worthy of a municipal incorporation bill, but lacking in power and majesty'.[5] And its history was at best a challenge, if not a burden: a story of conflict between French and English colonialists and of the oppression of its Indigenous Peoples. It was easy to understand why the federal government, in one of its innumerable proposals for national renewal, seemed to want to wipe the slate clean, erasing the memory of Wolfe's victory at Quebec City – and much else:

> Too many outdated myths and old hang-ups persist in various parts of the country. They are like millstones around our necks: we must break the chains that bind us to them. Let us forget once and for all about the Plains of Abraham: the vanquished and the vanquishers are dead. Let us 'decolonize' Quebec in our own minds.[6]

In this vein, Canadian federalists had been seeking out new symbols for this young country: since the end of World War II it had acquired – after much argument – a new flag, a new anthem and a new 'brand' for the federal government. All the while, it became increasingly anomalous that Canadians did not have their constitutional future in their own hands: the Westminster Parliament retained the authority to amend the British North America Act. It was an obvious, but perilous, next step for federalists to renew their bid for sovereignty by patriating the constitution.

Did the uneasy accommodation between French and English amount to a 'Canadian way'? Was it enough to proclaim that the federation derived strength from its diversity, a country of immigrants peacefully co-existing? It was far from clear that this mortar was strong enough to hold the federal edifice in place. Perhaps more promising was the claim that Canadians had values in common, values which had been translated into practical, tangible action. After all, they seemed to believe in mutual support, as witnessed by the universal healthcare system, the federal pension plan and the equalisation payments which subsidised the poorer provinces. Canadians may be sparsely scattered across half a continent, but their experiences of the land, of the frozen north and of the struggle against the climate are common experiences. As Margaret Atwood has shown, survival is the essential *leitmotif* of Canadian literature.[7] And if common experience and common values were not enough to define the nation, federalists could always resort to defining Canada in contrast to its neighbour. Canada was not wracked by ethnic strife; Canada did not leave its poor and sick to depend on handouts from charity; Canada was not scarred by gun violence; and Canada had not become embroiled in Vietnam.

[5] Justice, file 251600-16, vol 4, pouch C, nr 2, Submission by the Committee to Democratize the Constitutional Debate to the Special Joint Committee, nd [1980].

[6] *A Time for Action. Towards the Renewal of the Canadian Federation* (Ottawa, Canadian Ministry of Supply and Services, 1978) 2.

[7] Margaret Atwood, *Survival. A Thematic Guide to Canadian Literature* (Toronto, McClelland & Stewart, 2004).

And so the federalist cause was far from hopeless, but in 1967 it had not yet found a defining theme. Over the next decade it was to face new challenges: the rise of interest group politics, Indigenous demands for self-determination, a strengthening of regionalist sentiment and an economic recession that put new pressure on an enfeebled federal treasury. Federalists feared that they were searching for unity in a fissiparous community. No wonder that the Pepin-Robarts taskforce was to ask plaintively, 'Why are we drifting apart?'[8]

II. Enter Trudeau

Pierre Trudeau had been in Parliament for less than two years when the centenary began. He had arrived in Ottawa at the 1965 election as one of the 'three wise men' from Quebec, a package deal negotiated by the Federal Liberal Party of which the prize was thought to be Jean Marchand, the trade unionist. But it was Trudeau who caught the eye. Appointed as Minister of Justice under Pearson, he set about driving the state out of the nation's bedrooms[9] – liberalising the law on divorce, abortion, contraception and homosexuality. The former professor of constitutional law began to learn a new profession. The easy fluency which had characterised his essays in *Cité Libre* would also be his signature in high office, but his directness and combativeness, assets for an essayist, would now cost him many friends. And his career prior to entering federal politics had given plenty of hostages to fortune: his contempt for the West was returned in kind; his refusal to fight in World War II was not forgotten in English Canada; and Quebec separatists were all too willing to quote back to him his 1962 characterisation of French Canada as economically destitute and culturally, intellectually and spiritually retarded.[10] In the eyes of his partisans he would later be credited with saving the country from schism, but even amongst federalists there were some who would always remember him as 'the hateful demagogue PE Trudeau'.[11]

Trudeau's spell as an academic has prompted some to analyse his views as one might trace the intellectual development of a detached philosopher diagnosing the ills of his nation. And it is true that his early statements as a Minister do read more like academic texts than political propositions. But it is problematic if we see him as an academic, still more as a philosopher. Even before he came to Ottawa,

[8] The Task Force on Canadian Unity, *A Future Together. Observations and Recommendations* (Hull, Quebec, Supply and Services Canada, 1979).

[9] Trudeau took the phrase from a newspaper headline and claimed it as his own.

[10] On a visit to the West as Prime Minister he famously thumbed his nose at the prairies. For the length of memories of his record during the war see, eg, Justice, file 251600-16, vol 4, pouch C, nr 1, letter to the Special Joint Committee from VH Coley of Edmonton, 19 November 1980. For his comments on French Canada in 1962, see Pierre Elliott Trudeau in Gérard Pelletier (ed), *Against the Current. Selected Writings 1939–1996* (Toronto, McClelland & Stewart, 1996) 170.

[11] Justice, file 251600-16, vol 4, pouch A, letter to the Special Joint Committee from EF Allistone of Vancouver, 17 November 1980.

he was a player, not a spectator, arguing a case, challenging opponents to a duel of wits. Once in government his life was the stuff of priorities, hard choices and political pressures. And he was in office during a time of rapid social change: by 1984, the year of his retirement, he was seeking to resolve problems which were unrecognisable from those which confronted him when he first came to Ottawa. If one neglects this context, his writing and his speeches seem inconsistent and perplexing. Even if one allows for the context there are tensions and changes in his thought which are difficult to reconcile.[12] Notoriously private, he would surprise even his closest advisers by a sudden change of tack or by the choice of a new line of argument.[13] But before we pick up the story of the constitutional negotiations initiated in 1967 it is worth piecing together some of the principal beliefs and theories that characterised his political career, even if we have immediately to add the rider that his thought changed over time, sometimes in ways which he was reluctant to concede.

The first, and most obvious observation, is that Trudeau was a liberal in the Lockean tradition. A belief in individual fulfilment and in the rights of the individual was central to his thought.[14] Only an individual could have rights; those rights could best be enjoyed in supportive communities but it was the individual, not the community, that was endowed with rights.[15] And those rights were shared by all equally: the essence of citizenship was the participation of equals in a community.

Trudeau's individualist liberalism was married to – and at times in tension with – his commitment to personalism. Shaped by the work of Jacques Maritain and Emmanuel Mounier, this Catholic creed constituted a call to social action, inspiring individuals to work for the common good. Man was not a mere vessel endowed with rights which defined his relations with others, but a spiritual being who found fulfilment within a community. The common good was not exclusively a matter for the community or for the individual: it was for both. André Burelle, a personalist who worked closely with Trudeau before breaking with him over constitutional reform, points up the communal emphasis of the doctrine and struggles to reconcile this with his friend's focus on the primacy of the individual. Burelle argues that the latter was to win out over the former from 1980 onwards. But his attempts to explain the change – citing, variously, the pressures of office, the American education of his advisers in his final term and the broader political context – are not wholly convincing. Even Burelle seems to acknowledge as much when he reluctantly concludes that Trudeau was, in his head, a personalist but in his heart he

[12] For those difficulties, see the considered analysis of Trudeau's thought by one of his former collaborators: André Burelle, *Pierre Elliott Trudeau. L'intellectuel et le politique* (Montreal, Éditions Fides, 2005).

[13] Roger Tassé, interview with the author, 25 May 1980.

[14] See, eg, *The Constitution and the People of Canada. An Approach to the Objectives of Confederation, the Rights of People and the Institutions of Government* (Ottawa, Government of Canada, 1969) 8, 14.

[15] Pierre Elliott Trudeau, 'The Values of a Just Society' in Thomas S Axworthy and Pierre Elliott Trudeau (eds), *Towards a Just Society. The Trudeau Years* (Toronto, Penguin, 2000) 408.

was an individualist.[16] If this attribution is correct, the evidence would suggest (surprisingly) that Trudeau – who prized reason and logic – was ruled more by his heart than his head. He would, at times, appear open to the concept of *collective* rights, but he would more commonly argue that rights were the exclusive preserve of individuals. This, as we shall see, was his approach before and after 1980, the year in which Burelle maintains he lost his way.

If Trudeau was clear that all citizens had certain fundamental rights, he was less emphatic about the identity of those rights. Beyond a core of political and legal rights he showed himself to be flexible as to which rights should earn constitutional protection. This flexibility was partly a response to changing circumstances and partly an indication that, for him, the enumeration of the rights beyond the core was not a first order question. During his time in government he was willing to propose human rights charters which were modest in their scope and in their probable effect.[17] This cannot be explained exclusively by reference to pragmatism – although this most intellectually rigorous of politicians learned, reluctantly, to trim. Even when he was at the height of his powers he would surprise his staff by his lack of interest in the detail and extent of proposed charters.[18]

Trudeau was clear – and consistent – in arguing that the principle of entrenching rights guarantees in the constitution *was* a first order question. This conviction – as so much else in his thought – had been shaped in the 1950s by his experience of the repressive regime of Union Nationale leader and Quebec premier Maurice Duplessis. He saw at first hand the tyranny and corruption of majoritarian rule – the persecution of labour, the denial of civil liberties and the abuse of minorities. Influenced by Frank Scott's advocacy of a constitutionally entrenched charter which was beyond easy reach of legislators, Trudeau took up a cause which he was to champion throughout his political career. There were times on the constitutional journey through the 1970s when, for political reasons, he set the charter aside but his belief in the necessity of entrenched rights did not waver. He had no difficulty with the notion that parliament should continue to determine the law on capital punishment or on abortion, but he wanted to remove fundamental principles of natural justice from the political fray.[19] The risk that the majority would abuse those principles at the expense of minorities was simply too great.

If Trudeau's commitment to a charter was forged by his experience of the Union Nationale administration, it was the Quiet Revolution of the 1960s – in which so many of his contemporaries took part – that confirmed his view that

[16] André Burelle, *Pierre Elliott Trudeau. L'intellectuel et le politique* (Montreal, Éditions Fides, 2005) 68.

[17] For one measure of the distance travelled on the Charter during Trudeau's time in government, compare Pierre Elliott Trudeau, *A Canadian Charter of Human Rights* (Ottawa, Information Canada, 1968) with the Charter as finally agreed. For a second measure, see the degree of movement on fundamental issues in the Charter that is evident in the successive drafts prepared by officials in the late 1970s: Justice, file 249318, Constitutional Revisions – Charter of Fundamental Rights and Freedoms.

[18] Barry Strayer, interview with the author, 30 May 2006.

[19] Otto Lang, interview with the author, 27 May 2006.

ethnic nationalism was a narrowing and corrupting creed. It was, he maintained, an emotional response to a set of political choices best resolved by the application of reason. By the time he left for Harvard in 1944 he had already travelled a long way from the fascist sympathies of his youth.[20] By then he was an internationalist: the nameplate on his student room announced him as 'Pierre Elliott Trudeau, Citizen of the World'. The nation state was at best irrelevant, but more commonly it was a cause of human misery. It was the product of nineteenth century ethnic nationalism and its champions; and it had brought the world conflicts on a scale previously unimaginable. In a nation state an ethnic community asserted an illegitimate claim to sovereignty; the collective was usurping the legitimate claim of the individual. He inveighed against the denial of opportunities to Francophones in English Canada;[21] but he came to feel more keenly and more urgently the threat from the nationalist impulse in Quebec. The separatist movement grew in response to oppression, but when its moment of opportunity arrived, it turned in on itself, protecting its own rather than reaching out to others. It chose to construct its own ghetto.

Trudeau's rejection of ethnic nationalism was not a denial of the worth of ethnicity nor of community life. The individual derived benefit from the community: he or she was enriched by its cultural life, was supported by it, and his or her sense of identity was enlarged by association with something that endured over time and extended beyond the immediate locality. Hence it was Trudeau's Government in 1971 that committed Canada to multiculturalism, sponsoring programmes to support the distinctive cultural identities of Canada's diverse population. And it was Trudeau's Government that had earlier passed into law the Official Languages Act in 1969, derived from the recommendations of the Bilingualism and Biculturalism Commission established earlier under his predecessor, Lester Pearson. French and English were to be the languages of the federal government and Ottawa began the slow, tortuous process of requiring its employees to be fluent in both languages and to deliver services in them.[22] Trudeau was clear that the federal state would fail if French Canadians could not claim parity with their English-speaking compatriots. The promotion of official bilingualism across the country was to become central to Trudeau's concept of a pan-Canadian identity. When successive Quebec governments acted to strengthen education in French within the province, he responded by stressing that *all* of Canada should respect the language rights of English- and French-speaking minorities. In the struggle against the ethnic partition of the country, it was imperative that Anglophones prospered within Quebec and that

[20] For his earlier views, see Max and Monique Nemni, *Young Trudeau. Son of Quebec, Father of Canada, 1919–1944,* vol 1 (Toronto, McClelland & Stewart, 2006).

[21] Lorraine E Weinrib, 'Trudeau and the Canadian Charter of Rights and Freedoms: A Question of Constitutional Maturation' in Andrew Cohen and JL Granatstein, *Trudeau's Shadow. The Life and Legacy of Pierre Elliott Trudeau* (Toronto, Random House Canada, 1998) 263.

[22] The story of bilingualism is best told in Graham Fraser, *Sorry, I Don't Speak French. Confronting the Canadian Crisis that Won't Go Away* (Toronto, McClelland & Stewart, 2006).

Francophone communities survived beyond its borders.[23] And so the language rights of minority linguistic populations were to be protected in each province: the Charter was to provide the vehicle through which this could be secured.

If language rights were so central to his concept of the Canadian future, it might seem surprising that he should be inconsistent in his approach to their entrenchment. As Minister of Justice in 1968 he published a version of the charter which contained only modest protection for the linguistic rights of the two 'founding peoples'.[24] But by 1980 he had come to see language rights as central to the Charter project: they had found their way into the irreducible core upon which he was most insistent.[25] Equally, he did, on occasions, depart from his standard argument that the right of a citizen to communicate and be understood was an individual entitlement. In 1977, and again in 1980, Trudeau appeared to concede that French Canadians – a collective entity – had rights *as an entity*. How are we to explain this inconsistency? The first point to make is, quite simply, that his thinking – and his policies – changed over time. Language rights came to assume greater importance as he became locked into a competitive struggle with the separatists: language was the most potent symbol of, and vehicle for, the promotion of Francophones throughout Canada. His acknowledgment of the collective character of linguistic rights in 1977 and 1980 is perhaps best understood as a tactical manoeuvre brought about in both cases by his need to reach out to the separatists – first in the wake of the PQ's election and later in the aftermath of the Quebec referendum. In both cases there must be some question as to the sincerity of the gesture, not least because he would soon revert to type. It is another reminder that Trudeau was a political actor, not a detached spectator. He was forced to accept that the rights to minority language education had a collective dimension, in so much as access to it would depend on numerical demand. But again, this should be understood as a concession made in the course of negotiations. His core conviction was that individuals, not communities, had rights – including rights to language. And he was particularly resistant to any suggestion that language rights might be associated with a particular community living in a particular location. For him, that smacked of ethnic nationalism. For many in Quebec it was no more than the recognition of an historical and sociological reality.

We can see the same animus to collective rights in Trudeau's resistance to the notion that Indigenous Peoples had a special status in Canada or were deserving of special treatment. Whatever wrongs had been done in the past were in the past: national policy could not become a quest for restitution for past wrongs. And so he railed against the Indian Act and the Department of Indian and Northern Affairs – the legal and bureaucratic infrastructure for the Indigenous Peoples. The policy choice was stark: either the state could build higher walls around the Indigenous

[23] Gordon Robertson, interview with the author, 26 May 2006.
[24] Pierre Elliott Trudeau, *A Canadian Charter of Human Rights* (Ottawa, Information Canada, 1968).
[25] Barry Strayer, interview with the author, 30 May 2006.

ghetto, or it could entice the Indigenous Peoples out, encouraging them to share in a common Canadian citizenship. That might mean the loss of some of their traditions, but his brusque assessment was that was a small price to pay in return for full citizenship in the national community.[26] He never entirely abandoned this view but over time, and with the encouragement of Gordon Robertson, his first Cabinet Secretary, he softened his rhetoric and accepted that his government's policy towards the Indigenous Peoples had to change.[27] The Indian Act withstood his onslaught – for reasons that were pragmatic rather than principled.

In his account of Trudeau's constitutional reforms, Kenneth McRoberts argues that as Prime Minister he was systematically pursuing an elaborate national unity strategy. The components were, in their own right, ambitious: official bilingualism in federal and, if possible, provincial government; multiculturalism; reform of federalism to include greater prominence for Ottawa and the equality of the provinces; and the patriation of the constitution to include an entrenched charter of rights.[28] This chapter will focus primarily on patriation and the charter, but it is worth pausing here to consider the way Trudeau thought about the nation and its future.

Throughout his public life Trudeau was motivated by an intellectual and visceral opposition to ethnic nationalism, an opposition incubated by his early experience of Quebec. Separatists were exponents of this 'narrow nationalism' and they had to be defeated: he had to save Canada from this fate. It is one of the complaints of his critics that he was unable to conceive of Quebec nationalism in any other terms. André Burelle has commented on this, bemoaning the simplifying logic that was characteristic of Trudeau's thought:

> A brilliant man and a redoubtable dialectician, he practised a binary logic of black and white … In his improvised, warlike line of argument, the 'separatist' camp became a focus of ethnic division, of racism and of fascism.[29]

It is possible to understand much of Trudeau's public life – including each of the policy strands identified by McRoberts – as a struggle to overcome this opposing camp. Throughout his career he was at pains to spell out to his compatriots the perils of the alternative visions for Canada. Separatism was the most obvious threat but more insidious was the acceptance by some federalists of the *deux nations* concept, which acknowledged that the French Canadians were a distinct

[26] Pierre Elliott Trudeau, Remarks at the Vancouver Liberal Association Dinner, 8 August 1969: Pierre Elliott Trudeau in Ron Graham (ed), *The Essential Trudeau* (Toronto, McClelland & Stewart, 1998) 83–4.

[27] Gordon Robertson, interview with the author, 26 May 2006. The change in policy was influenced in part by the strength of the reaction against the 1969 White Paper and in part by the Supreme Court's recognition of Indigenous title in the Calder case in 1973.

[28] Kenneth McRoberts, *Misconceiving Canada. The Struggle for National Unity* (Toronto, Oxford University Press, 1997) 176.

[29] André Burelle, *Pierre Elliott Trudeau. L'intellectuel et le politique* (Montreal, Éditions Fides, 2005) 83. Free translation by the author.

nation within the Canadian nation. It would, he argued, lead to a country divided by ethnicity, a country in which communities turned in on themselves – a bifurcation of the mind if not of the country's political geography.[30] But if Quebec was the most urgent challenge to national unity, Trudeau was also preoccupied by the rise of regionalism, especially in the prosperous West. In a 1981 interview with CBC he took aim at the decentralisation advocated by some provincial premiers, arguing that 'some of [them] see Canada as a confederation of shopping centers. I don't. I think there is such a thing as the national will from which none of us can opt out'.[31]

If the fissiparous tendencies within Canada were to be overcome, federal Canada had to compete with the siren voices of ethnic nationalism. Federal Canada was to make an offer to its citizens which could not be matched by Quebec, or for that matter, by any other province. It was to offer an enhanced citizenship, a distinctively Canadian citizenship, to be enjoyed by all throughout Canada. Individual rights for all were to be articulated and then protected from depredation by legislators – in Ottawa and in the provinces. And the very act of articulating those rights would require Canada to express its common values. Those rights, as enshrined in the constitution, would constitute a statement of the nation's common purpose.[32] Hence the Charter was at the heart of Trudeau's response to separatism.

This approach was to be buttressed by practical evidence that the federal government would do more to support its citizens, even if this strayed into policy realms previously considered the responsibility of the provinces. Hence the Trudeau governments of the 1970s created an urban affairs department and instituted a new stream of funding direct to municipalities. It also began to offer support to new constituencies, including women, consumers and environmentalists.[33] Canadians of both traditions – and those who did not identify with the two 'founding peoples' – had to receive tangible benefits in return for their commitment to the nation.

But there would be little point in developing this counter-offer if citizens did not recognise it. Hence he promoted the federal 'brand' and his Government was at pains to communicate the benefits of federal programmes, not least in Quebec. He always recognised that it might be necessary to win the battle for the public's

[30] Look, for example, at the way in which he attacked Bob Stanfield, the Progressive Conservative leader, for his advocacy of the *deux nations* concept during the 1968 election campaign.

[31] LAC John, MG26 0 19, vol 161, folder on Constitution: PM's Conference on the Constitution 2 November 1981, transcript of *News Special*, CBC TV, 16 April 1981.

[32] See, eg, LAC John, MG26 0 19, vol 161, folder on Constitution: PM's Conference on the Constitution 2 November 1981, Statement by the Prime Minister on the Constitution, 2 October 1980 and LAC John, MG26 0 19, vol 161, folder on Constitution: Supreme Court Decision on Constitutional Reference 1981, Prime Minister's Speech to the House of Commons, 23 March 1981. See also *The Constitution and the People of Canada. An Approach to the Objectives of Confederation, the Rights of People and the Institutions of Government* (Ottawa, Government of Canada, 1969) 4 and Pierre Elliott Trudeau, *A Canadian Charter of Human Rights* (Ottawa, Information Canada, 1968) *passim*.

[33] Kenneth McRoberts, *Misconceiving Canada. The Struggle for National Unity* (Toronto, Oxford University Press, 1997) 140.

imagination. When still Minister of Justice he wrote of the need for national symbols:

> One way of offsetting the appeal of separatism is by investing tremendous amounts of time, energy and money in nationalism, *at the federal level.* A national image must be created that will have such an appeal as to make any image of a separatist group unattractive. Resources must be diverted into such things as national flags, anthems, education, arts council, broadcasting corporations, film boards; the territory must be bound together by a network of railways, highways, airlines; the national culture and economy must be protected by taxes and tariffs; ownership of resources and industry by nationals must be made a matter of policy.[34]

But early in his career his first instinct was to win over Canadians by articulating – and delivering – a new citizenship. And so after the passage just cited from *Federalism and the French Canadians*, he goes on to argue that it is preferable to win the support of citizens by force of reason rather than by conjuring up attractive symbols for the nation. He is open to the thought that this approach might fail, but his choice of reason over emotion is clear. But over time he came to place greater emphasis on the need to win citizens' affection, strengthening the emotional bond with them while loosening the ties that bound them to their provincial loyalties.[35] Emotion did not win out over reason, but the two were harnessed to the same purpose.

In the second half of his premiership – and particularly in his final term – his appeal for Canadians' loyalty and support was increasingly characterised by a rhetoric which focused on the primacy of the Canadian nation. He spoke of the national will, he emphasised the unity of Canada and he urged on Canadians the importance of a strong, unifying federal government. He stopped short of advocating a unitary state, but the primacy of Ottawa was asserted: the federal bureaucracy was the instrument through which the will of the Canadian people – manifested in general elections – was to be put into effect. Decentralisation would imperil this vision. Here, unquestionably, one has evidence of an exercise in nation-building, not simply the defeat of Quebec separatism.[36] By the time of his final bid for patriation, if not before, Trudeau had cast off the federalism he espoused in the 1960s, a federalism in which power was dispersed within the federation as a bulwark against oppression by government. He was advancing the case for a pan-Canadian nationalism to unite the country. This was a civic nationalism, embracing diversity and engaging with Canada's moral purpose in the world, but it was nationalism all the same. He had travelled a long way from his earlier misgivings about the

[34] Pierre Elliott Trudeau, *Federalism and the French Canadians* (Toronto, Macmillan of Canada, 1968) 193.

[35] Jeremy Webber, *Reimagining Canada. Language, Culture, Community, and the Canadian Constitution* (Kingston & Montreal, McGill-Queen's University Press, 1994) 58.

[36] See, eg, the terms of the press release in which he confirmed his unilateral bid for patriation: Alberta, Lougheed, accession 85.401, box 27, item 278, 'Statement by the Prime Minister, Ottawa, October 2, 1980'.

nation. The man who once discussed the Canadian federation in detached terms, as a possible but not necessary, solution to Canada's problems had now become its most strident advocate.[37]

It is unclear whether Trudeau was pursuing a consistent national unity strategy throughout his time as Prime Minister. We have already seen that he could be inconsistent, adopting policy positions which were contingent rather than strategic. Trudeau's approach to each of the policy strands enumerated by McRoberts was undoubtedly shaped by his determination to overcome separatism. But the terms in which he conceived of Canada changed over time. By his final term he was unquestionably bent on nation-building and his constitutional ambitions were central to that enterprise. As we shall see, those ambitions also varied over time. This was in part a reflection of what he judged to be practical politics. And however much he may have wanted to dictate the terms of the constitutional game, he was rarely free to do so: to take just one example, the dramatic rise in oil prices in the early 1970s sharpened provincial demands for a realignment of federal-provincial powers in respect of trade and the economy.

When the wind was in his sails, Trudeau would aspire to an expansive constitutional agenda. This included, on and off, a statement of the fundamental objectives of the federation. But he was clear that this was not essential: when its drafting proved more difficult than he had hoped, he set it aside. Even though his view of the federation and of the nation were to change profoundly during his time in his office, two elements of his constitutional agenda were constant. The constitution was to be put under Canadian control. If the country aspired to full sovereignty it could do no less. This was both a necessary part of his re-ordering of the constitution and a move pregnant with symbolic potential. The second component was, of course, a charter guaranteeing rights in equal measure, right across the country. By participating in this project, the next stage in the country's national journey, citizens would be sharing in something their provinces could not give them. Canada would be dedicated to the fulfilment of each of its citizens and that fulfilment would be promoted through the protection of their rights and through the enrichment that could only come from living in a multicultural, diverse community. If this community was to thrive it was imperative that both of the 'founding peoples' should prosper and so their language rights had to be respected across the country.

For Trudeau the charter was both an article of faith *and* an instrumental political tool. As we shall see, those two purposes were at times in tension. Towards the end of his career he came to think of the charter primarily as a means of binding the nation together. He had other constitutional tools which served the same purpose – the patriation of the constitution itself, equalisation and the preamble – but it was the charter which was his hope for the future of the federation.

[37] See André Burelle, *Pierre Elliott Trudeau. L'intellectuel et le politique* (Montreal, Éditions Fides, 2005) 52–5, 474; Kenneth McRoberts, *Misconceiving Canada. The Struggle for National Unity* (Toronto, Oxford University Press, 1997) 63, 172.

The charter was a tool of sufficient flexibility to appeal both to reason *and* emotion. It was an affirmation of a single, unifying Canadian identity, an assertion of the rights and values held in common by all Canadians. As Jeremy Webber has observed:

> A charter would not only protect individual rights, it would help focus attention on each citizen's individual relationship to Canada as a whole; it would emphasize the oneness of Canada and of Canadian citizenship, implicitly undermining concepts of Canada that treated citizens not simply as members of the whole, but also as members of distinct and cohesive groups with their own publicly recognised identity.[38]

The charter's symbolic and practical utility as a means of unifying the nation was to be emphasised particularly sharply in Trudeau's final term – and in his interventions in constitutional politics once he had retired.

III. From the Centenary to Victoria

The apparent success and visibility of the *Confederation of Tomorrow* conference in 1967 – the first provincial premiers' gathering to have been televised – provoked Lester Pearson into a response. A planned federal-provincial conference on the criminal code would be expanded to include the constitution. It would now consider the rights of the citizen and, inevitably, it would seek an agreement on the patriation of the Canadian constitution. For most purposes, Canada's independence from Britain had been formalised by the Statute of Westminster in 1931, but for as long as the Canadian constitution was to be found in a British statute, Canada had to ask British parliamentarians to approve amendments. Canada had made eight previous attempts at patriation, the last of them in 1964. All the efforts had come to naught because the federal and provincial governments could not agree how the constitution should be amended once it was in Canadian hands. The ninth attempt was to last, on and off, for 15 years.

The federal-provincial conference met in February 1968 and it resolved on a maximalist approach. The governments committed themselves to the search for a new constitution: an amending formula, citizen rights, governmental powers and federal institutions were all up for review. A Continuing Committee of Officials on the Constitution would work towards solutions, reporting back to periodic federal-provincial conferences. In 1969 it was agreed that officials' labours should be supplemented by standing committees of ministers with mandates to examine official languages, fundamental rights, the judiciary and the Senate. The enterprise set in train was to be an exercise in executive federalism: governments would seek to resolve the issue amongst themselves. Any involvement by the public was to be strictly passive. The more dedicated might watch the televised conference sessions,

[38] Jeremy Webber, *Reimagining Canada. Language, Culture, Community, and the Canadian Constitution* (Kingston & Montreal, McGill-Queen's University Press, 1994) 96.

a habit encouraged by the drama of Trudeau's clashes with the Quebec premier Daniel Johnson in February 1968, or they might thumb through the federal Minister of Justice's treatise, *A Canadian Charter of Human Rights*. As if addressing a national audience of undergraduates, Trudeau set out his stall; he rehearsed the intellectual justification for the charter and he identified the rights that should be entrenched in the new constitution. Published on the eve of the February 1968 conference, it was intended to set the agenda for the talks. It allowed for unqualified rights and it gave the courts significant discretion. But in retrospect, his prospectus is also notable for its limited scope: it focused on political and legal rights; its proposals for anti-discrimination rights were modest; it had nothing to say about economic rights; and it had little to offer on linguistic rights. More predictably for a Trudeau document, it was silent on the rights of Indigenous Peoples and of ethnic communities.[39]

But before long even this agenda seemed beyond the reach of the constitutional review process. Common ground was difficult to find; the provinces saw no urgency in the process; and the television cameras brought out the worst in delegates, not least Trudeau. He was to move centre stage at the conferences when he replaced the more emollient Pearson as Prime Minister in April 1968. Never afraid to show his impatience, he felt trapped in a process which seemed doomed to a long, fractious demise.

From the outset, Trudeau's relations with the Quebec delegation at the talks had been strained; they were suspicious of him and he questioned the determination of successive Quebec administrations to face down the separatist movement. His reputation in Quebec – let alone his credentials as a defender of civil liberties – was to suffer permanent damage for his handling of the October Crisis in 1970. Acts of terrorism by the Front de la Libération du Québec (FLQ) culminated in the kidnapping of the Quebec Cabinet Minister Pierre Laporte and the British Trade Commissioner James Cross. Laporte was later murdered. Trudeau told reporters that he would not tolerate terrorism and that he would act decisively to restore order. He concluded the interview with the invitation, 'Just watch me'. And nobody could question the vigour with which he acted: he invoked the War Measures Act, put troops onto the streets of Montreal and sanctioned the arrest and detention of suspects without trial. He acted at the invitation of the Mayor of Montreal and with the consent of the Quebec Premier Robert Bourassa, whose Liberal administration had come to power in April 1970. But all of this was lost in the heat of the moment. Trudeau, the self-proclaimed champion of human rights, had shown scant regard for the civil liberties of the Quebec detainees and he had resorted to force to get his own way on the streets of Montreal. Trudeau may have secured praise in Anglophone Canada, but in Quebec separatists and federalists were united in their condemnation.

[39] See the discussion in BL Strayer, 'In the Beginning …: the Origins of Section 15 of the Charter' (2006) 5 *Journal of Law and Equality* 13.

It was against this background that Gordon Robertson and Marc Lalonde, then Trudeau's principal political adviser, proposed to the Prime Minister that he should make one final effort to bring the constitutional review process to a conclusion. He was understandably reluctant, questioning the prospects for success and pointing up the risks of failure. But Trudeau, commonly regarded as arrogant and intellectually overbearing, was willing to listen to unwelcome advice from his team. He agreed to another round of talks if ministers and officials were able to establish that an agreement might be reached. Preparatory work led by Justice Minister John Turner provided sufficient reassurance that a deal might be in prospect and so the scene was set for a conference at Victoria, British Columbia in June 1971.[40]

The deal on offer at Victoria fell far short of the ambitions sketched out at the first conference in February 1968. The institutions of the federation were to be left unreformed and the distribution of powers was to be untouched. But the constitution was to be placed under Canadian control and, finally, there was a proposed amending formula which the 10 provinces and the federal government all seemed willing to accept. Amendments were to be approved by the federal parliament and, on a regional basis, by the provincial legislatures; Ontario and Quebec would each have a veto. The deal included a charter of rights which was broad in scope, but legislatures would be able to make incursions on fundamental freedoms as long as those restrictions were 'reasonably justifiable in a democratic society'. And the rights it provided were not uniform across the country: in accepting it, Trudeau was accepting a 'checkerboard Canada'. But it was a deal of sorts, it was a riposte – of sorts – to radical nationalism and it would, at last, put an end to the interminable round of conferences.

The meeting at Victoria seemed to bear out Lalonde and Robertson's judgement that an agreement was within reach. Eight of the provinces signalled their consent at the time and Alberta and British Columbia did so subsequently. But when Robert Bourassa presented the package to his Cabinet in Quebec City, Claude Castonguay argued that Quebec should have greater powers over social policy. Faced with a revolt by two of his ministers, Bourassa buckled: he went back to Ottawa and asked for more. Trudeau refused. The deal was off.[41]

The failure of Victoria shaped the course of constitutional politics for the remainder of the decade. Bourassa's climbdown captured perfectly the federalists' dilemma in Quebec. Had he stuck by the agreement he would have risked much more than the loss of two ministers. He would have faced the charge that he had sold the province short, committing it to a constitutional future within an over-centralised federation. Already weakened by the October crisis and by public sector strikes, he chose to give way. The damage done to his relations with Ottawa was irreparable. Trudeau and Lalonde were confirmed in their view that Bourassa

[40] Marc Lalonde, interview with the author, 23 May 2006.

[41] ibid. See also Peter H Russell, *Constitutional Odyssey. Can Canadians Become a Sovereign People?* (Toronto, University of Toronto Press, 2004) 87–91.

was without principle, a man unfit for public office.[42] Consequently Trudeau took the view that a new constitutional settlement was all but inconceivable while Bourassa was in power in Quebec City. Bourassa had demonstrated to Trudeau's satisfaction that a deal could not be reached if the central dynamic was a provincial quest for greater powers. It was never clear how much decentralisation would be 'enough' and one of their number – most probably Quebec – would always come back for more.

IV. Stasis

In the aftermath of Victoria, the momentum towards a constitutional settlement stalled. The components for a deal were to hand: there was little that was surprising or novel about the agreement which was finally to be celebrated in April 1982. Even the 'notwithstanding' clause, which allowed legislatures to override some of the provisions of the Charter, was discussed in the early 1970s and Trudeau indicated to his Minister of Justice privately that he might be willing to accept it.[43] This is not to belittle the achievement in 1982: the assembly of the component parts of the deal was genuinely difficult. But the principal obstacle after Victoria had little to do with the design of an agreement. Rather, it was that the principal participants did not have the incentives or authority needed to bring matters to a conclusion. Trudeau and the federal Liberals had other preoccupations: their government was returned to power in the 1972 federal election, but it lost its majority and until 1974 it depended on New Democratic Party (NDP) support to take business through the House of Commons. And even after the 1974 election, when it recovered its majority, there was little to encourage it to return to the question of constitutional reform. Not only were there plenty of other priorities competing for attention – not least an ailing economy – but the prospects for a deal with Quebec looked even worse than they had done three years before.

Bourassa's Liberal administration had survived its own trip to the polls in October 1973 and in the following year it introduced Bill 22, a measure designed to strengthen the French language in the conduct of business and in education. The political incentive to do so was clear: after the 1973 election the PQ became the official opposition in the Quebec Assembly. The disincentive for Bourassa to seek a deal with Ottawa was now even greater than it had been in Victoria. Instead, he was drawn into a domestic competition for Francophone support and he responded to the PQ's identity politics by offering an alternative brand of his own. Trudeau feared that this was a race towards a unilingual Quebec and an abandonment of the pan-Canadian Francophone community. As the Quebec Liberals and

[42] Gordon Robertson, interview with the author, 26 May 2006. Marc Lalonde, interview with the author, 23 May 2006.

[43] Otto Lang, interview with the author, 27 May 2006.

the PQ focussed their attention on the promotion of French within the province, so Trudeau was confirmed in his view that what was needed were language guarantees for both minorities in each of the provinces. For him, language became a totemic issue: the protection of the languages of the two 'founding peoples' would hold the country together by sustaining minorities and stemming the slide towards ethnic sectarianism.

Constitutional dialogue continued through this period, but it was often little more than a formulaic exchange of demands intended to pander to partisans. A Joint Parliamentary Committee in 1972 had served to keep the issue in the public's mind, but it achieved little else. Committees of federal and provincial ministers continued to consider possible constitutional reforms, but there was little to show for their labours. And the pressure from the provinces for greater control over their destiny had taken on a new impetus after the sharp increases in the worldwide price of oil in 1973. The value of the Western oil reserves rose dramatically, provoking a conflict between the provinces' determination to maximise the benefit from the resources under their control and the federal desire to secure advantage for consumers and taxpayers across the country. This, in turn, heightened pre-existing tension over federal control over interprovincial trade.[44] Alberta, which stood to gain most, had elected Peter Lougheed as its premier in 1971 and he was to prove an effective advocate of the provincial cause. For Trudeau – whose party was chronically weak in the West – this development reinforced his opposition to provincial parochialism.

When, in 1975, Trudeau invited provincial premiers to a conference to discuss the patriation of the constitution, their response was predictable. They were willing to do so, but they argued that the issue was best tackled in the context of the decentralisation of powers and the assertion of provincial control over resources. Trudeau demurred. He tried again the following year, offering alternative ways forward and apparently signalling that he might settle for a deal that did not include a charter or even an amending formula. These were tactical manoeuvres: he was searching for a way out of a stalemate and he did not have the leverage to find an exit on his own terms. His philosophical commitment to the charter remained undiminished.

V. From PQ Victory to Liberal Defeat

The realignment of political forces that eventually made the April 1982 constitution possible began with the PQ's dramatic victory in the November 1976 Quebec election. Canada now had two nation-building projects. Trudeau still hoped to bring

[44] For just one example of the long-running, and intertwined, disputes over control of resources and of trade, see Statement by Premier Allan Blakeney on Amendments to the Constitutional Resolution, 9 February 1981 (Alberta, Lougheed, accession 6R1985.0401; item 278; box 27).

the Canadian nation to maturity in a new constitutional settlement. Meanwhile, René Lévesque, the new Quebec premier, sought to realise his party's ambitions for Quebec nationhood. Bill 101 further reinforced the place of French in Quebec schools. And the argument for sovereignty-association was rehearsed: Quebec would be free to manage its own affairs but it would have close economic and commercial relationships with the rest of Canada. A referendum would ultimately be held to give the PQ the mandate to pursue sovereignty-association.

With the PQ in power, the dynamics of constitutional reform were decisively changed. A deal with Bourassa would have been difficult; but a deal which excluded a Quebec Liberal administration would have been inconceivable. A deal with Lévesque, for whom Trudeau had little regard and less respect, was probably out of reach. And in the short-term, it was difficult to see how the PQ could conclude any agreement with Ottawa: everybody knew that its primary objective was to win a referendum to secure a mandate for sovereignty-association. Hence Quebec's role in the negotiations in the latter part of the decade was at best ambiguous. From Ottawa's point of view, the PQ's election was significant because thereafter it became possible to conceive of a deal *without* Quebec.

In the wake of the Quebec election, the message that was sent through the bureaucracy was that the priority now was to save the nation from dissolution. At the political level, efforts were to be coordinated by Marc Lalonde, who had been appointed to the new post of Minister of Federal-Provincial Relations. The ostensible purpose was to synchronise all of Ottawa's dealings with the provinces, but the principal focus of Lalonde's work was Quebec: he was charged with the Quebec-proofing of federal policy and with the promotion in the province of a coherent, attractive image of the federation and, in particular, of the federal government. The communication of Ottawa's message was put in the hands of a new arm of the federal government, the Canadian Unity Information Office. At the official level, Lalonde was assisted by Paul Tellier, who led a small group of senior officials from across the bureaucracy whose loosely defined brief was to put Ottawa in the best position possible to win a future referendum in Quebec. They planned, they plotted, they predicted and, above all, they analysed intelligence from Quebec.[45]

Its most recent constitutional initiatives having been spurned by the premiers, in July 1977 Ottawa seemed to set off on a new tack. It established the Task Force on Canadian Unity under the chairmanship of John Robarts, formerly premier of Ontario, and Jean-Luc Pepin, formerly a minister in Trudeau's Cabinet. In a country accustomed to formal commissions of inquiry, this was a curious hybrid. It was to travel the land, listening to the views of Canadians on the future of their nation. It had no mandate to produce a report, let alone recommendations on the way forward. Rather, it was to provide a space for national reflection.

[45] Marc Lalonde, interview with the author, 23 May 2006. David Cameron, interview with the author, 16 June 2006.

But the Government was not alone in seeking a way through Canada's constitutional impasse. The Canadian Bar Association established a commission to work over the same ground. The Quebec Liberal Party did likewise, ultimately producing its Beige Paper, a vision of a decentralised Canada that did nothing for relations with Trudeau's federal party. Provincial governments launched similar initiatives and in 1977 *Options for Canada* provided yet another forum in which interested citizens could debate their future.

McRoberts and Burelle have suggested that the appointment of the Taskforce was indicative of a new openness on Trudeau's part. They buttress this argument by reference to the Prime Minister's speech in Quebec City in January 1977, three months after the PQ had come to power. Trudeau's only stated precondition for constitutional renewal was the charter. He even suggested that rights might 'probably' extend to the *collective* aspect of human rights. But the evidence here is mixed: his grudging nod to collective rights was combined by reference to a choice in allegiance – between Quebec and Canada. It was not a prospectus to give much encouragement to those who believed in the possibility of complementary identities within a federal union.[46] Equally, Trudeau was soon to demonstrate that he regarded the Pepin Robarts Taskforce as little more than a 'safety valve', first dismissing its report and subsequently ignoring it altogether.[47]

What was striking about this frenzy of constitutional introspection is that the process itself was new: executive federalism was being diluted by input from civic society. The development stopped far short of mass popular engagement and in appointing the Taskforce Trudeau had made it clear that Ottawa was not yielding control of the policy process to anyone. But there was an opportunity for the politically engaged and, above all, for interest groups to put forward their proposals or (more commonly) their demands. They were able to do so because the terms of the debate were changing. This was no longer a discussion of the best constitutional fix for the federation but an examination of the country's future – if, indeed, it had a future together. In that context, women's groups, Indigenous organisations and others saw the need to press their claims for greater recognition within a reformulated federation. The greater the uncertainty, the greater their potential opportunity.

In the autumn of 1977, as the Taskforce set about its business, the Government was already preparing the way for its next constitutional initiative.[48] Its new agenda was set out in the overheated prose of *A Time for Action*, which was published the following year. Readers were taken on a rapid tour of Canadian history and

[46] Kenneth McRoberts, *Misconceiving Canada. The Struggle for National Unity* (Toronto, Oxford University Press, 1997) 148–9; André Burelle, *Pierre Elliott Trudeau. L'intellectuel et le politique* (Montreal, Éditions Fides, 2005) 57–60.

[47] The phrase is David Cameron's. Cameron was director of research for the Task Force. David Cameron, interview with the author, 16 June 2006.

[48] See Justice, file 249318, vol 1, correspondence on development of Charter and on phasing of reform packages (for an example of the latter, see Barry Strayer minute to Minister, 19 December 1977.

geography in the course of which they were told that, 'Indians and Inuit are not the only ones enraptured by the boreal magic of our northlands. The strange sense of boundless horizons does not rouse only Westerners, nor does the relentless drift of eternal glaciers move only the people of our mountains.'[49] The persistent reader would discern that the future of the nation was at stake and that it was time to renew its mythology – and its constitution. The renewal was to be based on an assertion of contemporary Canadian values: the primacy of citizens and of their rights; respect for the dignity *and rights* of Indigenous Peoples; the language rights of the 'founding peoples'; multiculturalism; regionalism; economic integration; mutual support; and federalism. The list was, by now, familiar although the accent on Indigenous rights was new and one can only assume that officials persuaded Trudeau to accept the more inclusive tone. More striking were the proposed tactics. A new constitution would be delivered by 1981 – in two phases. In the first, the federal government would make those changes that were within the competence of Parliament. Legislation to that end would be passed by July 1979. After further consultation with the provinces and with the public, the remaining changes would follow. If agreement on an amending formula were reached in time it would be in phase one. A charter would also appear in phase one, but it would bear only on federal government.[50] The Government had initially wanted to bundle language rights into the first phase, but it eventually opted for a more cautious line.[51]

A Time for Action should best be understood as another federal attempt to do that which was possible. With every month that passed Trudeau felt greater pressure to do something to show that the federal government could head off the threat from the sovereigntists who now controlled the provincial government in Quebec. He did not want to wait for a Task Force whose report he could not control and which, ultimately, was to dwell on the duality and regionalism of a fractured country.[52] The political scene was changing around him, not least with the passage of Bill 101 in Quebec, and his own Government was in difficulties on other fronts. *A Time for Action* was an attempt to generate momentum by a Prime Minister who feared his time was running out.

It was soon in trouble. Opposed by the provinces and by the Progressive Conservatives in Parliament, the two-stage strategy had been dropped by February 1978. But the Government persisted with its attempt at unilateral action, introducing Bill C60 to the House of Commons in June. This promised sweeping reform of federal institutions, a charter which would redefine the relationship between citizens and federal government and a new statement of the federation's objectives.

[49] *A Time for Action. Towards the Renewal of the Canadian Federation* (Ottawa, Canadian Ministry of Supply and Services, 1978) 1.

[50] ibid, 1–12, 19–25.

[51] For the development of the Government's thinking, see Justice, file 249318, vol 1, Barry Strayer to D Thorson, 24 November 1977; Strayer to Minister, 12 December 1977; and Strayer to Minister, 10 January 1978.

[52] Ultimately, he simply brushed the Task Force's report aside.

Of the many points of contention, the most fruitful for the opposition was the proposed creation of a House of Federation, a new upper house of Parliament to be jointly elected by the provinces and by the Commons. The provinces objected that Parliament could not replace the Senate without their consent and a legal challenge was soon under way.

The House of Federation may have acted like a lightning rod for the opposition, but it is worth considering for a moment the proposed statement of the federation's objectives. It exemplified the difficulties that were to befall all such drafts. Trudeau had called for something inspirational but the preparation of Bill C-60 had been put in the hands of a draftsman whose most recent assignment had been the preparation of income tax legislation and he was evidently better suited to the rhetorical demands of his previous task.[53] Trudeau's aspiration was understandable, but successive attempts over the next three years proved to be lame, awkward circumlocutions, striving to draft their way around Canada's constitutional feuds. Phrases which would have been innocuous in other constitutions were pregnant with contentious meaning in the Canadian context. Was a reference to the 'nation' a denial of the Anglo-French duality? Was an assertion of unity a slight on Canadian diversity? The questions mounted and successive draftsmen wilted. The strain showed clearly in a June 1980 draft which referred to the 'meeting of the English and French presence on the North American soil'. Poetry had been sacrificed on the altar of blandness. And when he came to express the purpose of governments and legislatures the draftsman found that Thomas Jefferson had all the best lines. They were to 'have no other purpose than to strive for the happiness and fulfilment of each and all of us'.[54] Marc Lalonde commented subsequently that he always thought that the preamble was no more than 'literature'.[55] There was popular pressure for a statement that captured the essence of Canada in clear, powerful terms: the Government was lobbied to accept this phrase or that principle.[56] But in the end it all proved too difficult. There were so many other differences to resolve that the preamble was an argument that did not need to be had. Canada could not have a simple statement of its objectives because it could not agree what they were. The April 1982 text included a one line preamble, itself the result of a political compromise. The Cardinal Archbishop of Toronto urged the Prime Minister to grant God a place in the new constitution. Trudeau judged the pressure to be irresistible and so He was allowed in. But His arrival presented the drafters with a new problem. He could not preside in isolation over the new constitution and so a search began for something to accompany Him, something which would not prompt further disputes. A common denominator was found and Canada entered

[53] For the Prime Minister's brief, see Justice, file 249318, vol 1, Fred Jordan to Minister, 23 January 1978.

[54] LAC John, MG26 0 19, vol. 160, statement of constitutional principles, 10 June 1980.

[55] Marc Lalonde, interview with the author 23 May 2006.

[56] See, eg, Justice, file 251600-16, vol 4, pouch C, nr 2, Submission by the *Conseil pour l'unité canadienne*, June 1980.

its new constitutional era with the briefest of preambles: 'Canada is founded upon principles that recognize the supremacy of God and the rule of law.'[57]

But in early 1979 the drafting of the preamble was the least of Trudeau's problems. Having already dropped the second stage of the strategy advocated in *A Time for Action*, the first stage was brusquely denied him by the Supreme Court. It ruled that Parliament did not have the right to act unilaterally to reform the Senate. Bill C 60 was dead.

Trudeau was on the back foot. The economy was in trouble and an election was imminent. The Government's best hope was to drive home the message that the nation's survival was at stake, a theme that Trudeau would work and re-work over his remaining years in power. But even some of his Cabinet colleagues questioned whether that argument would work in English Canada. Others wanted to raise the profile of the issue by challenging the provincial premiers at the constitutional conference to be held in February 1979. But Trudeau and Lalonde were becoming more cautious; they were all too aware of their weakness. The Prime Minister argued that 'the Government must first do its utmost to be seen as seeking agreement with the provinces before either moving unilaterally or towards a confrontation. Thus the Government must first appear to be reasonable.'[58]

At the February conference the Prime Minister was a man at bay. He found himself drawn ineluctably into the 'more powers' game he so abhorred. The premiers, sensing that the momentum was with them, pressed for greater decentralisation. Trudeau was forced to yield ground but he was unable to reach an agreement. He went to the polls in May, with nothing to show for 13 years of constitutional politics. The nation did not rally to his appeal for national unity. The modest, unassuming Albertan Joe Clark led his Progressive Conservative Party into power for the first time since 1963. Clark's first task was to establish the Conservatives' competence in government and then he would go to the country again to secure the majority that had eluded him in the May election.

Trudeau's political career was at its lowest ebb. His reputation as Prime Minister was insecure, despite 12 years in office. Quebec remained on course for a referendum on sovereignty-association. His constitutional labours had come to nothing.

He resigned the Liberal Party leadership and the Party prepared to find a new leader. Trudeau, at the age of 60, faced up to retirement. He spoke of spending more time with his three boys – who remained in his custody after the painful, public collapse of his marriage. He was able to spend more time canoeing. And he gave a candid interview to the CBC in which he described constitutional reform as his greatest failure. It seemed time to add a new name to the roll call of Canadian political reputations broken by the search for a new constitution.

[57] Strictly, this serves as the preamble to the Constitution Act 1982; the preamble of the Constitution Act 1867 (formerly known as the British North America Act) remained undisturbed.

[58] PCO, ATI – AA – 2003 – 0017, Cabinet Minutes, 18 January 1979.

VI. A Final Chance

And then Joe Clark stumbled. It was never going to be easy to secure parliamentary approval for his minority Government's budget but the new administration bungled the vote in December 1979. The Government fell. Canada was to go the polls in February. The fall came sooner than expected and Clark had not had a chance to do much more than initiate a series of policy reviews. Constitutional reform was no further forward, but the provinces had welcomed the more inclusive, less abrasive tone adopted by the Conservatives. In official Ottawa the expectation was that the Liberals would be back before long and there was a reluctance to engage in new policy initiatives for fear that they would be fruitless.[59]

When the Government fell Trudeau had not yet been replaced as Liberal leader. He did not renounce retirement immediately. He took time to consult his closest supporters, weighing his options. He then announced that he would lead the Liberal Party through the election *and* he would remain to lead the victors in government. Canoeing would have to wait.

In returning to frontline politics, Trudeau was clear that he had been given one last chance. If he won the election he would serve one term and no more. This was his final chance to secure his legacy and his reputation. In reflecting on his 1974–79 Government, he had told Lalonde that the administration had lost its way; it had been compromised by tactical accommodations. Were he to have another spell as Prime Minister he would stick to his principles and would focus relentlessly on seeing a couple of big things through to a conclusion.[60]

He led the Liberals back into office in February, securing a comfortable majority and winning 74 out of 75 seats in Quebec.[61] Once in power he made it clear – clearer than he had done during the election – that he had two priorities: the negotiation of a National Energy Program (NEP) and the search for a new constitutional settlement which would unify the nation. The NEP would involve head-on conflict with oil-rich Alberta. And the constitutional agenda had, if anything, become more difficult since he left office the previous year. Lévesque had alighted on 20 May for the Quebec referendum and he stuck with his preference even after the federal election was called.[62] If the Yes campaign won, Trudeau's hope of a last mandate reprieve would have been snuffed out. The first priority was to do what he and the federal government could do to secure a No vote on 20 May. But even if that hazard were negotiated, he still had to persuade English Canada to come to an agreement and, in particular, he had to find a way of carrying the West. His Party

[59] Fred Jordan, interview with the author, 29 May 2006.

[60] Marc Lalonde, interview with the author, 23 May 2006.

[61] The Bloc Québécois – a sovereigntist party contesting federal elections – was not formed until 1990.

[62] From his point of view this was probably a mistake, since the federal and provincial campaigns blurred into one another to the disadvantage of the Yes cause.

had won just two seats in the four western provinces in the February election, and none west of Winnipeg. It was a fragile platform on which to build national unity.

Before turning to the Quebec referendum, Trudeau took two decisions which showed that, in his final search for a constitutional settlement, he would steer a bold course. His first was to invite Ed Broadbent, leader of the NDP, to join the Liberals in a coalition. Broadbent said that his small Party would want a number of Cabinet seats, a couple of them senior posts. Trudeau was willing to meet his terms but Broadbent backed away, knowing that the Liberals did not need NDP votes for a majority in the Commons and so the NDP might be dropped as quickly as it was embraced.[63] But what is interesting here is that Trudeau was willing to sacrifice Cabinet seats and (presumably) part of his programme even though he had won a majority. His rationale was simple: if he had the NDP's support for his constitutional reforms he would be able to argue that he had the endorsement of the West, where the NDP was strong. The coalition ploy failed, but the courtship of the NDP was to continue.

The second move was to put in place a new team to run Ottawa's strategic and tactical approach to the constitutional question. Michael Pitfield, whom Trudeau had appointed Cabinet Secretary and head of the Privy Council Office (PCO) in 1975 was to return to that post, having been dropped by the Conservatives. Gordon Robertson, who been at Trudeau's side throughout the constitutional initiatives that followed the PQ victory in 1976, wanted to return to his old job as head of the Federal-Provincial Relations Office (FPRO). But Trudeau judged Robertson too much of a 'gentleman' for the next round of work. Instead he opted for Michael Kirby, the former Dalhousie mathematics professor, who had worked as an adviser to Trudeau in 1974–76 but who was new to the constitutional portfolio. Kirby brought to the role a keen brain, sharp elbows and a feisty temperament. His approach was straightforward, and its impact soon felt by the provinces: 'I don't go looking for fights. But I don't run from them either. Because in a war you can't do that.'[64] The metaphor was apt: he removed some FPRO officials whom he judged 'inherently pacifist' and he set about the planning and execution of a concerted campaign to overcome the opposition. He rapidly established the capability he judged necessary to secure victory: a sophisticated polling operation, an advertising programme to sell the government's message and access to legal counsel who might have might be more willing to take risks than were lawyers in the Department of Justice. But Justice was to continue to serve as the government's principal source of constitutional expertise. Its Minister, Jean Chrétien, was to become the public face of the Government's negotiating team but he was not free to direct the course of those operations. He had no choice but to tolerate the close

[63] Ed Broadbent, interview with the author, May 2006; Ted Johnson, interview with the author, 24 May 2006.

[64] Michael Kirby, interview with the author, 25 May 2006.

attention of the Prime Minister but, more tryingly, he also had to accept direction from Kirby himself.[65]

Trudeau had not appointed a Minister of Federal-Provincial Relations and so Kirby reported direct to him and had day-to-day responsibility for the tactics and organisation of the Government's constitutional efforts. He had the confidence of the Prime Minister and could speak with his authority when dealing with Ministers, officials or the provinces. But the key strategic decisions were taken by Trudeau. To state this is not simply to affirm a constitutional convention: Trudeau had a grip on the detail of this brief; he was always ready to take papers on the issue, he read them rapidly and commented on them liberally. And he took advice from multiple sources. He listened to Ministers, especially Marc Lalonde (now leading on the NEP) and the Deputy Prime Minister Allan MacEachen. The Cabinet as a whole was respectful of Trudeau's judgement on the constitution, but he was a good chairman, giving colleagues the opportunity to express their views, and working assiduously to carry them with him. He was equally diligent in listening to the mood of the Party caucus, finding time for weekly lunches with backbenchers at the Prime Minister's residence, 24 Sussex Drive. Pitfield always had ready access to the Prime Minister and although Kirby would brief Trudeau with just a private secretary in the room, the PCO continued to provide its own, separate stream of advice direct to the Prime Minister on constitutional issues.[66] Ottawa's constitutional operations were not necessarily a comfortable place to work after the 1980 election, but the team as a whole was unquestionably formidable. Joe Clark later acknowledged ruefully that it was a 'comprehensive, calculated, smart' operation.[67]

VII. Quebec Votes

It fell to the leader of the Quebec opposition and leader of the province's Liberals, Claude Ryan, to become the head of the No campaign in the run-up to the referendum on 20 May. This presented Ottawa with some immediate difficulties, given the long-standing enmity between Trudeau and Ryan. The Prime Minister found it difficult to take the former journalist seriously as a politician and he refused to dance attendance on the 'Pope of St Sacrament Street'.[68] And so it was Chrétien who was despatched to see Ryan – and was forced to wait for two hours before

[65] Fred Jordan, interview with the author, 29 May 2006; see also PCO, ATI – AA – 2002 – 2002/I, Note of Prime Minister's staff meeting on 18 October 1980, 20 October 1980.

[66] It is not possible yet (if it ever will be) to come to a definitive view on the balance of influence between the PCO and the FPRO because the PCO's advice is not yet publicly available. This paragraph reflects the evidence of interviews and of those records which have been released to date.

[67] Joe Clark, interview with the author, May 2006.

[68] Ryan had been editor of the Quebec paper *Le Devoir*, whose editorial offices were based in St Sacrament Street.

he was granted a papal audience.[69] But in the end the federal Government got its way on the issues that mattered to it most. Ryan would be the public face of the campaign. But whether Ryan liked it or not, Chrétien, supported by the Ottawa machine, would shape the campaign's themes, its publicity and its polling. It was to be direct, unsophisticated stuff: Chrétien toured the province, tirelessly emphasising the risks of sovereignty and the prospects for local jobs and fuel prices if Quebec left the federation.[70]

It has been suggested that Trudeau and Chrétien bought Ryan's complicity during the campaign: if he allowed the federal government influence over the campaign they would use the Beige Paper as the basis for a constitutional deal with Quebec. In the absence of any proof, it seems best to discount this theory. Trudeau and Chrétien were fundamentally opposed to the decentralisation advocated by the Beige Paper and it was, in any event, a negotiating document crafted by Raynold Langlois to represent the Quebec Party's opening bid. Langlois never thought that Ottawa would accept it *in toto.*[71] But in the unlikely event that Trudeau swallowed it whole, surely it would have been to the No campaign's electoral advantage to have made the deal public, to persuade swing voters that Ottawa was willing to listen to Quebec's reasonable demands. A more credible explanation is that Ottawa got its way by working around Ryan, collaborating with his team and tolerating, with more or less good grace, his performances on the stump. Insofar as an understanding was reached with Ryan it was that the campaign should do what successful No campaigns customarily do: it should attack the proposition before the electors. This they did successfully.

The second, and more persistent, theory about the referendum campaign concerns one of Trudeau's four direct interventions. On 16 May he spoke at the Paul Sauvé arena in Montreal. In a passage that was apparently *ex tempore*, he said:

> I know that I can make a solemn commitment that following a 'No' vote we will immediately take action to renew the constitution and we will not stop until we have done that.[72]

He did not elaborate what he meant. Before many weeks had passed the sovereigntists were to fasten on this commitment as evidence that Trudeau had dishonestly suggested that he would grant Quebec's traditional demands. As Claude Morin, Lévesque's Constitutional Affairs Minister later put it:

> He played with words and knowingly tricked the population, something, moreover, which was subsequently conceded by federalist politicians from Quebec who had been deceived by what was later delivered: they, in effect, realised that Trudeau had his own reform agenda and it wasn't what Quebec expected.[73]

[69] Serge Joyal, interview with the author, May 2006.

[70] For the campaign, see Graham Fraser, *René Lévesque and the Part Québécois in Power*, 2nd edn (Montreal, McGill-Queen's University Press, 2001) 219–21.

[71] Raynold Langlois, interview with the author, 23 May 2006.

[72] Cited in Peter H Russell, *Constitutional Odyssey. Can Canadians Become a Sovereign People?* (Toronto, University of Toronto Press, 2004) 109.

[73] Claude Morin to the author, August 2006. Translation by the author.

Trudeau loyalists dismiss this interpretation as fanciful. Where, they ask, was there the slightest evidence that Trudeau was going to yield to Quebec's demands? It would have run contrary to his whole career; there was no hint of decentralisation in the Liberals' election campaign; and nor was there any suggestion of it in the Throne Speech in April which described the Government's programme.[74] This is all fair, but it might be objected that Trudeau *did* already have a plan for constitutional renewal but it was not one he bothered to share with the electorate at the federal poll and nor was it one that he made explicit in the Quebec campaign. A careful reading of Trudeau's speeches in the 1979 election might have prepared voters for what was about to happen, but this was, at best, an indirect way of communicating to the Canadian public his intentions in early 1980.

The most compelling explanation of Trudeau's approach is that after the 1979 poll he felt no pressing need to explain his plans. In the first instance, his defeat rendered the plans irrelevant. In the February 1980 election he ran against Clark's record. Once he was back in power he knew what he wanted to do and he judged that it would serve his purposes better if he seized the initiative immediately after a No vote. That was best secured by dismantling the sovereigntists' proposition. His reference to the renewal of the constitution was unquestionably ambiguous and he might easily have provided clarification of the contentious phrase. He chose not to do so and he did not appear troubled by the prospect of securing electoral advantage from his ambiguity.[75] But only the most credulous voter could have seen the short passage in the Paul Sauvé speech as evidence that Trudeau had been converted to decentralisation.

In any event, it is far from clear that Trudeau's intervention had a significant effect on the vote on 20 May. The No Campaign was already on course to victory by 16 May and it ultimately secured 59.6 per cent of the vote.[76] Trudeau had cleared his first hurdle and the way was now clear for his final, and most audacious bid to reform the Canadian constitution.

VIII. Constitutional Reform in the Wake of the No Vote

Chrétien was summoned to see Trudeau the morning after the referendum result. The Prime Minister made scant reference to the victory: his focus had already shifted to his grander reform plans.[77] To that end Chrétien was to begin an immediate tour of provincial capitals to test their appetite for radical change.

[74] Eddie Goldenberg, interview with the author, 26 May 2006. David Ablett, interview with the author, 14 June 2006.

[75] His willingness to encourage the hopes of Québécois did not stop in May. His July 1980 open letter to Québécois was notably conciliatory in tone, even making reference to Quebec's 'distinct society'.

[76] The PQ's own polls showed the Yes vote in decline from 51% in late March to 45% by late April.

[77] Eddie Goldenberg, interview with the author, 26 May 2006.

It is worth pausing here a moment to assess the impact which the No vote had had on the political context. Had it brought about a realignment of the principal players, opening up the prospect which Trudeau and his team would take later the following year? The moment was auspicious for a decisive move by Trudeau: he had just won an election and a referendum on the bounce, he was back from the dead politically and his poll numbers were high. Equally importantly, the Government felt good about itself: it told itself that it had momentum and its caucus was in excellent spirits.[78] But none of this did much to make the provinces more tractable. René Lévesque had suffered a stinging rebuff, but his administration was no less committed to sovereignty-association. Its current mandate still had some way to run and even if it were defeated, the prospects of Ryan as premier would have done little for morale in Ottawa. English Canada was mightily relieved that Quebec had drawn back from the brink but the premiers did not draw the conclusion that it was now necessary to bring the constitutional process to a rapid conclusion. If anything, they saw Trudeau's urgency as a sign of weakness: he needed an outcome more than they did and they were willing to use this as an opportunity to press their demands for decentralisation. By May 1980 most of the nine provinces were led by experienced, canny politicians who knew Trudeau well. Negotiating with Trudeau was a bruising experience and by this stage in the process, personal enmity had infected the relationships with Ottawa. When, in September 1980, Brian Peckford of Newfoundland was challenged publicly to choose between Trudeau's vision for Canada and Lévesque's, he had no hesitation in opting for the latter. Peckford had not become a sovereigntist, but he was not going to miss an opportunity of snubbing the Prime Minister. The premiers did not yet feel under pressure to deal on Trudeau's terms and they, like Ottawa, read the polls. The public may have been in love with Trudeau again but it did not see the need for a hasty constitutional settlement, nor did it warm to the idea of unilateral action by Ottawa to bring it about.

In his tour of the country, Chrétien was soon to discover that the conditions were not yet propitious for a deal. But Trudeau was not in the mood to wait for events to move his way: he was determined to make the political weather. In his final bid for a settlement he was ready to gamble with the political stability of the country – and his own reputation. It is a truism that new constitutions are generally the result of a national crisis – a revolution or a civil war. The strategy adopted by Trudeau would ultimately engender a sense of crisis across Canada.

Trudeau's gamble was threefold. First, he was willing to resolve the matter unilaterally. He had the votes in Parliament and the sense of momentum needed to carry a resolution against Conservative and provincial opposition.[79] And he would put pressure on the British Government to take the necessary legislation through the Westminster Parliament to sever the constitutional link with Canada once and

[78] For ministerial support for Trudeau, see PCO, ATI – AA – 2003 – 0017 Cabinet Minutes, 18 September 1980 (74–80 CBM).

[79] PCO, ATI – AA – 2003 – 0017 Cabinet Minutes, 2 October 1980 (76–80 CBM); and Michael Kirby, interview with the author, 25 May 2006.

for all. He did not seek a unilateral solution if an agreement could be reached; and in the summer of 1980 it is clear that his preference – as expressed in public and in private – was for a deal.[80] But his calculation was that an agreement was more likely if the provinces understood that he had a choice. He could terminate the talks and go to Westminster. To be effective, this had to be a realistic option which he was willing to see through in the face of any number of political or legal threats. He had formed this view before the Quebec referendum and he ensured that his advisers made it clear to the provincial negotiators that a unilateral plan was under development.[81] The package was to be recast to avoid the rocks on which Bill C 60 had foundered and his lawyers told him that the new course would probably, but not certainly, survive challenge.[82]

The second gamble concerned the presentation of the reforms. They were to be sold over the head of politicians. As Marc Lalonde later observed, 'The Charter of Rights has the advantage of appealing to any citizen who is basically suspicious of politicians, whether [the citizen] is on the right or the left.'[83] The distrust of governments was to be exploited in an aggressive public relations campaign run by the Canadian Unity Information Office. This, in turn, sparked competitive campaigns by the provincial governments. Critics have charged Trudeau with disrespect for Canadian federalism: he was appealing to the nation as though it were one national whole. That was just the point: by 1980, if not earlier, he had come to believe that there was *one* national community which needed to take a collective view on the fundamental choices, especially if that view happened to coincide with his own.

The third gamble was tactical. Trudeau and his advisers had taken a fresh view of what was essential and what was desirable. The essential components were, inevitably, the Charter of Rights, patriation and the amending formula. The charter was to be broadly cast and linguistic rights (defined to include the language of education) had become part of the irreducible core.[84] This agenda, now branded the 'people's package', was to be addressed first in the negotiations in the summer of 1980. The second agenda concerned the redistribution of powers between federal and provincial government. To telegraph the message that the Government attached less priority to an agreement on this front, it earned the label 'the powers package'. There was to be no trading between the two packages.

[80] For the Prime Minister's thinking, see PCO, ATI – A – 2000 – 0195 Cabinet Minutes, 31 July 1980 (71–80 CBM). See also his July 1980 open letter to Québécois: André Burelle, *Pierre Elliott Trudeau. L'intellectuel et le politique* (Montreal, Éditions Fides, 2005) 437.

[81] Barry Strayer, interview with the author, 30 May 2006.

[82] Any suggestion of continuing vulnerability to court challenge remained a cause of anxiety. See Justice, file 260349, part one, Roger Tassé to Michael Kirby, 15 August 1980 and Michael Kirby to Prime Minister, 26 August 1980. Senior Justice officials have subsequently confirmed that they were confident that unilateral patriation was lawful; but questions remained as to whether it was in accordance with convention. See Roger Tassé, interview with the author, 25 May 2006 and Barry Strayer, interview with the author, 30 May 2006.

[83] Marc Lalonde, interview with the author, 23 May 2006.

[84] Barry Strayer, interview with the author, 30 May 2006. Ted Johnson, interview with the author, 24 May 2006.

The distribution of powers had formerly been the provinces' territory, but to upset the dynamic of the earlier negotiations Ottawa now withdrew some of the concessions it had made in the talks before the 1979 election. It also pressed its own economic agenda harder, seeking the removal of barriers to interprovincial trade and commerce: it demanded that the provinces yield authority and create a Canadian economic union.[85] The negotiations on powers were now to be about a two-way exchange, not simply the retreat of Ottawa in the face of provincial pressure. Eddie Goldenberg, Chrétien's political adviser, remembers with pleasure that this stiffening of the federal position, 'hit like a bombshell'.[86] At one and the same time Ottawa was willing to threaten the provinces with unilateralism and to deny them the progress they most dearly sought. Taken together, these gambles increased the risk of another constitutional impasse. To mitigate this, the federal team was open to deals as long as they did not imperil the people's package. If tactical advantage was to be secured, concessions would be made. If it took concessions on natural resources to bring Broadbent into the fold, he was to have them; if the provinces could not come to an agreement on property rights in the charter, they should be dropped; and if it helped to have equalisation payments as part of the people's package, they were to be smuggled in.[87] Trudeau might have winced at some of the concessions, and he may have regretted the abandonment of any plans for the reform of federal institutions, but his focus did not shift from the achievement of those reforms which he judged necessary to secure a settlement.

A federal-provincial conference in June agreed that the Continuing Committee of Ministers on the Constitution (CCMC) – a cumbersome piece of negotiating machinery first cranked into action in 1978 – should be revived. It was to spend the summer in an intensive round of negotiations on a 12-point agenda. The Prime Minster and the premiers would reconvene in September to take stock of progress and, if possible, finalise an agreement. Chrétien, shadowed everywhere by Kirby and his team, did his best to keep to the agreed strategy: Ottawa was happy to discuss any item on the broad agenda but it would give priority to the people's package.[88] It would urge economic union in those parts of the talks which dealt with federal-provincial powers. All the while, Kirby's team was sounding out provincial delegations, assessing how best to entice them.[89] It was soon clear that

85 For a snapshot of its negotiating stance, see PCO, ATI – A – 2000 – 0195 Cabinet Minutes, 31 July 1980 (71–80 CBM).

86 Eddie Goldenberg, interview with the author, 26 May 2006.

87 For an indication of the flexibilities in the federal position, see PCO, ATI – A – 2000 – 0195, The Federal Government's Approach to Constitutional Reform and its Initial Negotiating Position on the Twelve Items, 27 June 1980.

88 Derek Ablett, interview with the author, 14 June 2006.

89 This testing of provincial negotiating positions continued for the rest of 1980 and through until the First Ministers' Conference in November 1981. For one of the final, and most comprehensive, examples see LAC John. MG26 0 19, vol 160, folder – First Ministers' Conference on the Constitution, October [sic] 1981 – Briefing Book.

Ontario and New Brunswick were ready for Ottawa's embrace. Ontario had long seen itself as having national responsibilities, as the senior, if not the oldest, province. Richard Hatfield, the New Brunswick premier, was committed to improving the lot of the large Francophone community in the province and he wanted a settlement to entrench their language rights, a concession Trudeau was all too happy to grant. Throughout the summer the FPRO searched for a third province to seduce. Saskatchewan seemed the most vulnerable to Ottawa's charms. It was the only province to be held by the NDP and its premier, Allan Blakeney was sharp-witted and apparently open to a deal. The courtship was almost consummated under tropical skies later that year, when a deal was put to Blakeney on holiday in Hawaii, but at the last moment he thought better of it.[90] The FPRO also judged British Columbia and Nova Scotia to be open to persuasion, but little progress had been made with them by the time of the First Ministers' Conference in September.

In regular reports to Ministers, the FPRO faithfully chronicled the negotiating position of all 10 provinces. Even Quebec, which joined the CCMC talks although it had refused to see Chrétien in June, was the subject of these assessments. But the FPRO would, inevitably, pay particular attention to those provinces which might come over to Ottawa's side. Their task, short of a unilateral solution, was to create an ever-larger coalition of support. Implicitly this meant that their focus was on a deal with those provinces which were tractable. There is nothing to suggest that in the summer of 1980 they had already written off Quebec or any other province. But the package which was taking shape bore the contours of deals, or potential deals, with those provinces which seemed most open to persuasion by Ottawa. It was not such a big step to begin to contemplate a deal to which one or more provinces were not a party.

If Ottawa were eventually to take the unilateral course, it had to know that the British would not flinch from passing the necessary legislation. They might have to do so to the sound of protests from the Canadian provinces, the Progressive Conservative Party and any number of interest groups. Would the British feel the need to look behind the resolution, prompted by some vestigial sense of responsibility to the people of the former Dominion?

To manage this risk, the Canadian High Commission in London opened a second front in the fight for a new constitution.[91] It began an intensive lobbying campaign of Mrs Thatcher's Government and of parliamentarians. Trudeau himself secured a commitment from the British Prime Minister that the Conservative Party in the Commons would back the legislation. In the House of Lords, the Government would do its best to help, but it could not guarantee the outcome. Mrs Thatcher's colleagues were even less reassuring: a Bill of Rights might excite opposition in the Commons and it would be difficult to meet Ottawa's preferred timetable (on which

[90] Roy Romanow, interview with the author, 25 May 2006.

[91] Strictly, the team was in the Canadian High Commission but the staff working on the operation reported direct to Kirby (Michael Kirby, interview with the author, 25 May 2006).

Ottawa was insistent, until domestic considerations forced delays).[92] The more that the British looked at the Canadian proposition, the more complicated it became. The Foreign Affairs Select Committee concluded that Britain did, indeed, still have an imperial responsibility to scrutinise Canadian legislation.[93] And liberal peers began to ask about the rights of Canadian Indigenous Peoples. Some of these queries were home-grown in London, but others were planted by the provinces, who had now launched their own lobbying operation in London. Susceptible MPs and peers were to grow fat in the winter of 1980–81, as they were wined and dined competitively by the federal and provincial governments of Canada. The longer the process went on, the more the British came to wonder whether it was right and proper to accept Trudeau's invitation to 'hold their noses' and pass whatever it was that Ottawa eventually sent them. Reporting on talks in September 1980, a senior official in the Department of External Affairs reported that even their erstwhile allies in London were slipping away from them. The legal adviser to the British Foreign Office 'was like a novice bride in his reaction to what he described as a "more extensive proposition than anticipated"'.[94] The British would do their best but they did not want to be blamed: 'In the new Canadian confederation, it seems that the midwives are anxious to ensure that the sins of the fathers not be visited upon them.'[95]

IX. Going it Alone

Trudeau and his Cabinet had approved the federal negotiating brief at the CCMC talks but the execution had been left to Kirby and Chrétien. Trudeau received periodic reports but he was not going to allow the talks to ruin his summer. When Chrétien made his initial assessment of the prospects of a deal in advance of the First Ministers Conference, Trudeau was a voice of caution. A deal was possible, but not probable: the government should not close down the possibility of agreement, nor should it move now to determine the scope of a unilateral package, not least because it would need all the friends it could get if it were to go down that route.[96]

The September conference proved to be no more than a ritual display of policy differences and personal enmities. The pre-conference dinner gave a flavour of

[92] Norman StJohn Stevas (Leader of the House of Commons in the UK) was reported to have said to his Canadian counterpart in October 1980 that Britain would not be helpful, emphasising that the Bill of Rights would be particularly difficult for the British. His opinion caused angst in Ottawa. Justice file 260349, Patriation, part one.

[93] Foreign Affairs Committee, *The British North America Acts: The Role of Parliament. First Report, 30 January 1981.*

[94] Justice, file 260349, part one, Legal Talks with British Authorities, a minute by LH Legault to DMM [de Montigny Marchand], 29 September 1980.

[95] ibid.

[96] PCO, ATI – A – 2000 – 0195, Cabinet Minutes, 31 July 1980 (71–80 CBM). For a robust assessment of the progress made by the federal government through the adoption of its more aggressive negotiating stance, see the assessment at PCO, ATI – A – 2000 – 0195, Discussion Paper. Progress Report on the

what was to follow. Trudeau enquired loudly of the Governor-General, as host, how quickly he might leave so that he could get away from the premiers. Lévesque, delighting in the discomfort of his old foe, remarked in a stage whisper that 'the princeling is in high dudgeon tonight'.[97] The conference's collapse was accompanied by the leaking of a policy document drafted by the Quebec delegation said to describe a common stand by the provinces. Trudeau was infuriated by the so-called Chateau Consensus, seeing in it the provinces' readiness – egged on by Quebec – to reheat old arguments.[98]

But the Government was not terribly surprised by the failure of the conference. The talks in the summer of 1980 had served a useful purpose: the provinces were on notice that the Government wanted to focus on the people's package, that it expected a quid pro quo for any transfer of powers and that it was contemplating the unilateral option. Ottawa had begun to sell its new message to the people and it had persuaded Mrs Thatcher that she should do the right thing when the moment came. Ottawa would, of course, have been delighted if the provinces had come to an agreement by September, but that could not yet be expected; the components of a deal were to hand but the provinces still did not feel under sufficient pressure to bring the process to a conclusion.

On 2 October Trudeau ratcheted up the pressure on the provinces. He gave a televised address to the nation in which he announced that the Government would take the unilateral route. It would secure parliamentary approval for the people's package, which now included equalisation, and then it would take the resolution to London. This was not a tactical ploy: the Prime Minister was willing to see this through to the end. If it persuaded the provinces to treat that would be advantageous, but that was no longer a necessary objective. If progress was to be made – by any route – it was essential to establish that provincial agreement was no longer a prerequisite.

Trudeau had been preparing for this moment since his return to office in February. After the failure of the conference in September he took the temperature of his Cabinet colleagues and he listened to the mood of his caucus.[99] Both were supportive. But when he went on television to announce the unilateral course, he was taking a huge risk. He had been told that he could not count on any support

Three Weeks of Constitutional Negotiation in Montreal, Toronto and Vancouver, 28 July 1980 (FPRO-1-80DP). The influence of Kirby on the draft is clear.

[97] Roy McMurtry, interview with the author, 28 May 2006. Roy Romanow, interview with the author, 25 May 2006. On the eve of the conference a federal strategy paper (to be known popularly as the 'Kirby memorandum') was leaked to the Quebec delegation, who shared it with the world, pointing up that the Government was contemplating unilateralism. The leak attracted much attention but it cannot be blamed for the failure of the conference. The provinces already knew that government lawyers were working on unilateralism. After the initial embarrassment, the Government probably derived some benefit from the leak: it pressed home the point that it might go it alone.

[98] André Burelle, *Pierre Elliott Trudeau. L'intellectuel et le politique* (Montreal, Éditions Fides, 2005) 64–5.

[99] David Cameron, interview with the author, 16 June 2006. Christopher Page, *The Roles of Public Opinion in Canadian Government* (Toronto, University of Toronto Press, 2006) 82–3.

from the provinces;[100] it was probable that there would be a fresh legal challenge; the Progressive Conservatives would do their best to hinder Trudeau in the Commons; the British might back away; and the public remained hostile to unilateralism. If the project lost momentum and the Government became entangled in lengthy political, legal or diplomatic wrangles, support for the charter might ebb away and Trudeau's gambit might be seen as divisive and reckless.

The Government did what it could to mitigate those risks. It concluded a deal with Broadbent, securing the support of most of the NDP caucus in Parliament.[101] In his appeals to the nation, and in his entreaties to the British, Trudeau could now claim a measure of support in the West. He also hoped that the agreement with Broadbent would improve the prospects of persuading Blakeney, the NDP premier of Saskatchewan, to support the federal cause. But he was to be disappointed: relations between Broadbent and Blakeney were not close and the Saskatchewan Government felt a sense of pique that it was Broadbent who had secured concessions in respect of provincial control over resources. Discussions with Ontario and New Brunswick were more fruitful: both came out publicly in support of Ottawa. In Quebec, by contrast, the Government could not even persuade the Liberal opposition to take its side. Trudeau would not call Claude Ryan in person and so Serge Joyal, a Quebec MP was deputed to telephone Ryan while Trudeau listened in. Concessions were offered and Ryan agreed to consult his caucus. If Trudeau needed any evidence to confirm his view of Ryan as a naïve tyro, it came in the subsequent call. Ryan told Joyal that his caucus wanted the concessions – but it would not sanction the deal. The concessions were withdrawn.[102]

Ottawa had raised its game in 1980, assembling a strong and combative team, adopting tougher tactics and taking more audacious risks. Now the provinces responded. Later in October six of the dissenting provinces announced they would work in concert to oppose Ottawa's unilateralism. In time they were to be joined by the other two – Nova Scotia and Saskatchewan. The 'Gang of Eight' recognised that they were now engaged in a war which had to be fought simultaneously on many fronts. They launched three court challenges, each of which argued that the Government's ploy was unconstitutional: provincial consent was needed if the constitution was to be amended. They increased their presence in London. They worked with Joe Clark, encouraging him to filibuster in the Commons to win time for their legal challenges.[103] And they appealed to their electorates to support them in their resistance to Trudeau's coup.[104]

[100] PCO, ATI – AA – 2002 – 0002/I, Cabinet Minutes, 2 October 1980 (76–80 CBM).

[101] Ed Broadbent, interview with the author, May 2006. PCO, ATI – AA – 2003 – 0017, Memorandum for Cabinet from Jean Chrétien, 25 November 1980 (656 80 MC(E)). Broadbent's ability to command his caucus remained in doubt: see PCO, ATI – AA – 2002 – 0002/I, Premier Blakeney's Position on the Constitution [draft], Michael Kirby to Prime Minister, 16 January 1981.

[102] Serge Joyal, interview with the author, May 2006.

[103] Peter Lougheed, interview with the author, 3 August 2006. Richard Clippingdale, interview with the author, 31 May 2006. Joe Clark, interview with the author, May 2006.

[104] See, eg, *British Columbia Government News*, vol 25, nr 8, Special Issue, September 1980.

If we set aside the noise and fury of the provincial counter-attack, we can make out three consistent themes in their opposition. First they argued that the process chosen by Ottawa undermined its alleged objectives. As Dick Johnston, the Albertan Minister of Federal and Intergovernmental Affairs put it:

> For the act of patriation to have any meaning, it must foster in Canadians a greater spirit of nationhood and promote national unity. To proceed unilaterally with patriation, over the objections raised by a majority of provinces, could prove to be more disruptive than unifying, adding to the already considerable strains on the fabric of Canadian unity.[105]

Their second argument struck directly at the proposed charter. They protested that they were, in principle, in favour of measures to promote the rights of their constituents. The federal government had passed a Bill of Rights as early as 1960 and in time all provinces were to pass legislation safeguarding, to a greater or lesser extent, the rights of their citizens. Their objection was to the entrenchment of rights legislation in the constitution, beyond easy amendment by legislatures. From Allan Blakeney on the left to Sterling Lyon on the right, the premiers rallied to the cause of parliamentary sovereignty.[106]

Last – and certainly not least – they saw the package as an assault on the rights of the provinces and, by extension, on the nature of the federation. This was expressed in different ways by each of the premiers, but they had two common reference points. The Government's proposed amending formula included a deadlock-breaking referendum which usurped the rights of provincial legislatures in sanctioning constitutional change. And the charter was to apply to rights which were within provincial rather than federal control. Its provisions on the language of education, for example, would effectively cede power from provincial legislatures to the courts. One way or another, the charter was seen as a centralising move by Trudeau. For some premiers, it was the language provisions that they most resented; for others it was the anti-discrimination rights.[107] But they were united in seeing the package as an erosion of provincial authority.

The eight were as one on these core principles, but their alliance was never an entirely comfortable one. In belatedly joining the others Saskatchewan had given the common front no more than qualified support: its objective was to challenge the *process* through which the Government wanted to effect change. And Quebec's participation was driven by short-term tactical considerations. Lévesque was shaken by the defeat in the referendum, his administration was in disarray and his Cabinet gloomily contemplated a defeat at the next provincial election.

[105] PCO, ATI – AA – 2002 – 0002/I, Dick Johnston to Jean Chrétien, 4 December 1980.

[106] Their reasons for taking this stance were quite different. Blakeney, who was sympathetic to the rights agenda, was fearful that the courts would be too conservative. Lyon, by contrast, was a more thoroughgoing opponent of entrenched rights.

[107] To illustrate the provincial resistance to the anti-discrimination provisions, see, eg, PCO, ATI – AA – 2003 – 0017, Howard Leeson to Michael Kirby, 21 October 1980 and Memorandum for Cabinet from Jean Chrétien, 25 November 1980 (656 80 MC) (discussion in respect of age discrimination).

They concluded that Claude Morin should participate in the CCMC talks because not to do so would risk an even more resounding defeat in the elections: Quebec voters would see it as a neglect of the province's interests. They had no choice but to accept the referendum result and they hoped that they might put pressure on Trudeau to honour his commitment to constitutional renewal. They would wait on events, they would defend provincial rights – and they would hope that something would turn up.[108] It was not a negotiating strategy, nor was it a tactic calculated to secure a particular outcome: it was no more than the short-term response of an administration on the back foot.

But Peter Lougheed, who emerged as the de facto leader of the Gang of Eight, had come to the conclusion that the provinces would lose the battle for public opinion if they did nothing other than block Ottawa's progress. They had to have an alternative approach to offer the Canadian people.[109] With that end in mind, the eight premiers met in Ottawa in April 1981 to hammer out a common programme for constitutional change. Lévesque was amongst their number, having just been returned to office after a remarkable recovery from his referendum defeat the year before. After a difficult negotiation, they ultimately concluded a deal whose interpretation is critical to our understanding of the agreement later in the year with Ottawa. The Eight declared that they supported patriation with an amendment formula. Any new constitutional initiative, including a charter of rights, would have to wait until after the constitution was under Canadian control and subject to the new formula. This was to be based on the equality of the provinces. But if a province did not approve of an amendment it had the right to opt out – and to receive financial compensation for doing so. This provision was included at the insistence of Quebec. Traditionally, it had laid claim to a right of veto, but if this were to be set aside it wanted an alternative which was equally protective of its interests. An opt-out, backed by compensation, might even be more advantageous because it could be used without provoking the ire of its provincial partners: a veto could only be used if Quebec were willing to prevent action sought by the other provinces.[110]

When the parties to the April Accord later reflected on what it meant, there was little common ground. It does seem to have been generally understood that if a province was to contemplate parting company with the Eight, it was first required to inform its partners of its intentions. But there the consensus stopped. Later, Lougheed was clear that in April the premiers had achieved their goal of offering the country an alternative agenda to Trudeau's. But the understanding reached was inherently defensive in nature.[111] It was a device to force Ottawa to the negotiating table. If Trudeau abandoned unilateralism and showed a willingness to trade,

[108] Claude Morin, 'Le grand mensonge de 1980' in *Cégep Maisonneuve de Montréal* (1980). Claude Morin, 'Notes sur certains points particuliers' (unpublished, nd). Claude Morin to author, August 2006.
[109] Peter Lougheed, interview with the author, 3 August 2006.
[110] Claude Morin to author, August 2006.
[111] Peter Lougheed, interview with the author, 3 August 2006.

each province would be free to take a view as to the best way forward. The pact would have served its purpose. This, it must be said, is a wholly plausible interpretation of the April Accord but it must just as readily be conceded that the words of the agreement do not explicitly support Lougheed's view. How could they tell the world that this was simply a tactical device to be used to deter Ottawa from its unilateralist course?

Morin was later to rebut Lougheed's view. The text expressed the intentions of the premiers: they had entered a firm commitment to a complete package which could not be dismantled. And he went further, suggesting that the Quebec had not abandoned its traditional claim to a veto. It was always 'understood', he maintained, that if the Accord formula were not secured, Quebec would revert to the veto.[112] This argument, like Lougheed's, cannot be verified by reference to the text. It is quite possible that the Accord meant different things to different provinces from the moment it was signed. It was achievement enough to have reached an agreement after a long and difficult negotiation in which Quebec had resisted the suggestion that an opt-out would only be allowed if it were supported by two-thirds of a legislature. Whether it was tactically prudent of Quebec to have settled for the Accord is itself questionable. It was seen to have abandoned the veto and its later protests that it had done nothing of the sort were to persuade few outside the PQ. Lévesque who came to the meeting in Ottawa just two days after his election victory, was tired and preoccupied. He won an opt-out deal which was practical and potentially valuable, but the abandonment of the veto was a strategic error.

By the spring of 1981, it was clear to the premiers that the game might be slipping away from them. Their court challenges enjoyed mixed fortunes. Of the three cases they had launched, two were decided in Ottawa's favour and only the Newfoundland court ruled that the Government required provincial consent to proceed with its plans. All three cases were now bound for the Supreme Court. But the Government had not waited on the legal action in the provinces. It had presented its draft resolution to the Commons in October and sought to make brisk progress before moving onto London. But Joe Clark had fought an effective rearguard action. He had, of course, been weakened by the Tories' defeat in February, there were murmurings about his leadership and his parliamentary party was split on constitutional reform. And so he played for time, seeking to take tactical advantage where he could and taking a common stance with the Progressive Conservative premiers. The Government wanted the resolution debated, amended and approved on the floor of the Commons. The Conservatives mounted a filibuster, frustrating the Government. It was no part of the Government's plan that the resolution be remitted to a joint committee of both houses, still less that the proceedings be televised and it certainly did not want the sittings to run into the New Year. But it had to concede on each of these points.

[112] Claude Morin to author, August 2006. Claude Morin, 'Pour vraiment en finir avec une sottise' in *Le Devoir*, 10 June 1998.

From November to February the Joint Committee of both Houses became the focal point of a national conversation about Canada's constitutional future. The Taskforce on Canadian Unity had been a modest experiment with popular engagement. The Joint Committee's hearings were interest group politics on a grand scale. Over 56 hearing days and 267 televised hours of discussion, the Government's resolution was weighed, found wanting and comprehensively revised. The Committee took written submissions from 941 individuals and 294 organisations. In all, 67 amendments to the resolution were approved. Executive federalism would return to public prominence, but for a time the conventional machinery of constitutional reform was set aside. Some of the provincial premiers did give evidence to the Committee but for the moment they had become supplicants, seeking a place at the table.

The Joint Committee took its energy and momentum from the interest groups who beat a path to Ottawa. The Committee was asked to slow the process down, to heal Canada's divisions, to establish a constituent assembly and to stand firm in the face of the judicialisation of politics.[113] But above all, organisations pressed for amendments to the resolution, making special provision for their particular interest. Parliamentary committees in Ottawa were not new to lobbying but everybody understood that this time the participants were playing for keeps. Win at this Committee and they might get a permanent foothold in the constitution. Women wanted the gender equality provisions strengthened; the disabled wanted protection from discrimination; the Catholic Church sought an end to abortion; and ethnic minorities protested that languages other than French and English should be given constitutional status. Barry Strayer, a senior official at the Department of Justice, recalls wearily that the process was one of 'ascending paranoia': even when interests were protected by the draft there was competitive pressure to seek ever stronger language, however nugatory that might be.[114]

The Government had not sought this process but it soon learned to play by the new rules. If it were able to make concessions to interest groups it was to its political advantage to do so: a noisy charter lobby with a stake in the proposed resolution would be to its advantage in its struggle to face down the premiers. And so it worked closely with the Committee – behind the scenes and in open session – to reformulate the resolution.[115] This was rough and tumble retail politics. If an interest group put its case cogently and if its proposal did not endanger Ottawa's compacts with Ontario, New Brunswick and the NDP it would receive favourable consideration. The Government was even willing to support some groups in the hope that they would be able to put their case across more effectively. But even

[113] See, eg, Justice, file 251600-16, vol 4, pouch C, nr 1, Submission by the Citizens for More Time Committee to the Special Joint Committee, 16 December 1980. Justice, file 251600-16, vol 4, pouch C, nr 2, Submission by the Committee to Democratize the Constitutional Debate to the Special Joint Committee, nd [1980].

[114] Barry Strayer, interview with the author, 30 May 2006.

[115] Barry Strayer, interview with the author, 30 May 2006. Serge Joyal, interview with the author, May 2006.

federal funding could do little to heal the divisions which were all too apparent within the Indigenous lobby.[116]

The Government had good reason to be pleased with the Joint Committee's amended resolution. Left to its own devices the Government would have stuck with a more modest text. But the key decisions made by the Committee had the blessing of the Cabinet, if not always of the Department of Justice.[117] The Government had secured all 58 of its amendments in committee; the other two parties chalked up just nine between them. The Committee had fought shy of concessions which would have been politically toxic for the Government: a ban on abortion, for example, was not going to succeed however hard the Catholics lobbied. And some of the amendments were more a matter of gesture than of substance. But the draft resolution which returned to the Commons in February had a more muscular charter. The limitation clause – which defined the context in which rights may exist – had been narrowed, making it more difficult to justify an encroachment on the charter's provisions. The anti-discrimination grounds had been broadened; the minority language provisions had deftly been strengthened; gender equality had been asserted; multiculturalism had been affirmed; and even the ill-organised Indigenous lobby had earned a nod in the direction of their special status.[118] It was no wonder that the provincial premiers felt the need to mount a counter-attack when they met in April.

It looked briefly as though the Government might now choose to brush the court challenges aside, rushing the resolution through its remaining stages in Parliament and taking it on its way to London before the Supreme Court had the chance to rule. But the Progressive Conservatives were no more inclined to speed now than in the autumn of 1980. And the Supreme Court had no desire to be sidelined: it brought forward its consideration of the appeals. Judgment would be given in late September, coinciding with a trip which Trudeau was to make to South Korea and Australia. Politicians and officials headed for their summer cottages knowing that the constitutional future of the country rested on the Court's decision.

Bora Laskin, the Chief Justice, acknowledged the intense public interest in the case by allowing television cameras in to the Supreme Court to film the denouement. The CBC was to carry the session live, with an expert panel of commentators charged with giving pre- and post-match analysis to the waiting nation. But the proceedings had not even kicked off before they descended into farce. In taking

[116] Ed Broadbent, interview with the author, May 2006.

[117] For the Government's deliberations on changes during the Joint Committee, see PCO, ATI – AA – 2003 – 0017, Memorandum for Cabinet from Jean Chrétien, 25 November 1980 (656 80 MC(E)); Report of Decisions of Cabinet Committee on Priorities and Planning, 10 December 1980 (80-656-80MC(E)); Record of Cabinet Decision, Meeting of 11 December 1980 (656-80RD(E)); Report of Committee Decision, Possible Amendments to Proposed Resolution on Constitution of Canada, 17 December 1980 (719-80CR MEO).

[118] *Minutes of Proceedings and Evidence of the Special Joint Committee of the Senate and of the House of Commons on the Constitution of Canada. Report to Parliament* (1st Session of the 32nd Parliament, 1980–81, issue 57).

his seat at the bench, one of the justices had tripped on a cable, disconnecting the microphones. And so the nation had to lip-read as the judgments were read out. The CBC panel did its best to analyse the mime, but even they were dependent on what a technician had been able to hear as he listened at the closed door of the court.

The result was as skilful as it was remarkable. The Court found, by a majority of seven to two, that Parliament would be acting lawfully if it acted unilaterally to seek action in Westminster to amend the constitution. But a six to three majority concluded that constitutional *convention* required that Parliament should first obtain the agreement of the provinces: 'a *substantial degree of provincial consent* – to be determined by the politicians and not the courts – was conventionally required for the amendment of the Canadian Constitution'.[119]

The Ministers and officials gathered in the Department of Justice were stunned.[120] But that was hard to discern from Jean Chrétien's bullish press conference: the Government had been vindicated. Joe Clark was quick to condemn this as legal trickery: the nation was in crisis and the Liberals were to blame.

In Seoul, the Prime Minister and two of his advisers waited up late at night to get word of the judgment from Ottawa. The Prime Minister's initial reaction seems to have been that more concessions would have to be given: their pyrrhic victory on the legality of unilateralism might cost them half of the charter. But Chrétien was handling the immediate reaction and so there was no reason to do anything precipitously. And so Trudeau went to bed, leaving his officials to clarify exactly what it was that the Supreme Court had said – and the nation to wait on the word from Seoul. Overnight Ottawa counselled caution:

> It seems to us that it is very important that you do not go overboard with a simplistic and aggressive 'we won' attitude … Your task is to diminish [the] drama with patience, concern and a cheerful outlook for Canadians.[121]

The Prime Minister's Office knew all too well that Trudeau was not naturally inclined to exhibit patience and concern. But in his morning press conference he seemed to have heeded their advice. He was sure-footed, placatory and reasonable – until the very last minute. To the delight of his critics and the dismay of his supporters he could not resist one final line: 'Just watch me'.

By the time Trudeau had reached Melbourne, on the next leg of his trip, the story in Canada had moved on. The premiers had claimed victory and Kirby was warning him that their attack on the 'immorality' of unilateralism would hurt and

[119] Emphasis added. Supreme Court of Canada, Re: Resolution to amend the constitution, [1981] 1 SCR 753; 28 September 1981. The substantive consent argument had been advanced in the hearings by Roy Romanow, the Attorney General of Saskatchewan.

[120] Eddie Goldenberg, interview with the author, 26 May 2006.

[121] LAC John. MG26 0 19, vol 160, folder on Constitutional Events during Australia trip 1981, Telex from Joyce Fairbairn, Prime Minister's Office, to Pierre Elliott Trudeau, 28 September 1981. (Original text was telegrammatic in style. Quotation used here has been slightly modified.)

that it 'will be hard to refute'.[122] The press reaction was mixed but the Cabinet, the caucus, Ontario and New Brunswick were all standing firm. Lévesque was about to launch a new advertising campaign against the Government's constitutional proposals but, more damagingly, he was to put a motion of condemnation to the Quebec National Assembly. Ryan was to support him.

Trudeau was angry at what he saw as the Court's meddling in politics. He was puzzled as to why the Court should go beyond the clear terms of the question put to them.[123] But he put this aside in the short-term. His initial focus was on how best to safeguard the resolution. To press on regardless and to despatch the matter to Westminster would risk uproar at home and even greater opposition in London. Another conference, even an unsuccessful one, would demonstrate to Canadians and to the House of Lords that he had done all in his power to find a consensus. After an ill-tempered game of cat-and-mouse with the provinces, all parties finally agreed to assemble in Ottawa on 2–5 November.

X. One Last Try

Two versions of the November conference have entered the history books. One tells of lies, deception and treachery. The other of triumph, hope and regret. There are stark differences of interpretation – and of fact. When discussed almost a quarter of a century later, the memories of the participants had become blurred and many of the most significant exchanges did not leave a written record. The account that follows constructs the most credible narrative from the available evidence, scraping away the encrusted mythology and pointing up the gaps in the evidence.

The story begins from the moment it became clear that there was to be one more federal-provincial conference. Ottawa was hard at work sounding out the participants, testing their flexibility and taking their temperature in the wake of the Supreme Court's judgment. There was nothing surprising or sinister about this operation. One way or another it had been under way since the Liberals' return to power the previous year. And it was not always conducted through formal approaches. The relations between Chrétien and the provincial ministers of justice were cordial, having been established during the negotiations in the summer of 1980. And so when, in July 1981, he found himself in Cambridge at a conference with Roy Romanow of Saskatchewan and Roy McMurtry of Ontario it was natural that the three of them should discuss how a deal might be brought about. The FPRO's activities in October took a similar course, but they paid particular attention to Saskatchewan and British Columbia. They remained the most tractable of

[122] LAC John. MG26 0 19, vol 160, folder on Constitutional Events during Australia trip 1981, Telex from Michael Kirby to Prime Minister, 29 September 1981.

[123] Ted Johnson, interview with the author, 5 June 2006 and correspondence with the author, August 2020. For Trudeau's views 10 years later, see the Convocation Speech at the Opening of the Bora Laskin Law Library, University of Toronto (21 March 1991) in Pierre Elliott Trudeau, *Fatal Tilt: Speaking out about Sovereignty* (Toronto, Harper Collins, 1991).

the provinces and Bill Bennett of British Columbia was now the premiers' chairman. Neither province had come to an understanding with Ottawa before their delegations set off for the capital and there is no evidence to suggest that either had reneged on the April Accord.[124]

In the weeks before the conference Trudeau took every opportunity to turn up the heat on the premiers. He was open to an agreement but he had not abandoned unilateralism. And he wondered aloud at the motivation of the premiers whose focus was on the transfer of ever greater powers to the provinces:

> I don't think people are going to say well: We can't get more powers, therefore we don't want our constitution. We don't want to be independent. We don't want to have our fundamental rights guaranteed. And that's naturally their judgment. And, if I'm wrong, the Canadian people will defeat our party at the next election and they will change the constitution and they will get rid of the bill of rights. They can even send the constitution back to Britain.[125]

These were the words of a man whose political instinct was confirmed by the polls: patriation and the charter remained popular in every province of the federation. The Canadian people had not become any more enthusiastic about unilateralism, but there is no reason to doubt that Trudeau would have followed through on his threat: he would have risked provincial outrage and public opprobrium by going to London on his own if the premiers had not come with him.[126] He had no choice: if he backed away from unilateralism he was denying himself his best hope of securing a deal with the provinces. Without a credible threat of going it alone, he would have lost his leverage with the provinces.

On the eve of the conference the underlying circumstances were, at long last, favourable for a deal. The passage of time had begun to change the combatants' attitudes. Trudeau was almost 20 months into his final term of office: time was beginning to run out. The public was tired of the constitution – and of the perpetual wrangling amongst their governments. The premiers of English Canada did not want to face their electors having failed yet again to come to an agreement. If Trudeau did take the unilateralist route he might do himself irreparable damage, but he would also tip the country into constitutional crisis. Having already fought two Supreme Court cases over the constitution within less than three years, nobody in English Canada had the appetite for a third.

But it was the Supreme Court that had brought about the decisive realignment amongst the governments. Its strictures on constitutional convention may have caused fury in Ottawa, but it had endorsed the doctrine of 'substantive consent'. Ottawa was now freed from any obligation to seek unanimous consent and it was

[124] Claude Morin takes a different view: Claude Morin to author, August 2006.

[125] LAC John. MG26 019, vol 160, folder Constitution, part III, Transcript of the Prime Minister's interview with Jim Munson of CTV Television, 2 October 1981.

[126] For polling evidence see LAC John. MG26 019, vol 160, folder Constitution: Supreme Court Decision on Constitutional Reference 1981, Michael Kirby to Prime Minister, 9 September 1981, Appendix B. See also Michael Kirby, interview with the author, 25 May 2006.

well placed to brush away any suggestion that the larger provinces had a veto. The Court did not say when consent became substantive consent: it presumably required more than a bare majority and the threshold was not as high as nine or ten. Trudeau seems to have concluded that seven provinces representing at least 50 per cent of the population would suffice.[127] In any event, it was now reasonable for Ottawa to proceed on the basis that it no longer needed Quebec's agreement to proceed. It did not exclude Quebec from its pre-conference diplomacy but it was, as before, concentrating its efforts on the provinces most likely to constitute a federal-provincial coalition. By the time the premiers took their seats in the Federal Conference Centre on 2 November most of them had strong incentives to come to an agreement. For the first time they were operating on terms which would maximise the chance of a successful outcome.

Canada was wearily familiar with federal-provincial conferences on the constitution. The apparent obsession of their leaders with a nineteenth century British Act of Parliament was not shared by all Canadians. But the Supreme Court's ruling had dramatised the choice facing the country. Ottawa and the provinces had launched renewed advertising campaigns as each rallied support one more time.[128] Trudeau and the premiers had toured the television and radio studios staking out their position. By 2 November all of Canada knew that the nation's constitutional order might be about to be put to its greatest test.

A citizen watching the opening sessions on television would have searched in vain for some sign of inspiration or novelty from the nation's leaders. Familiar postures were struck. Tired lines were rehearsed. Old rivalries were rekindled.

Things did not get much better on the second day, with the conference now in closed session. Trudeau clashed with Lévesque. Bill Davis locked horns with Peter Lougheed.[129] A ritual was being played out.

The familiar routine finally gave way to substantive negotiations on the third day, 4 November. The proceedings were to conclude the following day and if a deal were to be reached, the real business could be delayed no longer. At the Gang of Eight's breakfast meeting Bennett of British Columbia said that he wanted to float a possible solution, having tried and failed to secure support for another deal the previous day. Blakeney of Saskatchewan, whose Gang membership had always been provisional, said that he, too, wanted to see if he could build common ground between the parties.

[127] This was Trudeau's brief to Chrétien during the November conference: Jean Chrétien, interview with the author, 24 May 2006.

[128] Peter Lougheed, interview with the author, 3 August 2006. For federal publicity efforts, see LAC John. MG26 0 019, vol 160, folder Constitution, part two, Michael Kirby to Prime Minister, 2 November 1981.

[129] LAC John. MG26 019, vol 160, folder Constitution, part two, Unofficial transcript of the First Ministers' Conference, morning of 3 November 1981. Davis and Lougheed were both spoken of as potential successors to Joe Clark. They represented quite different strands of conservatism. Davis was a patrician and a traditional nationalist. Lougheed was the champion of the new West, emboldened by its new wealth and committed to free market economics.

But it was Trudeau, not the premiers, who was to break the logjam. In the run-up to the conference he had been toying with the notion of a referendum to validate the charter.[130] The idea was not fully worked-up but it did not need to be: it was a tactical ploy whose sole purpose was to give the premiers a jolt, shaking them out of their well-established negotiating positions. He knew that most of them would be appalled: the charter was overwhelmingly popular. And if the referendum were to be based on regions, the very idea would be sure to turn provinces against one another; just as they found it difficult to settle on an amending formula, so they would struggle to agree on the structure of a referendum. The risk in Trudeau's ploy was that he would upset Davis and Hatfield, his only provincial allies. But by the morning of the third day, he judged this to be a risk worth taking, a political judgement Chrétien understood instinctively.[131] Trudeau proposed that the British be asked to make provision for two referendums, one on the charter, the other on the amending formula. In each case, the threshold for approval would be a majority of Canadians *and* a majority in each of four regions (the Atlantic, Quebec, Ontario and the West).

The Gang of Eight dissolved on impact. Faced by Trudeau's challenge, Lévesque's *amour propre* got the better of his political judgement: without reference to his colleagues in the Gang, he accepted the idea. Trudeau, recognising the significance of the moment, adjourned the session. Leaving the room, he dug his knuckles into an aide's back and twisted them, giddy with excitement. He called an impromptu press conference and announced to a bemused world the new alliance between Ottawa and Quebec. When the conference resumed and Trudeau was asked to clarify his proposal, the Prime Minister was, we must assume, forced to extemporise. Any referendum would be held after Canada had patriated the constitution, adopted an amending formula and entrenched the charter. Lévesque at once withdrew his support, condemning this sequence as undemocratic. But the damage was done.

Twenty-four hours after Trudeau proposed the referendum, Lévesque claimed that it had 'become in reality no more than a balloon, inflated so it could be deflated'.[132] But he had spotted it 24 hours too late. He would later do further damage to his reputation for political nous, by asking how he could have done other than accept: he believed in the concept of the referendum and he was confident he could defeat Trudeau in Quebec. This was to miss the point by some margin. To achieve his goals at the conference Lévesque had to focus on one thing and one thing only: he had to prevent a cigarette paper being inserted between him

[130] Michael Kirby, interview with the author, 25 May 2006. Roy McMurtry, interview with the author, 28 May 2006.

[131] Jean Chrétien, interview with author, 10 July 2020.

[132] Canadian Intergovernmental Conference Secretariat, *Federal-Provincial Conference of the First Ministers on the Constitution. Verbatim Transcript. Ottawa. November 2–5, 1981* (unpublished photocopy held by Library and Archives Canada, Ottawa) 106. The text cited here is the author's translation.

and the other members of the Gang of Eight. But at the first invitation from his old foe he had broken with his colleagues.

For Claude Morin, the issue was simple: Trudeau had made an offer he could not sustain, he had been found out and the ploy had collapsed. Years later Morin was to go further, arguing that Lévesque's rapid abandonment of the referendum should have left the Gang of Eight stronger than it had been before: a sinner had repented and returned to the fold.[133] But this shows how little the Quebec delegation must have understood their partners. None was enamoured of Ottawa, still less of Trudeau. But most of them now wanted a deal. Lévesque's flirtation with a referendum was not important in itself but it confirmed for the Gang that the ice floe was cracking under their feet. Quebec had not betrayed the Gang of Eight any more than Saskatchewan, which floated its own solution on 4 November and was subsequently accused of treachery by Morin.[134] But Trudeau's offer, as much as Lévesque's response, suggested that, at long last, the trading had begun. The April Accord had served its defensive, tactical purpose: Trudeau was now negotiating and so it was now for each premier to look out for his own province's interests.[135]

The referendum ploy was a brilliant device, played to good effect by Trudeau. But it was no more than a device. It did not – as some have suggested – deliver a deal. It moved the conference on from its ritualised opening to its second, substantive phase. More important than the ploy was the response to it: it was significant that it was Quebec which took the bait. The alliance between the separatist government and its seven partners had always been an uneasy, tactically convenient union. Lévesque's folly made it easier for the other seven to distance themselves from Quebec over the coming 24 hours.

The precise sequence of events during the remainder of 4 November and the night that followed will never be reconstructed with confidence. The closed session of the conference was not formally minuted and, in any event, the principal exchanges were to happen away from the open session – either in the corridors of the conference centre, at 24 Sussex Drive or in the premiers' suites at the Chateau Laurier hotel.[136] What is clear is that by late on the afternoon of 4 November,

[133] For Morin's views at the time, see Roy Romanow, interview with the author, 25 May 2006. For his views subsequently, see Claude Morin, 'Des myths persistants', *Le Devoir*, 24 April 2002.

[134] Claude Morin to Dick Johnston, 6 November 1981 (Correspondence supplied to the author by Peter Lougheed, 2 August 2006). René Lévesque also took up the charge against Saskatchewan: see Lésveque to Peter Lougheed, 5 May 1982 (correspondence supplied to author by Peter Lougheed, 2 August 2006).

[135] In his subsequent correspondence with René Lévesque, Peter Lougheed stresses two characteristics of the pact reached in April. First, it was provisional, a device intended to force Trudeau to abandon unilateralism. Second, it was agreed on the eve of the November conference that none of the eight should take the others by surprise during the proceedings. Lévesque seems to have misunderstood the first point and to have neglected the second. See Alberta, Lougheed: Peter Lougheed to René Lévesque, 8 March 1982 (accession GR1985.0401, item 3763, box 215).

[136] The author's interviews with most of the principal players in 2006 reveal almost comical confusion about who was where and who said what to whom. The most convincing explanation of this has nothing to do with conscious deception: over time memories cloud over and it is all too easy to begin to remember events as one would have prefer them to have been.

an outline of a deal was in play. Brian Peckford had put together one version and Jean Chrétien, Roy Romanow and Roy McMurtry had cooked up a second.[137] Allan Blakeney took it upon himself to promote an agreement in discussions with his colleagues. It soon gathered momentum: by early evening there was support from Ontario, Saskatchewan, British Columbia and the four Maritime provinces.[138] And Dick Johnson, acting for Peter Lougheed, signalled that Alberta viewed the emerging plan positively. The deal was worked and reworked in an all-night drafting session, much of which took place in Bill Davis's suite. Michael Kirby spoke for Trudeau, Chrétien having gone home after a meeting at 24 Sussex Drive. For the second time in this drama, the Prime Minister retired to bed, content to wait on events. But before doing so he had taken a call from Bill Davis who sketched out the deal, which was to include a charter with a notwithstanding clause allowing a legislative override of charter rights. Davis indicated that he was ready to accept the legislative override and that if Trudeau did not, Ontario would no longer back him.[139] The Prime Minister did not yield immediately but he told Chrétien that evening that if the deal had sufficient support he would, reluctantly, accept the notwithstanding clause.[140]

Peter Lougheed saw the deal shortly before the Gang's 8am breakfast meeting. He confirmed what Johnson had said; Alberta would sign up.[141] It was the eighth province to accept the terms. The exceptions were Manitoba and Quebec. Sterling Lyon, premier of Manitoba and a vigorous opponent of the charter, had had to fly back to Winnipeg to resume his campaign for re-election. Gerald Mercier, his Attorney General, had stayed behind to protect Manitoba's interests, and he, cautiously, inserted a caveat in respect of minority language education rights alongside the charter text. Lyon was defeated in the election and his successor withdrew the caveat in a telephone call.[142] Quebec stood alone.

Lévesque arrived late at the breakfast meeting, having travelled across the Ottawa River from Hull, where he had spent the night.[143] Lougheed explained the deal to him and spent some time before the conference resumed trying to persuade him to agree.[144] Later that morning, when Lévesque publicly rejected the terms on offer, he spoke with sadness of the demise of the provincial alliance. Before the day was out Quebec and its former partners had both tried their hand at a first draft of history. Depending on one's taste, the night of 4–5 November was either a testament to Quebec's regrettable intransigence or it was the Night of the Long Knives,

[137] The second deal has entered Canadian mythology as the Kitchen Accord because it was developed by the three principals in a meeting in the conference centre pantry. It seems best to regard it as a sign that the weather was changing rather than a cause of climactic change.

[138] Jean Chrétien, interview with the author, 24 May 2006.

[139] Roy McMurtry, interview with the author, 28 May 2006. Roy Romanow, interview with the author, 25 May 2006.

[140] Jean Chrétien, interview with the author, 24 May 2006.

[141] Peter Lougheed, interview with the author, 3 August 2006.

[142] Roy McMurtry, interview with the author, 28 May 2006.

[143] Hull is on the Quebec side of the river and Lévesque always stayed there when he came to Ottawa.

[144] Peter Lougheed, interview with the author, 3 August 2006.

in which English Canada indulged in a shameful betrayal. Why was Quebec not at the meetings in the Chateau Laurier? According to one's preference, one could choose to believe that it declined to attend or that it was purposely excluded.[145] The truth may be somewhere in between. When Lévesque and Morin set off for Hull on the evening of 4 November they knew that a deal was in the air and that the conference was to conclude the following day. If they had wanted to participate in the process they could easily have done so. There may, or may not, have been an invitation to the Quebec delegation to come to the Chateau Laurier but one suspects that the other provinces did not exert themselves to involve Lévesque and Morin in the talks. And the federal team had already become used to the notion that seven or eight provinces would be sufficient for its purposes. By the night of 4–5 November, 10 of the participants to the talks shared a common incentive; and the eleventh had another. The 10 wanted an agreed outcome and they were each making judgements as to how to maximise their own advantage in the deal.[146] It was politically more attractive to the eleventh to stand aside from the process: the terms of any deal were unlikely to be acceptable to the PQ Government and if the discussions were seen to have happened in its absence it would be that much easier to denounce the outcome as a betrayal.

The deal which emerged on the morning of 5 November was neither novel nor surprising. Most of the charter had survived, but part of it was to be subject to a notwithstanding clause.[147] If a legislature – federal or provincial – chose to override charter rights it could do so for a maximum of five years. It was then required to seek fresh approval of the mandate or to let it expire. Entrenched rights had been squared with parliamentary supremacy. Trudeau's calculation was that legislatures would have to think twice before suspending the constitutional protections given to citizens: the provinces had secured a tool which would be difficult to use. And the language provisions – including language of education – stood outside the scope of the notwithstanding clause. The principle of equalisation of wealth between provinces was to be entrenched. Ottawa had to accept most, but not all, of the amending formula in the April Accord. The equality of the provinces had been upheld: on most issues, an amendment required the support of Parliament and of seven provincial legislatures representing at least 50 per cent of the population.[148] But the federal Government had been able to mitigate the risk of a checkerboard

[145] Contrasting accounts are given to this day by Lougheed and Morin. Peter Lougheed, interview with the author, 3 August 2006. Claude Morin to author, August 2006.

[146] Manitoba's position was more ambiguous. Sterling Lyon's principal preoccupation was his (unsuccessful) bid for re-election and he was, in any event, a strong opponent of an entrenched charter. But it seems fair to categorise Manitoba with the others because, as events showed, the notwithstanding clause cleared the way for Attorney General Mercier to sign up, while reserving the right of the Manitoba legislature to take a final view on the matter.

[147] The day before the Conference opened Trudeau indicated to Ministerial colleagues that he might still be willing to narrow the terms of the charter if that was what was needed to secure a deal: see PCO, ATI – AA – 2002 – 0002/I, Cabinet Minutes, 3 November 1981 (37(B) – 81CBM).

[148] As incorporated into the Constitution Act 1982, the amendment formula is complex and on some provisions each province has a veto. These include amendments relating to the monarch, to the Governor-General, to provincial representation in Parliament, to the use of English and French (other than

Canada by stripping out the provision in the April formula which guaranteed financial compensation to a province which opted-out of an amendment. Any opt-out would now be at the province's own expense.

Having cavilled at aspects of the deal when it was put to him in the morning, Trudeau relented, knowing that the agreement was good enough. He closed the conference before he stretched the patience of the participants too far:

> I don't think I will open the meeting for any afterthoughts because we had better grab the signatures, this piece of paper, and run before anyone changes his mind.[149]

Trudeau and nine of the 10 provincial premiers put their signatures to a short statement recording their principal points of agreement and the deal was – almost – done.

The Department of Justice's team had spent the night trying to draft a proposal to give effect to Trudeau's referendum proposal of 4 November.[150] Early on 5 November they were told that the story had moved on. The referendum was now the stuff of prehistory and they were to start work on a comprehensive revision of the text of the constitutional resolution. At the end of the afternoon it was presented to a meeting of officials from each of the signatories. The federal team had no intention of reopening the negotiation, but it soon became clear that there was a measure of confusion about what had been agreed between the principals.[151] It was eventually concluded that although discrimination on grounds of gender was proscribed, the additional guarantee of gender equality – conceded by the Government before the Joint Committee – was to be dropped. Similarly, the text was to be silent on the rights of the Indigenous Peoples.

Canada was soon reminded that the charter lobbies – so noisy at the Joint Committee the previous winter – had lost none of their energy. Chrétien pointed out to Allan Blakeney that unless he wanted women's groups from across Canada to descend on Regina, he had better drop his province's opposition to the gender equality provision.[152] Blakeney took the point and the guarantee was put back into the text, but not before he, in turn, pressed for the restoration of the clause recognising Indigenous rights.[153]

Indigenous organisations had been swift to condemn the Government for abandoning them and many had drawn the conclusion (wrongly) that Trudeau had reverted to type. The federal Government was not particularly wedded to the entrenched protection of Indigenous rights, not least because its lawyers

provisions relating to one or more, but not all, provinces), the composition of the Supreme Court and procedures for amending the constitution.

[149] Canadian Intergovernmental Conference Secretariat, *Federal-Provincial Conference*, 133 *of the First Ministers on the Constitution. Verbatim Transcript. Ottawa. November 2–5, 1981* (unpublished photocopy held by the Library and Archives Canada, Ottawa).

[150] Mary Dawson, interview with the author, 29 May 2006. Barry Strayer, interview with the author, 30 May 2006.

[151] James Ross Hurley, interview with the author, May 2006.

[152] Jean Chrétien, interview with the author, 24 May 2006.

[153] Roy Romanow, interview with the author, 25 May 2006.

were worried that it did not know the extent of those rights, but it was resistance from the provinces which had caused the provision to be dropped. It was only restored after Peter Lougheed suggested the text refer to the 'existing' rights of Indigenous Peoples, thereby excluding the possibility that dormant rights might be resuscitated.[154]

In parallel with this process, efforts were made to make the deal more palatable in Quebec. Reflecting on these talks later, Michael Kirby termed them 'window-dressing': the PQ Government had taken its decision and it was not to be persuaded.[155] This interpretation tallies with the recollection of PQ Cabinet Ministers: some were troubled by Lévesque's tactics but they rallied to him all the same. There was no suggestion that they should succumb to Ottawa's embrace.[156] But Ottawa wanted to build up public and parliamentary support for the deal, before it was despatched to London. The prospects for a smooth passage at Westminster had improved immeasurably, but when the joint resolution was finally passed in Ottawa in December it still faced legal challenges and hostile lobbying on both sides of the Atlantic. With this in mind, Ottawa had made two concessions to Quebec. First, it bowed to pressure from the Progressive Conservatives and agreed that if an amendment were to deprive a province of authority over education or cultural matters, financial compensation was to be paid to the province which opted-out. Ostensibly a concession to all provinces, this was only likely to be of any value to Quebec. Second, the impact of the minority language education rights in Quebec was softened by suspending one of the two provisions through which Anglophone Canadian children could claim a right to instruction in English. This concession, purposely hidden at the end of the Constitution Act, lessened but did not remove the conflict between the new constitution and Bill 101.[157] The concessions made no impression on the Quebec administration. Lévesque and Trudeau briefly traded correspondence, each practising lines which were to become all too familiar to Canadians over the years to come. Lévesque reasserted his province's claim to a veto on constitutional change; Trudeau directed him to the Supreme Court reference; Lévesque returned to the charge, calling for a pause, allowing the Supreme Court to rule on Quebec's veto; Trudeau demurred, this time reminding his sparring partner that he had himself abandoned his claim to a veto when he signed up to the April Accord. The resolution went on its way to London.[158]

The deal struck by Ottawa and the nine provinces was fashioned out of compromise. Each of the parties had an eye to guiding principles and to aspirations for the nation's future, but in the final stages they had to bargain for the best deal that

[154] Peter Lougheed, interview with the author, 3 August 2006.

[155] Michael Kirby, interview with the author, 25 May 2006.

[156] Bernard Landry, interview with the author, 28 June 2006. Claude Morin to author, August 2006.

[157] Constitution Act 1982, s 59. The Act allowed for the theoretical possibility that Quebec would want to opt into the second of the two minority language provisions.

[158] The Supreme Court would eventually address Quebec's argument in December 1982, ruling that the province did not have a veto, in law or in convention.

they could get. Even Trudeau knew that he had to yield ground, all the while questioning the intellectual merit of the arguments ranged against him. And he had to accept painful reverses. For example, he had hoped that Ontario might join the federal government, Quebec and New Brunswick in entrenching bilingualism in their courts and legislatures. But Bill Davis ultimately backed away from the move, fearful of local resistance in his overwhelmingly Anglophone province. Even when it came to language rights – the glue that was to hold the federation together – Trudeau was unable to dictate terms.

Might it have been possible to have framed a deal to which Lévesque would have been a signatory? In seeking to answer that question we should first remind ourselves that Ottawa and the provinces had come a long way since the federal election in February 1980. Over the following 21 months, the political circumstances began to favour an agreement. But there was nothing certain about a deal when the conference opened on 2 November and if Ottawa had mishandled the final round of negotiations, it might have faced the prospect of a unilateralist solution, without even the support of Ontario and New Brunswick.

Claude Morin has suggested that Ottawa chose to exclude Quebec from the final deal, proposing to the other provinces that it should be barred from the talks on the night of 4–5 November.[159] But in the absence of any firm evidence to support this argument, it seems reasonable to conclude that Quebec's 'exclusion' was not something orchestrated by Ottawa. We do know that Kirby, Goldenberg and others on the federal team privately doubted whether the PQ Government would ever conclude an agreement with a Trudeau-led Government.[160] Relations between Ottawa and Quebec had long since been corroded by personal bitterness, accusations of betrayal and mistrust. None of this was conducive to an agreement, but none of it serves as proof that Ottawa did not want a deal with Quebec. As late as August 1980 the federal team was exploring the prospect for a compromise with the *péquistes*. But by the summer of 1981, if not before, its formal assessments of the PQ's intentions made for gloomy reading.[161] And the briefing to Trudeau on the eve of the November conference concluded that the PQ was sitting on its hands, 'satisfied that it has Ryan in its pocket [and] convinced that it has the support of Quebeckers'.[162] As we have seen, Ottawa had come to focus its efforts on those provinces which seemed to be more tractable and it was reasonable to conclude that the Supreme Court had legitimised this tactic. Had Quebec shown itself to be more open to a deal there is every reason to believe that Ottawa would have worked harder to embrace it in the agreement. But amongst the negotiating teams the common assumption was that Quebec would always remain apart: and the

[159] Claude Morin to author, August 2006.

[160] Eddie Goldenberg, interview with the author, 26 May 2006. Michael Kirby, interview with the author, 25 May 2006.

[161] PCO, ATI – AA – 2002 – 0002/I, Memorandum for Prime Minister, [unsigned], 29 June 1981.

[162] LAC John. MG26 0 19, vol 160, folder: First Ministers' Conference on the Constitution, Oct. 1981, Briefing Book, Summary of premiers' negotiating positions. Translation by author.

Quebec delegation confirmed this in private conversations.[163] By the summer of 1981 the PQ no longer had any electoral incentive to court Anglophone Québécois: it was secure in office for another three years. Lévesque's principal political challenge was how best to hold the sovereigntists together as he plotted a new, more circuitous course towards sovereignty-association. An accommodation with the rest of Canada, however temporary, exposed Lévesque to the risk of turbulence within his party. This was to be demonstrated in 1984 when he announced that the PQ would not fight the forthcoming provincial election on the basis of sovereignty-association. A quarter of his Cabinet resigned in protest and he was fatally weakened by the fall-out. How much greater would have been the risk to Lévesque in November 1981 of a long-term settlement binding Quebec to a future within the federation? In any event, it is far from clear how that deal might have been constructed: the PQ would have baulked at a federal charter which had any purchase in Quebec and they were not willing even to accept the modest language provisions which survived in the final text. Had these two provisions been further eroded Trudeau would have been unable to argue with any conviction that the deal was consistent with his nation-building project.

In all likelihood Ottawa faced a choice between, on the one hand, a partial deal delivering a charter and minority language education rights and, on the other, no deal at all. Trudeau may have been furious at the Supreme Court's patriation ruling but it was Lévesque who was undone by it. Stripped of the protection of unanimous provincial consent, Quebec's alliance with English Canada came under a strain it could not bear. Quebec had been able to construct a defensive alliance but it was unable to do more. Indeed, it misunderstood and misconstrued the intentions of the other provinces, asserting that they shared Ottawa's conception of Canada's future.[164] It was little wonder that the April Accord collapsed. The wonder is that it lasted for all of seven months.

XI. Aftermath

The Westminster Parliament duly removed itself from any further involvement in the Canadian constitution, passing the Canada Act in March 1982. Lévesque had made a final appeal for a delay, this time to the British Prime Minister. She was no more tractable than her Canadian counterpart. A last gasp challenge had sought to interest the British courts in the UK's continuing responsibilities to the Indigenous Peoples. But the invitation had been declined. The legislation moved

[163] Jean Chrétien, interview with the author, 24 May 2006. Roy Romanow, interview with the author, 25 May 2006. Barry Strayer, interview with the author, 30 May 2006 and correspondence with the author, 5 January 2009.

[164] See, eg, Claude Morin, 'Le 'rapatriement' de 1982: une mise en perspective', *Le Soleil*, 18 February 2002.

speedily through Commons and Lords, leaving the way open for the Queen to sign the proclamation in Ottawa in April.

Some four decades after the pageantry on Parliament Hill, the merits and consequences of the patriation package remain fiercely contested. Participants and observers adopt different conceptual and temporal vantage points to argue their case. Two examples illustrate the point. Richard Gwyn, one of the keepers of Trudeau's flame, points us to the national unity record as it stood in 1984: the Quebec referendum had been won; the PQ was heading for defeat in the next provincial elections; federalists were about to resume control in Quebec City; and Reform, a right-wing protest movement focussed on the promotion of Western interests, had yet to be founded.[165] Claude Morin winds the clock further forward to take in Brian Mulroney's efforts at a new constitutional settlement. For Morin, the engagement of English Canada in this process is evidence enough that the other provinces had a bad conscience about the events of 1982.[166] They had betrayed Quebec and now they sought to make amends.

Just as it is questionable when one should start an account of the patriation, it is open to argument when a discussion of it should conclude. On the one hand April 1982 is clearly premature, but on the other it might be argued that even 2020 is too early to assess such a profound change to a country's constitution, its politics and its culture. Before considering some of the consequences of patriation, we will simply attempt a brief survey of what has happened to the Canadian constitution since April 1982.

The Charter of Rights, now celebrated by liberal constitutionalists the world over, got off to a stumbling start. It was not until autumn 1981 that the Department of Justice fully absorbed the implications of the Government's unilateralist tactics; the Department had no more than six months to prepare to implement a fundamental change to Canada's legal system.[167] As that moment drew closer, the tension between the Department's charter advocates and charter sceptics became more pronounced.[168] The latter echoed the complaints of the police and criminal justice system that criminals would go free because of the charter. The Department responded by giving messages of reassurance, emphasising that the world would continue to turn and that criminals would continue to be convicted. This process went so far that Eddie Goldenberg felt moved to remind officials that his understanding was that the charter was supposed to change things, not to leave them

[165] Richard Gwyn, 'Trudeau: The Idea of Canadianism' in Andrew Cohen and JL Granatstein, *Trudeau's Shadow. The Life and Legacy of Pierre Elliott Trudeau* (Toronto, Random House Canada, 1998) 28.

[166] Claude Morin to author, August 2006.

[167] See Justice, file 249318, vols two and three, *passim*. Volume two includes an initial work plan dated 18 August 1981 but the Ministry seems only to have focused hard on implementation after the breakthrough came in November.

[168] See, eg, Justice, file 249318, vol four, Fred Jordan to EG Ewaschuk, 29 March 1982. For Ewaschuk's doubts about the merits of an entrenched charter, see Justice, file 249318, vol one, EG Ewaschuk to Roger Tassé, 13 August 1980.

undisturbed.[169] And so the pendulum swung back. Within government, the Department found that it had to balance its role as charter-architect with a realisation that a generous interpretation of the charter would leave ministries exposed to defeat in charter court cases.[170]

All the while the Department had to respond to the emerging charter jurisprudence. The charter had been purposely framed by its drafters to encourage a cautious judiciary to make use of the fundamental principles enshrined in the text.[171] Judges and officials were trained in what the charter meant. And, crucially, the Government made available funds to litigants wishing to take charter points in their cases.[172] Decisions on abortion and on the extension of charter rights to refugees were soon prompting concerns about 'activist judges' reaching excessively liberal conclusions. Nobody familiar with the charter's text could reasonably express surprise that the text was being re-interpreted over time in the context of changing social and political circumstances: it had been drafted to have just this effect.[173] The Supreme Court became more accustomed, however reluctantly, to a central position in Canadian public life. Its more controversial judgments on criminal cases have earned it public opprobrium. But the Court itself, and the judiciary in general, continue to be held in high esteem by the public.

Trudeau's judgement on the notwithstanding clause has been vindicated.[174] It has not yet been used by the federal Parliament and provincial legislatures have only resorted to it on rare occasions. The charter is now all but inviolable. As a token of this, Paul Martin, the Liberal Party leader, proposed in the 2006 federal election that the notwithstanding clause be revoked. Martin made the move as a despairing gesture late in a campaign he was losing. It made no difference to his fortunes but it is significant that he thought the charter might save him – and that he could do so without igniting renewed agonising over parliamentary sovereignty.

In the immediate aftermath of the November 1981 conference, Québécois were slow to rally to the charge that their province had been betrayed. Polls showed that 49 per cent of Québécois disagreed with the stance taken by Lévesque; just 34 per cent agreed with him.[175] But over time, voters were to hear *péquistes* and

[169] Justice, file 249318, vol three, Eddie Goldenberg to Fred Jordan, 5 January 1981.

[170] Frank Iacobucci, interview with the author, 19 May 2006.

[171] For Justice's doubts about the activism of the judiciary, see PCO, ATI - AA - 2003 - 0017, Memorandum for Cabinet from Jean Chrétien, 25 November 1980 (656-80 MC).

[172] See Charles Epp, *The Rights Revolution: Lawyers, Activists and Supreme Courts in Comparative Perspective* (Chicago, University of Chicago Press, 1997) 156–96.

[173] One of the critical choices made in the preparation of the text – and a point of contention between the federal government and the provinces – was the rejection of an exhaustive list of equality rights. Instead, some rights were stated but the courts were given the flexibility to interpret the equality provisions more broadly in the light of changing circumstances.

[174] Although there has been an increase in use – or threatened use – of the clause in the last couple of years.

[175] Canadian Institute of Public Opinion, *The Gallup Report*, 10 December 1981. Support for the stance was stronger among Francophones: see Kenneth McRoberts, *Misconceiving Canada. The Struggle for National Unity* (Toronto, Oxford University Press, 1997) 182.

Quebec Liberals consistently working and reworking the theme that the province's traditional rights had been ignored. Brian Mulroney, who led the Progressive Conservative Government elected in 1984, was to confirm that message, launching a new constitutional process aimed at reconciliation with Quebec. The Meech Lake Accord, the product of a renewed round of executive federalism, acknowledged Quebec as a 'distinct society'. Trudeau emerged from retirement to savage the deal as a betrayal of the charter. If it were to be interpreted in accordance with the 'distinct society' provision, the result would be a checkerboard Canada, a subordination of individual rights to collective interests and a subversion of the single, unified Canadian citizenship. No less potent out of office, his intervention helped to sink the accord and to prompt renewed charges in Quebec that it had been betrayed by English Canada.

Trudeau was no more enthusiastic about the Charlottetown Accord. Mulroney's second attempt at constitutional reconciliation was quite different from his first. Guided by Joe Clark, now the Minister of Constitutional Affairs, Charlottetown was a much more inclusive and ambitious process. Indeed, one of the principal criticisms of the 1992 agreement was that the interests of the nation as a whole had been lost in a series of concessions to Quebec, to the Indigenous Peoples and to the provinces. It was rejected in referendums in October 1992, one in Quebec, the other in the rest of Canada.

It is little wonder that Jean Chrétien, who returned to government as Prime Minister in 1993, vowed that he would set the constitution to one side to concentrate on other issues. For the most part he succeeded, but in 1995 he was faced with a constitutional challenge he could not avoid: a second Quebec referendum. The PQ Government of Jacques Parizeau took quite a different approach to the 1980 referendum. Elected the previous year, it moved swiftly to put sovereignty to the vote, eschewing the long, deliberate build-up of 1976–1980. And the proposition before the voters was somewhat clearer than the one they had considered 15 years earlier. This time they were asked if they agreed that Quebec should become sovereign after it had first made an offer to the rest of Canada of a new political and economic partnership. The result was remarkable. On a turnout of 93.5 per cent, the Yes cause secured 49.4 per cent of the votes cast and No won 50.6 per cent. The proposition had been defeated by just 54,288 votes. In the immediate aftermath of the 1995 referendum it seemed inconceivable that Quebec would be reconciled to the new constitution. A third constitution seemed inevitable. Quebec politics remain volatile but viewed from 2020, another sovereignty referendum now seems a distant possibility.

XII. Consequences

Ottawa did not stint in its promotion of the patriation deal in general and the charter in particular. A booklet describing the new constitution was sent to

8m households, its every word scrutinised by Michael Kirby.[176] But the charter had already captured the public imagination and over the years its popularity has increased, even if there continues to be a deal of confusion about exactly what it means. In Quebec, as in other provinces, the public has responded positively to the charter. It is secure in the popular consciousness as an expression of the values the country holds in common.[177]

This achievement alone is hailed by Trudeau's partisans as a vindication of his constitutional labours. He risked his government and his reputation in pursuit of a constitutional settlement which would, he determined, deliver a renewed citizenship, endowing all Canadians with the same benefits and requiring them to take on the same burdens. That much he achieved. And he brought to a decisive conclusion Canada's ninth foray into constitutional renewal since 1927, delivering a solution – something which had escaped all of his predecessors. Canada had acquired full sovereignty: it was no longer beholden to anyone in determining its constitutional future.

All of this is true, and all of it fair. But even if we restrict ourselves to the consequences of patriation and of the charter, it will immediately be clear that Trudeau's essay in nation-building has a larger, and more complex, balance sheet. Canada's ninth exercise in constitutional reform – a tortuous, exhausting 15-year journey – did deliver patriation with an entrenched charter. But it also spawned the tenth exercise at Meech Lake, the eleventh at Charlottetown and, possibly, a twelfth once a future federal government again has the appetite and incentive to return to the question. It was to Trudeau's manifest fury that the Progressive Conservative Governments of Brian Mulroney reopened business that he regarded as having been closed once and for all on Parliament Hill in April 1982. But Mulroney was not alone in arguing there was a job still to be done. And even though his own reforms foundered, the very fact that he tried (twice) reinforced the notion that the task is incomplete.

Trudeau's successors face a hurdle even more daunting than the one he cleared in 1982. They must play by the rules instituted in 1982: they are dealing with an entrenched constitution whose amendment is governed by complex formulae which probably put some reforms out of reach for ever and a day. But just as important as the rule changes is the shift in public attitudes towards the constitution and its reform. The 1982 settlement has shone a light on the constitution, investing it with a symbolic importance which arises from, but is not restricted to, the charter. Reformers after Trudeau are attempting to rework a public document,

[176] See, eg, Justice, file 260349, pouch of annexures, Hershell E Ezrin to Michael Kirby, 12 February 1982 and Kirby's textual comments of 25 February 1982.

[177] See, eg, Centre for Research and Information on Canada, *The CRIC Papers 5. The Charter: Dividing or Uniting Canadians?* (Montreal, CRIC, 2002). The poll found the highest rate of approval for the Charter was in Quebec (91%). For reaction in Quebec in the 1980s, see Kenneth McRoberts, *Misconceiving Canada. The Struggle for National Unity* (Toronto, Oxford University Press, 1997) 184.

not simply renewing a private conversation amongst elites. And the perspective of future reformers has ineluctably been shaped by the experience of 1982. Most significant has been the cost not just to constitutional reform but to Canadian unity of a settlement to which Quebec was not a party. After all, this was an agreement rejected not just by the PQ administration, but also by a 70–38 vote in the Quebec National Assembly. Quebec sentiment on the nature of the deal was to harden quickly: in 1984 the federal Liberals were decisively rejected in the province. Voters opted instead for Mulroney's offer to find a way in which Quebec could accede to the constitution 'with honour and enthusiasm'. The sense of failure and recrimination in the province was further sharpened by the demise of Meech Lake, an event which caused a spike in support for sovereignty. McRoberts has gone further, arguing that Trudeau's failure to win support in Quebec has been mirrored by the relative success of his broader national unity strategy in English Canada. With old notions of allegiance to Britain in decline, Trudeau's vision of a pan-Canadian nationalism won adherents outside Quebec, widening the gulf with the province.[178] Indeed, once McRoberts introduces the wider strategy into the balance sheet, his verdict is damning. Official bilingualism in Ottawa was welcomed in Quebec, but its application in other provinces was at best a second order question for Francophones in Quebec. Their primary concerns over language were about the status of their mother tongue within their own province and there they came to understand that the PQ's language laws were in tension with the charter. Multiculturalism, which was understood in English Canada to be a generous policy was viewed with suspicion by many in Quebec: it was a rejection not only of the recommendations of the Biculturalism and Bilingualism Commission but of the dualist conception of Canada.[179] McRoberts' underlying critique is that Trudeau was playing the wrong game: Quebec's problems with the federation were not primarily about rights. They were about the recognition sought by a province with a cultural and linguistic identity which marked it as distinct from the rest of Canada. The 'one Canada' mindset encouraged by Trudeau was inflexible and prevented the federation from adopting a sufficiently generous approach to Quebec. Jeremy Webber takes up the charge: the conceptual framework imposed by Trudeau failed to accommodate the complex realities of Canada, a country whose peoples experience competing allegiances and where national and cultural communities overlap one another.[180] The final word on the charge sheet comes from Burelle: Trudeau's model has condemned Quebec and the rest of Canada to an ideological prison.[181] In short, he made matters worse.

[178] Kenneth McRoberts, *Misconceiving Canada. The Struggle for National Unity* (Toronto, Oxford University Press, 1997) 184–6.

[179] ibid, 125–9, 135, 164.

[180] Jeremy Webber, *Reimagining Canada. Language, Culture, Community, and the Canadian Constitution* (Kingston & Montreal, McGill-Queen's University Press, 1994) 119–20, 224.

[181] André Burelle, *Pierre Elliott Trudeau. L'intellectuel et le politique* (Montreal, Éditions Fides, 2005) 469.

It is worth pausing in our own consideration of the 1982 balance sheet to note that many previous attempts to conduct an audit of 1982 might, more accurately be described as attempts to attribute blame. Trudeau was a divisive figure before, during and after his long spell in office; and he remains so to this day. But the determination with which even the most thoughtful and incisive commentators have sought to pin blame on him has obscured analysis of the 1982 settlement. He was the pre-eminent politician of his generation and he was able to exert remarkable influence on events. But he was one player amongst many and he, like his contemporaries, was operating within a political, economic and social context which generated changes he could not control. Other actors have to answer for their own contributions. Hence it is for the PCs and the NDP – not Trudeau – to answer for their abandonment of the *deux nations* doctrine in the late 1960s; it is for the provincial governments – not Trudeau – to answer for their failure to embrace official bilingualism; and is for those who came after him to answer for their attempts to reopen the settlement and to encourage a sense of grievance in Quebec. Above all, we must be clear on the respective roles played by the PQ and by Ottawa in shaping the 1982 settlement. Blame – and mythology – have obscured our understanding of the events of 1980–82 and so it is important to state this conclusion precisely. The approach selected by the federal government made it probable that one or more provinces would not be signed up to the patriation package. And Quebec was always the most likely to remain outside a deal. Ottawa did not 'exclude' Quebec from the deal; but it did not maximise the chances of drawing it in. Any such effort would probably have been fruitless and so Ottawa's actions were perfectly rational. Once the Supreme Court indicated the hurdle over which Ottawa had to jump, it played by the rules. It did not agonise about the consequences of leaving Quebec in the cold; indeed, by November 1981 it had become accustomed to the idea that Quebec was unpersuadable. And in all of this Lévesque's administration must be held responsible for its own actions. It chose to take the separatist course; it chose to misconstrue the objectives of the other provinces; it bungled the November 1981 conference; and it did all it could to turn public opinion in Quebec against the settlement, helping to ensure that the province would still be outside the deal four decades later.

It was unquestionably Trudeau who ultimately dictated the manner and speed of the final route to a settlement in 1980–82. The process as a whole, from 1967 to 1982 cannot satisfactorily be characterised as executive federalism because there was a measure of popular engagement in the wake of the PQ's victory in 1976 and the Joint Committee mobilised interest group activity of an intensity Canada had not previously witnessed. But success was only achieved in 1980–82 after a bravura display of executive authority. Leaving aside the terms of the settlement, the price paid for the speed of this approach – by Canada, not just the Government – was significant. The country did not have a mature, considered debate about the merits of moving from parliamentary supremacy to constitutional supremacy. The issues were articulated by a prescient few, but their voices were lost in the hubbub. Canada's adoption of an entrenched bill of rights was, for good or ill, a leap of faith.

Some of its most ardent advocates have been forced to acknowledge that they are bemused at the policy consequences of the original text. Even Senator Serge Joyal, one of the most outspoken advocates of the charter, has expressed his surprise that the judiciary have discerned an inherent right to Indigenous self-government in the text.[182]

Trudeau's critics have suggested that it would have been possible to have secured a constitutional settlement through other means, arriving at a more inclusive agreement. The process, for example, might have been more reflective and more open, allowing for wider participation by citizens. These ideas were mooted at the time. The Pepin-Robarts Taskforce had discussed the merits of a constitutional commission or, more radically, of a constituent assembly. And the Joint Committee received submissions from the Citizens for More Time Committee and from the Committee to Democratize the Constitutional Debate.[183] But these were voices at the margins, their views given little time by any of the governments. Given the history of repeated failures and delays since 1967, let alone since 1927, it is easy to understand why there would have been scepticism about the merits of an approach which might have seemed to offer more delay and greater complexity.

As for a settlement on different terms, McRoberts has argued cogently that an agreement which embraced the dualist conception of Canada would have ultimately been more likely to have delivered the national unity sought by Trudeau.[184] As he recognises, this begs a number of counterfactual questions, not least whether English Canada would have been open to such a deal and, more crudely, whether the separatists would have regarded such an outcome as anything other than a staging post to their ultimate destination. But more importantly, one is left to ask whether Trudeau and the federal government would ever have accepted any such deal. The flirtations with dualism or with collective rights were no more than temporary, tactical deviations from the course Trudeau pursued throughout his time in office. It is inconceivable that he would have been a party to a dualist settlement. Concede this and McRoberts' counterfactual proposition becomes even more speculative: a deal might have been done on other terms if Trudeau was not Prime Minister. This is to heap speculation upon speculation and, indeed, it distracts from McRoberts' central proposition that Trudeau's whole strategy was ill-conceived and damaging for the country.

The history of constitutional reform since 1967 and the known preferences of the provincial governments should make us deeply sceptical as to whether there was an alternative at hand. The tactics chosen by Ottawa were costly. Trudeau had once railed at the premiers who were willing to trade 'fish for rights' in an

[182] Serge Joyal, interview with the author, May 2006.

[183] Justice, file 251600-16, vol 4, pouch C, nr 1, Submission by the Citizens for More Time Committee to the Special Joint Committee, 16 Dec. 1980. Justice, file 251600-16, vol 4, pouch C, nr 2, Submission by the Committee to Democratize the Constitutional Debate to the Special Joint Committee, nd [1980].

[184] Kenneth McRoberts, *Misconceiving Canada. The Struggle for National Unity* (Toronto, Oxford University Press, 1997) 249–50.

undignified scramble to enhance their powers. Ottawa showed itself to be equally instrumental in the way it played its hand. When the President of the Native Council of Canada wrote to Trudeau in June 1981 rejecting the terms on offer to the Indigenous Peoples, Kirby's advice to the Prime Minister was revealing. The draft reply brushed aside the complaints. Kirby explained this by noting that the constitutional reforms were now before the Supreme Court and so 'the political support of the Indigenous Peoples for patriation is but of academic interest'.[185] Whatever one makes of this high-handed cynicism, it is hard to avoid the conclusion that if a deal was to be made within the foreseeable future, the approach adopted in Trudeau's final term maximised the chances of success. Only fierce determination on the part of Ottawa was going to clear the path to a settlement. Only by confronting the premiers with the threat of unilateralism would they be brought to compromise. Only by risking a constitutional crisis and exhausting the patience of most citizens, was it possible to bring the players – or most of them – to an agreement. Trudeau's tactical judgement was vindicated by the ceremony on Parliament Hill.

Leaving aside the brilliance and the instrumentality of the tactics, the bigger question is what one makes of the balance sheet itself. What are we to make of Trudeau's essay in nation-building? Canadians were to raise their sights from petty nationalistic or provincial concerns, recognising that their prospects for self-fulfillment would be immeasurably greater if they participated wholeheartedly in a community which nurtured diversity.

The charter soon won favour with citizens across the country, including Quebec; and it has retained its popularity through the vicissitudes of the province's politics. There has been a profound change in the political and judicial culture of the country: entrenched rights are valued and the Supreme Court, as their ultimate guardian, has won public respect, even if some of its judgments have caused controversy. But Quebec is no more securely bound to the country than it was when the deal was struck. Asked to choose between a French Canadian, Québécois and Canadian identity, Francophones in Quebec have moved decisively towards a provincial allegiance: 31 per cent chose Québécois in 1977, rising to 59 per cent in 1990. Over the same period those identifying themselves as Canadian halved – from 18 per cent to 9 per cent. All the while, their sense of association to the Francophone communities elsewhere in Canada has atrophied: their affiliation is with a linguistic and cultural community in one part of the country. It is precisely the intersection of language and territory that Trudeau most wanted to resist. Support for separatism among Québécois has fluctuated over the four decades but in its fourth decade the Charter seems to have secured a place in the hearts of Canadians and the unity of the country is no longer under immediate threat. A 2016 poll found that 65 per cent of Canadians said they 'had a deep emotional

[185] LAC Trud. MG26 0 10, vol 832, docs 1153 182; 1159, 113 and 1159, 115, Michael Kirby to Prime Minister, 12 June 1981.

attachment to the country. [They loved] the country and what it [stood] for]'. The Quebec response stood at 37 per cent; and 69 per cent of Quebec residents thought that Quebec should stay in Canada.[186]

Those who came after Trudeau – separatists and federalists – must accept their share of responsibility for the instability inherent in the Canadian federation. But the central thrust of McRoberts' critique is hard to rebut. Trudeau's achievement was to bring about constitutional change where all others before him had failed. The constitution signed on 12 April 1982 was a powerful expression of contemporary Canadian values: respect for individual rights, mutual support, multiculturalism, a commitment to nurture the languages of the 'founding peoples' and a recognition of Canada's obligations to its Indigenous citizens. The constitution not only reflected Canadian aspirations, but it changed the nation's sense of itself and of its responsibilities towards its citizens. Outside Quebec, the charter and, by extension, the constitution itself, have become a focus for Canadians' allegiance: English Canada has embraced Trudeau's vision of a single, unifying pan-Canadian citizenship.[187] But the 1982 settlement failed to resolve the tension at the heart of the federation.

In addressing the Pepin-Robarts Task Force, one Canadian citizen argued that, 'It takes a dream to fight a dream.'[188] Trudeau ultimately offered the nation a dream of civic nationalism, a dream which he hoped would be more alluring than the prospectus of the *péquistes*. His offer was to reshape citizens' understanding of what it is to be Canadian. But those who believe in the federation are still seeking a solution which guarantees its future. Any solution must surmount four decades of grievance and recrimination. And, in the words of Joe Clark, 'if Canada wants to hold Quebec, wants to hold the West, wants "new" Canadians to prize the country they are joining, the sense of Canada must be as positive and compelling to Canadians as the sense of Quebec is today to Quebecers'.[189]

XIII. The Sesquicentenary of Confederation

The 150th anniversary of confederation in 2017 provided Canada with the opportunity to take stock of the state of the country and, in particular, of the impact of the fervid nation-building of the late twentieth century. If the ceremony on Parliament Hill in April 1982 was characteristically Canadian, so was the memorialising in 2017.

[186] Angus Reid Institute/CBC poll, *What makes us Canadian? A study of values, beliefs, priorities and identity* (3 November 2016). See also Kenneth McRoberts, *Misconceiving Canada. The Struggle for National Unity* (Toronto, Oxford University Press, 1997) 36, 180, 183.

[187] Jeremy Webber, *Reimagining Canada. Language, Culture, Community, and the Canadian Constitution* (Kingston & Montreal, McGill-Queen's University Press, 1994) 116–7.

[188] Task Force, *A Future Together* 37.

[189] Joe Clark, *A Nation Too Good to Lose: Renewing the Purpose of Canada* (Toronto, Key Porter Books, 1994) 114.

Opinion polls on Canadian identity were commissioned; national introspection was sanctioned; and there was even a Trudeau to preside over it all.

The proceedings served to validate Robertson Davies' line that Canada was a country to worry about. The Indigenous People complained that the whole jamboree overlooked 14,000 years of their history; Canadians told pollsters that they wanted immigrants to do more to 'fit in'; there were rumblings from the alt-Right; sub-national identities were beginning to eclipse Canadian identity for some; Quebec remained unhappy with its lot. And Canadian historians were at war, as they had been for much of the previous 20 years. The battle lines were predictable: younger scholars argued for a more diverse choice of topic whereas their opponents maintained that Canada's military history and its gallery of heroic men were being neglected. The opening of the Canadian War Museum in 2005 had provided a focus for this clash, in which Stephen Harper, formerly Canadian Prime Minister had chosen to participate personally.[190] Critics argued that it tried to create a sense of the Canadian self 'inseparable from the nation's military history'.[191]

But it is hard to think of another nation on earth which would have interpreted the evidence in this way. Trudeau's political and constitutional legacy was secure, not least because his son was now Prime Minister. Ottawa defended multiculturalism, inclusion and diversity. Canadian unity was not under threat. And a poll in 2016 showed that 64 per cent of Canadians were satisfied with 'how things are going [in your country] today'. This was the highest score of any of the eight countries in which opinion was tested. The British lagged some 24 points behind.[192]

[190] See, eg, Mark Sholdice, 'The History Wars in Canada' (*The Toronto Review of Books*, 2013) 5.

[191] See the discussion in Ian McKay and Jamie Swift, *The Vimy Trap* (Toronto, Between the Lines, 2017) 235–46 and especially note 82. See also Ian McKay and Jamie Swift, *Warrior Nation* (Toronto, Between the Lines, 2012).

[192] Canadian data from 2016 poll by Angus Reid Institute; data from other countries from 2014 poll by Pew Research Center.

4

'A Small But Significant Step': Australia and the Republic

The Republican proposition in Australia was a simple one. The Queen should be replaced as Head of State by a President chosen by Parliament. The changes to the constitution would be kept to the minimum needed to realise this objective; executive authority would remain with the Prime Minister and the Cabinet. But the country would, for the first time, have one of its own as its constitutional figurehead. Malcolm Turnbull, head of the Australian Republican Movement (ARM) captured the idea succinctly in a speech in October 1999:

> We should have a resident for President. Someone who lives among us, breathes the air we breathe, hurts when we hurt, cheers when we win, encourages us when we lose and always barracks for Australia. Someone who can represent our nation both to its own people and to the world. Only an Australian can do that.[1]

What could be simpler? How could Australians, a self-confident people who had long had sovereign authority over their own affairs, tolerate any other arrangement?

But by the time that Turnbull made that speech the proposition was already slipping inexorably to defeat in the referendum of November 1999. Its demise was noisy and bad-tempered; the air was thick with charges of betrayal, of deceit and of villainy in high places. But in truth the Republic was not overcome by sudden or dramatic setbacks. Rather, it slipped slowly below the waves, its stately decline the result of its internal contradictions, of political mismanagement and of the sheer difficulty of securing any form of constitutional change in Australia.

This is not simply the tale of a flawed political proposition. It is also a story about Australian national identity, about an attempt to re-fashion it through constitutional change – and about the perils of doing so peremptorily.

I. The Combatants

It all started so promisingly. At a lunch in Sydney in December 1990 a group of friends and acquaintances – from politics, business, the arts and the media –

[1] Speech, 13 October 1999 cited in Malcolm Turnbull, *Fighting for the Republic. The Ultimate Insider's Account* (South Yarra, Hardie Grant Books, 1999) 195.

mulled over the prospects for a Republican decade. They explored the prospects for a political crusade culminating in the appointment of an Australian Head of State at the dawn of the new millennium. This, surely, was an idea whose time had come. Support for the monarchy was in secular decline. From its highpoint in 1954, when Australia swooned at the visit of its young Queen, popular regard for the monarchy (but not for the Queen) had ebbed away. And by 1992 Australians would tell pollsters that for the first time fewer than half of them supported the monarchy.[2] Australia had severed all of its other constitutional links to Britain in 1986; it had cast off its White Australia policy in 1966 and it took an increasing proportion of its immigrants from Asia. Media coverage of marital break-ups had tarnished the Royal Family's image. And Britain's entry into the European Community had given a clear signal to Australia that the former bonds between the two nations were loosening.

And so the moment seemed propitious. The friends gathered around the lunch table had good reason to think that they could make a success of this enterprise. They had brains, they had money and they had connections.

Seven months later the Australian Republican Movement (ARM) was launched. It was an elite organisation with an elite mission: 'to influence the influencers'. It was constituted as a corporation and had no ambition to become a mass movement. On the contrary, it wanted to remain exclusive to eliminate the risk that it would be hijacked for other purposes.[3] When Turnbull became chair in 1994 he signalled a desire to broaden the movement's membership, reaching out to women and to Indigenous Peoples.[4] But progress was modest and the ARM remained vulnerable to the charge that it was an unrepresentative clique; it was dominated by Sydney, by new money and by 'the top end of town'.[5]

Whatever miscalculations may be laid at their door, the ARM's founders cannot fairly be charged with complacency. They knew from the outset that they would only secure their prize if they learned the lessons of previous attempts to reform the constitution. The hurdle they faced was formidable; amendments had to be approved first by the Commonwealth Parliament and then by a popular majority in a national referendum *and* by a majority of the electors in a majority of the states. Just eight of the 42 proposals put to a vote since federation in 1901 had succeeded. Most recently, the Hawke Government had put forward four proposals in the wake of the Constitutional Commission it had established. All four were defeated in a 1988 referendum.

[2] Morgan Gallup poll for *Time*, (6 April 1992). Support for the monarchy had slipped 7% since July 1991 to 49%. There had been little change in the years 1975–88 but there had been a steady erosion in support in the years following the bicentenary.

[3] See, eg, the anxieties of Franca Arena that the movement might be hijacked, Thomas Keneally, *Our Republic* (Port Melbourne, William Heinemann Australia, 1993) 94.

[4] 'Message from new Chairman', *Newsletter* (Sydney, Australian Republican Movement, 25 March 1994) 1–2.

[5] The characterisation is by John Hirst, who led the Victorian branch of the ARM.

The ARM's leadership drew three lessons from this history. First, they had to be disciplined in their objective. This must not mutate into a broader campaign for constitutional renewal. They wanted simply to replace a monarch with a president. Other distractions, however alluring, were to be ignored.[6] Second, they had to be disciplined in their tactics. They were not to criticise the Queen, not so much out of respect for her, but because the opinion polls showed that her personal popularity remained above that of the monarchy.[7] And third, they had to build a cross-party coalition in support of change. The record showed that if a proposal was put to a vote without the support of both major parties, it would be defeated. This, as we will see, proved to be a particular challenge for the ARM, not least because the Australian Labor Party (ALP) had long been identified with republicanism and their opponents – the Liberal and National Parties – were supporters of the status quo. Hence Thomas Keneally, the first chair of the ARM, was at pains to distance the new movement from the ALP, chiding it for its partisan approach to the republican question.

The ARM did not always abide by its own strictures on questions of tactics. Thomas Keneally's colourful turn of phrase may have delighted his literary admirers but it was a political liability. In the warm embrace of a St Patrick's Day celebration he chose to compare the Queen to a colostomy bag on the body politic. We can only guess at his colleagues' reaction to the media coverage sparked by the remark. But leaving aside these tactical diversions, the ARM did maintain its focus on its objective through thick and thin. Indeed it had alighted upon its preferred model for a republican presidency within 12 months of its launch. As early as February 1992, Malcolm Turnbull was advocating to his colleagues the election of the president by Parliament, rather than by the public. By 1993 the ARM's preferred model followed the same pattern, albeit with the additional proviso that the appointment, or dismissal, of the president would require support from two-thirds of a joint sitting of Parliament.[8] It was this model, give or take some refinements, which survived to be put to the vote in November 1999.

Keneally, buoyed by the media's welcome of this new venture, spoke of the republican promise with millennial extravagance. He brushed aside the thought that there might be an alternative route to victory. And for a while, his optimism seemed to be justified: polls in 1992 and early 1993 encouraged the view that the republican proposition had momentum.[9] But even before that progress slackened

[6] See, eg, Donald Horne's emphasis on crafting a proposition which would succeed: RAC, submissions folder 2, S0110, Donald Horne, 'A Comparative Evaluation of Scare Factors. Submission to the Republic Advisory Committee'.

[7] State Lib. NSW, Collins, MLMSS 7442/71-6, box 74, ARM Candidates and Campaign Manual, [1998].

[8] State Lib. NSW, ARM, box 1, folder 1(7), Turnbull to ARM Committee members, 27 February 1992 and Turnbull, 'Why we need a Republic', speech to the National Press Club, 18 March 1992; box 1, folder 1(20), ARM submission to the RAC [1993].

[9] Since 1953, the Morgan Poll had asked Australians if their country should remain a monarchy – or become a republic with an elected presidency. Support for the second option moved from 36% in July 1991 to 52% in April 1993. Over the same period support for the monarchy declined from 56% to 38%.

there were warning signs for those who cared to look. Two messages were clear: women were not attracted to the republican cause as much as men; and when offered the choice Australians expressed a clear preference for direct election over indirect election through Parliament. Poll after poll told the same story through the rest of the decade, but neither problem had been overcome by November 1999.

The choice between direct and indirect election was not a matter of constitutional nicety. Real republicans, as they were to term themselves, argued that only popular election would be an authentic expression of republicanism: sovereignty rests with the people and so they should choose their head of state. Indirect election would offer the solution most likely to preserve the Westminster system, whereby the executive is led by a Prime Minister, who is in turn accountable to the legislature. Some of the advocates of direct election expressly wanted to challenge the Westminster system, creating a popular mandate for a president who would be directly accountable to the people and who would have the authority (implicit or explicit) to check the excesses of Prime Ministerial government.

This cleavage in republican thought served as a reminder that Australian republicanism was not summoned into being over a good lunch in December 1990. It was older than the federation and it had taken many forms over the years. Keneally wrote about the tradition of Irish and, especially, Irish Catholic republicanism as though it were an historical episode which had passed into memory. But the Irish resentment of the British – which had long been expressed through the ALP – provided fertile ground for the ARM in the 1990s. A visceral dislike of the British, of their snobbery and pomposity, was cheerfully expressed by Keneally himself who was ready to point up any slight by perfidious Albion, whether real or imagined.[10]

If republicanism's deepest roots were ethnic, its revival in the second half of the century owes much to a search for civic renewal. This strain of republicanism was nurtured by Donald Horne, the journalist and public intellectual, who raised the standard for modern republicanism in the 1960s. After Gough Whitlam's Labor Government had been controversially dismissed by the Governor-General in 1975 Horne founded Citizens for Democracy to campaign for democratic reforms to the constitution. It did not begin life as a republican organisation, but by 1977 it was sailing under republican colours.

Horne was one of the authors of the ARM's approach: he fully accepted the need to focus on that which was attainable rather than on that which might be desirable. But other reformers took a more expansive view of the republican cause. Not only did they maintain that they had reason on their side in advocating radical reform – and in particular a directly-elected presidency – but the opinion polls encouraged them in their view that there was advantage in doing so. In choosing to commit itself to indirect election, the ARM was making a hardnosed political

The December 1993 poll (in the wake of the RAC's report) seemed to show the trend arrested: 44% for a Republic and 48% for the monarchy.

[10] See, eg, Thomas Keneally, *Our Republic* (Port Melbourne, William Heinemann Australia, 1993) 192.

calculation that this was the right solution for Australian democracy *and* that it was the approach most likely to win. But in making that choice it was cutting itself off from many who would describe themselves as republicans.

If the ARM was a coalition, the same could be said of its principal opponents, the Australians for a Constitutional Monarchy (ACM). Its supporters were called into the field by the President of the New South Wales Court of Appeal Michael Kirby, who took the view that the ARM should not win the argument by default.[11] Like the ARM, the ACM aspired to be bipartisan but it, too, struggled to achieve this in practice, not least because it was contrary to ALP rules for a party member to campaign against an element of the party's policy platform. The ACM's natural allies were conservatives and during Kerry Jones's time as Director the organisation's sympathy for the Liberal-National coalition was plain to see.[12] Turnbull notes that Tony Abbott's appointment as Executive Director of the ACM had brought a sharpness to relations with the ARM. As events were to prove, these were only the opening shots in the unhappy coincidence of Abbott and Turnbull.[13]

The group initially established by Kirby represented a wide range of conservative constitutional opinion. For some, the cause was straightforward: Australia owed its stability and prosperity to the Crown and, more generally, to Britain. The nation should honour that heritage and, in particular, should respect the Queen who had served Australia so well for so long. Kirby himself would focus less on the officeholder and more on the merits of a constitutional system which was neutral and above politics. In an interview in 2006 he argued that 'By divorcing ultimate, symbolic power from the whims of popular movements and committing it in theory to representing everyone you have a symbolic value that you have to be careful before you toss aside.'[14] Kirby dissented when the organisation proposed that its new slogan be 'Leadership above politics'. He did not see the monarch as an *active* leader and he noted that heredity, because it was illegitimate, was more likely to act as a check on a monarch, encouraging caution and prudence. Others took an orthodox Burkean view: they were not wedded to the status quo, but they had not been persuaded that the alternatives had greater merit and so they would stick with the system they knew.[15]

The differences between these lines of thought were not tested as sternly as those amongst republicans, not least because the ACM's task was simpler. It did not have to mount an argument for change and to defend it against all-comers: it simply had to hold together an alliance of those who thought change was a mistake.

[11] Michael Kirby, 'The Australian Republican Referendum 1999 – Ten Lessons', lecture at the University of Buckingham (3 March 2000) at www.lawfoundation.net.au/resources/kirby/papers/20000303_referendum.html (last accessed 24 May 2005).

[12] See, eg, Kerry Jones' editorial in *Australian Constitutional Monarchy* (December 2004) 2.

[13] Turnbull was ousted by Abbott as Liberal leader in 2009; Turnbull repaid the favour in 2015. Earlier in Abbott's career he was Executive Director of the ACM from 1992–94. He was replaced by Kerry Jones. For the Turnbull-Abbott tension, see Malcolm Turnbull, *A Bigger Picture* (Richmond, Victoria, Hardie Grant Books, 2020).

[14] Michael Kirby, interview with the author, 14 March 2006.

[15] See, eg, JB Paul, 'An Australian Republic? But why?' (1991) 35(9) *Quadrant* 279.

For some its task was tactical and defensive. For others, like Alan Atkinson, it was engaged in nothing less than a fight for the soul of the nation:

> Broadly speaking, the republic aims to draw on the visionary riches of the future, and it sees those riches largely in commercial terms. It aims at the redefinition of Australia as a player in the world at large. The monarchy, properly managed, draws on the inner riches of the past and present – the Australian past and present – and on the principles of shared effort and the common good.[16]

Whether the ACM's supporters necessarily supported this conception of their cause, they were able to unite against a common enemy. And they were helped in doing so by the ARM's profile as a scion of the urban elites. The ACM's own organisational myth was that it was a rank and file movement, the voice of ordinary voters alienated by the rich and the powerful. This might seem a surprising approach for an organisation dedicated to the defence of an hereditary monarchy and it was belied by the ACM's own access to wealth and power. But the myth was supported by the movement's undoubted success in building a national membership, which peaked at more than 30,000 and had active branches across each of the states and territories. And the myth was expressed in the manner (if not the origins) of its director, Kerry Jones. Her awkward, stiff bearing in studios or on public platforms contrasted sharply with the brilliant fluency of Malcolm Turnbull, the overbearing figurehead of the ARM. Turnbull was the quicker, more effective debater but his superiority over Jones did little to endear him to his audience. The ACM, Jones would argue, was the underdog, treated unfairly by the media and by government. But it would not be silenced.[17]

The ACM was never as media-savvy as its opponents, but it showed a sure touch in steering the debate. Long before the referendum campaign had begun, it was clear that the battle would not be won if it came down to a defence of the monarchy. Loyalty to the Crown and, in particular, affection for the Queen were important to the ACM – and especially to its activists – but these sentiments were wasting assets. And so the ACM trained its guns on the republican proposition. It was divisive; it was risky; and it was big. This was not a minimalist change; it threatened to unravel the Australian constitution with consequences that were hard to imagine, let alone predict. The country's entire constitutional edifice might collapse. Australia would have to reapply to join the Commonwealth – and it might be rebuffed. Australian athletes might be denied their habitual triumphs in the Commonwealth Games. And the advent of a republic would encourage the constitutional radicals to tear down the remaining symbols of old, Anglo-Australia. The flag itself was not safe. Australians should not trust the glib reassurances of their politicians: their republican rhetoric masked a power-grab by MPs keen to control the appointment of the new president. If this were not enough, one National Party

[16] Alan Atkinson, *The Muddle-Headed Republic* (Oxford, Oxford University Press, 1993) 126.

[17] See, eg, Kerry Jones, *The People's Protest. Being a True and Accurate Account of the Republic Debate, 1992–1999 and the Republic Referendum* (Sydney, ACM Publishing, 2000) 54.

Senator conjured up the spectre of bloodshed in the streets if Australia succumbed to republicanism.[18]

These fears were effectively voiced by Kerry Jones, but she was able to support her claims with testimony by senior figures who had a plausible claim to expertise. Sir Harry Gibbs, formerly the chief justice of the High Court, warned that a presidential system might open the way to dictatorship.[19] And Sir David Smith, formerly official secretary to the Governor-General who dismissed the Whitlam Government, carved out a second career arguing that the whole republican argument was misdirected. The Queen was not the Australian Head of State: the Governor-General held that office and so the nation already had one of its own in the top job.[20] As if this were not fanciful enough, the ACM went one better, claiming that the Queen herself was not a foreigner. By implication, she was an Australian.[21] Constitutionalists may have frowned at the first claim, and public credulity may have snapped at the second – but both served a useful purpose. Australians were encouraged to believe that the republican cause was more complicated than it first seemed and that perhaps its advocates were not telling them the full truth.

II. Enter Paul Keating

From July 1992 the ACM had a new foe, and it could not have asked for a more promising target. In the previous December Paul Keating had finally replaced Bob Hawke as Prime Minister. The ALP, already in office for eight years, was half-way through a parliamentary term. The polls were bleak and Keating, a tough, reformist finance minister, was seen as a divisive figure. Clever, aggressive and immodest, he delighted his backbenchers by his attacks on the coalition front bench; ALP loyalists cheered as he called the Liberal leader 'a shiver waiting for a spine to run up' but others recoiled at the violence of his language and at his boundless self-confidence.[22] Keating was instinctively, tribally Labor: he was born into party, it was the only life he had known and he had an intuitive understanding of its rank and file members. He may have acquired a taste for sharp suits and fine antiques, he may have pushed through the liberalisation of the Australian economy, provoking 'the recession we needed to have', but his values remained those of an Irish Catholic brought up in the suburbs of Sydney.

[18] The doom-monger was Senator Bill O'Chee. See 'Mixed reaction of anger, praise greets report' *Sydney Morning Herald* (6 October 1993).

[19] 'Ex-Judge Warns of Dictatorship' *The Advertiser* (5 June 1993).

[20] David Smith, *Head of State. The Governor-General, the Monarchy, the Republic and the Dismissal* (Sydney, Macleay Press, 2005) 85–116.

[21] Australians for Constitutional Monarchy, *The Australians for Constitutional Monarchy Handbook. Key Facts and Opinions for the Republic Debate in Australia* (December 1996) 31.

[22] The phrase has been attributed to a number of politicians, including Neil Kinnock, the British Labour Party leader and Winifred Ewing, the Scottish Nationalist.

It was those values that shone through when he rounded on Coalition MPs at Question Time in February 1992. He raged at their toadying, cringing attitude towards Britain. And then he went further, accusing Britain of abandoning Australia to its fate after the fall of Malaya and Singapore in 1942. For the British, a tabloid villain was born, a Pom-hating larrikin with a sharp tongue. For Australian monarchists, a foe from central casting was about to step onto the stage.[23]

There was nothing inevitable about Keating's journey from his Question Time tirade in February to his declaration in July that he wanted Australia to become a republic. He had long been a republican and his party had first adopted a republican policy when Bill Hayden was leader. But Hayden and his successor, Bob Hawke, had both side-stepped the issue; it was, said Hawke, a second-order issue.[24] The same route was open to Keating. The most likely explanation of his outburst in February was that he got carried away: he excelled in bravura displays of aggression at the Dispatch Box and now, for the first time as Prime Minister, he had rallied his backbenchers, who cheered him on to ever more colourful rhetoric. It was not artifice: British condescension irritated Keating almost as much as did the Australians who paid homage to their former colonial master. Keating was an Australian nationalist, but his views about Britain were more nuanced than the tabloids would allow: this was not a man who was driven blindly by national enmities.

His announcement in July was a product of careful calculation. It had some short-term political appeal: it could be used as a wedge issue against the Liberals. The party of Menzies, still wedded to support of the monarchy, would be wrong-footed. They now numbered many republicans within their ranks and it was thought that John Hewson, their leader, privately favoured a republic. A republican campaign would make the Liberals look outdated and disunited, and would shift the focus from the economy, which continued to struggle.

These considerations no doubt weighed with Keating, but they were not decisive. This was a politician who got his energy from big ideas and he had come to the view that for Australia, none was bigger than this. Encouraged and, at times, cajoled by his speechwriter, Don Watson, Keating began to develop his Big Picture. It was of an Australia reborn, economically, psychologically and culturally. A country whose economy was ever more integrated with those of Asia; a regional power; an open democracy, multicultural and ever more ethnically diverse; a country reconciled with its Indigenous Peoples; a creative, culturally vibrant nation. There was much in this vision that was neither new nor novel: under Hawke, Australia had begun to 'enmesh' its economy with those of east Asia; the White Australia policy had been dropped under Harold Holt, a Liberal; and Malcolm Fraser, another

[23] Don Watson, *Recollections of a Bleeding Heart. A Portrait of Paul Keating PM* (Milsons Point, NSW, Vintage, 2003 edn) 121.

[24] Bob Hawke, interview with the author, 14 March 2006.

Liberal, had championed multiculturalism when Prime Minister. The accent on the arts and the emphasis on reconciliation, invited comparisons with Whitlam. But the presentation of the policies as a coherent whole was new – and distinctively Keating's. This was evident to all in his powerful speech on reconciliation at Redfern in December 1992 and in his Government's skilful response to the High Court's ruling in the Mabo native title case.[25]

Two inter-connected arguments ran through Keating's Big Picture. First, Australia had the chance to seize the future, and to create 'the good society', or it could let the opportunity slip through its fingers. As Watson put it:

> He wanted it to be universally understood that the country had to make its own way. On that perception depended the courage to make radically new choices about the future. He thought from this clearing of national decks might come the energy to make the whole Australian experiment exciting again.[26]

Second, and consequently, if Australia was to face its destiny it had to do so on its own, without any backward glances to Europe. A sovereign nation at the other end of the world from Britain could not have a Briton as head of state without confusing itself – and its Asian partners – as to the true nature of its national identity. The Queen may have no substantive power under the Australian constitution but the monarch's presence was a shackle to a past which was no longer relevant.

Keating has since said that it was his declaration in favour of a Republic that transformed it from 'an after dinner mint' talking-point to a serious political proposition. This is fair; but it is not the whole story. When the Prime Minister threw his weight behind the cause, he moved it to centre stage and kept it there, pledging in his federal election address in 1993 that the ALP, if re-elected, would launch an expert inquiry into how best to create a republic. But Keating's intervention undoubtedly gave a boost to the opposing cause, and his advocacy may have put some voters beyond the republicans' reach. This rapidly became *Keating's* Republic. This was a Prime Minister who polled badly amongst women, whose time as Treasurer was bitterly resented by many and who had earned the determined opposition of Liberal and National supporters. And he had offered them a generous target: the argument over the Republic would have yielded sufficient controversy but Keating had woven it into a more elaborate narrative of Australia's future. Brimming with ambition, angular with challenges, there was something in this to offend anybody who wanted to be offended.

[25] The High Court overturned the doctrine of *terra nullius*, whereby native land rights had been denied. The Government passed the Native Title Act 1993 to clarify land rights in the light of the Mabo ruling.

[26] Don Watson, *Recollections of a Bleeding Heart. A Portrait of Paul Keating PM* (Milsons Point, NSW, Vintage, 2003 edn) 123.

Keating's prosecution of the case did nothing to dispel the notion that this was a partisan crusade. Periodically he would recall that success in a referendum depended on cross-party support and he would make overtures to the opposition, hinting at a future constitutional convention or offering them the chance of cooperating in a joint endeavour. But the offers never tempted his opponents, who saw little comfort in his embrace.[27] And before long he would revert to his customary approach, using the Republic – like everything else – to secure competitive advantage over the coalition. He knew that this might imperil the republican project, but his opponents offered him targets that were just too tempting: first John Hewson, a social liberal ill at ease with his party's constitutional conservatism; then Alexander Downer, eviscerated by Keating at the Dispatch Box and seeking refuge from the republic in a suggestion that there should be a people's convention to decide the issue; and finally, John Howard, a committed monarchist whose frontbencher colleagues were beginning to come out as republicans.[28]

Keating's endorsement of republicanism had an additional, equally important consequence. He would occasionally hint that a republic might usher in further reform, but at heart he was a constitutional conservative; he believed in the Westminster system; he wanted to uphold the authority of the Prime Minister; and he did not want to yield any further influence to the upper house, the Senate. The Dismissal of 1975 might have shaken the Australian system to its foundations, but he put the failures down to the behaviour of individuals: he trusted the system.[29] Hence he favoured the surgical removal of the Queen from the constitution, the transfer of the powers of Governor-General to the President and the election of the President by Parliament. The reserve powers – hitherto exercised by the Governor-General but in future to be wielded by the President – should remain uncodified or, at most, should be subject to limited codification. In short, he was a natural ally of the ARM and, crucially, he bolstered their brand of minimalism. By the time of the 1993 election Turnbull and Keating between them had put minimalism in the ascendancy: more radical variants of republicanism might have commanded popular support but they had yet to find a champion.

[27] Keating held out the prospect of a constitutional conference in his letter of April 1993 inviting John Hewson to nominate a representative to the RAC. In a press release on 29 April, he reacted to Hewson's refusal to nominate by declaring that it demonstrated 'a lack of understanding on Dr Hewson's part of the weight of the issue and the approach of the Government'. In May 1993 Keating's offer to adopt a bipartisan approach on the issue only provoked wider divisions in John Hewson's Liberal ranks. See, Michael Millett in *The Sydney Morning Herald* (13 May 1993) and Ross Peake in *Canberra Times* (13 May 1993). By the winter, Keating's offer to Downer, the new leader, was made conditional on his acceptance of the principle of a Republic. See Mark Baker, *The Age* (25 July 1994).

[28] Author's interview with senior ALP politician, 10 March 2006.

[29] He has subsequently suggested that in 1975 the Prime Minister should have arrested the Governor-General.

III. Mapping the Course: The Republic Advisory Committee

Keating won the 1993 election in what he dubbed 'a victory for true believers'. This was a sweet moment; he had come from behind, defied the opinion polls and had won a mandate in his own right, strengthening Labor's hold on the House of Representatives. He had a full term of three years in which to begin to realise his vision for a new Australia.

He moved swiftly to appoint an expert committee on the republican question. His handling of its appointment and management was telling. He considered, but rejected, the idea of an arms-length operation run by an independent foundation. Instead, he opted for a government committee coordinated by civil servants and working to a narrow brief: it was to prepare 'an options paper which describes the minimum constitutional changes necessary to achieve a viable Federal Republic of Australia, maintaining the effect of our current conventions and principles of government'.[30] The committee was to chart the possible courses to a minimalist solution, it was to abjure recommendations and it was not to argue the case for republicanism one way or another.

This might have been a technical exercise mapping out the options, but at the heart of the Republic Advisory Committee (RAC) were true believers – in minimalism. Turnbull took the chair; and he was joined by George Winterton, the intellectual father of minimalism, and John Hirst, a conservative historian who argued the case for 'generous minimalism'. This was a heresy, but a benign one as far as the ARM was concerned. Hirst was a supporter of modest institutional change, but he did want the constitution redrafted in terms relevant and accessible to modern Australians. With a constitution its people could understand, prefaced by an inspiring preamble, the advent of the Republic might be used to revive Australian civic culture.[31]

Turnbull, Winterton and Hirst, in a somewhat uneasy alliance, dominated the proceedings of the Committee; their colleagues either lacked the expertise or the interest to challenge them.[32] Hewson declined to put forward a Liberal nominee for the Committee, but Nick Greiner, the Liberal former premier of New South Wales, was appointed. Geoffrey Blainey, the conservative historian and scourge of the liberal establishment, was proposed by Jeff Kennett (the Liberal premier of Victoria) but his appointment was not supported by the other state premiers.

The deliberations of the RAC are revealing about the challenges facing the republicans. Turnbull, Winterton and Hirst may have occupied a narrow

[30] RAC, *An Australian Republic. The Options – the Report* (Canberra, Australian Government Publishing Service, 1993) iv.

[31] See John Hirst, *A Republican Manifesto* (Oxford, Oxford University Press, 1994).

[32] The papers of the RAC show, for example, that it was Turnbull, Winterton and Hirst who took the labouring oar when it came to working up draft chapters.

ideological range on the republican spectrum but even they struggled to agree a common approach. Turnbull, whose bullying manner raised hackles amongst his colleagues, had floated the idea that if the Senate declined to pass a government finance bill both houses should automatically be dissolved. Had this provision been in place in 1975 the Governor-General would not have had to have intervened; the Whitlam Government would have fallen because it could not secure supply. But this provision would have represented a shift of constitutional authority to the Senate – and to the minority parties which typically held the balance of power there.[33] Turnbull's colleagues on the RAC were not persuaded. On another occasion Turnbull suggested partial codification of the president's powers, a move which might have been seen as giving the office a stronger hand in a future dispute with the Prime Minister. Hirst's response was terse; 'Have you forgotten we are reporting to a Labor government?'[34]

Hirst had rather more success when he promoted the idea of a new preamble to the constitution. Arguably it was outside the Committee's terms of reference and even though the report stopped short of advocating a preamble, there is more than a hint of Hirst's generous minimalism about it.[35] In pressing his point with his RAC colleagues Hirst captured the minimalists' dilemma precisely:

> The rationale for minimalism is that the republican case will be endangered by attempting more; the danger of minimalism is that it can aim at less than what the people would support and expect. There is a lot of idealism invested in this movement. The minimalist approach is already causing disappointment. Some of this is no bad thing in that it makes us the moderates, but we should not needlessly turn idealism sour. Let's be generous minimalists[36]

Over the course of the next six years this tension in minimalism was often exposed, but never resolved. In their cautious, technocratic mode the minimalists would fail to excite their potential supporters. When, occasionally, they lapsed into grandiloquent flourishes, they would excite suspicion and fear.

The responses to the RAC also provided a foretaste of the trials which were to await republicans later in the decade. Monarchists responded to the exercise with confected anger: they accused the Government of rigging the exercise. But the Government was doing no more than it had said it would do in its election programme; it is far from clear that the addition to the RAC of avowed monarchists would have helped in the production of a report mapping out routes to a republic. But Malcolm Turnbull gave them what they wanted: he replied in kind, threatening to field Republican candidates against monarchists at the next general election. Away from the media's glare, Turnbull took a different tack, trying to entice Daryl Williams, the Shadow Attorney General, into participating informally

[33] John Hirst, *A Republican Manifesto* (Oxford, Oxford University Press, 1994) 68.
[34] RAC, folder of miscellaneous papers, Hirst to Turnbull, 20 August 1993.
[35] See, eg, RAC, *An Australian Republic*, 133–41.
[36] Hirst to RAC members, 24 May 1993.

in the RAC's proceedings. Williams, privately a republican, had no choice but to decline the offer. The Liberals, Williams confided in Turnbull, just wanted the issue to go away.[37]

For the most part the public reacted with indifference. The Committee members did its best to draw them in: they appeared on talkback radio; and they travelled the length and breadth of the country to speak to public meetings. Some citizens took the chance to register a protest at the Government; a few risked a public argument with Malcolm Turnbull; others questioned whether the whole exercise was treacherous; and still more wanted reassurance that the flag would not be changed. Public understanding of the issues, it is fair to say, was not well developed.[38]

The RAC's report was clear, authoritative and dull. The Committee had delivered what was asked of it: not quite a blueprint, but a narrowing of the options which would lead to a minimalist solution. It served to establish an ideological orthodoxy, but it did nothing to quicken the pulse. And the polls continued to show that direct election was much more popular amongst voters. Republicans said it was time to start a national debate; monarchists pressed for an early referendum to finish the matter.

IV. Becalmed

Keating's response was to play it long. Ostensibly, he was a Prime Minister in a rush. He had grand ambitions for his country and little time in which to achieve them: he had cheated the political fates once and might not survive the next election. But at the time it was the ACM, not the ARM, which was pressing for a rapid move to a vote. Republicans were proposing a period of reflection, hoping to boost understanding of the issue (not to mention awareness of the constitution itself). George Winterton, for one, endorsed the idea of a constitutional convention, an idea also championed by the independent Constitutional Centenary Foundation. Republican caution was undoubtedly influenced by tactical as well as substantive considerations. Their advance in the polls had, apparently, been checked. Keating's own briefing in late 1993 suggested that the anti-republican vote had a clear lead but that a significant proportion of voters remained undecided.[39]

Keating's first step was an orthodox one: he established a Cabinet Committee and set it to work through the remaining political choices. And it did so, slowly. The ARM and Malcolm Turnbull were kept at arm's length while Keating and his

[37] RAC, folder of miscellaneous papers, Hirst to Committee members, 24 May 1993. Daryl Williams, interview with the author, 3 March 2006.

[38] The shortcomings in understanding is apparent from the submissions sent to the Committee. One of them, from the Christian Leaders in Waverley, went so far as to suggest that the whole exercise might constitute treason: RAC, Submissions folder two, S0167.

[39] PM&C, Briefing for the Prime Minister, 'Developments since release of the Turnbull Report' (November or December 1993).

senior colleagues weighed their options. They did not reach a conclusion until the winter of 1995, in the final year of Keating's term of office.

Keating's second step, in June 1994, was to appoint a committee of experts to consider the state of civics education. The RAC had confirmed what the Constitutional Commission had reported just five years before; Australians did not understand their constitution and a majority even questioned whether their country had one at all.[40] Most public-minded citizens would have been disturbed by this, but it was the republican project which gave the issue its salience. Australians are obliged to vote in referendums and the evidence is clear that those who do not understand the proposition before them tend, reasonably enough, to vote No. This was troubling in itself, but public ignorance also threatened to undermine Keating's grander ambitions. How could Australians renew their image of themselves and of their place in the world if they did not understand the most basic features of the Australian state or of civic life?

The Civics Experts Group (CEG) confirmed the scale of the problem: only 18 per cent of Australians had *any* knowledge of the constitution. Ignorance was greatest amongst the young, those from non-English speaking backgrounds, the unskilled, the less well-educated and women. For republicans the message was stark: their proposal had not been understood and key sections of the electorate – those who had remained resistant to republican blandishments – had a poor grasp on the way they were governed. Just 3 per cent thought that a republic would foster national pride and identity, but most reluctantly conceded that it would probably come to pass anyway – because government and the media wanted it. A tenuous basis on which to build a referendum campaign, let alone a renewal of the nation.

The Government considered the findings diligently and its policy response, when it came, was serious. The Commonwealth would make $25m available over four years to support an improved understanding of democracy, rights and citizenship.[41] The lion's share of the money would go to schools and the remainder would be used to induct new citizens and others.

Sober and sensible. But in the context of the republican debate – and the Keating Prime Ministership – the CEG was the source of controversy from the start. When it was first appointed the monarchists identified it as a republican stalking horse. They were quick to point out that its chair, Stuart Macintyre, a former communist, took a radical, post-modern view of Australia's national story. The Government's initial response to the CEG's report, in December 1994, degenerated into a parliamentary brawl.[42] Tony Abbott – once of the ACM and later on the Liberal frontbench, ultimately as Prime Minister – had already set the tone for the debate. When the Government had said it was contemplating a programme of

[40] *Final Report of the Constitutional Commission. Volume One* (Canberra, Australian Government Publishing Service, 1988) 43, paras 1.56 and 1.57.

[41] Under the Australian constitution, education is a matter for the states and the Commonwealth (federal) government has had to force – and spend – its way into education policy.

[42] Gerard Henderson, *Brisbane Courier Mail* (30 December 1994).

public education on the constitution, Abbott had labelled the move 'a form of ideological child abuse'.[43] The combatants on both side of the republican debate knew their lines and they stuck to them: initiatives by their foes were to be regarded with suspicion and traduced wherever possible.

Keating made his formal response to the CEG on 6 June 1995. He studiously avoided making any link to the Republic, but his speech made clear that he believed government could and should have a role in forging a new civic purpose. If anybody had missed the link between civics and the Republic, it was there in the timing of the announcement. The very next day the Prime Minister gave the Government's formal response to the RAC report. Almost two years in the making, it was hard to resist the judgement that the Cabinet Committee had laboured hard to bring forth a mouse. Nobody familiar with the RAC report would have been surprised by Keating's endorsement of indirect election or by his response to the argument that the president's powers to appoint or dismiss a Prime Minister could not be left undefined. There was nothing generous about his model: this was a steerage class republic, stripped of all extraneous features. The political tactics were clear. The determination to protect the Westminster system shone through: codification of the reserve powers, urged on Keating by Turnbull earlier that month, was rebuffed. This was a restrained republic and, quite literally, a cheerless one: its advent would not be greeted by the 'beating of drums – or chests'.[44]

As at each stage in the republican journey, the June speech was accompanied by partisan acrimony. In one version of events, Keating called John Howard, now in his second term as Liberal leader, and offered to give him the time in which to consider the announcement carefully before responding. Howard rebuffed him.[45] Whatever the precise details might have been, Keating redrafted his speech to include a stinging personal attack on the leader of the opposition. Only a threat of resignation from Don Watson saw the passage removed; its excision was, said one adviser, 'like taking meat off the table of a starving man'.[46] But even the final, more placatory text did nothing to assuage Howard. Labor backbenchers, who had had precious little comfort in recent months, cheered their republican hero to the echo; Howard left the chamber while the Prime Minister was still on his feet.

Keating's speech explored the republican dilemma but it did not resolve it. He situated the project within his own grand vision for Australia, but the course he charted for his countrymen was both sober and modest. This would be 'a small, but significant step': it would unlock the future but it would not sever Australia from its traditions of parliamentary democracy. In the course of his announcement he pointed to no fewer than 14 features of the Australian constitution which

[43] Michael Millett, Geoff Kitney and Julie Lewis, report in *The Sydney Morning Herald* (17 May 1994).

[44] Don Watson, *Recollections of a Bleeding Heart. A Portrait of Paul Keating PM* (Milsons Point, NSW, Vintage, 2003 edn) 586.

[45] Author interview with senior ALP politician, 10 March 2006.

[46] Greg Wood, interview with the author, 14 March 2006. Don Watson, *Recollections of a Bleeding Heart. A Portrait of Paul Keating PM* (Milsons Point, NSW, Vintage, 2003 edn) 584–7.

would remain unchanged. For those who might (reasonably) wonder what all the fuss was about he returned to an argument he had used before: Australia was not yet a sovereign country. To go forward it could not remain 'a political or cultural appendage to another country's past'. This was a perilous route: in his quest to remake Australia's self-image he was suggesting not only that there was a greater future awaiting it, but that this prosperous, successful, self-confident society had not yet reached full nationhood.

John Howard's predecessor had committed the Liberals to a people's convention. The move was defensive: the party was split over the republic and this was a ploy to stall the argument, allowing it to seek the moral high ground by arguing that citizens should decide the way forward, not politicians. In the course of his ill-fated leadership, Alexander Downer never managed to scramble to the moral heights, but in his response to Keating, Howard just about made it there. This, he warned, was a big question, fraught with risk, and so the people should be given a choice. Keating had not quite closed the door on the idea, but the Prime Minister was quite clear that any decisions – prior to a referendum – were for Parliament. Earlier in the year he had considered a fresh approach, opening the process up to wider participation, but he came back to the orthodox view that this was a matter for parliamentarians as representatives of the people. Howard's advocacy of a convention was politically astute and it began to command some public support. Before the general election of 1996 Keating had been forced to concede that a referendum would be preceded by non-binding plebiscites to test the public's mood. But this was a last-minute, involuntary concession. And the electorate would soon determine that Keating's own contribution to the republican cause was almost at an end.

Why did Keating take so long before he announced the Government's policy and why did he not press home his case thereafter? He may have taken the reasonable view that the minimalist cause could not win a quick victory: every poll on the question confirmed that direct election remained stubbornly popular. And, in any event, it would not be possible to take through referendum legislation and to hold a referendum until the other side of the 1996 general election, and so a quick solution was simply not available. But there is also a simpler, and complementary, explanation. Keating kept the Republic under his close personal control; it was his project and it was not to be advanced by any of his ministerial colleagues.[47] Consequently, the Republic had to wait its turn in the crowded Prime Ministerial in-tray. Internationally, he was investing time in the establishment of the Asia-Pacific Economic Co-operation leaders' group; domestically, he was steering an embattled administration that seemed doomed to defeat, not least after its loss of the 'unlosable' Canberra by-election of March 1995. Without his advocacy the cause inched forward; had he put more energy into it he might have excited

[47] Greg Wood, interview with the author, 14 March 2006. Author interview with senior ALP politician, 10 March 2006.

tougher resistance. As it was, 'we launched the republic and immediately it was becalmed'.[48]

V. John Howard and the Republic

Some commentators have traced the defeat of the Republic to the general election of 1996. Keating had predicted that the proposal would not have 'a snowball in hell's chance' if the Prime Minister of the day was known to oppose it. And on 2 March 1996 John Winston Howard's coalition swept to power, crushing the ALP and sending Paul Keating into retirement. Thereafter, the argument runs, Howard did all in his considerable power to undermine the republican cause.

Before testing the strength of this interpretation it is worth pausing briefly to ask whether the Republic would have prospered after a Keating victory. We have seen that there were contradictions within the republican proposition and that the public could be forgiven for asking whether this was a 'small' or a 'significant' step. We have seen that the opposition forces were canny and well organised. And we know that Keating polarised opinion. In implementing his election programme, he would, presumably, have held a plebiscite to confirm the public's preference for a Republic. Had he received the result for which he hoped, his next step – according to his election platform – would have been to refer the question to a joint parliamentary committee. The consequences of this move are harder to predict. If the committee had championed minimalism, would he have engineered a referendum before the next general election? If the parliamentarians had conjured up a directly elected presidency, how would he have reacted? We cannot know the answers to these questions, but this counterfactual diversion does demonstrate that a Keating victory in 1996 would have brought fresh headaches for the Republican project. Republicans had little cause for comfort on election night 1996, but it would be wrong to focus on the result when seeking the cause of the republic's demise.

Howard's victory was a personal triumph. His first stint as Liberal leader had ended in an ignominious ambush by party colleagues; few would have thought it possible that he could return seven years later to claim the ultimate prize. That he should do so in a contest with Paul Keating, his long-time adversary, made the moment all the sweeter.

A 40-seat majority in the House of Representatives constituted a clear endorsement of the new Prime Minister. But when it came to the Republic he knew that his mandate was more ambiguous. The issue had not featured significantly in the campaign. Some of his Cabinet colleagues had already come out in favour of a Republic and more were to do so over the next couple of years. In short, the coalition's commitment to a convention remained as much a political necessity in government as it had been in opposition.

[48] Don Watson, *Recollections of a Bleeding Heart. A Portrait of Paul Keating PM* (Milsons Point, NSW, Vintage, 2003 edn) 589.

Howard has been a source of confusion for political commentators (and opponents). Many have sought to categorise him as a relic of the past, yearning for the social and political certainties of the 1950s, nostalgic for a homogeneous Australia, in which parents brought up sports-loving children in suburban houses, a Holden in the drive and washing drying on a Hills Hoist in the back yard, all to the hum of a Victa mower at work. An Anglo-Australia, respectful of authority and, above all, of the Crown. An Australia under the benign guidance of the ever-present Robert Menzies, founder of the modern Liberal Party.

But this is no more than a caricature. It is at its most misleading when Howard is likened to Menzies. Implicitly and explicitly he has invited the comparison; only Menzies served longer as Prime Minister and Howard has angrily defended Menzies' reputation against his critics. But Howard is quite clear that Menzies was a product of his age, a son of the British Empire; when Menzies spoke of 'the people' he meant the British family, of which Australians were but a part. Howard is an Anglophile inasmuch as he respects the institutions and legal system which his country has inherited from its former colonial master. But he is, above all else, an Australian nationalist, proud of what he insistently terms 'the Australian achievement'. He is a confirmed monarchist not because he particularly wants to retain a Briton as head of state, but because he can see no better alternative. A presidency would upset the balance of the Westminster system and, in particular, would represent a challenge to the office of Prime Minister.

Howard's critics (and there are many) begrudgingly concede that he was a brilliant tactician. After a more than decade in power it would be hard to deny him that. But the concession does not recognise his full impact on Australian politics. Howard sought to remake the Liberals as the party of the nation, a role hitherto filled by the ALP. His Liberal Party was the party of the battlers, the party of the ordinary, hard-working families. In the run-up to the 1996 election he repositioned the Liberals as the voice of this majority. There is, he said:

> a frustrated mainstream in Australia today which sees government decisions increasingly driven by the noisy, self-interested clamour of powerful vested interests with scant regard for the national interest ... Increasingly Australians have been exhorted to think of themselves as sub-groups. The focus so often has been on where we are different – not on what we have in common.[49]

His target was clear: the cosmopolitan, urban, liberal elites. He regarded them as disproportionately powerful, advocates of minority interests; apostles of multiculturalism and of diversity.

In office, he refashioned – but did not abandon – multiculturalism, emphasising the primary commitment of all citizens to Australia and to its common values. He stiffened immigration policy and, in the face of intense controversy, Australia took a more restrictive approach to asylum-seekers. And through it all

[49] John Howard, 'The Role of Government: A Modern Liberal Approach', speech given at the Menzies Research Centre (6 June 1995).

he promoted the nation and its symbols, prompting one conservative to object that the flag-bedecked capital had become redolent of Nuremburg.[50] Howard's governments were at pains to celebrate Australian achievements – not least on the sports field – and to memorialise Australian sacrifices. During Howard's decade, it was the Prime Minister, not the Queen or the Governor-General, who represented the nation to itself: it was the Prime Minister who bade farewell to departing troops and welcomed them on their return; and it was the Prime Minister who lead the mourning for the fallen or rushed to the bedside of the victims of terrorism.[51]

The 'nationalisation' of the Liberal Party struck a chord with many Australians. The 1996 election results showed that the Liberals had made progress with blue collar voters – and especially with white men. Howard had stolen the ALP's rhetoric as the party of the people; and he had made inroads into their core vote. And if some commentators wrinkled their noses at his flag-waving nationalism, it was far from clear that this was a sentiment shared by the majority. At the start of Howard's Prime Ministership the campaign for a new Australian flag had reasonable prospects for success. By the time he left office it was inconceivable that the country would abandon its most potent visual symbol.

Seen in this light, Howard's attachment to the monarchy may be viewed not as nostalgia for a former age but as a strategic necessity – and as political opportunism. It would have been discordant, if not bizarre, for Howard to have combined social conservatism with a bid to do away with the institutional – and personal – emblem of the established order. It would have been unnecessary, if not foolhardy, to have created a ceremonial presidency just as the Prime Minister was stepping into the same space, inaugurating new war memorials and celebrating the success of Australian athletes. And it would have been careless, if not dumb, to pass up the opportunity afforded by the Republic. It distilled the frustrations of Howard and his battlers: the Republic was not, in Howard's words, 'a barbecue-stopper'. It was a non-issue dreamt up by an unrepresentative elite, encouraged by a fawning media and promoted by a Prime Minister out of touch with his electorate. And it divided the nation. Throughout Howard's observations on the Republic (and on much else) he returned time and time again to the need for national unity. He would gather the nation behind him, whereas Keating was splintering it into self-interested factions. Even at the Constitutional Convention, which was marked by acrimony and feuding amongst the competing groups, Howard claimed that what united the delegates – and the nation – was more important than what divided them. They were all Australians: 'we all smell the same eucalypt, we all know the same dust and we all feel the same salt in the ocean'.[52]

[50] Greg Craven, interview with the author, 2 March 2006.

[51] For Howard's emphasis on Australia's military tradition, see Robert Manne, 'Little America. How John Howard has Changed Australia' (2006) 10 *The Monthly* 20–32.

[52] *Report of the Constitutional Convention. Old Parliament House Canberra. 2–13 February 1998. Volume 4. Transcript of Proceedings. Week Two, 9–13 February 1998* (1998), 997.

If Keating may reasonably be criticised for partisanship, the same charge may be levelled at Howard. While in opposition, Howard had nothing to gain by helping Keating to take the heat out of the issue. To do so would remove its political value to Howard and so he declined any offers to negotiate a truce.

In office, Howard allowed his new Cabinet to discuss the issue and members remained free to speak their minds in public, but he retained personal control over the Government's strategy. Daryl Williams, the new Attorney General, was to have ministerial responsibility for any referendum and so Howard balanced him with an ardent monarchist, Senator Minchin. The two of them 'watched each other like hawks'.[53] And all the while, the Prime Minister – supported by a team in his own department – took the key decisions in the run-up to the Constitutional Convention, not least when it came to the selection of delegates.[54] In preparing for the Convention, Howard might have made greater use of an independent foundation with proven expertise but, like Keating before him, he decided that the Republic was a matter for government and, in particular, for the Prime Minister.[55]

Republicans called foul at Howard's role: they protested that the Convention was rigged and that the subsequent referendum question was unfair. Some of this may be discounted: they were in a rough and tumble contest in which the other side also protested at the unfairness of the process.[56] And it is specious to suggest, as some republicans have done, that the public funding of the 'Yes' and 'No' campaigns was unfair because it reduced the advantage hitherto enjoyed by the richer ARM. Republicans were right to be fearful of Howard's interventions – but it was his public pronouncements as much as his private manoeuvring which endangered their cause. Ostensibly, he stood back from the debate, allowing his Ministers to steer a neutral process. But every so often he would remind the public of his personal preferences, of the gravity of the choice they faced – and of the risks associated with change.[57] It was a consummate performance, restrained and yet deadly.

VI. The Convention

Until November 1997, the Republic debate may fairly be characterised as an exercise in elite-driven change. It would not have secured momentum if public attitudes to the monarchy had not been changing, but the direction and energy of the campaign had come from the ARM and, above all, from Paul Keating. In committing the Liberals

[53] Daryl Williams, interview with the author, 3 March 2006.

[54] Author interview with official on the Prime Minister and Cabinet team, 14 March 2006.

[55] Cheryl Saunders, 'The Constitutional Centenary Foundation' in Timothy LH McCormack and Cheryl Saunders (eds), *Sir Ninian Stephen: A Tribute* (Melbourne, The Miegunyah Press, 2007) 72–3.

[56] See, eg, David Smith, 'The Referendum: a Post-Mortem' in *Upholding the Australian Constitution. Volume Twelve. Proceedings of the Twelfth Conference of the Samuel Griffith Society* (2000) ch 7.

[57] See, eg, John Howard, 'Search for Symbolism in Road Towards Republic' *The Age* (24 January 1998).

to a people's convention Alexander Downer had simply hoped to deny Keating one of his many points of attack. It was not intended as an experiment in participative democracy: but that was its eventual consequence. The election of delegates took place in November and December 1997 and the Convention delegates were finally called to order in Old Parliament House, Canberra on 2 February 1998.

This was not Athens under a southern sky. The bill establishing the Convention had been the source of fierce controversy, especially in the Senate. Republicans saw treachery in the use of a voluntary, postal vote: Senator Minchin was either paving the way for the wider use of voluntary voting (a move likely to help the Liberals)[58] or he was manipulating it in the hope that monarchists would be more motivated to vote than republicans. For their part, the monarchists were to protest that the postal ballot was vulnerable to manipulation and that the trade union supporters of the Republic were experts in electoral fraud.[59] In any event, just 76 – half – of the delegates were to be elected. The remainder were in the gift of the Prime Minister. He clearly made efforts to make his appointments representative of the population as possible. But the voting record shows that the appointed delegates were more supportive of the status quo than were their elected counterparts.

Nevertheless, the election did give the people their first chance to vote expressly on the Republican question – and almost 47 per cent of them did so. And the Convention itself focused public attention on the choices the country faced. It was raucous and untidy; tempers flared and threats were made. But amidst the noise – perhaps because of it – the arguments were set out and the nation began to sit up and take notice. The ABC carried the proceedings live throughout the fortnight and citizens came from across the country to watch from the public gallery. By the second week, the queues stretched around Old Parliament House. When asked why she had come, one of those waiting in line said simply, 'I want to witness history being made.'[60]

The Convention almost foundered before it was properly under way. On the second day the ARM voted in a way which seemed to rule out a directly elected presidency. The direct electionists teetered on the brink of pulling out. The Convention's Resolutions Group had to indulge in a crude re-writing of the rules to revive the chance that the direct electionists might yet win the day. The Convention stayed in business, but the relations between the ARM and its fellow republicans, never good, had been soured.

The ARM's approach at the Convention remained dirigiste. It had its favoured model and it would tolerate little variation from it; those elected on an ARM ticket would be expected to vote to an ARM line, dictated by a small steering group. This much might have been expected. But what was more surprising was that the ARM was badly prepared for the Convention.

[58] Australia has had compulsory voting at parliamentary elections since 1924.
[59] David Flint, interview with the author, 8 March 2006.
[60] George Williams, interview with the author, 10 March 2006.

It had cause for concern from the moment the Convention election results were declared. It was the largest single group, with 27 of the 76 elected delegates and more than 30 per cent of the vote; the ACM had 19 delegates from a share of 22.5 per cent. But the other republicans – mostly direct electionists – had 20 delegates between them. It was true that that they were not a single entity – the Direct Election Group was not formed until the second day of the Convention – but their votes would be critical if the ARM was to carry the day. Simple arithmetic should have said as much; failing that, political acumen should have alerted the ARM to the opportunity – and threat – posed by the Direct Electionists. Somehow they missed it.

The Convention's agenda had been set out by John Howard at the second reading of the Convention Bill. It was to take a view on:

- whether or not Australia should become a republic;
- which republic model should be put to the electorate to consider against the status quo; and
- in what timeframe and under what circumstances might any change be considered.[61]

If the ARM were to secure majority support for their answer to the second question, they would have to treat, either with the direct electionists or with the republicans on their other wing. These were the supporters of the model put forward by Richard McGarvie, the former governor of Victoria. It was, as one of its advocates cheerfully acknowledged, 'miserably conservative': a president would be appointed by a council of the great and the good. The president would have the same powers as the governor-general. This was super-minimalism: a gerontocracy would replace a monarchy.[62]

The ARM made some effort to woo both factions, but in truth its heart was not in it. It professed itself open to alternative solutions to its own, but its actions said otherwise. Mary Delahunty's pitch to the direct electionists captured the ARM's ambivalence. She protested that she – and the ARM – had an open mind but then she proceeded to say that a directly elected presidency would constitute 'a crisis of civic confidence'. As if this were not challenge enough, she then appealed to the direct electionists to 'convince me we are not seeking a saint [as president under their model]; that we are not asking too much of any single human being'.[63]

Over the course of the fortnight, there was just one unity meeting amongst all the republicans – and that was not called by the ARM. For the rest of the time they feuded with their co-republicans, whom they regarded as naïve populists,

[61] *Report of the Constitutional Convention. Old Parliament House Canberra. 2–13 February 1998. Volume 1. Report of Proceedings*, 14.

[62] The model's questionable democratic credentials are perhaps best captured in the draft minutes of one of the Convention's working groups. There an unwitting notetaker refers to the 'Mugabi [sic] model': NAA, Con. Con. A11734/1, working groups, papers from day one.

[63] *Report of the Constitutional Convention. Old Parliament House Canberra. 2–13 February 1998. Volume 3. Transcript of Proceedings. Week One, 2–6 February 1998* (1998), 309.

untutored in the harsh lessons of constitutional referendums.[64] In his account of the Convention, Turnbull pointedly cites Greg Craven's description of the direct electionists as 'a tub of lizards'.[65]

Talks with the McGarvie group came closer to agreement. Indeed, Craven for the super-minimalists thought he had a deal with the ARM which he might even be able to sell to the monarchists. This proved to be false optimism. Craven was further dismayed when Turnbull, with whom the deal had been done, publicly disavowed Craven's modifications to the presidential appointment process.[66] Turnbull's last minute volte face enraged the McGarvie camp and left his own ARM colleagues confused.[67]

Before the end of the Convention, the ARM had agreed to some changes to its model, but they were insufficient to command majority support. In its failed attempt to win over the direct electionists it had modified the front-end of its model, to allow the public to nominate candidates. But it also made an ill-considered amendment to the process by which the president might be dismissed, apparently handing full control over the process to the Prime Minister. The prospect that the president might become simply a puppet of the Prime Minister alarmed many and even George Winterton – who had first conceived of the ARM's model seven years before – felt obliged to condemn this development. At the end of the Convention, as at the beginning, the republicans were in disarray.

When the Convention came to vote, the ARM's model won more support than three other republican variants *and* the status quo. Asked whether, if Australia became a republic, it should do so on the basis of the modified ARM model, the Convention came within two votes of giving the proposition majority support. One can only imagine the mood in ARM ranks at the news that four delegates had abstained, including Greg Craven. Asked to choose between the ARM model and the status quo, an indirectly elected presidency again came out on top – but once more it fell short of an overall majority. It is hard to escape the conclusion that the handful of votes needed to secure a decisive ARM victory were there if Turnbull and his colleagues had worked harder and earlier to persuade their fellow republicans.[68]

As it was, the Prime Minister took the view that the Convention had expressed a 'clear view', even if not a majority view. The Government would bring forward legislation for a constitutional referendum, to be held in the following year. The minimalist model had, at least, secured its place on the ballot paper.

[64] Moira Rayner, 'A View from the Fringe' (1998) 4(2) *The 1998 Constitutional Convention: An Experiment in Popular Reform. The University of New South Wales Law Journal Forum* 27–30.

[65] Malcolm Turnbull, *Fighting for the Republic. The Ultimate Insider's Account* (South Yarra, Hardie Grant Books, 1999) 79.

[66] Greg Craven, interview with the author, 2 March 2006.

[67] Steve Vizard, *Two Weeks in Lilliput. Bear-baiting and Backbiting at the Constitutional Convention* (Ringwood, Victoria, Penguin, 1998) 302–04, 320–23.

[68] For the votes, see *Report of the Constitutional Convention, Old Parliament House Canberra, 2–13 February 1998* (1998), vol 1, 38–40; vol 4, 929–30, 983–84.

Steve Vizard concludes his full-throated diary of the Convention by saying that everybody was a winner: Republicans were to have their referendum; the ARM had its model; the ACM would finally have a contest with a model it knew to be flawed; and the Prime Minister's convention had reached a successful outcome, delivering a republican solution which he believed would be rejected in a referendum. And the process had given Australians a taste for direct, participatory democracy: it had been 'a fresh, volatile, unpredictable outpouring of middle Australia, crisp in its honesty, brilliant in its naivety, breath-taking in its spontaneity'.[69] This is all fair, but the Convention had an additional legacy. Forced by John Howard to come to a decision over the best model, republicans had torn themselves apart. Turnbull and others blamed the Prime Minister for the wounds they inflicted on one another during that fortnight in Canberra. Others would suggest that it was the republicans trading blows who were culpable. Either way, the wounds would not heal quickly. In the months that followed, the ARM did make some progress in building a broader coalition. The burgeoning Liberal support – evident in the Convention – was to spawn Liberals for a Republic. Faced with a binary choice between the ARM model and no republic, some erstwhile opponents rallied to the Yes cause. On the Right, Greg Craven was to become influential in the newly minted Conservatives for an Australian Head of State. On the Left, the ALP state leaders in Queensland, West Australia, South Australia and Tasmania, all of whom had supported a directly elected presidency, reconciled themselves to the indirect alternative. But the core of the direct electionists was not assuaged. They were bitter at their treatment by the 'Chardonnay oligarchs' in the ARM; they knew that the opinion polls showed that their model was more popular; and they saw that a Yes vote in 1999 was likely to resolve the issue once and for all, denying Australia any hope of a directly elected presidency. By contrast, a rejection of indirect election would leave open the hope of a later referendum on their, more popular alternative. The ARM was to argue that it would be folly for the nation to pass up its only chance of a republic in 100 years of federation in the hope that another one would be along shortly. But John Howard gave enough encouragement to the idea of a second vote to make it seem credible. The scene had been set for a bloody referendum campaign.

VII. Australia Votes No

The *Australian* newspaper, always prominent in the Republic's media chorus, organised a number of campaign debates between the Yes and No campaigns. The series culminated in Sydney on 31 October 1999, as the two teams were making their final push for victory. Both were in no doubt as to its potential significance;

[69] Steve Vizard, *Two Weeks in Lilliput. Bear-baiting and Backbiting at the Constitutional Convention* (Ringwood, Victoria, Penguin, 1998) 358.

the No cause was holding a lead, but the result of the referendum on 6 November still seemed to be in the balance. The two hours of debate in Sydney town hall were to reveal the strengths and weaknesses of both campaigns.

The Yes team had prepared thoroughly, using their local network of connections assiduously. Vote Yes banners had been hung from every lamppost in the city centre: a gesture ordained by the Lord Mayor and his Deputy, Lucy Hughes – Mrs Malcolm Turnbull. Their platform party did not lack in talent: Turnbull was in the lead, supported by two star turns – the art critic Robert Hughes (uncle of Lucy Hughes) and Bob Hawke, who had not planned to be part of the campaign but who had responded to a belated plea for help. Turnbull, who had carried the burden of the campaign – as much through his cheque book as his tireless advocacy – was visibly weary. But once again he nimbly constructed the republican case, brushing aside the suggestion that a Yes would usher in a 'politicians' republic': he demonstrated that it was *direct* election which was more likely to deliver a politician as president, not least because the political parties would participate in any national poll for head of state. Robert Hughes, still on crutches after a car crash earlier in the campaign, was passionate and fluent, if short on specifics. But it was Hawke who took the eye. Like a champion boxer called out of retirement for one final bout, he strutted about the ring. Trouncing the hecklers in the fractious audience, he made a brilliant, *ex tempore* plea for Australia to listen to the Yes case.

Theirs was a dazzling display. By comparison, the No team was pedestrian and crude. Hawke recalled, years later, that at the debate Tony Abbott had 'squibbed it'; it was a fair assessment of a lame performance. Kerry Jones, never comfortable on the public stage, stuck stolidly to her script, repeating her stock lines as if by rote. The poet Les Murray was to have been the third member of their team. Perhaps prudently, he failed to show up, and had his lines read for him by an uncomfortable, last minute stand-in.[70]

The Yes campaign had the brains, the fluency and the more subtle arguments. But the performance was horribly misjudged. Their line-up would have warmed the hearts of an ARM loyalist, but it did nothing to reach out to the undecided voter. The public's adverse reaction to Turnbull had been confirmed in a number of opinion polls; Hughes, a resident of Manhattan, was poorly placed to persuade Australians to realise their destiny; and Hawke, even in retirement, was an ALP partisan unlikely to attract coalition voters to the cause. In the closing stages of the campaign, the Yes campaign was talking to the converted.

The No team did not inspire, but their message was simple and effective – and they had a woman to communicate it. Jones worked and reworked a handful of themes. The proposition before the electorate was unsafe and would take the country into constitutional danger. The proposition would deliver a presidency in the gift of politicians – and one held by a politician. The proposition, if passed, would

[70] Murray's other contribution to the exercise was to have cooperated with the Prime Minister on early drafts of the Preamble. He subsequently disavowed this work.

kill off the hopes of those who would prefer a directly elected presidency: a second referendum after a Yes vote was inconceivable. And finally, the proposition was complicated; and anybody uncertain about it should do the safe thing – vote No. Negative, simplistic and crude – but the message was carefully crafted to appeal to a wide cross-section of the population. The unlikely coalition between monarchists and direct electionists had come about after the Constitutional Convention, encouraged by Bill Hayden, formerly leader of the ALP and, latterly, Governor-General. During the Convention the ACM had stood aloof from tactical alliances: it had voted according to its beliefs rather than attempting to secure the outcome most disadvantageous to republican interests. But in the months that followed, Hayden – who had promoted a direct election model at the Convention – helped to persuade the ACM leadership that they now had to respond to a different challenge. They had to provide leadership to a broadly based No campaign and to reach out to the disaffected direct electionists. They did both, building a cohesive and effective No campaign team which did not suffer from the fratricidal enmities which periodically erupted in the rival camp. This was achieved by following the basic rule of No campaigns: their role was to oppose – it was not for them to chart Australia's constitutional future, nor were they under any obligation to remain in coalition the day after the referendum was won. Hence Kerry Jones and her fellow monarchists took a vow of silence: the Queen was all but absent from Vote No literature. As Paul Keating acidly remarked, loyalty to the Crown had become 'the love that dare not speak its name'.

The No campaign had the easier task; and they set about it competently. The Yes team struggled to reach out beyond its core vote; and its tactics alienated the undecided. Its use of celebrities in its advertisements proved to be a flop; and its direct attack on Prince Charles was counter-productive. Despite the advice of the best pollsters and public relations advice that money could buy, the Yes team had a tin ear when it came to judging the public mood. It thought, for example, that it would be a boon to bring together Malcolm Fraser and Gough Whitlam – the two great foes of the 1970s – in a joint endorsement of the Republic. Here, at last, was bipartisanship at work. But the public reaction was simple: for once in their lives Fraser and Whitlam were in agreement about something – and so perhaps there was something in the charge that this was a politicians' republic. The ALP, watching on as political amateurs steered the Yes campaign unerringly for the rocks, launched its own, supplementary campaign in favour of a Yes vote. And it did so to the theme tune 'It's time' – the battle hymn of Gough Whitlam's famous 1972 ALP campaign. Nothing was better calculated to fix in the public's mind the thought that this was a partisan conflict, redolent of old political enmities.

Just as republicans alleged that the Convention had been rigged by John Howard, so they protested that his subsequent interventions undermined their prospects for success.[71] There can be no doubt that the Prime Minister helped

[71] Malcolm Turnbull, *Fighting for the Republic. The Ultimate Insider's Account* (South Yarra, Hardie Grant Books, 1999) 85, 139 and 219.

secure a majority for the No cause, but it is much more difficult to prove that his interventions were decisive, still less that they were illegitimate. Late in the campaign he made a carefully worded statement of support for a No vote. Deliberately understated and generous in its praise for patriots in the Yes camp, it reminded all who cared to listen that the Prime Minister thought the status quo worked well, that the republican model on offer was flawed and that the Governor-General was, in effect, the Head of State.[72] The No campaign could not have asked for more. But by most estimates the race was already won by the time of Howard's article: if anything, voters swung back to the Yes cause in the last couple of weeks.

More important was Howard's role in the wording of the question that ultimately appeared on the ballot paper. He fought hard for a formulation that avoided any reference to the appointment of an Australian as head of state, phrasing which might have boosted the Yes vote by as much as 4 per cent. The wording was contested in Parliament and its final form was the result, as much as anything else, of a lack of nerve by the Australian Democrats. The Yes cause was denied its preference, but it would be hard to call the outcome unfair. Voters were asked whether they wanted

> to establish the Commonwealth of Australia as a republic with the Queen and Governor-General being replaced by a President appointed by a two-thirds majority of the members of the Commonwealth Parliament.[73]

More fanciful is the suggestion that Howard chipped away at republican support by putting a second question on the ballot paper. The inclusion of a second issue – a new preamble to the constitution – may have been done something to confuse the argument and so helped the No cause to argue that those in doubt should play safe. But it is a stretch to argue that this was all part of a plot by Howard. After all, he invested political capital in the preparation of the preamble: he even drafted the original text in collaboration with the poet Les Murray. The sentiments it expressed were true to his own conception of Australian national identity – up to and including its attempt to introduce the term 'mateship' to the constitutional lexicon. He was mocked when a spatchcocked version of the eccentric original was disowned by Murray. Prime Ministers do not willingly invite derision – least of all those who have just made heavy weather of their own re-election. Howard blames the Australian Democrats for the inadequacy of the revised text and for the 'political correctness' that prompted the exclusion of 'mateship'. And he remains critical of the ALP for its opposition to a preamble which did not adhere to its preferred formula for Indigenous reconciliation. The preamble was to suffer an even worse defeat than the core republican proposition, winning support from less than 40 per cent of the electorate.[74]

[72] Statement by Prime Minister John Howard on the Republic Referendum (27 October 1999).
[73] Australian Electoral Commission, *Yes/No Referendum '99. Your Official Referendum Pamphlet* (1999).
[74] John Howard, *Lazarus Rising* (Sydney, Harper Collins, 2010) 328–29, 333.

The final charge levelled at Howard is that he manipulated the public education campaign which preceded the referendum. The funds voted by Parliament were to be used to educate citizens on the issues, before the formal start of campaigning. An expert advisory committee took a view on questions of balance, but the members of the committee were deeply divided and the outcomes on which they were able to agree were not particularly helpful for informing the public.[75] There can be little doubt that the Prime Minister took a close interest in the preparation of the publicity materials and that he pressed for the inclusion of the argument that the Governor-General was really the Head of State. But he failed. There is no evidence linking him to the campaign's brush with controversy. Official publicity illustrated the choice facing Australians with a picture of a fork in the road. Republicans protested that that this over-dramatised the issue; after all, their slogan was that a Republic was 'a small step, important and safe'. Those preparing the neutral public information on the issues had an unrewarding task. Their draft of the voters' leaflet explained that there would be a referendum on 6 November to determine if the Queen should be replaced as Head of State by a President. The Yes campaign complained that the text should refer to an *Australian* President. The No campaign protested that the Queen was not Head of State.[76]

The Prime Minister was entitled to use his political influence to help the No cause and he did so, skilfully. There is no reason to believe that he acted illegitimately. But on referendum night Malcolm Turnbull called it differently. In a bitter close to an angry, bruising campaign he railed at Howard for suggesting in bad faith that supporters of a direct election could expect a second vote on their preferred model if the minimalist model was defeated. He invited Australians to think of Howard as 'the Prime Minister who broke a nation's heart'.[77]

VIII. Why the Republic was Lost

On the night of 6 November the Republic went down to a heavy defeat: just 45.1 per cent of voters supported it. Not a single state gave it a majority. The Preamble won only 42 per cent of the popular vote.[78]

Pundits and participants were quick to explain the reasons for the Republic's demise – and to speculate about the prospects for a second coming. Early analysis

[75] Malcolm Turnbull, interview with the author, 10 March 2006. Cheryl Saunders, interview with the author, 16 January 2006.

[76] Author interview with official on the Prime Minister & Cabinet team, 14 March 2006.

[77] Malcolm Turnbull, *Fighting for the Republic. The Ultimate Insider's Account* (South Yarra, Hardie Grant Books, 1999) 245.

[78] The Australian Capital Territory did back the Republic – by 63.3% to 36.7% – but to achieve the second half of a double majority, a proposition has to win in a majority of *states*: territories do not count.

focussed on questions of process and of tactics. Turnbull lamented the poor level of public understanding of the issues, complained that the electorate had been rushed, admitted that the model had been misunderstood and inveighed against his tormentor in chief, John Howard.[79] Old political hands queued up to attribute the blame to the naïvety and unpopularity of Malcolm Turnbull.[80] The No campaign exulted in the good sense of the Australian people and, privately, congratulated themselves on a campaign which had encouraged voters to fear the consequences of a republic.

This emphasis on process is understandable. We have seen how the ARM and its allies had failed to overcome the key strategic challenges it had faced from its outset. It had not been able to build a broad coalition and although it had engaged in fierce debate with its opponents, it was a debate which left much of the population confused and alienated – and did nothing to draw in those who already felt distanced by the political process.[81] Its choice of indirect election was made and sustained for cogent reasons; and it repeatedly demonstrated that it was its model which was most likely to deliver a non-party figure as president and to leave the Westminster system undisturbed. Cogent it may have been, but this cold, clear analysis did little to win over the public: Greg Craven commented later that to win a referendum vote, a republican proposition has to be all brains or all sex – and that the one on offer in 1999 was neither.[82] In polls taken in the two months before the referendum, indirect election commanded no more than 15 per cent support, far behind direct election and the status quo.[83] And so before we place too much emphasis on tactical failure, it is as well to put our eye to the other end of the telescope: the Yes Campaign managed to persuade some 30 per cent of the electorate to vote for their proposal even though it was not their first preference.

Beyond the discussion of tactics and personalities, there is a more interesting narrative of republican failure – one that does not deny a role to political mismanagement but one which helps explain why Paul Keating and the ARM had such a hard time persuading Australia of the merits of their republic. Paul Kelly, who had used his editorship of *The Australian* to champion the republican cause, was quick to discern a pattern in the demographics of the vote. As the results were coming in he concluded that

> The defeat of the republic exposes Australia as two different societies – a confident, educated, city-based middle class and a pessimistic, urban and rural battler constituency hostile to the 1990s change agenda.[84]

[79] Malcolm Turnbull, *Fighting for the Republic. The Ultimate Insider's Account* (South Yarra, Hardie Grant Books, 1999) 85, 118, 247.

[80] Bob Hawke, interview with the author, 14 March 2006.

[81] For the (lack of) significance of the Republic to those whose first language was not English, see NLA, CCF, 6.10.1, nr 93, Referendum – file 4, Emigré Multicultural Communications for the Referendum Taskforce (May 1999).

[82] Greg Craven, interview with the author, 2 March 2006.

[83] Newspoll Market Research opinion poll for *The Australian* (September and October 1999).

[84] *The Australian* (8 November 1999).

Subsequent analysis of the voting returns and of opinion polls has given Kelly's election night assessment greater definition and nuance, but the principal features of his diagnosis have been confirmed. The Republic struggled to make headway amongst blue-collar voters, amongst those with the most limited education, amongst women and the elderly. The socially conservative, suburban white working class voters – John Howard Liberals – were sceptical about the proposal. Voters who did not trust government and the governing elite voted No, as did those who still valued the traditional links to Britain.[85]

John Howard did not want the 1999 referendum to divide the nation: but the demographics of the Republican defeat show a clear pattern of social and economic division. This was not simply a divide between the prosperous and the socially disadvantaged; nor was the nation divided along conventional left-right lines. By the time of the referendum many Liberals had chosen to vote for the Republic; and of the 17 Liberal constituencies to opt for change, one of them was Bennelong in Sydney – for whom the sitting member was John Howard. Katharine Betts has demonstrated that the rejection of the Republic was a product not just of economic disadvantage but of the rejection of the broader social and cultural change agenda of the 1980s and 1990s.[86] This was a reaction against the dominance of the new class, defined by Kelly as 'a coalition of white-collar professionals – teachers, social workers, university lecturers, journalists, reformist lawyers, environmentalists, civil servants and union officials' plus some of the 'opinion-making elite in the media, business and the banks'.[87] Betts concedes that this dynamic does not explain all factors at play in the referendum but she successfully shows that on 6 November the socially conservative working and lower-middle classes – who took pride in their nation as it was – took their revenge on the cosmopolitan agenda which had come to the fore when Paul Keating was Prime Minister. Three years after he had been driven from office, why did his Big Picture continue to excite such enmity? Some had bitter memories of the recession at the end of the 1980s; for others there was an enduring opposition to the man himself – but three years into his retirement, we need better explanations as to why a polarised nation voted as it did.

In searching for answers we should begin with the contradictions in the republican proposition itself. In the mouths of its advocates, this Republic was a colourless beast, a constitutional soporific. So determined was the ARM to strip the proposal of all threat that it went into the 1997 Convention elections on a platform which promised no change to the anthem, no change to the flag, no change to Australia's membership of the Commonwealth and no change to her participation in the Commonwealth Games. And it topped this off with a paean of praise to

[85] See especially the analysis of the results in Ian McAllister, 'Election without Cues: The 1999 Australian Republic Referendum' (2010) 36(2) *Australian Journal of Political Science* 247–69.

[86] Katharine Betts, 'The Cosmopolitan Social Agenda and the Referendum on the Republic' (1999) 7(4) *People and Place* 32–41.

[87] ibid, 34–5.

Her Majesty the Queen.[88] Peter Collins, the Liberal leader in the New South Wales legislature and a prominent member of the ARM, had gone one better and even suggested that the Queen did not need to go. A Republic would be secured and, in a show of respect to the present monarch, legislation would be passed granting her the honorific title 'Queen of Australia'.[89] At the Convention Janet Holmes à Court even went so far as to declare that it was the very modesty of the ARM proposal, its smallness that attracted her to it.

Why anyone should feel moved to vote for this titivation of the existing order was not fully explained. Or, more accurately, it was not consistently explained. Seduced by the presence of fellow believers, even the most politically astute minimalists would suggest that a Republic would bring with it the rebirth of the nation. Hence Keating, in his address to the annual dinner of the ARM in November 1995 promised that a Republic would fuse the Australian past to the Australian present.[90] The more maladroit republicans would have no such inhibitions and they would beckon the faithful to the promised land. Hence Keneally suggested that

> we will use the Republic as the light by which we review everything, from our relationship to our antediluvian continent, to our position with its indigenous peoples, to the question of our international relations. Delivered of colonialism at last, and finally cured of the twitches of dependence, we will be able to see ourselves in a real light for the first time. We will have settled or at least embarked on the question which for so long has persecuted us: What is an Australian? The fruits may be incalculable. Whereas we already know the staleness and limitations of the old way.[91]

These excesses were as rare as they were florid, but they provided the monarchists with just enough ammunition to persuade a distrustful public that the ARM wanted to smuggle through an altogether more revolutionary change.

Yet even if one sets aside this underlying tension about the scale of the proposition, the Republic of Paul Keating and the ARM begs as many questions as it answers. In the words of Don Watson, this was to be 'the first post-modern Republic': it was to symbolise Australia's leap from dominion to a twenty-first century open democracy, at ease with itself and its neighbours. But in a globalised community of ever greater interconnectedness, there must be some question as to how modern – let alone post-modern – it was to launch a political project whose focus was on the political character of the nation state. Republicans chose to ignore this conundrum rather than resolving it.

[88] NAA, Con. Con. A11737/1, *Republic Yes or No?* (ARM text in official election leaflet for Constitutional Convention elections).

[89] State Lib. NSW, Collins, box 72, folder 1(2), Peter Collins, speech, Adelaide (27 January 1997).

[90] NAA, Keating, M4014, item 737, Paul Keating, speech at Fifth Annual Dinner of the ARM (3 November 1995).

[91] Thomas Keneally, *Our Republic* (Port Melbourne, William Heinemann Australia, 1993) 272.

No political enterprises are without tensions and contradictions. But these matter less if their champions can demonstrate that their proposed solution is a viable remedy for a defined problem. But it was far from clear which problem the Republic was intended to solve. It was irrelevant to Australia's economic trials. Only the most deluded or the most imaginative believed that the sovereign retained the power to wreak havoc on Australia's democracy. And so republicans had to fall back on arguments which were subtle, if not tortured. Keating proposed to an incredulous nation that Asian countries were confused by Australia's retention of a Briton as head of state and this complicated its relations with its regional neighbours. Evidence of these complications was hard to find. Others stepped forward with the argument that with the Queen on the Australian throne the Australian nation was not yet fully national.[92] But this was rebutted by republicans like Peter Costello, John Howard's Deputy and then his heir apparent. His answer to the exam question was different: Australia's constitutional arrangements were no longer credible because they were discordant with contemporary Australian values. This was a more sustainable line of reasoning – and one less likely to be offensive to an Australian's sense of national pride – but it was hard to persuade voters that the alleged mismatch between Crown and values was a first order issue. For many, the Republic remained a solution in search of a problem.

Some four years before the referendum, the ARM's pollsters delivered a clear warning to the Republican leadership: the trend in favour of a Republic might not deliver victory in 1998/99. Strong, committed support was growing slowly. The ARM's message had not been heard by key demographic groups.[93] By 1997 the polling advice was even more uncomfortable: the movement had to excite interest by stating, plainly that the republican choice was about Australian values and Australian character. It was a question of national identity.[94] The ARM's leaders did not need to be told this – they had come into the movement for reasons of nationalism. But they were nervous about running a campaign which put the national identity front and central. This ran contrary to Turnbull's every political instinct: it would have meant that republicans would have been fighting on a broad, and ill-defined front.

But, like it or not, the minimalist proposition was intrinsically an exercise in identity politics. It was an attempt at a surgical incision in the constitution to remove one office holder and to replace her with another. The President would wield powers all but identical to those of the Governor-General. Australian

[92] State Lib. NSW, Collins, box 72, folder 1(2), collection of Peter Collins' speeches 1993–97, published under the title, *That Final Step towards Nationhood: the Republic*. Keneally would also argue that for as long as Australia retained the monarchy it was a 'stunted nation'. See, eg, State Lib. NSW, ARM, box 1, folder 1(1), Keneally's speech at the launch of the ARM, Sydney (7 July 1991). A similar line is developed in his article for *Australian Business Monthly* (November 1991).

[93] Syd, ARM, Martin James, 'Defining the Target Market for the Republican Movement' [1995 or later].

[94] Syd, ARM, Irving Saulwick and Associates, 'Attitudes to the Constitutional Convention. A Qualitative Study' (April 1997).

democracy would have been wiped clean of the taint of heredity. But the real energy for the idea came from the desire to replace a Briton with an Australian. In the ARM's early days this simple, reasonable ambition shone through – as in Turnbull's call for a 'resident for president'. Indeed the early ARM showed evidence of a more earthy, robust nationalism. Keneally, ever candid, had no hesitation in branding Dame Leonie Kramer, a monarchist, 'un-Australian' for her alleged prejudice against Australian literature. The term is a telling one; Keneally was sufficiently confident of his own sense of what it was to be Australian that he had no hesitation in defining its antonym. The US, a country with a long settled civic ideology, is no stranger to the term 'un-American' but Keneally's usage raised all manner of questions about whether there was a shared sense of Australian-ness. During the Yes campaign, republicans were to risk a return to a more direct appeal to national sentiment in its advertisements: the implicit message was that patriots should answer the call and vote for the Republic.

Turnbull was right to be nervous about a battle over the nature of modern Australia. If that was what the republican debate became there would be no chance of distinguishing it from the rights and wrongs of Keating's cosmopolitan agenda. And if that judgement needed confirmation, he had only to look at the point of attack chosen by John Howard. In 1993, when shadowing the industrial relations portfolio, Howard awarded himself the brief of cheerleader in chief for the monarchy. From the start he attacked the republic as a denial of Australian values and Australian history – in particular the Liberal contribution to the country's story. From the outset he sought a battle over the character of the nation not simply to defeat the Republic but to advance his broader political agenda in competition with Keating's.[95]

If Turnbull needed a lesson in the perils of identity politics his brief skirmish with the preamble provided it. For most of the decade he steered clear of it – and he urged the ARM to do likewise. But as chair of the RAC he received submissions calling for a new preamble. John Hirst urged him to embody Australian values in a new constitutional text. The Constitutional Commission in the 1980s had fought shy of the issue but it allowed itself the observation that if a new preamble were desired – a proposition it opposed – it should express 'fundamental sentiments' and those held in common. The Commission concluded that it was difficult to identify such sentiments, let alone express them in a 'concise and inspirational form'.[96] The RAC's troika – Turnbull, Hirst and Winterton – struggled when faced with the same challenge and so one could readily imagine the difficulties that the nation as a whole might have.[97] In particular, representatives of the Indigenous

[95] John Howard, 'Wrecker Keating is Mocking our Past' *Canberra Times* (21 May 1993). Norman Abjorensen report in *Canberra Times* (28 September 1993).

[96] RAC, folder for meeting on 21 July 1993, draft 'Background Paper on the Preamble', nd, 3–4.

[97] For differences between Committee members, see RAC, folder for meeting on 21 July 1993, Record of Committee Meeting (30 June 1993), annexed noted entitled 'Discussion on Preamble'.

Peoples urged on the Committee the need to recognise Indigenous rights and to commit the nation to reconciliation if not expiation for past wrongs.[98] Turnbull took the view that a preamble must have something to say about reconciliation but that it would be fatal to the project if it became entangled with the High Court's 1992 ruling in the Mabo native title case. The same arguments were re-run at the Convention some five years later, with equally inconclusive results. The debate over the preamble was everything that Turnbull did not want the republic debate to be: it was multifaceted; it engaged partisans with competing visions of the nation's future; and it offered the risk of alienating powerful interest groups in exchange for symbolic textual gestures.[99]

Ultimately Turnbull could only do so much to insulate the Republic from a broader battle over the future direction of Australian society. Not only was Paul Keating determined to unite the republican cause with his crusade for 'the good society', but John Howard was just as enthusiastic to fight along a broad and shifting front. It was central to his own project that he should characterise the struggle as one fought between, on the one hand, 'the New Class establishment and cultural iconoclasts who have held such sway in Australia in recent years' and, on the other, the patriotic, hard-working battlers, struggling to make ends meet under Keating.[100] From reconciliation to cultural policy, the Labor Prime Minister was creating division and disharmony as he slavishly advanced the interests of the New Class. In understanding how the Republic was inextricably linked to this wider conflict, it is worth considering two of the flashpoints along the battlefront: multiculturalism and the so-called History Wars.

In opposition Howard had made clear his unease over multiculturalism but he did, reluctantly, come to sanction it in office. His response to the Keating brand of multiculturalism was both strategic and tactical. His assault on the ALP was based on a critique of interest group politics which overlooked the needs of 'mainstream Australia'. For Howard, multiculturalism was a distillation of all that was wrong with Keating's Government. He took aim at its political correctness and at the suggestion of special treatment for minorities. And in doing so he knew that he was expressing the grievances of his target voters. In office he found that there was a more strident voice speaking out on multiculturalism. Pauline Hanson had been dropped by the Liberals during the 1996 election but she won election on a One Nation ticket. Once in Parliament her targets included the 'Aboriginal industry' and the threat to Australia posed by Asian immigration. Howard's response

[98] See, eg, RAC, submissions folder 3, S0209, submission by the Aboriginal and Torres Strait Islander Commission. RAC, folder for meeting on 21 July 1993, Record of Committee Meeting, 30 June 1993, annexed noted entitled 'Discussion on Preamble'.

[99] Most were agreed that a new preamble would be non-justiciable; its value would be exclusively declaratory.

[100] The quotation is from an address by John Howard to the Samuel Griffith Society. In this passage he was railing at the retreat from pride in Australian history. See John Howard, 'Mr. Keating's Mirage on the Hill: How the Republic, like the Cheshire Cat, Came and Went' in *Proceedings of the Samuel Griffith Society*, 3 (1994) ch 7.

was slow and awkward: having seen the Liberals make progress among the white working class he was reluctant to lose them to One Nation – which briefly threatened to become a force across the country. By the time of the 1998 election he had distanced the Liberals from Hanson but not before he had given battlers reassurance that he understood their grievances about policies which favoured minorities at the expense of the majority.

The tension in Howard's Government over multiculturalism was never fully resolved: in February 2006 there was a public disagreement between Peter Costello, the Treasurer, and Tony Abbott, then the Health Minister, over the merits of the approach.[101] But Howard's own acceptance that his Government should have a multicultural strategy is revealing. His rhetoric was quite different from Keating's and there were substantive differences in policy, but there was much common ground between the approach his administration set out in 1999 and the course followed by Keating.[102] The Howard Government maintained that all citizens owed a primary debt of loyalty to Australia – a recurring theme in Howard's thought, and one shared with Keating. Australians, it was asserted, are united by the English language, by shared democratic values and by the notion of the fair-go. Keating's Government would have placed the emphasis elsewhere and its handling of Indigenous issues was quite different: whereas Keating apologised for the wrongs done to Indigenous Peoples, Howard had resisted any suggestion of inter-generational guilt. But both Governments were seeking to establish, and inculcate, a civic ideology for the nation. Whereas Keating expressed his approach as a new, progressive creed that would transform the country, Howard's claim was that he was simply expressing the wisdom of the mainstream. He was articulating what everybody knew to be the case: that Australians were egalitarian, that they believed in the fair-go and that they were committed to parliamentary democracy. His was not a mission to transform Australian beliefs, but to clarify them and to protect them from neglect or from the noisy claims of minorities. But Keating and Howard were both responding to rapid global and national change; to dramatic increases in population movements; and to the economic imperative of closer ties with Asia. In an uncertain world both sought to provide direction by reference to fundamental values which should guide the nation. The progressive sought to do so in a rhetoric of modernisation and he attempted to capture the character of Australia in an emblematic change to its constitution. The conservative spoke of established truths, of common sense and of the unity of the nation. Their visions were different, although there was greater continuity between them than either would concede. But they were both groping towards a civic ideology to unite the people behind them.

[101] See, eg, Louise Dodson in *The West Australian* (2 March 2006) and Dennis Altman in *The Age* (1 March 2006).

[102] *A New Agenda for Multicultural Australia* (December 1999). See also *Multicultural Australia: United in Diversity. Updating the 1999 New Agenda for Multicultural Australia: Strategic directions for 2003–2006* (2003).

The same dynamic was at work in the so-called History Wars, the protracted argument over the teaching of Australian history – in schools, in the media and in museums. This acrimonious wrangle is not unique to Australia: there are parallels in the UK, where Mrs Thatcher pressed for the restoration of a 'traditional' approach to history, and in the US, where controversy erupted over the standards for the teaching of school history in 1994.[103] In each case the Right sought to fight back against what it saw as the denigration of the nation's past and a denial of its achievements in favour of a guilt-ridden focus on the oppression of minorities. And the combatants persuaded themselves that the stakes could not be higher; the Institute of Public Affairs in Australia felt moved to remind its readers of Orwell's dictum, 'he who controls the past controls the future'.[104] The battle over the curriculum became a battle for ideological supremacy.

The Australian sub-plot in this international drama is a story of attack and counter-attack.[105] The Right would argue that the provocation came from the Left. It was progressives, encouraged by the ALP, who plotted to mark the bicentenary of British settlement in 1788 with a multicultural jamboree under the soupy title 'Living Together'. The Right counter-charged that it was self-loathing intellectuals, led by the radical historian Manning Clark and championed by his student (and apostle on earth) Don Watson, who renounced their British inheritance and tarnished it with charges of racism. It was two justices from the left establishment who declared, in the Mabo case, that Australia's treatment of its Indigenous Peoples was a tale of 'unutterable shame'. It was Paul Keating who paid homage at Kokoda in preference to Gallipoli, long celebrated as the crucible of the nation but now denigrated as a scene of slaughter in a distant land in service of the British Empire. Kokoda, by contrast, was where Australians heroically turned back the Japanese march through Papua New Guinea; a sacrifice of Australian lives to protect the homeland so cruelly abandoned by the British.[106] It is a measure of Keating's appetite for risk that he championed the remembrance of Kokoda as a national shrine at the very time that Gallipoli was beginning to command increasing popular attention.

The counter-attack was first led by Geoffrey Blainey, the Melbourne historian whose appetite for controversy seemed to know no bounds. Through the 1980s he took aim at the re-writing of Australian history, at immigration policy, at multiculturalism and at the subversion of the Bicentenary. Along the way he was branded as a racist and, ultimately, was shunned by his Melbourne colleagues. In time he was joined by a new, and even more raucous, voice of dissent: Keith Windschuttle

[103] There were also echoes of the controversy in Canada, sparked by JL Granatstein's book, *Who Killed Canadian History?* These are discussed in the closing pages of chapter three above.

[104] Cited in Stuart Macintyre and Anna Clark, *The History Wars* (Carlton, Victoria, Melbourne University Press, 2003) 118.

[105] Far and away the best account of this episode is in Stuart Macintyre and Anna Clark, *The History Wars* (Carlton, Victoria, Melbourne University Press, 2003).

[106] Don Watson, *Recollections of a Bleeding Heart. A Portrait of Paul Keating PM* (Milsons Point, NSW, Vintage, 2003 edn) 181.

was to claim that white atrocities against Indigenous Peoples were exaggerated if not fictitious. There was a leftist bias running through the history establishment – in universities and in cultural institutions. Windschuttle and Blainey courted controversy – and were rarely disappointed. But it was Howard who gave the revisionist cause its political leadership. He did not hesitate to personalise his attack. Keating's ambitions were sinister; he was attempting a 'heist on Australian nationalism' and one of his tools was a 'negative, simplistic rewriting of history'.[107] In particular, Keating was 'intent on marginalising the liberal/conservative contribution to Australian history and the Australian achievement'.[108] Howard spoke up specifically for the reputation of Robert Menzies, but more ambitiously for Old Australia and for the values that all Australians held dear. Again, he positioned himself as the spokesman of the majority – and of the story the majority liked to tell themselves about their past.

Howard argued that he was the champion of the 'facts' against 'interpretation'; he had looked at the Australian balance sheet and he had found it in healthy surplus; it was now time to tell that positive story and to protect the nation from the 'professional purveyors of guilt'. This was authentic Howard: a plain-speaking man articulating common sense. But it also flew in the face of what a generation of Australian historians knew to be the case: history was not revealed truth; facts were contestable; and interpretation was not an optional extra, it was an obligation. But it was not easy to persuade the listeners of talkback radio to engage with the subtleties of the seminar room: Howard had judged his audience well and he knew that it yearned for the certainty and reassurance of a positive national narrative. Don Watson, who had trained as an historian, was left to lament that 'the need to win is greater than the need to reason, and ignorance far outweighs understanding; the debate, therefore, quickly takes on the farcical characteristics of the Inquisition or the Marx Brothers'.[109]

Howard continued to prosecute the History Wars in office. His campaign was made more difficult because the state governments – dominated by the ALP – controlled most of the levers of educational policy. But in federal government his revisionism met little resistance. Its advocates were promoted to the boards of the national cultural institutions; its followers developed new history curriculums; and the new National Museum of Australia – initially an exponent of a multifaceted, questioning version of the Australian story – was ultimately put on a shorter ideological rein.[110]

The debates over the Republic, Australian history and multiculturalism do not run neatly along party lines. Indeed, individuals straddled the debates

[107] John Howard, 'A Reflection on the National Identity Debate' (13 December 1995).

[108] Howard, 'Mr. Keating's Mirage' in *Proceedings of the Samuel Griffith Society* (1994) 3, ch 7.

[109] Don Watson, *Recollections of a Bleeding Heart. A Portrait of Paul Keating PM* (Milsons Point, NSW, Vintage, 2003 edn) 374.

[110] The National Museum proved to be one of the Government's trickier targets. Successive reviews did not generate the results the administration might have preferred. But the 'established' narrative of Australian history did, over time, secure greater prominence in the exhibits.

uncomfortably. Peter Costello, Howard's Treasurer, illustrates the point. He was a reluctant republican who ultimately supported a Yes vote in 1999. But he openly questioned government policy on multiculturalism, inviting Muslims unhappy with Australian values to go somewhere more in tune with their beliefs. And so John Howard was not able to command consistent and disciplined support for his social conservatism. But his counterattack against Keating's cosmopolitan vision reshaped Australian politics. He gave a voice – a plain-speaking voice – to a discontented, alienated constituency nostalgic for old certainties and fearful for its place in the new Australia. His assault on Keating was carefully constructed: he set out a series of mutually supportive policy positions which collectively constituted a coherent ideology. The Republic need not have been part of that construct. He might have chosen to regard it as a second order issue, one on which his own party was split. This would have been personally difficult for him: it would have been painful for him to preside over a divorce from the Crown. But Keating's promotion of the Republic gave the issue a symbolic value for Howard. The Republic was emblematic of the whole progressive agenda: attack the Republic and one would be launching an assault on that wider agenda. Conversely, a conservative alliance which rallied behind his critique of multiculturalism, reconciliation and revisionist history might just swing behind a defence of the current constitutional order. And so for reasons both principled and pragmatic Howard wove his constitutional conservatism into his grander ideological assault on Keating's Big Picture.

IX. Where Next for Republican Australia?

Two decades on from the referendum, some of the republican wounds have healed. The ARM staggered but did not fall and it ultimately re-emerged as a 'member-led organisation' with Peter FitzSimons, the high profile writer, as its chair. The ALP has remained committed to the cause; before its return to power in 2007, it said that it would test support for a Republic in a plebiscite in its first term, something it neglected to do. Support for the general proposition of an Australian Republic has fluctuated in opinion polls but the moment has never seemed right for another referendum. In 2015, Bill Shorten, then ALP leader, pledged a new vote *by 2025*. The Party's 2019 National platform had a modest pledged tucked away on page 209 of its commitments:

> Modernising our constitution also entails a transition to an Australian Republic, with an Australian head of state, who can fully represent our traditions, values and aspirations as a nation. Labor will hold a national vote to give every Australian voter a voice in the process of becoming a republic with an Australian Head of State. If the result is yes, Labor will consult with the Australian people, political parties and the States and Territories as to the form the Republic should take. A member of the Labor Ministry will promote community debate about the advantages and disadvantages of various republican models. When the detailed constitutional changes are prepared Labor will initiate an appropriate secondary referendum under section 128 of the Constitution.

Whatever other choices the party had made, it had clearly decided against poetry as a vehicle for its vision. But long before the ALP had alighted on this stolid prose Turnbull, *mirabile dictu*, had returned to centre stage, first as Liberal leader and then Prime Minister. Looking back on the campaign, Malcolm Turnbull did not think the ARM missed any tricks of consequence but they were undone by the rifts in Republican ranks, especially the divides between those who favoured indirect election and those who advocated popular election of the President.[111] One can understand why. Indeed, is anyone willing to risk a re-run of the November 1999 debacle in the foreseeable future?

It is perfectly possible that nothing will happen for a long time. Successive Prime Ministers have relegated the issue to the second order. Republicans do their best to keep their cause in the public eye and they periodically reheat old controversies with their adversaries in the ACM.[112] But for the moment this is no more than a sideshow on the margins of politics. There is no presenting problem: the day-to-day duties of a head of state are performed by the Governor-General; and the Queen's visits have been infrequent and well-received. The country is, in effect, a crowned republic: civic life bears little if any reminder that Australia is a monarchy. To borrow an analogy from Greg Craven, Australians' attitude towards their constitution is comparable to proof of the existence of God. A believer sees the works of God and has faith in His existence. A citizen sees that the country is peaceable and stable and concludes that its constitutional arrangements, though mysterious, must be sound. Unless a Prime Minister wishes to invest political capital on a gamble with a new referendum, there is every reason to believe that things will remain as they are for some time to come. It was once a maxim that Republicans would have their chance at the start of a new reign but even that seems uncertain now. And with Messrs Keating and Howard now in retirement the country seems, for the moment, less preoccupied by its cultural divides.[113]

This does not mean that republicans have been idle. On the contrary, they have been engaged in a perpetual search for the lessons from 1999. Malcolm Turnbull's conclusion is that the ARM made the right choices and they did not miss any tricks of consequence: the Republic failed because Australia did not want to back indirect election and it would have been irresponsible to have backed direct election.[114] Others discern new ways forward.

In 2003–04, a Senate Inquiry chaired by Nick Bolkus achieved the appearance of progress for the republican cause without making any substantive difference to the constitutional landscape. It came down in favour of plebiscites and constitutional education. The Government did not feel the need to respond to it.

[111] Malcolm Turnbull, interview with the author 10 March 2006 and correspondence with the author July 2020.

[112] See, eg, the furore over whether God Save the Queen should be played at the Commonwealth Games in Melbourne in February 2006.

[113] See, eg, Judith Brett's analysis of the Rudd Government after 12 months: 'Comment' (2008) 39 *The Monthly* 8–11.

[114] Malcolm Turnbull, interview with the author, 10 March 2006.

George Williams, a constitutionalist close to the ALP, has argued that the solution lies in engagement. He has advocated a fast-paced, community-based approach in which citizens are genuinely consulted about the way forward. He prays in aid the success of the public consultation in Victoria over state legislation on human rights. Sceptics questioned whether the public would pay attention but the six-month programme designed by Williams generated genuine interest and more than 2,500 public submissions. The commitment of the Victorian premier to take a rapid decision on the outcome may have helped to persuade citizens to take the process seriously. Turnbull was unpersuaded when this approach was put to him: the underlying issues would remain and no more than a tiny fraction of the population would ever participate in such exercises.

A quite different path has been advocated by John McMillan, formerly a professor of administrative law and Commonwealth Ombudsman. Analysing the results of past constitutional referendums he points to the obstacle that all progressive proposals have to overcome: the undecided and the ill-informed are more likely to vote No because they do not understand the proposition before them. He welcomes the prospect of improved civic education, but he points out that there is a simpler way through which is more likely to allow constitutional reform to proceed. If compulsory voting for referendums were to be abandoned propositions would be approved or rejected by those who had engaged with the questions and who felt sufficiently motivated to vote one way or the other; the Don't Knows would stay at home. The compulsory voting requirement is in statute law and so it may be lifted by Parliament. McMillan's argument is logical and his analysis of the referendum record incontrovertible. But he offers no guidance on how a government might avoid the charge that it was manipulating the voting system to usher in changes which would not command the support of a majority of the eligible electorate.[115]

If we turn from questions of process to the substance of the issue, it is far from clear that republicans are any further forward. There is a greater spirit of comity amongst them and the ARM is now open to different republican solutions. But the underlying choices are every bit as difficult and the answers offered by republicans every bit as discordant. Keep it simple, said Bob Hawke; don't over-intellectualise the question or link it to extraneous issues. Offer the Australians the chance to vote on becoming a republic *after the present reign is concluded*. That, he argued, would have mobilised popular support for the cause and would have paid due respect to the monarch for her service to the Australian people.[116] The political calculation behind the move is clear: an early move against the Queen, who remains popular, might be criticised as disrespectful. Prince Charles is more vulnerable. But whether it would be deemed respectful to move against Charles in the immediate

[115] John McMillan, 'Constitutional Reform – or Constitutional Delusion?' (2003) 14(5) *Public Law Review* 5–9.

[116] Bob Hawke, interview with the author, 14 March 2006.

aftermath of his mother's death must be a moot point. Contrast Hawke's prescription with Mark McKenna's pleas for an inspirational rallying cry for the nation. The monarchical symbolism should go; to be replaced by the symbolism of the modern republic as expressed in a new, bolder preamble.[117] The Republicans are not yet in a position, if they ever will be, to move decisively in the event of the Queen's death.

Optimists speak of a third way which will unite minimalists and direct electionists. A hybrid model will emerge, giving the public a say in their choice of president while protecting the Westminster system against a latter day bonapartist. But no such model has yet been described and attempts to do so have generally foundered when their advocates try to codify the Governor-General's reserve powers or to shift the balance of power between the Senate and the House of Representatives. The search for a hybrid solution continues, but in all likelihood a second referendum will be run either on a spruced-up version of the ARM's model or on a directly elected presidency. The polls confirm the popularity of the latter but the minimalists remain convinced that support for it would collapse during a campaign. What is more, many of them would seek to bring down the proposition to save the Westminster system: this time the minimalists, not the real republicans, would enter the ACM's grateful embrace.

Polling data on attitudes towards the Republic remains contradictory.[118] Three polls in April – May 2008 were open to quite different interpretation. But look at the Australian Election Study and the opponents of change have reason to take comfort: support for a Republic has slipped from its highpoint at the 1998 federal election (66 per cent) to a low of 49 per cent at the 2019 election.[119] These results should be interpreted with caution: the Republic has not been a significant electoral issue for some 20 years and neither the Republicans nor their opponents command intense support for their cause. It is unclear what will happen if or when the issue returns to centre stage.

Australia's political class is predominantly republican and constitutionally conservative. The electorate as a whole is predominantly republican and distrustful of its political class; consequently it expresses itself as open to radical, populist change to keep politicians in check. It remains to be seen whether such radicalism would survive a referendum campaign, let alone the scrutiny of the governing elite. It is all too easy to see how the fractures within the electorate – on questions of national identity as much as on constitutional reform – would reopen. For

[117] NLA, CCF, 6.9.5, speech by Mark McKenna, 6 February [1999].

[118] The discussion on the course of republicanism until 2009 owes much to John Warhurst, 'The Trajectory of the Australian Republic Debate', *Papers on Parliament, No 51, June 2009* at www.aph.gov.au/Senate/~/~/link.aspx?_id=5AA687831IBD423EB1E8AF076AF07CF0&_z=z (last accessed 21 May 2020).

[119] Sarah Cameron and Ian McAllister, 'Trends in Australian Political Opinion. Results from the Australian Election Study 1987–2019' (Australian National University). Respondents were asked if they favoured a Republic.

as long as there is this misalignment between the constitutional ambitions of the elite and the electorate, it seems best to bear in mind Gough Whitlam's dictum: in Australia, the way of the reformer is hard.[120]

X. Constitutional Change and National Identity

The Republican decade in Australia might be used by a cautious politician to explain why a cocktail of identity politics and constitutional reform should be avoided at all costs. But this chapter has shown that the lessons from this episode are more complicated. Some are generic; some are peculiar to Australia.

Keating was a politician attracted by big ideas and confident in his ability to realise them. He had huge ambitions for his country and he sought to bring about change in the way Australia earned its living, change in the way Australian communities related to one another, change in the way Australians saw their place in the world – and in the way in which they imagined their future. He knew that there were dangers in advancing quickly on such a broad front and so he seemed to slacken the pace on the Republic, as if waiting for the nation to catch up. But the shortness of the election cycle – just three years – and the weakness of the ALP's grip on power drove him forward. Change on this scale and at this speed – change which puts the very character of a country in play – encourages a reaction. It came in the unlikely form of John Howard, whose style was the antithesis of the flamboyant, stylish Prime Minister. But Howard was able to galvanise a formidable intellectual and political challenge to Keating, drawing on the reserves of alienation and bitterness generated by the Prime Minister's controversial agenda.

It seems improbable that Keating made a conscious choice that the Republic should symbolise his reforms. But it soon took on that status and he was not troubled by its elevation. It neatly expressed his desire to modernise Australian identity. But the Republic was, at core, a change to a political institution, whereas Australians' sense of themselves is predominantly about their social relations and their bond to an ancient continent. The political manifestations of Australian identity had changed over the course of the century – God Save the Queen had eventually given way to Advance Australia Fair; Empire Day had ceded pride of place to Australia Day before it expired altogether; and the oath of allegiance had been modernised. But these were slow changes, often the subject of controversy. And civic culture remained etiolated and sickly: citizenship ceremonies for new citizens were understated affairs and civics education in schools had been abandoned between the wars. It is almost as though Britain's withdrawal from its Dominion's life had been too smooth: Australia had not had to struggle for its

[120] Cited by George Winterton, 'Presidential Powers under Direct Election' in John Warhurst and Malcolm Mackerras (ed), *Constitutional Politics. The Republic Referendum and the Future* (St Lucia, Qld, University of Queensland Press, 2002) 227.

independence and it had not acquired the potent symbols of liberation. Britain had willingly quit the scene, leaving a void behind it.[121]

Keating's ambition was to fill this void with the symbolism of the Republic. This was doubly ambitious. To succeed, the Australian sense of self would have had to take on a new, more political character. But the ploy also assumed that Australians would embrace the politics of symbolism. For a notoriously practical people, this was an optimistic assumption. Throughout the Republican decade critics asked what substantive difference a republic would make. At the Constitutional Convention one delegate protested at republican attempts to stiffen Australian national identity:

> I am not one of those people who believes Australia suffers from an identity crisis. I believe that the Australian identity is so distinct and our shared values so robust, and so many of our achievements such a legitimate source of pride, that we don't need the seemingly endless hand wringing and navel gazing that occurs.[122]

His prescription for Australia was of a quite different order: Australians would feel better about themselves if the balance of payments was to improve, if the national debt were reduced, if its businesses competed more successfully in Asia – and if the Wallabies were to beat the All Blacks more often. John Howard had his sights set on a similar target when he condemned the 'cultural dieticians' who aspired to a new Australia, reborn, revitalised and reimagined. Theirs was a prescription vulnerable to caricature.

Howard's critique of the Republic might have led him to eschew the politics of national identity. But he has been every bit as determined as Keating to define Australian character and to extol Australian virtues. He tried to express an Australian creed; to articulate a set of values which all share – or should be brought to share. But he chose to do so in prosaic terms, addressing the people in a voice he hoped would resonate with them. Like Keating, he sought to underpin his version of Australian identity with a programme of civics education. Like Keating he tried to capture Australian identity in constitutional form. Like Keating he failed. The preamble he concocted with Les Murray earned widespread scorn. But behind the laboured text lay an ambition not so far apart from Keating's: to give enduring expression to what it was to be Australian at the dawn of a new millennium.

Keating and Howard may well have accepted the diagnosis of the Civics Experts Group that diversity was a national strength but it might not be a *civic* strength:

> difference may mean competing claims from claimants who have little faith in common citizenship … Australians have a better grasp of the ethics of tolerance and diversity

[121] John Hirst has written with particular insight on Australian civic culture and national identity. See, eg, 'The conservative case for an Australian Republic' (1991) 35(9) *Quadrant* 279. Donald Horne argued that Australia needed to construct a modern definition of Australian civic beliefs – replacing the outdated British legacy. See, eg, 'Out of empire, into what?' *Sydney Morning Herald* (8 July 1993).

[122] Geoffrey Hourn, *Constitutional Convention, Report of the Constitutional Convention. Old Parliament House Canberra. 2–13 February 1998. Volume 3. Transcript of Proceedings. Week One, 2–6 February 1998* (1998) 279.

> than of civics. Their capacity to recognise and accept difference outstrips their grasp of the decision-making processes whereby differences are negotiated and resolved.[123]

But it is one thing to diagnose the problem and another to alight on the three core values to be inculcated into the young. Democracy, social justice and ecological sustainability are all well and good but it is far from clear why they should be the foundation of a new Australian citizenship or why a committee of three experts should feel able to prescribe this remedy for the nation. One of the lessons of the Republican decade is that national identity is not readily malleable. Attempts to mould it, not least attempts to mould it through constitutional change, must be sympathetic to the national character – and they must be prosecuted slowly, deliberately and deftly.

Paul Kelly has taken this analysis further in his commanding survey of the period 1991 to 2007, the years of the Keating and Howard Prime Ministerships. In strategic terms he regards this as fundamentally a bipartisan episode, in which both Prime Ministers favoured de-regulation, the opening of the economy to competition and an inclusive egalitarian ethic. Both concluded that if Australia was to make a success of diversity, it needed to fashion a singular identity. Here, of course, they differed. As Kelly comments, Keating chose the riskier course:

> He dreamt of a better Australia but his identity project was liable to many interpretations. It was offensive to those who disagreed with him and risky given the Australian public's suspicion of the motives of politicians. Keating's identity improvisation was pursued too often with reckless regard for his electoral health. This was Keating as national therapist. He hoped that his vision – a cultural renewal amid a more dynamic economy – would carry the people across the psychological impasse that lay between themselves and their future.[124]

[123] *Whereas the People … Civics and Citizenship Education. Report of the Civics Expert Group* (Canberra, Australian Government Publishing Service, 1994) 15.

[124] Paul Kelly, *The March of Patriots. The struggle for modern Australia* (Melbourne University Press, 2009) 151.

5

'Power to The People'?: The UK Constitution After Blair

Having considered the Canadian and Australian exercises in using constitutional reform to re-engineer national identity, we now return to conclude the British story. By the time Gordon Brown became British Prime Minister most of the fundamental reforms in which he had a personal interest had already been undertaken. But the Blair administrations had expended little energy on providing the electorate with an overarching narrative for its reforms, let alone on explaining the significance of the reforms for the future of Britain or the other nations of the Union. The period from 2007 until Brown's defeat in 2010 was in good part the tidying of loose ends left behind by the departing Blair. Indeed, as we will see, the whole period since 2007 to the present day has been profoundly influenced by the reforms of Blair's first term. Only one issue – Brexit – broke that pattern and did so decisively.

We will first consider reform under Brown and, more briefly, in the decade that followed. Then we will allow ourselves to speculate briefly on what might come next for the British constitution. The chapter closes with an assessment of public engagement in New Labour's reforms.

I. Brown Arrives

Gordon Brown's commitment to constitutional reform had intermittently been on public view during his 10 years at the Treasury. But he was one of the few in the New Labour project who had pressed for an integrated reform programme underpinned by a coherent rationale. The case he made in his first Charter 88 lecture was repeated in a little noticed speech shortly after the 1997 election and was set out again in the months before he finally became Prime Minister in June 2007. This was, of course, no news to the constitutional reform lobby. The maximalists, as I have termed them in chapter two, had been disappointed by the piecemeal nature of reform under Tony Blair. But they kept the maximalist flame alight, waiting for Brown to enter into his inheritance. The centrepiece of their efforts was the Power Inquiry which got underway in 2004, prompted in part by anxiety at the exceptionally low turnout at the 2001 general election. Its final report came in 2006 when it pressed for decentralisation of power, some form of proportional voting system and the lowering of the voting age to 16. Tony Blair's spokesman was non-committal at the conclusion of the Inquiry. David Cameron, the new leader of the Conservative Party gave one of the keynote addresses at the May 2006 conference to herald the report, as did Sir Menzies Campbell, then leader of the Liberal Democrats. Labour was represented by Ed Miliband, who had only just made it onto the Labour frontbench. The warning was clear: if Brown were to ignore this agenda he would disappoint his natural allies and he might even be outflanked by the new Conservative leader.

As it was, Brown was emphatic that constitutional reform would be one of priorities of his premiership. National renewal, that New Labour trope of 1997, was dusted off once more. But this time it was to be about much more than institutional renewal: Brown called for a renewal of Britishness itself. Returning to what, for him, was a familiar theme he argued that Britain was a country defined by common values. But those values needed to be better understood, more clearly articulated and more securely grounded. This was to be achieved by establishing a bridge between the values and British history.

To the delight of reformers, Brown's Government took no time in publishing a new prospectus for change. Indeed, the speed of its production was confirmation that Brown's entourage in the Treasury had been moonlighting on constitutional reform in advance of Brown's accession. It fell to the Ministry of Justice stitch the Treasury's output into something coherent. Only the most dim-witted could have missed the message in the prospectus that this administration was going to do things differently from its predecessor. The Green Paper ran through a number of policy positions adopted by the Blair Government and either reversed them or said that they were now under review. Troops would not be deployed without parliamentary approval; the civil service would be put on a statutory footing; special advisers would no longer be able to give orders to civil servants; the role of the Attorney General would be subject to a review. Old favourites were not forgotten: the review of PR would be completed and Government would enact the will of the Commons on Lords reform. Even older favourites were taken down and put back in the spotlight: a Bill of Rights and Duties was again an option, taking Britain on the second stage of a journey begun with the Human Rights Act.

There was a good deal that was new. Experiments in direct democracy would be expanded. For example, public authorities might be required to consult local communities through citizens' juries. Throughout, there was a new emphasis on consultation, discussion and consensus-building. The new reforms would emerge from the people; they would not be handed down from government. But this was not all. The Green Paper closed with a coquettish wink in the direction of the maximalists:

> there is now a growing recognition of the need to clarify not just what it means to be British, but what it means to be the United Kingdom. This might in time lead to a concordat between the executive and Parliament or a written constitution.[1]

[1] *The Governance of Britain* (Cm 7170, July 2007) 62.

Reformers, fearful that the Government's enthusiasm for reform had long since dissipated, could scarcely believe their good fortune.

II. Britishness

There would be a national debate about the nature of Britishness, guided, but not led, by the Government. The objective would be to formulate a statement of British values. For Brown, Britishness was, of course, a return to familiar territory. From 2004 he had given speeches on Britain and the character of the British. Some dismissed this as a tactical manoeuvre on the part of a native of Scotland who was soon to become the Prime Minister of the UK. Others recognised that this was more than an exercise in presentation: he was setting out the principles which he wanted to underpin his premiership. His early intellectual formation as an historian was fundamental to who he was and his approach to the country's future.

Brown was clear that he was in search of a new definition of the nation, rejecting earlier concepts derived from blood, race or territory. He wanted to find the 'common glue' that would hold Britain together in the twenty-first century, allowing a new balance to be struck between diversity and integration. He claimed to have found it in British history. Over the centuries, the British story had been characterised by the quest for freedom, a commitment to fairness and a sense of duty to one another. These three values, he maintained, ran through British history like a golden thread. Why did this matter? Because he wanted these values to be at the heart of British citizenship, defining the duties and freedoms of everybody who chose to be a British citizen. And he wanted to use the concept to generate a policy agenda – for topics as diverse as national community service and the reform of local government.[2]

Commenting on Brown's Hugo Young lecture in December 2005, Timothy Garton Ash took issue with Brown's historical method, with its emphasis on the nobler episodes in Britain's story. But he acknowledged that there was a value in a political leader conjuring up an inspiring vision of the nation: 'I doubt that's who we really are, but it's a great idea for who we should want to be.'[3] Others questioned any attempt to divine common values. Ann Dummett, for example, challenged the suggestion that Britons held values in common: like it or not, the British are diverse and politicians have no choice but to work with what they have got: 'a government cannot create and then impose a sense of national identity: it needs, if considering constitutional change, to make use of existing aspirations and beliefs'.[4]

[2] Gordon Brown, Annual British Council Lecture, 7 July 2004; speech at Institute of Directors (24 November 2005); Hugo Young Memorial Lecture (13 December 2005); speech at Fabian New Year Conference (14 January 2006).

[3] Timothy Garton Ash, *Guardian* (15 December 2005).

[4] Ann Dummett, 'Citizenship and National Identity' in Robert Hazell (ed), *Constitutional Futures* (Oxford, Oxford University Press, 1999) 217–8.

Tariq Modood was equally sceptical, fearing that any statement of British values would either be divisive or it would retreat into blandness. He worried that Brown's project would call into question the plurality of British citizenship. He favoured a looser, evolutionary definition of national identity which would draw all citizens towards the nation rather than excluding them.[5]

Modood's prospectus for Britishness may have had its merits, but it would not have served as the basis for a new national project. Enthusiasts like Jonathan Freedland hankered after a bolder, more uplifting definition of what it was to be British. Inspired by the US, they yearned for nothing less than the rebirth of Britain, a rebirth brought about by a nationalism of ideas which would have caused us to reinvent our institutions, our symbols – and our constitution.[6]

For Freedland, the codification of the British constitution was central to any national project, giving the nation its defining statement of the ideals it holds in common.[7] Brown shared Freedland's admiration for the American model of nation-building but he was not necessarily driven to the same conclusion: it is as though the absence of a codified constitution prompted him to work all the harder to divine the country's shared values.[8] This difference turned on nothing more than a judgement of what was and what was not a practical political proposition. Brown may not have envisaged early codification as a priority, but his interest in Britishness was – and always had been – bound up with his commitment to constitutional reform. He had made this explicit in 2004:

> Take our constitution and all the great and continuing debates about the nature of the second chamber, the relationship of the legislative [sic] to the executive, the future of local and central government. Our approach to resolving each of these questions is governed by what sort of country we think we are and what sort of country we think we should become.[9]

In opposition and in government, Brown set out an overarching rationale for constitutional reform. Until he became Prime Minister these rationalisations were contributions to the debate, but they were marginal to policy-making. It was evidently his intention when he finally became premier to help the British people make sense of the reforms which were transforming their constitution. He wanted to do so by means of a narrative about Britain, its values and its future purpose. That narrative would embrace the reforms already made – and those yet to come.

[5] Tariq Modood, *Guardian* (23 May 2006).

[6] Jonathan Freedland, *Bringing Home the Revolution. How Britain can live the American Dream* (London, Fourth Estate, 1998) 227–9.

[7] ibid, 210–14.

[8] See, eg, Brown, British Council Lecture, 7 July 2004.

[9] ibid.

III. Governance of Britain

In the early days of the Brown premiership the new emphasis on a narrative, a definition of Britishness and an explanation of the prior reforms helped to mask the limited nature of the firm proposals set out by the Government. Perhaps this was consistent with the new emphasis on consultation and on listening, but it was hard to rebut the charge that the individual proposals under consideration did not and could not add up to a coherent programme. What, after all, was the link between circumscribing executive powers over war and the desire to put the civil service on a statutory footing?

If there was a common thread, it was to be found in the work to divine core British values. The ministerial lead on this – and on the Bill of Rights and Responsibilities – was given to the new Lord Chancellor, Jack Straw. As we have seen, Straw was not always the Government's greatest enthusiast for constitutional reform. He had periodically toyed with a Bill of Rights and Responsibilities and he now took up that brief again. Nominally, the same was true of Britishness but in practice he had little time for the project and he delegated the task to Michael Wills, his Minister of State. Wills was a close ministerial ally of the Prime Minister and a fully paid-up constitutional maximalist. He had a double first in history from Cambridge to his name and his doctoral research had been on aspects of British identity. Hence he seized the brief on Britishness with enthusiasm. Constitutional reform, he maintained, was not a side issue, marginal to daily politics.[10] It was about the distribution of power: it was about giving power to the people. He was concerned not just to advance the notion of a statement of British values but to do so in a manner which drew in the British people. Hence he had his officials prepare a deliberative process whereby citizens would be invited to discuss the whole notion of British values and, if supportive, they would then participate in a structured conversation to establish what those values should be.[11] The methods were borrowed, in part, from experiments overseas but they certainly broke new ground in the UK.

The Green Paper which heralded the work said that its purpose was to balance rights and responsibilities in a new national purpose.[12] There were two key questions to answer: how power was to be held to account and how to balance the rights and responsibilities of the citizen. Together this work was to strengthen the country in the face of globalisation. With a following wind, this might have yielded the coherence absent from the Blair reforms and it might have unified the new work on citizenship led by Lord Goldsmith (recently deposed as Attorney General) and the investigation of a Bill of Rights and Responsibilities. The new interest in citizenship picked up on a theme mostly absent from the Blair reforms. It might have

[10] Michael Wills, 'Power to the People' speech (2009).

[11] Author's interviews with Lord Wills (20 April 2020) and Peter Thompson (13 March 2020). See also Michael Wills, 'The politics of identity' speech (24 March 2008).

[12] *The Governance of Britain* (Cm 7170, July 2007), *passim*.

provided the glue to hold together the endeavours of Brown and his colleagues but Goldsmith's work remained semi-detached from the brief given to Straw and Wills. Citizenship was to remain a topic which periodically tempted Labour without ever engaging with it fully. Brown hinted at this in February 2008 when he spoke about the concept of earned citizenship, saying, 'Citizenship is not an abstract concept, or just access to a passport. I believe it is – and must be seen as – founded on shared values that define the character of our country.'[13] But over the long haul it was clear that the Prime Minister's preference was to use Britishness as the adhesive of choice holding the reform agenda together. The capacity of citizenship to unite Britons – old and new – remained largely unexploited by Labour and Brown's project was the poorer for it.

The work on Britishness was pursued with honest endeavour: a constitutional caravanserai travelled the land, seeking views on Britishness; papers were written; views were canvassed; but the work was never concluded.[14] The Constitutional Renewal Bill was deemed something of a damp squib when it was published in the summer of 2008. Work on the Bill of Rights and Responsibilities was hindered by Cabinet hostility towards the project. The Treasury, for example, had little time to spare for a measure which might lead ultimately to justiciable rights in social and economic provision.[15] To make matters worse, Brown's No 10 machine was rarely effective at corralling ministerial efforts.[16] The Prime Minister remained steadfast in his commitment to the cause but inevitably he was distracted by other things, not least the financial crash of 2008 and its aftermath. And the MPs' expenses scandal of 2009 left its mark: his exercise in reimagining the nation required time, space and trust. In the end, he simply ran out of political capital and ran out of time. He ran in the May 2010 general election on a manifesto which had much to say on democratic reform but which begged the question as to why progress has been so modest in the previous three years. Labour lost 90 seats and Brown resigned as Prime Minister after an attempt to remain in office with the help of the Liberal Democrats. They opted instead to enter a coalition with the Conservatives.

It seems unlikely that historians will dwell long on the products of Brown's reform initiatives. Work on the Bill of Rights and Responsibilities was still in train when the Government fell. It had been subject to the same deliberative process as Britishness but the outputs of the assemblies had not been fashioned into a statutory proposal: indeed, there would not have been ministerial support for any such measure.[17] The work on British values was incomplete and had not seized the imagination of the British people, although Brown did briefly, and surprisingly,

[13] Gordon Brown speech on 'Managed migration and earned citizenship' (20 February 2008).

[14] The most substantive output – more about the process than the outcome – was *People and power: shaping democracy, rights and responsibilities* (London. Ministry of Justice, 2009).

[15] Lord Wills, interview with the author, 20 April 2020.

[16] Jack Straw, *Last Man Standing. Memoirs of a Political Survivor* (Basingstoke, Macmillan, 2012) 500.

[17] Lord Wills, interview with the author, 20 April 2020.

enjoy some support from the Daily Telegraph for his endeavours.[18] Goldsmith's citizenship review was completed in good time but it sat oddly, almost a rival narrative to the one offered by Brown himself and the recommendations of his review were not adopted.[19] There was a Constitutional Renewal and Governance Act but it was passed as Parliament cleared the decks for the 2010 general election. And it contained an odd assortment of measures: from reform of the civil service through to changes to the powers of the regulator established in 2009 to clear up the scandal over Parliamentary expenses.

Brown had offered his narrative on the constitutional reforms with which Labour had begun its term in office. His search for a defining theme in Britishness was an attempt to fill the explanatory void left by his predecessor. And it was as likely to succeed as was any retrospective attempt. But the political circumstances could not have been less propitious. The attempt failed. But, as we will see, Brown's own contribution to Britain's constitutional journey was far from finished.

IV. The Coalition and Constitutional Reform

Constitutional reform did not feature prominently in the general election of 2010. But the same may have been said of the elections which immediately preceded it. The government which eventually emerged from the post-election negotiations was itself a novelty in that Britain was not used to coalitions. The coalition agreement had some constitutional echoes of what had gone before plus some pointers to the events to come.[20] The Conservative manifesto had much to say about constitutional reform; indeed at first blush there was a surprising degree of cross-party support for reform.[21] Whether that would be translated into action, time would tell. But it was clear the Conservatives intended to make peace with Labour's reforms.

The coalition agreement spoke of the need to 'clean up Westminster', a reference to the expenses scandal of the preceding year – one in which all parties shared culpability. Devolution caught the eye of some, with a commitment to a commission to address the West Lothian question; and an agreement to devolve further powers to Scotland and Wales. Another commission was to be used to examine the idea of a British Bill of Rights and it was made clear that this was to build on the Human Rights Act rather than to sweep it away. And the prize secured by the Liberal Democrats, if that is not a misnomer, was an agreement that there should be a referendum on the alternative vote (AV) electoral system. Parliaments would,

[18] See, eg, 'Ten core values of the British identity' *Telegraph* www.telegraph.co.uk/comment/telegraph-view/3618632/Ten-core-values-of-the-British-identity.html (last accessed 28 April 2020).

[19] Lord Goldsmith QC, *Citizenship Review. Citizenship: Our Common Bond* (London, 2008).

[20] *The Coalition: our programme for government:* https://assets.publishing.service.gov.uk/government/uploads/system/uploads/attachment_data/file/78977/coalition_programme_for_government.pdf (last accessed 28 April 2020).

[21] *Invitation to Join the Government* (Conservative and Unionist Party, 2010).

in future, last for fixed five-year terms. And there was a commitment, of sorts, to Lords reform.

What did all this add up to? Well, the final agreement was necessarily an act of compromise. The Liberal Democrats must have known that the AV system was loved by few even in their own ranks and that it would succumb to heavy defeat in a referendum, which it did. A commission on a Bill of Rights was convened with a balanced membership – and it duly failed to reach a united conclusion. Further investigation of Lords reform did not suggest to the observer that anybody thought a solution could be found in the near term. And it was not. As for the West Lothian question, it could not be solved without unpicking the devolution settlement and nobody had the political will to attempt that. Indeed, the Conservatives showed little enthusiasm for reopening New Labour's constitutional settlement, if that is what it was. They even showed signs of wanting to steal Labour's clothes much as they would deny it. If one looks at Cameron's speeches on Britishness and the Union they are not so very distant from Brown's own views.[22] Michael Gove, education secretary, sought to conclude the debate over British history and Britishness by formulating a statement of British values which would be woven into the national curriculum in England. Insofar as Britain has experienced battle in the so-called History Wars, the engagements were prompted more by the reform of the curriculum than they were by Brown's attempts to read positive values into British history. As we have seen, Brown's interventions were not welcomed by all, but it was Gove's approach which provoked the stronger resistance from the historical profession. The academy jibbed at what it saw as a return to an elitist narrative based on the lives of kings and queens.[23] It is probably fair to say that the efforts of the Royal Historical Society and others tempered some ministerial plans for reform of the school curriculum and the final diktat on values was inoffensive. As of 2014 schools had a duty to promote actively the 'fundamental British values of democracy, the rule of law, individual liberty and mutual respect and tolerance for those with different faiths and beliefs'.[24]

More notable in the long-term was the increased accent on Euro-scepticism in the Conservative manifesto, which found an echo in the Coalition's Programme for Government. The Conservatives, alert to the risk that they might be outflanked by UKIP pledged that there would be no further transfers of power to Europe without a referendum; that some powers would be restored to Westminster; that they would reject a federal Europe; that they would never enter the Eurozone; and they would seek to renegotiate the 2007 Lisbon Treaty which had provided the European Union with a new constitutional foundation. Perhaps most telling of all was the tone of the Conservative manifesto when it came to

[22] See, eg, Cameron's speech on the Union at Dynamic Earth in Edinburgh [nd] and Oliver Duggan, 'David Cameron: it's time to stop being 'bashful about our Britishness' *Daily Telegraph* (15 June 2014).

[23] See, eg, Richard J Evans, 'The Wonderfulness of Us' in *London Review of Books* (17 March 2011); 'It's old-school and old-fashioned: historians turn their fire on Gove' *The Observer* (17 February 2013); and 'Presidential letter', *Royal Historical Society Newsletter*, new series (13 May 2014).

[24] HM Government press release: *Guidance on promoting British values in schools* (27 November 2014).

Europe. It declared that 'the steady and unaccountable intrusion of the European Union into almost every aspect of our lives has gone too far'. And the policy on Europe appeared under the heading 'restore democratic control'. It was not so far removed from the slogan which would help win the Brexit referendum in 2016: 'take back control'.

But before they reached the 2015 election the Conservatives had good reason to be concerned about the coherence of the Union. In the Scottish election of 2011, the SNP won a majority for the first time and they soon proceeded to demand a referendum on independence. The Westminster government conceded this and the Unionist parties duly assembled a common front to fight off the secessionists. It was decided that Alistair Darling, Chancellor in the Brown administration, should lead the No vote campaign. When the referendum was called, few thought that it would be such a close-run thing. It is, after all, a political nostrum that it is easier to defeat a proposition than to succeed in standing one up. And this move by the SNP came within two decades of the establishment of a Scottish parliament while the process of devolution was still continuing. In early 2012 it was estimated support for independence was in the range 32 to 38 per cent.

But the polls tightened as the vote approached in September 2014. So much for George Robertson's oft-quoted claim that devolution would 'kill nationalism stone dead'.[25] The most striking intervention in the contest came late on when Gordon Brown returned to centre stage to articulate the positive case for the Union. His speech was a précis, albeit a vigorous one, of views put forward in his book published earlier that year *My Scotland, Our Britain*.[26] He argued it was perfectly possible to be both a loyal Scot and a believer in Britain. To withdraw from the Union, especially when further powers were likely to be devolved to Scotland, would be a pointless sacrifice. He acknowledged the post-war decline in attachment to Britain in Scotland but he maintained that Scots could find attachment to Britain if the UK could offer the world 'a model for how a more integrated globe that respects cultural diversity can work best'. The Scots were uniquely well placed to give to the UK their traditions of solidarity and sharing, helping Britain to 'lead the way in making sense of globalisation'.[27] He went on to define Britishness: 'at its best [it] is a passion for liberty matched by a strong sense of duty and social responsibility and a belief in fair play or fairness'.[28] In his speech in the latter stages of the referendum campaign he developed these themes into a rousing appeal for his compatriots to back the union for reasons which were both moral and practical. But more than that he bullied Unionist party leaders into a vow that there would

[25] Brian Taylor, the BBC's political editor in Scotland, claimed on 4 February 2015 that Robertson had originally made the prediction to him and it was specifically the SNP who would be killed off: www.bbc.co.uk/news/uk-scotland-31129382 (last accessed 29 April 2020).

[26] Gordon Brown, *My Scotland, Our Britain* (London, Simon and Schuster, 2014).

[27] ibid, 37.

[28] ibid, 195.

be further devolution to Scotland within a year. It is impossible to judge the impact of his intervention but the No cause emerged victorious by 55 to 45 per cent. Rancour was to follow. There was a spat over whether the referendum had resolved the issue for good. The Prime Minister, David Cameron provoked disunity amongst the victors when he pledged to introduce English votes for English legislation, the shorthand for curbing the powers of Scottish MPs to vote on English matters at Westminster. This ultimately culminated in relatively minor changes to Parliamentary procedure after the 2015 election and interest in the question subsequently dissipated. But the argument for a second independence referendum continues.

V. Brexit

This book does not seek to address Brexit at length. Instant histories of the Brexit story have already been written and it is too early to provide a considered account of its impact on the British constitution.[29] At the time of writing (April 2020) the final round of negotiations to determine the UK's future relationship with the EU has not yet begun and the COVID-19 crisis may yet delay its completion beyond the end of 2020. But our story cannot be left as though the referendum of 2016 had not even happened. To bring the British story to a close for now we should briefly conclude the narrative and then offer some observations on what the future might hold for the British constitution.

The coalition government duly ran its five years and to the surprise of some ended not in another hung parliament but in a narrow victory for the Conservatives. Consequently, David Cameron was faced with the consequences of the gamble he had taken in his election manifesto. In the face of renewed Conservative disunity on Europe and the electoral insurgency from UKIP, he promised that Britain would have an in-out referendum on membership of the European Union in 2016. As we all now know the referendum was won by 52–48 per cent by those campaigning for British exit from the EU. And Cameron quit the stage.

Looking at the immediate consequences of Brexit it would be hard to argue that New Labour brought about an enduring and stable constitutional settlement. Wherever one looks one can see centrifugal forces straining at the Union. The Scots voted by a clear majority to remain in the EU and their First Minister has taken the UK's departure from the EU as reason enough to press for a second independence referendum. The Johnson government has denied the request but it is hard to see that that will be an end of the matter.

At one point during the Brexit negotiations the then Prime Minister, Theresa May, said it would be unthinkable to have a customs border between Great Britain

[29] For a good, quick history, see Kevin O'Rourke, *A Short history of Brexit* (Pelican, London, 2019).

and Northern Ireland but that is effectively what we now have. And as Jonathan Powell has argued, Britain will diverge from the EU's regulatory regime over time and that in turn will cause Loyalists to feel that their British identity is under challenge.[30] Meanwhile the remarkable electoral progress of Sinn Fein in the Republic must enhance the prospect of a Border Poll on the future of Ireland, north and south.

It is most difficult to foresee what will become of Wales. Labour's reverses in Wales in the 2019 general election were less severe than in Scotland and the north of England and the nationalist cause commands modest support in Cardiff. It may be that the most likely outcome will be that the settlement in Wales will hold for the foreseeable future. And what of England? We will return shortly to the question of Englishness but the Johnson Government will undoubtedly face pressure to devolve additional powers to the North as part of its reward to those constituencies which 'lent the Conservatives their vote' in the 2019 election.

More generally, the Johnson administration stood on a manifesto proposing potentially far-reaching constitutional change to be considered by a commission.[31] Some on the Left have seen this as a potential threat to everything from the independence of the judiciary through to the Human Rights Act itself. This may have motivated some when the manifesto was drafted and it would be foolish to discount action on this front. If the commission is appointed, there must be a risk that it will 'inadvertently end up "fighting the last war" over Brexit'.[32] But it is perhaps more likely, not least in the light of the COVID-19 crisis, that action on this front will be modest.

The referendum data make for painful reading whichever side one supported in 2016. They show a country divided: by nation; by age; by education; by city against country. Overlay on them the results of the subsequent general election and one begins to see a country where the old loyalties of party and of class are losing their hold. Britain is becoming a country of nationalisms, not the least of which is the English variant. If that were not sobering enough, add in the findings of the 2019 Future of England Survey. A majority of Leave voters in England, Scotland and Wales expressed the view that violence towards MPs was a 'price worth paying' for Brexit. Majorities of Remain voters in all three countries were of the same view if violence towards MPs were to secure Remain. There is little comfort to be found in the observation that the majorities favouring violence were smaller amongst the Remain camp than the advocates of leaving.[33]

[30] Jonathan Powell: 'DUP justifiably aggrieved over Brexit deal' *Irish Times* (19 October 2019).

[31] *Get Brexit Done. The Conservative and Unionist Party Manifesto* (London, Conservative and Unionist Party, 2019) 48.

[32] The warning comes from Meg Russell and Alan Renwick, 'The government's proposed constitution, democracy and rights commission: what, why and how?' in *UK in a Changing Europe* https://ukandeu.ac.uk/the-governments-proposed-constitution-democracy-and-rights-commission-what-why-and-how/ (last accessed 30 April 2020).

[33] Richard Wyn Jones and Ailsa Henderson, 'Future of England Survey reveals public attitudes towards Brexit and the union' https://www.centreonconstitutionalchange.ac.uk/news-and-opinion/future-england-survey-reveals-public-attitudes-towards-brexit-and-union (last accessed 1 May 2020).

VI. What Next for the British Constitution?

There is a good reason why historians write about the past rather than speculating about the future. And so my thoughts about the future of the British constitution will be hedged around with caution and offered tentatively. Since I am writing this at the height of the COVID-19 crisis it would be particularly foolish to claim to predict the future with any confidence.

That said, it would be a surprise if certain trends were not to continue into the future. We are living at a time of increased voter volatility where the dominance of the two major parties is no longer assured. Indeed, the identity of those parties is undergoing fundamental change. Increasingly, Labour is the party of the young and of the more highly educated. And this identity has been buttressed by Labour's emergence, after much prevarication, as a Europhile party. For their part, the Conservatives are now emphatically a Eurosceptic party attached more to the countryside than to the large conurbations and they are the party of, and for, the older electorate. We will have to wait and see if the British constitution has the flexibility needed to cope with this de-alignment and re-alignment of party loyalties.[34]

One feature of the Brexit trauma which must call this into question. In assessing the damage caused to the British political system by Brexit, Jonathan Sumption has drawn attention to the strain it has placed on the country's 'shared political culture'. which he defines as 'the mutual acceptance that the constitution must be made to work in the interests not just of one side, but of the system as a whole'.[35] There must be some doubt as to whether this understanding – which is essential in a country without a codified constitution – can be recovered after the bitterness that has characterised the last four years.

Britain is now characterised by multiple nationalisms and the poll data do little to encourage the notion that Britishness has a commanding hold on the affections of any significant element of the population. The only exception to that is that ethnic minorities continue to find Britishness a more accommodating identity than they do Englishness, which remains freighted with the characteristics of narrow, ethnic nationalisms.

In 1991 Hugh Kearney noted that 'all but a small proportion of the inhabitants of the UK accept the term "British" when applied to them even if they do not apply it to themselves without some thought'.[36] His assessment was probably fair at the time, but by the end of the decade polls were telling a different story. Just 27 per cent of Welsh and 28 per cent of Scots said that they identified with Britain.[37] Surveys continued to pick up a dual affiliation – to England, Scotland, Wales *and*

[34] For the best discussion of voter volatility in Britain, see Edward Fieldhouse et al, *Electoral shocks. The volatile voter in a turbulent world* (Oxford, Oxford University Press, 2020).

[35] Jonathan Sumption, 'Brexit and the British constitution: on the Reflections on the Last Three Years and the Next Fifty' (2020) 91(1) *Political Quarterly* 107–15.

[36] Kearney, 'Four Nations or One' in Bernard Crick (ed), *National Identities* 3.

[37] MORI opinion poll (Sept 1999) for *The Economist* (4 November 1999).

to Britain, but in Scotland, in particular, there was growing evidence of a sense of nation which had little place for Britain.[38] Research by the Commission for Racial Equality (CRE) in 2005 confirmed that the Scots and Welsh were identifying more with their own nation than with Britain. But their reference group did not see the two identities as incompatible: it was simply that they reached more naturally for one rather than the other.[39] Britain was becoming less relevant to their lives. They were not rejecting it: it was simply slipping away from them.

The more that researchers probed popular understanding of Britishness, the more elusive it seemed to be. The CRE group reported that they rarely thought about it, finding it a 'tricky' concept. Ethnic minorities saw Britishness as descriptive of a multicultural, multi-ethnic society.[40] For a country which had been around for almost 300 years, British identity at the turn of the century was peculiarly plastic. Britishness was a capacious, flexible concept, capable of taking on new meanings. This may have been indicative of its potential – or of its weakness – but the debate over its potency was not fully joined during New Labour's first term. When it did attract attention, it did so for reasons that nobody could have expected. The issue was prompted by the terrorist attacks of September 2001 in the US and, particularly by those of July 2005 in the UK. If Muslims born and bred in Britain grew up to bomb their fellow citizens, what did that say about integration? What did it mean for the future of multiculturalism? What was it that British citizens held in common?

When those arguments were confronted during New Labour's second and third terms, they provoked elements of the Left to reconsider the purpose of nations within a modern world. This was uncomfortable territory for some, who retained an attachment to class solidarity in preference to national solidarity. This unease was captured by John Denham when he spoke of the need to *create* a national identity in Britain; he was wary of *rediscovering* it because of the more oppressive episodes in British history. What was needed was something new for the modern world.[41] At the end of the two decades or so since New Labour was first elected to office, liberal thinkers remain in search of a unifying purpose for Britain. That search first began post-war with the decline of Empire, once such a prominent aspect of Britishness. And the quest may have taken on new energy in the wake of Brexit, but it would be hard to argue that it is now much closer to a resolution.[42]

[38] John Curtice, 'Public Opinion and the Future of Devolution' in Alan Trench (ed), *Dynamics of Devolution: The State of the Nations* (Exeter, Imprint Academic, 2005) 124–05, 131. Ann Dummett, 'Citizenship and National Identity' in Robert Hazell (ed), *Constitutional Futures* (Oxford, Oxford University Press, 1999) 220.

[39] Commission for Racial Equality, *Citizenship and Belonging. What is Britishness?* (Commission for Racial Equality, 2005) 37.

[40] ibid, 18, 37. Linda Colley, *Britishness in the 21st Century*, Millennium Lecture at Number 10 (8 December 1999).

[41] John Denham, 'Who do you want to be?' (2005) 117(4) *Fabian Review* 6–8.

[42] For just one recent example, see William Waldegrave, *Three Circles into One* (London, Mensch Publishing, 2019).

David Reynolds has argued for the need for a new, post-Brexit, national narrative, linking our past, present and future. In suggesting how this might be done, he has, above all, suggested that it should be done with a nuance and flexibility wanting in earlier attempts at a national history.[43] Whatever the scholarly merits of Brown's vision of the British nation, his approach did not resonate with the British people. It is true that the breathless attempt to produce an 'answer' minimised his prospects for success but, equally, he overlooked the evidence that his compatriots' attachment to nation was not just about common values arising from our history. As his close political ally, Michael Wills, acknowledged, it was rooted 'in our values mediated through our institutions and our personal and national histories' – and was all the more elusive for that.[44]

One of the most significant questions surrounding Britain's political and constitutional destiny is whether Englishness will assert itself as the dominant identity chosen by citizens who live in, or associate themselves with, England. Bound up with that question is the future course to be steered by the Conservative party. Some would argue that it has already become an English nationalist party: Brexit has demonstrated the electoral advantages of that course. It is worse pausing here to consider the evidence on Englishness because it has not hitherto featured in our discussion of British identities.

Michael Kenny, the leading scholar of Englishness is something of a reluctant witness its rise. He notes the increased salience of identity and culture but adds the rider that they are not fully understood. And although he accepts that progressives regard Britishness as safer than Englishness because the latter is tainted with reactionary connotations, he is quick to add that in recent years there have been manifestations of a less defensive strain of Englishness. He also concedes that in the last 30 years, English tolerance towards their partners in the Unions is beginning to wear thin. In particular, there is growing evidence that the English are resentful that the Scots are getting a preferential deal out of devolution. In short, the evidence of a narrow nationalism in England is now unavoidable. Peter Kellner put it pithily: 'What distinguishes people who call themselves "English" is a passion for keeping other countries at arm's length.'[45]

And our discussion of Englishness should not be restricted to the British context. At its most extreme, Englishness may be seen as one species of the populist nationalisms which have enjoyed such electoral success in the last 15 years in Europe and the US. Whether this movement is one coherent whole with a common ideology remains debatable. The louder that Steve Bannon protests this it is one global movement the more that its diversity becomes apparent.[46] But what does

[43] David Reynolds, *Island Stories* (London, William Collins, 2019).

[44] Michael Wills, interview with the author, 22 May 2020.

[45] This paragraph draws heavily on Michael Kenny, *The Politics of English Nationhood* (Oxford, Oxford University Press, 2014). See also 'English resentment at "privileged" Scots grows' *The Guardian* (23 January 2012).

[46] See Joshua Green, *Devil's Bargain. Steve Bannon, Donald Trump, and the Nationalist Uprising* (New York, Penguin, 2018).

seem to be clear is that the populist nationalisms of recent years spring from a common source among those who have lost out, or feel they have lost out, in the globalised economy. It was this stratum of society which provided Brexit with so many of its foot soldiers in England. It is common in Britain to dismiss the risk from the far right as though the British policy has been inoculated against it. But in the light of Brexit and of the campaigns leading to it there can surely be little room for such complacency. Any remaining belief in British exceptionalism should surely be dispelled by a reading of Eatwell and Goodwin's recent study of populist nationalism.[47] They make a compelling case that the phenomenon – in England and elsewhere – is here to stay and that it represents a significant threat to liberal democracies. Combine this with what they term a crisis of social democracy and the looming global recession and we face a troubling future.

This outlook has prompted some to argue that now is the time to stiffen the defences of liberal democracy in the UK.[48] In other words, we need to seize the moment and to codify our constitution. One can understand the appeal to liberal voters stung by Brexit and now seeking safe harbour in an increasingly perilous world. But it is hard to see how this might come about. The Johnson government is an improbable promoter of codification, not least because it is unclear whether its own commitment to liberal norms is guaranteed. But leaving this aside, the creation of new constitutions typically occurs in the wake of war and revolution. In the absence of such extremities is hard to imagine the circumstances under which any government would commit the necessary political capital and Parliamentary time to codification.

VII. Public Engagement

Our discussion of New Labour's reforms has focussed primarily on high politics: the cast in the drama has been small, their motivations significant and their actions influential. But it would be a caricature to portray the reforms as an elite manoeuvre, executed exclusively by these players in Whitehall and Westminster, away from the public gaze. There was nothing secretive about the initial reform programme: each of its component parts was identified in the 1997 manifesto and, as we have seen, that blueprint was followed sedulously in the first term. Devolution was put to the public in votes in Scotland, Wales, Northern Ireland, London and the North East. Parliament and the public were given the opportunities to comment on draft bills; and changes were made after pre-legislative scrutiny. Not only did the Government ask for the public's views, but it found new ways of so, going beyond the routine of consultation papers and official responses.

[47] Roger Eatwell and Matthew Goodwin, *National Populism. The Revolt against Liberal Democracy* (London, Pelican, 2018).

[48] See, eg, Vernon Bogdanor, *Beyond Brexit. Towards a British Constitution* (London, IB Tauris, 2019).

It might, of course, have chosen to do more. It might have published more of its legislation in draft. It might have resisted the temptation to spring surprises: as Tony Blair himself recognised, to announce the abolition of the office of Lord Chancellor without prior consultation was ill advised. And it might have put greater energy into public education and advocacy. The Government's reticence to generate public debate is apparent in its handling of individual elements of the programme – most obviously human rights – *and* of the programme as a whole. To have provoked debate on the programme New Labour would have had to have had a clear, unifying rationale for its reforms. But as we have seen, the party never came under sustained, political pressure to defend or rationalise the reforms. Individual policies came under attack, and were defended or amended, but the programme itself was rarely challenged, not least because the party itself enjoyed such a long, untroubled ascendancy in the years following Blair's election as leader in 1994. In the absence of external pressure, a clear narrative for the reforms would only have been articulated if it had been in the interest of one group or other within the party to impose a rationale on the catalogue of reforms the party had assembled. But for New Labour pragmatists, the reforms were of secondary importance, rarely objectionable but only fleetingly demanding of attention. The most influential reformers in New Labour ranks, of whom Irvine is the best example, believed in the prosecution of the individual reforms and were sceptical about grand, overarching visions of constitutional renewal. Only the maximalists within the party aspired to a unifying rationale, but their voice was rarely heard.

And so New Labour only began to develop its explanatory story – or stories – long after it had begun to implement its reforms. As Jack Straw acknowledged in 2007: 'We are now having to come to terms with a better and stronger framework for our constitutional changes rather late in the day. Answering a question, "Why are we doing this?" rather late in the day.'[49] As we have seen, Irvine was the first to attempt to retrofit a rationale onto the reforms. His speeches during the first term show him in search of a compelling explanation for the programme. By 2000, he seemed to have accepted that it was necessary to advance a new rationale for the reforms, now identifying the renewal of citizenship as central to the enterprise.[50] Three years later, Falconer, his successor as Lord Chancellor, offered a three-fold rationale: the reforms were calculated to boost the credibility of public institutions; to strengthen public engagement; and to increase trust and accountability.[51] By 2007, Falconer was to argue that the whole programme was animated by egalitarianism.[52] One way or another, the reforms were no doubt about all of the themes selected by Irvine and Falconer, but in the first 10 years of New Labour no single, compelling rationale had emerged.

[49] Jack Straw, interview with the author, 7 January 2007.

[50] Lord Irvine of Lairg, *Human Rights, Constitutional Law and the Development of the English Legal System: Selected Essays* (Oxford, Hart Publishing, 2003) 76. He was subsequently to argue that the renewal of citizenship had been 'the major inarticulate premise' of the programme: Lord Irvine of Lairg, interview with the author, 27 October 2006.

[51] Lord Falconer, Constitution Unit Annual Lecture, University College London, 8 December 2003.

[52] Lord Falconer, 'Foreword' in Andrew McDonald (ed), *Reinventing Britain* (Politico's, London, 2007) v–vi.

Leaving aside the public presentation of their reforms, New Labour faced a more fundamental choice about the public's engagement in its reforms. Did it take the chance offered to it by its astonishing electoral good fortune to realise the most radical change to Britain's constitution for generations? Or did it proceed more slowly, raising understanding of the issues, generating debate and seeking to build popular support for reform? If the Government had taken the latter course it would undoubtedly have had less on the statute book by the end of its first term, but might the reforms have been underpinned by a stronger, more informed popular mandate? Irvine is clear that reformers had an historic chance open to them in 1997 and that the route taken by the Government was not just the quickest one but it was the only one likely to deliver such far-reaching change. Taking the Human Rights Act as an example, he describes it as doing good by stealth: it was important 'not to frighten the children'.[53] His message is clear: a slower, more deliberative process was fraught with risk. But the Government's preferred route was also perilous. By 2002, Irvine was calling – sadly – for a celebration of the Human Rights Act but it was all too easy to understand why the party was ill-attended. The public prospectus for the reforms had invited the conclusion that this was a modest, sensible step which would save litigants' time and money. And so a modest, sensible celebration was the most that might have been expected. But even that could not be held in peace: gatecrashers in the tabloid press tried to break up the party, complaining that the Act was anything but modest and sensible. Having neglected to mount and win a public argument that human rights offered the prospect of renewing British citizenship, the Government struggled to fend off these complaints. And its cause became immeasurably more difficult after 9/11 when it found itself balancing civil liberties and the new threats to national security.

The approach did change under Brown. Michael Wills championed a deliberative process for the statement of values and the Bill of Rights and Responsibilities. But it is striking that his approach was regarded as an exotic eccentricity on his part.[54] The deliberative approach had already been tried and tested, notably in Canada. When budgetary pressures began to bite, Jack Straw wasted no time in identifying the deliberative meetings as a candidate for cuts. But by 2008, the task of engaging the public was all but impossible. The financial crash and its aftermath commanded the headlines. And after his honeymoon with the voters in 2007, when he flirted with the idea of an early election, Brown's political capital drained away. It was all but impossible to engage the electorate in a debate over constitutional theory, still less the arcane search for Britishness. He did succeed in attracting some cross-party support for his endeavours but the whole enterprise was an easy target for Tory opponents who sensed that New Labour's time in office was coming to an end.

[53] Lord Irvine of Lairg, interview with the author, 27 October 2006.
[54] Lord Wills, interview with the author, 20 April 2020.

VIII. Public Reaction to the Reforms

The public may not have been engaged in a debate about the reform programme as a whole but that should not be taken as evidence of public ignorance of, or indifference to, individual reforms. Devolution to Edinburgh undoubtedly resonated with the people of Scotland, who gave emphatic support to the proposition in the 1997 referendum. The results in the polls in Wales and London were more equivocal: they were both won (the first narrowly) on low turnouts. And in the first couple of years that New Labour was in power, polls showed a recovery of confidence in government itself.[55]

Three years after New Labour's election, the polls began to show a more familiar story. The public expressed their unease about sleaze, cash-for-honours and dishonesty on the part of ministers. The executive was too powerful, Parliament too weak – and Britain was becoming less democratic.[56] By 2004, 63 per cent of those polled said that Britain's system of government could be improved, a return to the figure expressing the same view in 1991.[57] New Labour's election in 1997 had temporarily stemmed the long-term decline of trust in government, but the pattern soon reasserted itself.[58]

But if the public was uneasy about the quality of its democratic institutions – and of its politicians – that does not mean that it wanted to roll back the reforms. Early optimism about the legislatures in Scotland and Wales soon dissipated.[59] But the public seems to have interpreted the difficulties in Edinburgh and Cardiff as reason to strengthen the new institutions, not to abandon them. By 2004, 66 per cent of Scots and 49 per cent of the Welsh wanted further devolution from Westminster.[60] Asked to look into the future in 1999, Scottish voters expected the Westminster Parliament to become more marginal in the management of their affairs, a view echoed by the Welsh.[61] Support for independence in Scotland – running at 37 per cent in 1997 – had fallen back to 30 per cent by 2000. But by the end of the New Labour's second term it seems fair to conclude that devolution had had relatively little impact on Scottish or Welsh views on independence, or for that matter on the union. Devolution to Edinburgh and Cardiff continued to command majority support – in England as well as Scotland and Wales.[62] John Major has

[55] Patrick Dunleavy, Helen Margetts, Trevor Smith and Stuart Weir, *Voices of the People* (Politico's, London, 2005) 44 and 46.
[56] ICM – JRRT *State of the Nation 2005* opinion poll (October 2000).
[57] Patrick Dunleavy, Helen Margetts, Trevor Smith and Stuart Weir, *Voices of the People* (Politico's, London, 2005) 46.
[58] ibid, 15.
[59] John Curtice, 'Devolution and Democracy' in John Curtice, David McCrone, Alison Park and Lindsay Paterson, *New Scotland, New Society? Are Social and Political Ties Fragmenting?* (Edinburgh, Polygon, 2002) 146–50.
[60] ICM-JRRT, *State of the Nation 2004* opinion poll (May–June 2004).
[61] MORI opinion poll (September 1999) for *The Economist* (4 November 1999).
[62] John Curtice, 'Public Opinion and the Future of Devolution' in Alan Trench (ed), *Dynamics of Devolution: The State of the Nations* (Exeter, Imprint Academic, 2005) 117–35.

remained true to his original critique of devolution: he deemed it a reckless gamble with the Union. Indeed the subsequent pressure for independence for Scotland has confirmed him in his view. This is understandable, but his line of argument fails to address the possibility that independence would have garnered even more support if each and every move towards home rule had been frustrated.

Evidence of popular attitudes on the other big issues raised by the reform programme – Lords reform, PR and human rights – is more elusive. Either pollsters chose not to address the questions or, if they did, they did not test opinion in a way which allows us to draw firm conclusions on the popular mood. In the absence of sustained public debate on an issue it seems likely that popular opinion remained malleable.[63] The British were not hostile to constitutional reform and there is clear evidence that they favoured devolution to Scotland and Wales. But for the most part they had not been drawn into a debate on how the country was governed and how it might be governed in future.

IX. The Future of Britain

Before considering popular attitudes to Britain, it is worth remembering that the Blair administration did not have much to say about what Britain might mean in future. Britain did not come to the fore until Brown's premiership. Under Blair, devolution was primarily about Scotland and Wales – not Britain. When the Government did invoke Britain, it did so to defend the status quo: devolution would preserve the Union. Devolution would give expression to the plurality inherent in British identity. In Irvine's words:

> Devolution needs courage; but I say that it will forge a new Britain – a strong, multinational, multi-cultural, multi-ethnic country where our strength will come not from uniformity but from our diversity; not from a flattening process of programmed assimilation, but from a democratic renewal through mutual toleration and respect.[64]

In its first term New Labour rarely came under any pressure to develop its thinking about British identity – or identities. The Conservatives did explore the question of Englishness, toying with the notion of an English Parliament, but the Government felt sufficiently confident of its position simply to brush this aside. More troubling for ministers was the evidence, late in the first term, that its supporters were anxious that the influx of asylum-seekers was changing the nature of Britain. The party's private polls even caused some to question whether the issue might cost the

[63] Consider, eg, the evidence on attitudes to PR. Some polls apparently show consistent, majority support for the reform. But it is clear that the public's responses are conditioned by the way in which the question is put to them. See Patrick Dunleavy, Helen Margetts, Trevor Smith and Stuart Weir, *Voices of the People* (Politico's, London, 2005) 31–2, 97.

[64] Lord Irvine of Lairg, *Government's Programme of Constitutional Reform* (London, Constitution Unit, 1998) 12.

Government the next general election. This prompted a response – but on asylum policy, not on the nature of Britain.[65]

Matthew Taylor, one of the most influential voices in No 10 during the first term, recalls devolution as a missed opportunity: 'The thinking had all taken place in Scotland. There had been very, very little thinking at the UK-level about what it meant for the UK. It was just that the Scots had thought about it and they wanted it and so you gave it to them.'[66] But it is worth pausing to ask what might have been done if the Government had chosen, from the outset, to see constitutional renewal as an instrument for changing the way Britain saw itself. After all, the Government's programme in its first term was pregnant with questions about the meaning of Britain. This was an administration committed to the establishment of new national legislatures, devolution within England, the redefinition of Britons' rights and closer relationships with partners in the EU. Add in the strengthening of north-south relations in Ireland and the stirrings of interest in the meaning of citizenship, and it will be clear that the Government might have chosen to construct a vision for a redefined UK. In 2000 Derry Irvine even went so far as to sketch out how this might be done. In one of his periodic attempts to offer a compelling explanation of the programme he even went so far as to suggest that New Labour had always been motivated by a desire to reinvent Britain:

> [The reform programme] is designed to regenerate our national identity. By restoring people's sense of belonging to a country with a coherent vision of its past and its future, we will achieve a better engagement between people and government, and revive people's interest in public affairs … In planning these reforms we had a strong concept of what 'British' means. That gives them their coherence. It is also what will make them work for the people. Our constitutional renewal is a patriotic renewal.[67]

The British, Irvine argued, were a diverse people with a long history, outward-looking and fair-minded, committed to equality before the law and the rule of law. The reforms were consistent with the British character and they would allow British values to be expressed within modern institutions and within a modern citizenship.[68]

Irvine's lecture is important for three reasons. First, it is one of the few occasions when a senior New Labour figure made the intellectual link between the reforms and the meaning of Britain. Second, his use of common values to define Britain was to echo a theme which Gordon Brown favoured and to which he returned in his premiership. And third, Irvine was choosing to intervene in a growing debate – hitherto largely ignored by politicians – about the future of Britain in the coming millennium. Indeed Irvine explicitly took aim at Linda Colley, the historian whose 1992 account of the formation of Britain and Britishness had done

[65] Ed Owen, interview with the author, 31 May 2007.
[66] Matthew Taylor, interview with the author, 8 June 2007.
[67] Lord Irvine of Lairg, *Human Rights* 103.
[68] ibid 103–7.

much to generate the debate.[69] Colley was to argue that Britain had been founded in war; it had been defined by its religion and its enemies; and it drew strength from its empire and its monarchy. This was not a sustainable basis for a country faced by new challenges posed by the growth of the EU, by globalisation and by mass migration. As the new millennium drew nearer, writers competed with one another to develop Colley's thesis, offering their readers ever more gloomy accounts of British national disintegration and decay.[70] Reports by think-tanks and by the British Council agonised over the nature of Britishness, and sought to define British values. Colley herself was dismissive of the thought that British values could be expressed in a way which commanded widespread support. Her prescription, delivered in a Millennium Lecture at No 10 in December 1999, was to seek national renewal in the 'renovation' of British citizenship. Institutional change was all but irrelevant to the nation's survival. If anything, the reforms of the first term had given new salience to the question 'What is Britain for?' Colley herself sought to give an answer to this question in the lecture she was invited to give in Downing Street on the eve of the new millennium.[71]

But debating the future of Britain or the nature of Britishness remained a minority pastime for the electorate. The combined efforts of historians, doom-merchants, think tanks and even the Lord Chancellor could not capture the public imagination. Part of the reason may be found in popular attitudes towards Britain itself.

Much the most provocative contribution to the debate came from David Goodhart, the editor of *Prospect*. He argued that Britain and the British needed a reason to stick together. A society which was becoming ever more diverse would increasingly question the need to work together and to make sacrifices for the weak and the poor. Laissez faire multiculturalism was no longer a satisfactory or sufficient response. The Left needed to develop a progressive nationalism, which articulated the benefits and burdens of belonging to the national community. In particular, it had to project Britishness as a distinctive and attractive concept. Citizenship should only be granted after applicants had passed tougher tests of suitability and of fluency in English. British history should again become compulsory in schools, fostering an understanding of the national story. And there should be a holiday to celebrate Britishness.[72]

Goodhart was condemned by some for rejecting liberal multiculturalism, but his argument was influential in New Labour circles, providing the context for a determined attempt to embrace the nation as a force for social cohesion. David Blunkett, Jack Straw and Gordon Brown all joined in the effort to re-imagine

[69] Linda Colley, *Britons. Forging the Nation, 1707–1837* (New Haven, Yale University Press, 1992).

[70] See, eg, Richard Weight, *Patriots. National Identity in Britain 1940–2000* (Basingstoke, Macmillan, 2000). Andrew Marr, *The Day Britain Died* (London, Profile Books, 2000).

[71] Linda Colley, *Britishness in the 21st Century*, Millennium Lecture at Number 10 (8 December 1999).

[72] David Goodhart, *Progressive Nationalism: Citizenship and the Left* (London, Demos, 2006).

the nation.[73] Each of them conceived of it as a community defined by the values its members held in common.

X. Brown and the Constitution

At its inception, the Brown Government made a concerted attempt to fuse its constitutional ambitions with its commitment to national renewal. For a time, the constitution and the nature of British national identity were a political priority for the Government and the Prime Minister himself invested considerable energy in promoting his vision of constitutional change. But once the crash of 2008 had overtaken the Government, Brown could no longer make the political weather and it seems unlikely that his attempts to write a retrospective rationale for New Labour's reforms has left much lasting impact.

The more ambitious constitution-watchers have been tempted to raise a yet more demanding question: 'How are the reforms changing our sense of Britain and the British?' Again, we would be foolhardy if we rushed to answer. They almost certainly will change British national identity. But we should always remember that they were never proposed with that purpose in mind.

[73] David Blunkett, *A New England. An English Identity within Britain* (London, Institute for Public Policy Research, 2005). Jack Straw, Cyril Foster Lecture (25 January 2007).

6

Changing States, Changing Nations

This book has sought to understand three stories of constitutional change. To understand why were they attempted; how were they organised; why they succeeded – or failed; and what, indeed, qualifies as success? Our particular purpose was to understand better the reforms undertaken in Britain while Tony Blair was Prime Minister. The Canadian and Australian chapters have served that purpose but we have found ourselves drawn as much to the particular circumstances of each country as they we have been to the common themes they share. We will not attempt to force these tales into a single, comprehensive interpretative model; explanations of constitutional change typically lose their purchase if they aspire to universal currency or to global application.[1] The evidence presented here is not (or should not be) the stuff from which grand theories are constructed. But the commonalities in these stories are striking: the reforms originated in similar concerns and they prospered (or failed) for reasons which are relevant to all liberal democracies. This chapter seeks to tease apart what they have in common from that which is peculiar to each of them.

I. Three Stories: One Pattern?

In searching for patterns here, it is immediately apparent that constitutional change is a messy, noisy business. It bears the imprint of personal ambition, of opportunism and of the struggle for partisan advantage. In constitutional politics as much as any other branch of politics, leaders and their parties will choose to adopt policies for reasons of expediency. Constitutional policies may be taken up and put down again at will. That is not to suggest that politicians are without principle when they promote or resist constitutional change: each of these three stories provides proof that that is not the case. But their constitutional objectives may be secondary to another goal: constitutional law may be a species of higher law but that does not mean that those seeking its reform necessarily have superordinate ambitions. Constitutional politics are not always a continuation of politics as usual: the rules governing constitutional amendment can require, or at least encourage, politicians

[1] See, eg, Ran Hirschl, *Towards Juristocracy. The Origins and Consequences of the New Constitutionalism* (Cambridge, Mass, Harvard University Press, 2004).

to adopt tactics which are peculiar to constitutional reform. But the behaviours we associate with politics as usual do spill over into constitutional politics. To learn about the common themes in these stories we need to filter out the contingent and the tactical.

Apply that filter and it is clear that here are two explicit attempts – those from Canada and Australia – to use constitutional change to advance an argument about national identity. In the British story the reforms may not have originated in a concern with the nation, but the narrative which the Brown Government offered to explain constitutional renewal emphasised the renewal of Britain and of Britishness. The three episodes examined here command our attention because they were either the most significant reforms undertaken in the last 40 years – or they were as close as the countries came to formal constitutional change over that period. The Charter of Rights and Freedoms unquestionably represents the most profound constitutional reform in Canada. The Republic in Australia is the only reform to have been put to a referendum since 1988 and it is the only constitutional proposal to have seized the popular imagination in the last four decades. In the UK, the reforms introduced by the Blair administrations represent the most radical changes to the constitution since accession to the (then) Common Market in 1973. Withdrawal from the European Union would subsequently eclipse their significance but it is too early to draw anything but the most provisional conclusions on the full impact of Brexit.

Indeed, the reform debate has moved on in each of our three countries. The transformation wrought by Brexit in the UK is the most dramatic change, but constitutional politics in the other two countries look quite different now. The Republic in Australia is again a second order issue whereas the Charter in Canada has been absorbed into the political mainstream. The topic preoccupying reformers in both Australia and Canada is the attempt to secure constitutional recognition for the Indigenous Peoples/First Nations. The debates have been running for more than a decade in both countries and yet they still seem provisional and poorly defined. Should they culminate in substantive reform, which currently seems improbable, they will, of course, have implications for national identity.

We should be clear that not all constitutional change in these countries in the last 40 years originated in an argument about the character and future of the nation. Even if we confine our attention to the three stories told here, it will be readily apparent that nation-building (or re-building) was not the sole motivation of the principal actors. The British reforms were a loose assembly of policies which accumulated in successive Labour Party manifestos over more than two decades. Each was intended to cure a particular ill or to secure a particular electoral objective. Insofar as national identity was in play it was Scottish identity that preoccupied policy-makers, not British. The Republican project in Australia did, of course, originate in a proposition about the nation's future and the need to detach that future from its past. But in the end the project was only put to a vote because of a defensive manoeuvre by the Liberals in opposition: a constitutional convention was first proposed by Alex Downer when leader of the opposition as a means of deflecting Keating's use of the Republic as a weapon against his party. In the Canadian Charter we have a vessel for Trudeau's ambition that the nation be bound together in a common citizenship. But the vessel was also freighted with the ambitions of interest groups bent on securing their own ends rather than redefining Canadian values.

Nor are we suggesting that a preoccupation with the nation or with national values is peculiar to constitutional politics in the late twentieth century. After all, democratic constitutions record the rules within which societies choose to live. Social change might be expected to engender constitutional change: a constitution no longer in tune with the mores of its citizens is likely to change – whether through formal amendment or judicial reinterpretation. Only the most formidable procedural obstacles or the most resolute constructionism can preserve both the founding text *and* its original meaning. Look further back into the constitutional history of our three countries and we can readily identify earlier reforms to illustrate the point. For example, the 1967 amendment of the Australian constitution to admit Indigenous Peoples to full citizenship was a belated recognition that it was anomalous for a democracy to withhold rights on grounds of ethnicity. The debate was not framed in terms of national identity, but it was as much about the character of Australia as Keating's project in the 1990s.

And so we must allow that constitutional change in these three countries in the late twentieth century was not solely concerned with national identity; that the British rationalised their reforms after the event; and that the link between national identity and constitutional reform was not forged in the last quarter of the twentieth century. These are all important qualifications, but we are left with three stories which demonstrate the intimate relationship between constitutional reform and attempts to re-imagine the nation. This relationship may not be new, but it is significant that each of our constitutional moments took place in the last quarter of the century. In all three of the countries, not only is national identity now more contested but the whole conception of what it is to be a nation is being redefined. In the Charter, the Republic and, retrospectively, in the Blair reforms we can see politicians groping for a new source of national cohesion. Faced by ever-greater ethnic and cultural diversity and driven by the imperative to attract capital and labour in a globalised market, Canada, Australia and the UK are putting aside a sense of nation based on blood, history and culture. Cleaving to the old order risks anachronism at home and marginalisation abroad in the competition for talent and investment. In place of the old order, each is adopting a concept of the nation grounded in the values that its people share – or are said to share. The challenge to the prior conception of nation has, of course, been peculiarly vigorous in Canada. Only Canada has stared dissolution in the face. But this distinction is a matter of degree: the UK, another multinational state, has also experienced the return of ethnic nationalism within its borders.

As they search for a new nationalism, the Australians, Canadians and British find themselves doing battle with common foes: they struggle against disengagement from the democratic process, distrust of public institutions and ignorance of the rights and responsibilities of citizens. They search for ways of 'reconnecting' the elected and electors; of winning back ebbing confidence; and of inculcating understanding of civics. Not only is the nation being recast, but it is being promoted, celebrated and ceremonialised. Nations have congratulated themselves on their good fortune for as long as nations have been in business, but there is a particular urgency about the enterprises under way in Australia, Canada and the UK. Each wants to communicate the unique offer that it has to make to its existing citizens or to newcomers. No longer willing to rely on implicit, instinctive understandings arising from common kinship or shared history, they are fashioning a more explicit offer to citizens old and new. Each has felt disquiet – at its least – in the face of Muslim fundamentalism amongst its own citizens. Their response has included the articulation of the benefits of citizenship with an ever more forceful enumeration of its responsibilities. For once, policy-makers seem liberated to learn from one another, cheerfully stealing ideas as they fashion citizenship policies and rituals which are at once distinctive and competitive.

What of the US, which can hardly claim to have chanced across this new concept of the nation in the late twentieth century? The three others may not consciously be mimicking the values-based nationhood of the Americans, but the model which has begun to find favour in the UK, Australia and Canada has much in common with the example set by the first modern nation. In popular culture, the American myth remains in robust good health. But that does not mean that the US has been immune to the forces at play in Australia, Canada and the UK. The values which constitute the national myth may have remained constant, but their meaning has been the subject of vigorous debate. In recent years this debate has been sharpened by divisions over the war in Iraq and what some argue has been a betrayal of American values.[2] This type of ideological conflict is a persistent feature of nationhood based on values: define a people by a creed and the definition of the creed will become the subject of controversy. Partisans will seek to marginalise or expel opponents from the national community by interpreting the creed in a way which proscribes their behaviour or beliefs. The phenomenon may not be new but it has been given renewed impetus by increased diversity at home – fuelled most obviously by immigration from Latin America – and by the growing threat of competition from China and India. Some of the responses have been no more than a renewal of long-established features of American life: a reassertion of the importance of civics, an invocation of values held in common and an embrace of the flag. But some of the proposed solutions suggest a more radical reappraisal of what it is to be American. Can a nation of immigrants retain its prior identity once it has constructed a wall along its Mexican border? Could hyphenated American identity survive the adoption of an official language by state or federal government? And by

[2] For just one example of an attempt to state what those values should be in the wake of the war, see Anne-Marie Slaughter, *The Idea that is America. Keeping Faith with our Values in a Dangerous World* (New York, Basic Books, 2007).

the end of the first term of Trump's Presidency, commentators were asking whether the American project itself could survive the Presidency of a nativist and populist determined to denigrate the Americanism of his opponents, often in the most virulent terms? At the least one has to acknowledge that project is once again in flux, its trajectory in dispute. The details of the feud over the interpretation of values allegedly held in common may be peculiarly American but it has been sustained by anxieties over cohesion which are shared by the UK, Canada and Australia. Even the mythologising of the US flag is now echoed in some Commonwealth countries. Not the least remarkable feature of the reinvention of their nationhood is that their own national flags are now acquiring a ubiquity once unknown. And the UK and Australia there has even been serious discussion of a ban on flag-burning, a development which would once have been inconceivable.

The attempts to re-imagine the nation in our three countries are not the exclusive province of either Left or Right.

Consider the rival agenda of Paul Keating and John Howard – each trying to promote his vision of a renewed nation. Howard's proposed preamble to the constitution was as much an essay in national identity as Keating's grander vision. Listen to the terms in which Malcolm Turnbull looks back on the Republican campaign in his memoir:

> And at the heart of the success of the Australian project is that we don't define our nation by reference to one religion or race or cultural tradition. Every face, and every faith, can be Australian. What defines us, and unites us, is our commitment to common political values, more innate and better felt than they are defined.[3]

What is striking about this testament is not so much the unabashed multiculturalism from a leader of the Right but his cheerful ownership of a national 'project'.

Consider the attempts of the Mulroney governments to rework the settlement brought about by Trudeau's Liberals. It represented an attempt by the Right to re-imagine the concept of Canada.

Or in the UK, consider the stumbling efforts of the Conservatives to amend or remove the Human Rights Act, most commonly by introducing a British Bill of Rights, which might – or might not – have been accompanied by a decoupling from the European Convention on Human Rights.

In all three countries, Left and Right fight over the meaning of the nation, over its future destiny and over the interpretation of its past. Left and Right compete in the battle for popular sentiment, promoting their conception of the nation at the expense of any rival. They want their version of the national myth to be taught in schools, to be inculcated into new citizens. But they know that victories over the design of the school curriculum or citizenship ceremonies, however hard won, are transient. They aspire to victories which will endure, shaping civic life for decades to come, redefining the norm and recasting the consensus. It might be tempting to dismiss national identity 'projects' as politicians' *folies de grandeurs*. But to stitch

[3] Malcolm Turnbull, *A Bigger Picture* (Richmond, Victoria, Hardie Grant Books, 2020) 94.

one's perspective on national identity into the constitution offers the prospect of redefining the norm for years to come. In countries with a codified constitution just to attempt constitutional change is to label something as important. Even unsuccessful attempts at reform can earn ideological or political advantage for their promoters. And the prospect of success is seductive. Either the rules of national political life can be rewritten or the symbols of the state can be redefined. Even in an uncodified constitution, reform brings with it the hope of long-term change. Tit-for-tat reversals of major reforms are a hazardous business for one's political opponents; codified constitutions make a reversal all the more costly in political capital. At a time when the meaning of the nation is contested at home and the significance of the nation state is challenged abroad, it is little wonder that the advocates of a nationalism of ideas should seek to secure their ends through constitutional means.

II. Lessons for Reformers?

The prize for reformers may be alluring but constitutional politics is a perilous business for those promoting and resisting change; the obstacles to reform are purposely high and the electorate is commonly sceptical about attempts to rewrite the rules of the game. Paul Keating did not lose the 1996 election because of the Republic but his advocacy of his Big Picture helped the opposition to portray him as a Prime Minister who was detached from the sentiments and experience of average voters. The Charter was only secured in Canada after Trudeau had shown himself willing to gamble with the nation's future in an endgame which might easily have ended in the break up of the confederation. Only in the UK has constitutional reform had little fall-out for its advocates or opponents. The 1997 election was not influenced by the prospect of constitutional change; nor did voters choose to reward (or punish) its implementation at the subsequent general elections. The Brown Government's more explicit emphasis on a renewal of Britishness through constitutional reform aroused little support amongst the electorate in 2010.

The recurring choice facing reformers in these stories is whether to force the pace, moving ahead of public opinion in the hope that it would follow their lead, or to build a coalition for change, accepting that it will take time and that in the short-term the results might appear more modest.

Paul Keating recognised the dilemma but did not resolve it. His intervention transformed the republican debate, giving it energy and making the Republic a serious political proposition. His instinct – not always curbed – was to press on, to use the Republic as a weapon with which to bludgeon his opponents and to make progress before his own time in Kirribilli House ran out. But he understood the risks of acting hastily – and of being seen to act hastily. And so he asked an independent committee to deliberate on options; he established a group of experts to consider civic education; and the Cabinet Committee he chaired worked through the issues slowly and methodically. His critics would charge that he got it wrong both ways: he failed to make sufficient headway before his 1996 defeat *and* he failed to get credit for acting responsibly. But it is hard to see what a faster pace might have achieved. Keating's achievement was, as he modestly conceded, to move the Republic from 'an after-dinner mint' conversation to front page news. But in doing so it became *Keating's* Republic and its opponents took every opportunity to remind the public of the epithet. If he had kept up the early pace – a tall order for a Prime Minister in a struggling administration – he would have strengthened his opponents. And in any event, it was always unrealistic to expect a referendum to have been held before the 1996 general election. Keating found himself too far in advance of public opinion, promoting a proposition which was easier to oppose than to advocate. The brevity of Australian parliamentary cycles – just three years – presented the Prime Minister with a tactical conundrum which was all but insoluble. Ultimately he chose to play it long. And in so doing he ran the risk that it would be a monarchist, not a republican, who would preside over the referendum.

Pierre Trudeau's success in delivering constitutional change some 14 years after he first published a text for the Charter was a testament to his stubborn determination. But it cannot reasonably be seen as a conscious attempt to construct a consensus in favour of change. It might more accurately be characterised as serial attempts to wrench affairs in his preferred direction, imposing his will on others. His own political longevity and the hegemony of the Liberal Party afforded him the opportunity to make repeated bids for the prize. Each was intended to succeed; they were not planned as skirmishes in a grander, longer campaign. Their cumulative effect may have been to soften up provincial opposition and to win popular support for the Charter, but that had not been their purpose. When Trudeau made his final attempt at a constitutional settlement the circumstances were, finally, more propitious. But his basic tactical preference remained the same: he would coax and cajole the negotiating parties to come to a deal. What was different was that he was willing to play the game with a new recklessness: the country was now faced by an existential crisis and he was prepared to risk deepening it in one final bid to resolve it. That he was able to secure the support of interest groups with a stake in the Charter was a bonus. But he did not choose to enlist them and left to his own devices he would not have given them access to the reform process.

Tony Blair also faced tactical choices over the speed of reform, but they were not felt as keenly because constitutional reform was always a second order issue for New Labour, whether in opposition or in power. Insofar as he and his close colleagues agonised over the pace and nature of change, it was a matter of legislative tactics. How many constitutional bills could be fitted into each parliamentary session? Should Lords reform wait until devolution was through? At no stage did they contemplate a slower, popular campaign to build up a consensus in favour of change. Indeed, they were instinctively suspicious of Charter 88 – the noisiest advocates of grassroots mobilisation – because of Neil Kinnock's entanglement with Democracy Day in 1992. In the spring of 1997 New Labour still worried about winning the May general election. Only the most extravagant – or foolhardy – of reformers in New Labour's ranks would have sketched out a reform timetable running over two or even three Parliaments. Instead, they opted – like Derry Irvine – to do good by stealth; they supported early constitutional legislation, driving up the pulse rate of reformers, but failing to excite the nation as a whole.

Might the reformers in all three countries have enjoyed greater success in securing their reform if they had chosen to invest more time and energy in preparing the ground in advance, assembling a coalition of supporters willing to advocate change? First we should pause and consider what we mean by success. If it is taken to mean simply the approval of the reforms, it is plain to see that just two of our projects may be deemed successful. Or, more accurately, just two have succeeded to date. In years to come, we may yet be looking back on Keating's republican skirmishes as the first shots in a successful war to unseat the monarchy in Australia. If a Labor Government were to conjure up a referendum victory within the next 10 years Keating's early spadework might reasonably be seen to have laid the foundations for eventual victory, bringing the issue into the mainstream and beginning to reshape public opinion. We must allow for these possibilities, but let us judge the efficacy of the reform projects on the evidence to date.

It would be difficult to argue that the British and Canadian reforms would have had an easier or more secure route to the statute books if their authors had chosen to promote or even shape them through popular campaigns and consultation. Indeed, it would be hard to imagine a more efficient execution of constitutional radicalism than that seen in Britain from 1997 to 2001. Similarly, Trudeau's ultimate success was essentially an elite manoeuvre, executed by a small group of politicians and officials who took their chance skilfully and ruthlessly. Neither victory was achieved in a vacuum. Devolution to Scotland was undoubtedly made easier by the work of the Scottish Constitutional Convention, and by the long years of Tory rule which preceded the Convention. The sheer persistence of devolution as a Labour Party policy commitment helped bring about public acceptance of reform, even if it did not engender widespread enthusiasm for it. Similarly, the Canadian public gradually became accustomed to the notion of the patriation of the constitution, a rebalancing of federal-provincial relations and the Charter. By 1980 the Charter itself was unquestionably popular, but just as important was the sense of impatience across most of the country: voters were tired of their leaders' constitutional obsession and they wanted an end to it. The reformers' case in Britain and Canada was undoubtedly helped by the longevity of their cause: over time the public simply became more accustomed to the idea of change. But neither the British nor the Canadian case support the notion that popular mobilisation in favour of reform would have secured the desired changes any more effectively. And in the UK devolution was just one of the many reforms to find its way onto the statute book in the first term. The others were taken through, unremarked by most voters, on the back of a commanding parliamentary majority.

If we ask whether the Australian Republic might have prospered if it had been backed by popular campaigns, the evidence is no more compelling.

In Australia – the only country in our three to require a referendum to amend the constitution – it is true that the ARM might have been better placed to take on the monarchists if it had evolved into a mass membership organisation. But the ARM's leadership knew that to open up their campaign would risk a loss of control and of focus. The surgical operation to remove the monarch from the constitution, might soon have become a move to introduce direct democracy into the Australian system. Neither Malcolm Turnbull nor Paul Keating could have brought themselves to support that cause. Populism might have severed the republican head from the republican body. It is difficult to imagine that this would have helped secure a referendum victory in 1999 but it would have forced republicans to confront the fundamental tension between the conservatives and radicals in their ranks. As it was, the divisions were there for all to see during the Constitutional Convention, the highpoint of popular engagement en route to the referendum. The healing of those divisions did not begin until after the 1999 defeat and it remains a work in progress.

Broaden our focus still further and it remains hard to sustain the argument that popular engagement necessarily helps get constitutional reform across the line. Consider, for example, the Charlottetown Accord of 1992. The process which preceded it was admirable. Conferences were held across Canada; there were parliamentary hearings; interest groups were drawn into dialogue; Indigenous and territorial representatives were invited to join the talks for the first time; and the public was given candid daily briefings on the progress of the negotiations. The agreement of a wide-ranging constitutional pact by the premiers, the leaders of the federal territories and of the Indigenous organisations was but a prelude to the most striking innovation of all: a national referendum. Whereupon the Accord was rejected in six of the 10 provinces, securing just 44.6 per cent of the national vote.

Charlottetown shows the pitfalls of popular engagement. Misjudged and poorly focussed, it can become a liability for reformers. The evidence of our case studies suggest the uncomfortable lesson that constitutional change can be secured (or resisted) without investing in popular engagement. Interest groups seeking relatively modest reforms can often use their energies and resources more efficiently by influencing the influential. Freedom of Information in the UK, for example, was brought about through the efforts of a small, expert lobby which first persuaded the Labour Party to include the pledge in its manifesto in 1974. When it came to drafting each successive manifesto, campaigners ensured the commitment remained – little understood and largely unnoticed. FOI was popular in opposition (it always is); and opinion polls showed, unsurprisingly, that the public preferred openness to secrecy. But the question rarely caught the public's attention and campaigners struggled to make the connection between their cause and the everyday frustrations of citizens with public services. FOI appeared, as usual, in the 1997 manifesto and thereafter the lobby focussed its attention on ensuring the party in government remained true to its word in opposition. Legislation was passed in 2000.

It is important to distinguish between public awareness of an issue and genuine engagement in a popular campaign, driving up understanding and drawing citizens into advocacy. Popular recognition of a reform – not least one whose purpose is to reshape the popular image or perception of the nation – is generally a threshold which all successful constitutional reforms must clear. The issues studied here were, for the most part, all too familiar to voters by the time their fate was finally decided. By 1981 it would have been hard to have found a Canadian without views on patriation and the Charter. The notion of an Australian Republic had been gaining popular currency (if not acceptance) since the Republican rallies organised by the Campaign for Democracy in 1977. Only in Britain was the public unfamiliar with many of the proposed reforms. That was in part a function of their range and complexity, but it was also because the nation's political energies were otherwise engaged in 1997: above all, voters wanted to be rid of the Tories and to make a fresh start with New Labour. Devolution, the party's most urgent constitutional priority was, by now, a staple of political debate in Scotland and Wales. The trauma of devolution legislation during the Callaghan Government may have left its scars on the party, but it also served to introduce – or re-introduce – the public to the idea of home rule.

The stories examined here suggest that popular engagement was not a critical factor in determining whether propositions secured formal approval. This judgement is, in part, a simple reflection of the systems through which approval had to be secured. Only the Australian reformers faced an obligatory referendum and, as we have seen, their cause might have been helped if the ARM had somehow found a way of creating a mass movement while retaining elite support. The Blair administration chose to put devolution to referendums first in Scotland and then in Wales, enjoying a comfortable victory north of the border – where the proposals had support of all parties to the Convention – and coming within a whisker of losing the second vote. The referendums were a political necessity: it would have been unthinkable, after the issue had been put to voters in 1979, to have delivered devolution without them. The only controversy – intense at the time Tony Blair changed the policy – was whether to hold the votes before or after the legislation had been approved by Parliament. If the Welsh Labour Party had felt able to overcome its own differences earlier and to have reached out to other parties and to civil society, the referendum there might have been won more easily. But this process would undoubtedly have resulted in a different, more radical devolution proposition being put to voters. The leaders of the Welsh Labour Party, like their counterparts in the ARM, struggled to alight on a plan which would have caught the public's imagination without threatening their own principles – or interests. Popular engagement would have been as perilous for Welsh Labour as for the ARM. The origins of their respective difficulties lay as much in tensions within their own proposals as it did in their reluctance to enter dialogue with their critics. The long-term significance of the referendums in Scotland and Wales lay not so much in their influence on the parliamentary votes on the devolution legislation but in their long-term legacy. Devolution settlements which had been endorsed by popular votes could not be overturned without taking the issue back to the polls. Repeal would only be contemplated by the brave or the foolhardy.

Our stories suggest two further lessons. The first is a cautionary one for reformers: it is easier to mount a defence against a reform proposal than it is to secure its approval. Constitutions are, of course, inherently conservative: they are intended to foster stability and predictability. Codified constitutions secure that end by erecting barriers to amendments. But even if we set these hurdles to one side, the requirements facing a reformer remain exacting. They have to persuade decision-makers – whether they be provincial premiers, members of a legislature or individual citizens – that action is preferable to inaction. The challenge for reformers is greater if they neglect to resolve contradictions in their own base. Was the Republic a big change or a small one? Was it about the erasure of Australia's colonial past or about the modernisation of its constitution? Reformers were ineluctably drawn into a technical argument, robbing them of their strongest suit – outrage. Britain again is our exception: far-reaching reforms were taken through without strong resistance. It is one of the ironies of the British story that the Labour Party's conversion to constitutional reform was hastened by Mrs Thatcher's exploitation of her parliamentary majorities in the 1980s. New Labour took the chance afforded to it by Britain's uncodified constitution and by its 1997 landslide to drive through its reform programme with determination of which Mrs Thatcher herself would have been proud.

The second lesson is simple and it concerns political leadership, the decisive factor in each of our stories. Each of the successful combatants – John Howard, Tony Blair, Pierre Trudeau – showed acute judgement for what public opinion would, and would not, tolerate. Each had the political acumen needed to seize the moment to secure an advantage for their cause. And each of them was lucky, not least in their opponents.

III. Re-engineering National Identity

We know that constitutional reform can re-engineer the state, conferring or withholding citizenship, redistributing political power and assigning or denying rights. And we have seen that public engagement is not necessarily essential to the completion of the formalities of reform: the amendment of the constitution, whether codified or not. But what of the grander ambitions of our reformers? Most of those whose story we have told have wanted to change the way in which their fellow citizens thought about the nation. Before we consider the attempts to engage the public in these broader, less tangible enterprises, it is worth pausing to consider the nature of their ambition. After all, the re-engineering of national identity would once have been dismissed as the preserve of totalitarian regimes willing to indulge a fantasy that they could transform the nation by sporting success or displays of military prowess. And yet now we see liberal democracies apparently tempted by the same alchemy.

National identity is not a commodity which can be bought or sold; nor can its fluctuations be weighed in a balance. Identity is something that is experienced. My sense of my nation is refracted through my sense of who I am; I see Britain through a lens which is coloured by my values, my beliefs, by my hopes, my fears. National identity is rooted in the experience of individuals; it is a composite of their experience. And it is relational: it is about the relationship of the individual to the whole. This is a fluid, elusive concept. That does not mean that it is frivolous to care about national identity; nor that it is frivolous to want to change it. But we should be cautious if we try to assess the impact of a specific reform on national identity. How does one even attempt a summation of national identity as it is now – or as it might be tomorrow? Distillations of the popular mood are often no more than assertions, sometimes offered in the hope that their acuity or eloquence might earn them popular currency, helping to bring about the very change in identity which they are said to describe. Survey data can measure shifts in attitudes, but these aggregations are an inadequate substitute for the sum of our individual experiences.

Constitutional reformers who set out to change the way their nation sees itself are setting themselves a goal whose attainment is ultimately unknowable because progress towards it cannot be measured. And so they have to content themselves with proxies. They congratulate themselves on approval of their reforms by parliaments or referendums; they take comfort that their reforms have not been reversed; they point to opinion polls suggesting attitudinal shifts; and they claim that the popular mood is moving in their favour. And the more prudent amongst them wait – and listen. Listen to the testimony of individuals and to the representation of their nation in its art and its histories.

None of this is to suggest that reformers should set aside this ambition, but it is to recognise that any success they may enjoy can only ever be provisional. Characterisations of national identity will always be open to dispute, their claims derived from fragmentary glimpses of the experience of individuals.

What can reformers hope to achieve? A symbol burnished and its meaning redefined. A nation's future re-imagined. A national story re-told. A shared understanding of what it is to be a citizen. A recognition of values held in common. These were the goals sought by our reformers. Constitutional reform gave them (or would have given them) the prospect of securing lasting change to national institutions and public rituals, providing the opportunity to shift popular understanding of what it is to be a member of the national community. But it will be immediately apparent that constitutional reform may have been a necessary precondition for lasting change in national identity, but it would not have been sufficient by itself. Symbols have to be explained, false interpretations denied (or even proscribed). Stories have to be told – in school, in citizenship classes and in popular culture.

Myths have to be re-worked and renewed. New institutions have to come alive, to show that they have earned their place in national life. Once the reforming statute is approved, or the amendment confirmed, other agencies have to go to work: courts, litigants, teachers, copywriters, politicians all have to make the reforms live in the public consciousness. Some will act out of duty or conviction; others will need an incentive to participate in the re-fashioning of identity. But all have a role to play in shaping a narrative about what it is to be a citizen today, and what it might be tomorrow.

We can see this process at work most clearly in Canada. Using opinion surveys as a measure of shifts in national identity, we can conclude that the Charter caught the public mood. Many Canadians point to it as their preferred symbol of their country. This is testimony to Trudeau's confidence in the appeal of liberal constitutional values. But it is also testimony to the work of the interest groups who took Charter suits, to the Justice Department which funded them, to the judges who realised the Charter's potential – and to the relentless campaign run by Ottawa to remind Canadians of all ages, from all provinces, of how lucky they were to live in a country which had such comprehensive safeguards for the liberty of the individual.[4] The Charter may have been secured through executive federalism, but it came to life when Canadians across the country learned about it, used it and came to understand it as a defining feature of public life. The Charter may have taken Canadian social policy into territory few expected and many question, but it retains its popularity. Trudeau's first objective has been realised: the Charter has encouraged Canadians to take pride in their shared citizenship. But his ultimate ambition has been denied: the Charter has made Quebec's secession no less likely. Québécois, in common with their fellow Canadians, like the Charter – and make use of it. But the underlying level of support for secession has remained relatively stable over the last quarter of a century. Trudeau's nation-building project was one of two under way in Canada. The rival enterprise instigated by the PQ has retained the loyalty of the Québécois. They welcome the Charter, but at least a third of them still want to leave the confederation.

At the time of their introduction, Britain's constitutional reforms were not understood to be an exercise in the renewal of the national consciousness. This was a retrospective rationalisation of their (many) purposes. Brown's interest in British identity has undoubtedly been sharpened by the shift in popular attitudes he has witnessed in Scotland. There has been a decline in Scottish identification with Britain and a steady increase in those who regard themselves as more Scottish than British. A similar pattern is to be found in Wales.[5] Devolution has done little

[4] Charles R Epp, *The Rights Revolution: Lawyers, Activists, and Supreme Courts in Comparative Perspective* (Chicago, University of Chicago Press, 1998) chs 9 and 10.

[5] The trend in Wales is as in Scotland, but it is less marked. See John Curtice, 'Public Opinion and the Future of Devolution' in Alan Trench (ed), *The Dynamics of Devolution* (Exeter, Imprint Academic, 2005) 124–25.

to disturb the underlying pattern. It remains to be seen whether a more direct focus on Britain and British values has the capacity to capture the imagination of the Scots, the Welsh or, indeed, the English. National identity is in play in the UK, with the strengthening of sub-nationalisms, including Englishness, and the realignment of political allegiances prompted by Brexit.

It should be no surprise that politicians bent on re-engineering a nation's sense of itself should alight on constitutional reform as one of their preferred tools. Their ultimate success may remain a matter of conjecture, but if they aspire to enduring change to a nation's civic life, to a re-ordering of the public realm then they would be foolish to overlook constitutional reform. But they would be equally foolish if they considered their job done once an amendment is secured. The hard work – of introducing citizens to their new rights, of breathing life into new institutions – begins the moment the law is changed. The fight to capture the public's imagination is won over the long-haul, not in the heat of a referendum campaign or the parliamentary passage of a bill. A reform may find its way into law without the active engagement of the public, but if it is to reshape their understanding of their nation, they must be drawn into the enterprise. Indeed, it must become a shared enterprise, in which they make use of their new rights, they interact with their new institutions, they come to tell the national story afresh.

IV. Changing States, Changing Nations

This book has described episodes in the recent constitutional history of three liberal democracies. It will close with a speculation about the future of constitutional reform. History does not equip its students with the gift of prophesy but it can help us to understand who we are and can prompt us to think about who we might become in future.

It seems probable that reformers will continue to use constitutional reform to encourage us to think afresh about our nation and our place within it. For all the challenges to its role or even to its survival, the nation state remains remarkably durable and so political parties will continue to compete to shape its destiny. As our sense of the nation becomes ever more ideological in character, parties will fight to assert the primacy of the values which they believe are – or should be – the embodiment of national identity. And they will seek to lodge those values within our constitutions. Because it is in constitutions that communities express what they consider to be important about themselves: rules about inclusion and exclusion; the balance between government by the majority and the rights of minorities; and the distribution or concentration of power. Constitutions are themselves an expression of the enduring values of the community. Goodhart has argued persuasively that if democracies are to absorb successive waves of immigration successfully, then it is all the more important that they express a confident national identity to the newcomers.[6] Securing that identity in the constitution is one means to that end. Far better that reformers continue to strengthen the nation state and the national story against those who would divide our communities against themselves.

A national identity based on values is inherently contestable. In time, we might expect British, Canadian and Australian identity to be contested in the same fashion as it is in the US – a country which, ostensibly, has a shared set of values but which has a perpetual debate as to their meaning. The controversy over the teaching of national history provides a foretaste of what is to come. The contest will be played out in social policy, in immigration rules, in the arts, in the portrayal of ourselves in our national museums. But the promise of a more permanent victory will always draw the contestants back to constitutional reform.

A range of possibilities suggest themselves as we contemplate a future in which countries progressively adopt a values-based model of national identity.

The first is that some pre-existing features of national identity will not expire conveniently as the new model is asserted. Take the British example. It is currently a curious amalgam of history, culture and, unusually, institutions. The BBC and the NHS have taken root in the psyche of the British and they will not be readily moved. Suggest to a German that their health provider or public service broadcaster might have a similar status and they would consider the idea quaint, at best. National identity is often a combination of the local and the universal, and it is often the local which speaks most powerfully to its adherents.

And so we might be moving towards a future where the expression of national identity is not exclusively the work of some latter-day Madison, but a hybrid representing local need – multiculturalism in Canada; Indigenous reconciliation in Australia and universal healthcare in the UK – and global truths.

This outcome would, at least, still the fears of those who quail at the prospect of homogeneous statements of liberal values, each purporting to express the identity of their nations. I should add that there are worse prospects to keep one awake at night – as long as they are authentic expressions of national identity.

Globalisation will, at one and the same time, promote the adoption of common statements of national identity and it will temper disputes between those arguing over the meaning of values held in common. The nation state is now under ever greater treaty obligations to observe the rights of nationals and non-nationals. Over and above its obligations in law, the nation state has to be mindful of the imperatives of international trade: the market has expectations that national governments will observe basic norms in its regulation of commerce and of civil society. The market has the power, should it choose to exercise it, to enforce those norms more effectively than any international court or tribunal. But only the most optimistic would allow themselves to believe that an alliance of market

[6] David Goodhart, *The British Dream* (London, Atlantic Books, 2013) *passim*.

capitalism and international governance is about to secure the global triumph of liberal constitutional values. These forces may act as a check on constitutional variety within democracies – and aspirant democracies – but their influence remains uneven. Investors choose to look the other way; NGOs routinely point up the gap between treaty text and treaty observance. International obligations provide, at most, a partial framework within which national constitutions may be developed. Each state still has to determine its own answers to universal questions concerning the balance to be struck between majorities and minorities, between society and the individual, questions on which there is no consensus even amongst democratic countries. If democratic states cannot come to a common view on a question as fundamental as the death penalty, it will be clear that we are some way from having a shared consensus on liberal constitutional values. And constitutions have to do more than resolve universal, abstract choices; they must address the particular needs and circumstances of the national communities whose lives they govern. Hence the asymmetrical devolution of the Spanish constitution; and hence the aspiration to equity in public services in the South African constitution. However fine its intentions, however liberal its values, a constitution derived from an academic textbook or a manual on good governance cannot be an authentic expression of the values of a nation.

The particularity of constitutional change is readily apparent in the stories of this book. In each case the reform cause originated in circumstances which would have been difficult to imagine in the remainder of our sample. Only Canada has faced a crisis over its very survival. Only the Australians are preoccupied by the shedding of the last vestiges of their colonial past: the monarch's place in the Canadian constitution arouses far less interest.[7] New Labour's programme was the fruit of the long search for a formula which would secure its re-election. Over the years, each component was selected, refined or rejected, to achieve this so that the party could offer the country a programme for government which was at once credible and compelling.

And when the reforms examined here evoked public sympathy they did so for reasons particular to each society. The Republic provoked strong feelings – amongst opponents as well as supporters – because of the social changes which preceded the referendum, changes which had divided Australian society into winners and losers. The Charter gave English Canadians, fearful for their country's future, something to hold in common, a reason to hope for a Canadian future. Devolution to Scotland was a response to an ancient nationalism which had again found its voice.

We have seen that formal constitutional change can be achieved without enlisting a popular campaign in favour of it. But if reform is to be used as an instrument of national renewal, a means by which nations come to terms with who they are

[7] It is also technically more difficult to remove the monarch from the Canadian constitution than it is from the Australian constitution.

and who they want to be, reform cannot be imposed from above. Elites cannot expect to be thanked if they closet themselves away, study hard and then reveal to the people what they believe their common values to be. Constitutional renewal cannot be secured by intellectual effort on the part of a select few. The Civics Expert Group in Australia showed us as much. Reforms must resonate with the beliefs, the hopes and the passions of the people. There is no universal formula through which to achieve this. If the reforms are to be an authentic expression of national will, then the process is demanding for leaders and citizens alike. The discipline requires leaders to listen – not just to policy advisers and spin doctors – but to the people they aspire to represent. And it requires them to discover how best to involve the people, either to shape the reforms or give them life, to realise them in practice. For citizens it requires a willingness to participate, to recognise that we all have a responsibility to shape our common future.

Paul Keating recognised this need for partnership, describing it in a speech in June 1995:

> Government alone cannot put meaning and purpose into the lives of the young but they *can* help. They can certainly help create the conditions in which faith might flourish. If you teach history well you can help young people believe that they have a part in the nation's story. If you teach politics well you can help them to feel engaged. You can help them to feel that they have influence. We can help young people – and migrants – discover their attachment to this country and its traditions, and give them hope about its future and theirs. We can help them see that in the fulfilment of their hopes lies the hope of the country.[8]

Noble ambitions. Keating's own career was to demonstrate the hazards of reaching for them.

Nothing is more important to us than our sense of who we are. Constitutional reform has the potential to bring us to recognise ourselves and to strengthen the bonds which unite us. Few causes are more demanding, few offer such promise.

[8] Paul Keating, speech in response to the report of the Civics Expert Group (6 June 1995) NLA, CCF 7.3.11, folder two.

NOTE ON SOURCES

There are four principal sources for this book.

The first are archives and manuscript collections in the UK, Canada and Australia. These are listed in the table at the front of the book. These include Freedom of Information releases in all three countries. The second are interviews with scores of individuals, both participants and observers. These are detailed in the notes themselves. The third are monographs and articles. The monographs and collections of essays are listed in the select bibliography below. The fourth are official reports published by governments and other authorities. Again, these are described in the notes.

SELECT BIBLIOGRAPHY

I. Nationalism; National Identity; Constitutional Theory; Historiography

Ackerman, Bruce. *We, the People*. Cambridge, Mass.: Belknap Press. 1991.

Anderson, Benedict. *Imagined Communities: Reflections on the Origin and Spread of Nationalism*. London: Verso. 1991.

Appiah, Kwame Anthony. *The lies that bind: Creed, country, colour, class, culture*. London: Profile. 2018.

Banting, Keith G and Simeon, Richard. *The politics of constitutional change in industrial nations: Redesigning the state*. London: Macmillan Press. 1985.

Billig, Michael. *Banal Nationalism*. London: Sage. 1995.

Cannadine David. *History in our time*. New Haven: Yale University Press. 1998.

——. *The undivided past: History beyond our differences*. London: Allen Lane. 2013.

Cannadine, David, Keating, Jenny and Sheldon, Nicola. *The right kind of history: Teaching the past in twentieth century England*. Basingstoke: Palgrave Macmillan. 2011.

Clark, Anna and Ashton, Paul. *Australian history now*. Sydney: NewSouth. 2013.

Collier, Paul. *Exodus: Immigration and multiculturalism in the 21st century*. London: Allen Lane. 2013.

Eatwell, Roger and Goodwin, Matthew. *National Populism: The revolt against liberal democracy*. London: Pelican. 2018.

Goodhart, David. *Progressive Nationalism: Citizenship and the Left*. London: Demos. 2006.

Granatstein, JL. *Who killed Canadian history?* Toronto: Phyllis Bruce Perennial. 2007.

Green, Joshua. *Devil's Bargain: Steve Bannon, Donald Trump, and the nationalist uprising*. New York: Penguin. 2018.

Griffiths, Tom. *The art of time travel: Historians and their craft*. Carlton, Victoria: Black Inc. 2016.

Hechter, Michael. *Containing nationalism*. Oxford: Oxford University Press. 2000.

Hirschl, Ran. *Towards juristocracy: The origins and consequences of the new constitutionalism*. Cambridge, Mass.: Harvard University Press. 2004.

Judis, John B. *The nationalist revival: Trade, immigration, and the revolt against globalization*. New York: Columbia Global Reports. 2018.

Kagan, Robert. *Adversarial Legalism*. Cambridge, Mass.: Harvard University Press. 2001.

Levitsky, Steven and Ziblatt, Daniel. *How democracies die: What history reveals about our future*. New York: Viking. 2018.

Macintyre, Stuart and Clark, Anna. *The history wars*. Carlton, Victoria: Melbourne University Press. 2004.

Miller, David. *Citizenship and National Identity*. Cambridge: Polity. 2000.

Müller, Jans-Werner. *What is populism?* London: Penguin. 2017.

Oliver, Dawn and Fusaro, Carlo (eds). *How constitutions change: A comparative study*. Oxford: Hart Publishing. 2013.

Orwell, George. *Notes on Nationalism*. London: Penguin. 2018.

Runciman, David. *How democracy ends*. London: Profile. 2018.

Smith, Anthony D. *Nationalism: Theory, Ideology, History*. Cambridge: Polity. 2001.

Sunstein, Cass R. *Designing Democracy: What Constitutions Do*. New York: Oxford University Press. 2001.

Tamir, Yael. *Why nationalism*. Princeton: Princeton University Press. 2019.

Vose, Clement E. *Constitutional Change: Amendment Politics and Supreme Court Legislation.* Lexington: Lexington Books. 1972.
Wilson, Keith. *Forging the Collective Memory.* Providence, RI: Berghahn Books. 1996.
Winters, Jay. *War beyond words: Languages of remembrances from the Great War to the present.* Cambridge: Cambridge University Press. 2017.

II. United Kingdom

Ashdown, Paddy. *The Ashdown Diaries: Volume I: 1988–1997.* London: Penguin. 2000.
——. *The Ashdown Diaries: Volume II: 1997–1999.* London: Allen Lane. 2002.
Bogdanor, Vernon. *Beyond Brexit: Towards a British constitution.* London: I.B. Tauris. 2019.
Brooks, Thom. *Becoming British: UK citizenship examined.* London: Biteback. 2016.
Brown, Gordon. *My life, our times.* London: Vintage. 2017.
——. *My Scotland, our Britain: A future worth sharing.* London: Simon Schuster. 2014.
Colley, Linda. *Britons: Forging the nation, 1707–1837.* New Haven: Yale University Press. 1992.
Cook, Robin and Maclennan, Robert. *Looking back, looking forward: The Cook-Maclennan agreement eight years on.* London: New Politics Network. 2005.
Crick, Bernard (ed). *National identities: The constitution of the United Kingdom.* Oxford: Blackwell. 1991.
Dorling, Danny and Tomlinson, Sally. *Brexit and the end of Empire: Rule Britannia.* London: Biteback. 2019.
Goodhart, David. *The British dream: Successes and failures of post-war immigration.* London: Atlantic. 2013.
Freedland, Jonathan. *Bringing the revolution home: How Britain can live the American dream.* London: Fourth Estate. 1998.
Hirsch, Afua. *Brit(ish): On race, identity and belonging.* London: Jonathan Cape. 2018.
Irvine, Derry. *Human Rights, Constitutional law and the development of the English legal system: selected essays.* Oxford: Hart Publishing. 2003.
Jones, Janet. *Labour of love: The 'partly-political' diary of a cabinet minister's wife.* London: Politico's. 1999.
Kenny, Michael. *The politics of English Nationhood.* Oxford: Oxford University Press. 2014.
King, Anthony. *Does the United Kingdom still have a constitution?* London: Sweet and Maxwell. 2001.
——. *The British Constitution.* Oxford: Oxford University Press. 2007.
McDonald, Andrew (ed). *Reinventing Britain: Constitutional change under New Labour.* London: Methuen. 2007.
Major, John. *The autobiography.* London: Harper Collins. 1999.
Mandelson, Peter. *The Blair revolution revisited.* London: Politico's. 2002.
Mitchell, James. *The Scottish question.* Oxford: Oxford University Press. 2014.
Morrison, John. *Reforming Britain: New Labour, new constitution?* Edinburgh: Pearson Education. 2001.
O'Rourke, Kevin. *A short history of Brexit.* London: Pelican. 2019.
Rawnsley, Andrew. *Servants of the people: The inside story of New Labour.* London: Penguin. 2001.
Reynolds, David. *Island stories: Britain and its history in the age of Brexit.* London: William Collins. 2019.
Seldon, Anthony (ed). *The Blair effect: The Blair Government 1997–2001.* London: Little, Brown. 2001.
Sutherland, Keith. *The rape of the constitution?* Thorverton: Imprint Academic. 2000.
Rentoul, John. *Tony Blair: Prime Minister.* London: Time Warner. 2002.
Seldon, Anthony and Kavanagh, Dennis (eds). *The Blair effect 2001–5.* Cambridge: Cambridge University Press. 2005.
—— and Lodge, Guy. *Brown at 10.* London: Biteback. 2010.

Trench, Alan (ed). *The dynamics of devolution: The state of the nation 2005.* Exeter: Imprint Academic. 2005.
Trevor-Roper, Hugh. *The invention of Scotland.* New Haven: Yale University Press. 2008.
Trewin, Ion (ed). *The Hugo Young papers: Thirty years of British politics – off the record.* London: Allen Lane. 2008.
Waldegrave, William. *Three circles into one.* London: Mensch. 2019.

III. Canada

Atwood, Margaret. *Survival: A Thematic Guide to Canadian Literature.* Toronto: McClelland and Stewart. 2004.
Axworthy, Thomas S and Trudeau, Pierre Elliott (eds). *Towards a just society: The Trudeau years.* Toronto: Penguin. 2000.
Burelle, André. *Pierre Elliott Trudeau: L'intellectuel et le politique.* Montreal: Editions Fides. 2005.
Canadian Ministry of Supply and Services. *A time for action: Towards the renewal of the Canadian federation.* Ottawa: Canadian Ministry of Supply and Services. 1978.
Clark, Joe. *A nation too good to lose: Renewing the purpose of Canada.* Toronto: Key Porter Books. 1994.
Fraser, Graham. *Sorry, I don't speak French: Confronting the Canadian crisis that won't go away.* Toronto: McClelland and Stewart. 2006.
Lamontagne, Maurice. *Le Federalisme Canadien: Evolution et problemes.* Sainte-Foy: Presses de l'Université Laval. 1954.
McRoberts, Kenneth. *Misconceiving Canada: The Struggle for National Unity.* Toronto: Oxford University Press. 1997.
Nemni, Max and Monique. *Young Trudeau: Son of Quebec, Father of Canada, 1919–1944, vol.1.* Toronto: McClelland and Stewart. 2006.
Oliver, Peter C. *The Constitution of Independence: The Development of Constitutional Theory in Australia, Canada and New Zealand.* Oxford: Oxford University Press. 2005.
Pelletier, Gerard (ed). *Pierre Elliott Trudeau: Against the tide: Selected writings 1939–1996.* Toronto: McClelland and Stewart. 1996.
Russell, Peter H. *Constitutional Odyssey: Can Canadians become a sovereign people?* Toronto: University of Toronto Press. 2004.
Taskforce on Canadian Unity. *A future together: Observations and recommendations.* Hull, Ottawa: Canadian Ministry of Supply and Services. 1979.
Trudeau, Pierre Elliott. 'The values of a just society' in Thomas S Axworthy and Pierre Elliott Trudeau (eds), *Towards a Just Society: The Trudeau Years.* Toronto: Penguin. 2000.
——. *A Canadian Charter of Human Rights.* Ottawa: Information Canada. 1968.
——. *Federalism and the French Canadians.* Toronto: Macmillan of Canada. 1968.
Webber, Jeremy. *Reimagining Canada: Language, Culture, Community and the Canadian Constitution.* Kingston and Montreal: McGill-Queen's University Press. 1994.

IV. Australia

Atkinson, Alan. *The Muddle-Headed Republic.* Oxford: Oxford University Press. 1993.
Hirst, John. *A Republican Manifesto.* Oxford: Oxford University Press. 1994.
Howard, John. *Lazarus rising: A personal and political autobiography.* Sydney: Harper Collins. 2010.
Jones, Kerry. *The People's Protest: Being a true and accurate account of the Republic debate, 1992–1999 and the Republic Referendum.* Sydney: ACM Publishing. 2000.

Kelly, Paul. *The March of Patriots: The Struggle for Modern Australia*. Carlton, Victoria: Melbourne University Press. 2009.

——. *Triumph and demise: The broken promise of a Labor generation*. Carlton, Victoria: Melbourne University Press. 2014.

Keneally, Thomas. *Our Republic*. Port Melbourne: William Heinemann Australia. 1993.

Manning, Paddy. *Born to rule: The unauthorised biography of Malcolm Turnbull*. Carlton, Victoria: Melbourne University Press. 2015.

O'Brien, Kerry. *Keating*. Sydney: Allen and Unwin. 2015.

Republic Advisory Committee. *An Australian Republic: The Options – the report*. Canberra: Australian Government Publishing Service. 1993.

Smith, David. *Head of State: The Governor-General, the Monarchy, the Republic and the Dismissal*. Sydney: Macleay Press. 2005.

Turnbull, Malcolm. *Fighting for the Republic: The Ultimate Insider's Account*. South Yarra: Hardie Grant Books. 1999.

——. *A Bigger Picture*. Richmond, Victoria: Hardie Grant Books. 2020.

Vizard, Steve. *Two Weeks in Lilliput: Bear-Baiting and Backbiting at the Constitutional Convention*. Ringwood, Victoria: Penguin. 1998.

Warhurst, John and Mackerras, Malcolm (eds). *Constitutional politics: The Republic referendum and the future*. St Lucia, Queensland: University of Queensland Press. 2002.

Watson, Don. *Recollections of a Bleeding Heart: A Portrait of Paul Keating PM*. Milsons Point, NSW: Vintage. 2003.

V. Other Countries

Balfour, Sebastian and Quiroga Alejandro. *The reinvention of Spain: Nation and identity since democracy*. Oxford: Oxford University Press. 2007.

Bernhard, Michael and Kubik, Jan. *Twenty years after communism: The politics of memory and commemoration*. Oxford: Oxford University Press. 2014.

Elliott, JH. *Scots and Catalans: Union and Disunion*. New Haven: Yale University Press. 2018.

Elster, Jon; Offe, Claus; Preuss, Ulrich K. *Institutional Design in Post-Communist Societies: Rebuilding the Ship at Sea*. New York: Cambridge University Press. 1998.

Epp, Charles R. *The Rights Revolution: Lawyers, Activists, and Supreme Courts in Comparative Perspective*. Chicago: University of Chicago Press. 1998.

Huntington, Samuel P. *Who are we? The Challenges to America's Identity*. New York: Simon and Schuster. 2004.

Kamen, Henry. *Imagining Spain: Historical myth and national identity*. New Haven: Yale University Press. 2008.

Ostrovsky, Arkady. *The invention of Russia: The journey from Gorbachev's freedom to Putin's war*. London: Atlantic. 2015.

Persily, Nathaniel; Citrin, Jack; and Egan, Patrick J. *Public opinion and constitutional controversy*. New York: Oxford University Press. 2008.

Slaughter, Anne-Marie. *The Idea that is America*. New York: Basic Books. 2007.

Snyder, Timothy. *The road to unfreedom: Russia, Europe, America*. London: Bodley Head. 2018.

——. *The reconstruction of nations: Poland, Ukraine, Lithuania, Belarus, 1569–1999*. New Haven: Yale University Press. 2003.

Suny, Ronald Grigor and Martin, Terry (eds). *A state of nations: Empire and nation-making in the age of Lenin and Stalin*. Oxford: Oxford University Press. 2001.

INDEX

A

Australian republicanism

see also **Canada – patriation of the constitution**; **United Kingdom**

ACM as principal opponents, 154–6

Canberra Convention 1998

ARM's dirigiste approach, 170–2

'clear' if not majority view expressed by Convention, 172–3

declaration of election results, 171

experiment in participative democracy, 169–70

choice between direct and indirect election, 153

conjuring up of new national vision, 14–15

future prospects for republicanism

misalignment between elite and electorate, 190–1

need for different republican solutions, 189–90

re-emergence of ARM, 187–8

relegation of issue by successive Prime Ministers, 188

search for lessons from 1999, 188–9

talk of a third way, 190

Horne's focus on the attainable, 153–4

Howard and the impact of his election victory

attachment to monarchy as strategic necessity, 168

brilliant tactician, 167

clear endorsement of policy, 166

comparisons with Menzies, 167

criticisms of partisanship, 169

emphasis on multiculturalism, 167–8

'nationalisation' of Liberal Party, 168

Keating's response to RAC report

appointment of Committee of Experts, 163–4

de;lay in announcing government policy, 165–6

establishment of Cabinet Committee, 162–3

Howard's commitment to people's convention, 165

response to Committee of Experts, 164–5

launching of ARM, 151–2

lessons for reformers

Keating's failures, 221–2

need for better preparation and popular engagement, 223–5

media's welcome of new venture, 152–3

national myths and symbols

Keating's desire to modernise Australian identity, 191–3

national war memorial, 12

need to avoid identity politics and constitutional reform, 191–3

Paul Keating as Prime Minister

consequences of his endorsement of republicanism, 158

development of Big Picture, 157–8

key values, 156

from Question Time tirade in February to declaration in July, 157

promising start at Sydney lunch 1990, 150

rationale for choice as case study, 5–9

reasons for referendum No vote

absence of defined problem to be solved, 181

contradiction with post-modern notion of nation states, 180

contradictions in the republican proposition itself, 179–80

exercise in identity politics exercise in identity politics, 181–2

pattern of social and economic division, 179

political mismanagement, 178–9

process and of tactics, 178

story of attack and counter-attack between Right and Liberals, 185–7

tensions over multiculuralism, 184–5

Turnbull's skirmish with preamble to new constitution, 182–3

referendum campaign and rejection of republicanism

campaign debates, 173–4

heavy defeat for republicans, 177

No team approach, 174–5
republican protests at Howard's interventions, 175–7
Turnbull's influence for No vote, 177
Yes team approach, 174
referendum on Republic under coalition government, 5
Republic Advisory Committee (RAC)
appointment by Keating, 160
challenges facing the republicans, 160–1
domination of proceedings by Turnbull, Winterton and Hirst, 160
final report, 162
Hirst's proposal for new preamble to the constitution, 161
Monarchist responses, 161–2
public indifference, 162
search for civic renewal, 153
searching for patterns and common themes
character and future of the nations, 217–18
impact of social change, 218
national identity, 217
search for a new nationalism, 218–21
support for republicanism under Keating, 4–5
underlying proposition, 150

B
Brexit
immediate consequences, 203–4
impact on Blair reforms, 194, 217
nature of Britishness, 14
new energy for unifying purpose, 206–7
opportunity to explore past and consider future, 10
realignment of political allegiances, 229
role of populist nationalism, 208
significance to historians and political scientists historians and political scientists, 1
strain placed on 'shared political culture, 205
'take back control' referendum slogan, 202

C
Canada - patriation of the constitution
see also **Australian republicanism**
aftermath of November conference 1981
Charter of Rights and Freedoms, 140–1
merits and consequences of package, 140
passing of Canada Act in March 1982, 139–40
Québécois response, 141–2
return of Chrétien as PM, 142
Canada's coming of age under Trudeau, 88–9
Charter of Rights and Freedoms, 3–4, 140–1
Confederation of Tomorrow conference 1968, 89, 101–2
consequences of patriation deal
complex balance sheet, 143–5
consideration of alternatives, 146–7
effect of entrenched constitution, 143–5
instability inherent in Canadian federation, 148
price paid for speedy settlement, 145–6
promotion by Ottowa, 142–3
Trudeau's essay in nation-building, 147–8
vindication of Trudeau, 143
failure of Clark's government, 111
failure of early attempts, 101
impact of PQ's dramatic election victory 1976
contention and ensuing troubles, 108–10
dilution of executive federalism, 107
priority to save nation from dissolution, 106
publication of *Time for Action*, 107–8
Task Force on Canadian Unity, 106–7
Trudeau on the back foot, 110
two new nation-building projects, 105–6
lessons for reformers
need for better preparation and popular engagement, 223–5
re-working of national myths, 228
Trudeau's success, 222
November conference 1981 and Trudeau's last attempt at a deal
breaking of logjam by Trudeau, 132–3
compromise by Ottowa and nine provinces, 137–9
differences of interpretation, 129
doctrine of 'substantive consent', 130–1
early discussions, 129–30
efforts to make deal more palatable in Quebec, 137
emergence of a deal, 134–6
final closed session, 133–4
from lack of inspiration and novelty to substantive negotiations, 131
popular support for patriation, 130
responses to deal from interest groups, 136–7
Trudeau's pressure on premiers, 130
Pierre Trudeau the man
academic influences, 92–3
commitment to personalism, 93–4

importance of language rights, 95–6
liberal in Lockean tradition, 93
the nation and its future, 97–101
one of the 'three wise men' from Quebec, 92
opposition to ethnic nationalism, 94–5
status of Indigenous Peoples, 96–7
views on fundamental rights, 94
Quebec referendum
Ryan as head of 'No' campaign, 113–14
Trudeau's final chance, 112–13
Trudeau's four direct interventions, 114–15
rationale for choice as case study, 5–9
reform in the wake of 'No' vote
Chrétien tour of country, 115–16
negotiating position of provinces, 119–20
political impact of vote, 116
redistribution of powers, 118
revival of Continuing Committee of Ministers on the Constitution, 118
Trudeau's three-fold gamble, 116–17
searching for patterns and common themes
character and future of the nations, 217–18
impact of social change, 218
national identity, 217
search for a new nationalism, 218–21
sesquicentenary celebrations, 148–9
stalling of momentum after Victoria, 104–5
sustainability as a nation
challenges to French and English colonialism, 90–1
fears of Anglo-Tories, 90
growing force of separatism, 90
inexorable lure of the US, 89–90
Trudeau's final chance
invitation to Broadbent, 112
National Energy Program (NEP), 111
new team to run Ottawa's strategic approach, 112–13
Trudeau's invitation to provincial premiers in 1975, 104–5
Trudeau's lone attempts at a deal
April accord, 124–5
concessions to interest groups, 126
Joint Committee of both houses, 126–7
Lougheed as leader of Gang of Eight, 124
mixed fortunes of court challenges, 125–9
outcome of September conference, 120–1
rachetting up of pressure on provinces, 121–2
response from responses, 122–4
Trudeau's response to court 'meddling', 129
Trudeau's national unity strategy, 97–101
Victoria conference 1971, 102–4
Case studies, 5–9
Citizenship
Australia
ceremonies for new citizens, 191
Citizens for Democracy, 153
Committee of Experts, 192
Commonwealth grant, 163
debt of loyalty to Australia, 184
three core values, 193
Canada
publication of *Time for Action*, 108
support from federalism, 98
Trudeau's Lockean beliefs, 93
debates on the future of Britain, 213
Hungary, 16
searching for patterns and common themes, 218
UK Labour Party's constitutional reform programme
assessment of New Labour reforms, 86
assessment of New Labour's first term, 77
Cook-Maclennan; talks with Liberal Democrats, 54
Foundation 1989, 33
Labour's maximalism during 1987 Parliament, 29
New Labour's modified stance on reform, 46–7
New Labour's second term, 81–2
New Labour's third term – Blair's final years, 85–6
policy-making in wake of 1992 defeat, 33
UK reform under Brown, 196, 199–200
Coalition politics
Australia
Paul Keating as Prime Minister, 156–62
referendum on Republican government, 5
Canada, 112
UK Labour Party's constitutional reform programme
Cook-Maclennan; talks with Liberal Democrats, 49–56
turning point in relations with the Liberal Democrats, 73–5
UK reform under coalition government
Conservative concerns about devolution, 202–3
increased accent on Euro-scepticism in Conservative manifesto, 201–2
necessary compromise, 201
need to 'clean up Westminster', 200

Communitarianism, 40
Comparative studies
examples of constitutional reforms, 3
methodology, 21–2
rationale for choice of case studies, 5–9
Constitutional reform
Australia *see* **Australia**
Canada *see* **Canada**
challenge to a coherent national identity from diversity, 22–3
comparative studies, 3
future of constitutional reform
encouragement to think about nation and national identity, 229–31
need for public support and partnership, 231–2
growing importance of national identity, 1–2, 15–21
lessons for reformers, 221–6
national identity
change to an unknowable goal, 227
disputes over characterisation, 227
nature of reformer's ambition, 227–8
preferred tool of reformers, 229
re-working of national myths, 228
retrospective rationalisation in the case of UK, 228–9
something that is experienced, 227
nature of reformer's ambition, 226–7
rationale for choice of case studies, 5–9
searching for patterns and common themes
character and future of the nations, 217–18
impact of social change, 218
messy, noisy business, 216–17
national identity, 217
search for a new nationalism, 218–21
United Kingdom *see* **United Kingdom**

D
Decentralisation
see also **Federalism**
Canada
1975 premiers conference, 105
preference for Lévesque's vision of Canada, 116
Quebec's demands, 104
Trudeau's opposition to, 98–9, 114–15
Labour Party's constitutional reform programme
assessment of New Labour's first term, 76
Cook-Maclennan; talks with Liberal Democrats, 55
manifesto of 2001, 78–9
New Labour's second term, 80–1
New Labour's third term – Blair's final years, 84
Labour's maximalism during 1987 Parliament, 28
New Labour's modified stance on reform, 42–3, 46
UK
Charter 88 Democracy campaign, 55
Power Inquiry 2006, 194
United Kingdom, 195
Brown's commitment to constitutional reform, 194–6
Devolution
constitutional reform under coalition government
Conservative concerns about devolution, 202–3
West Lothian question, 200–1
debates on the future of Britain, 212–13
impact of Brexit, 203–4
Labour Party's constitutional reform programme
assessment of New Labour reforms, 86
assessment of New Labour's first term, 77
Blair's first Cabinet post, 59
Cook-Maclennan; talks with Liberal Democrats, 51–2
Labour's maximalism during 1987 Parliament, 30
New Labour government committees, 60
New Labour – May 1997 to November 1998, 62–3
New Labour – November 1998 to November 1999, 72–3
New Labour's first Queen's speech first Queen's Speech, 60, 60–1
New Labour's modified stance on reform, 44–6
New Labour's third term – Blair's final years, 85
Labour's maximalism during 1987 Parliament, 28
lessons for reformers, 223, 225–6
public engagement in New Labour's reforms, 208–9
public reaction to New Labour reforms, 211–12

E
Executive federalism *see* **Canada – patriation of the constitution**

F
Federalism
see also **Decentralisation**
distribution of powers, 89
isolation of Quebec, 89
need for a defining theme, 92
Pierre Trudeau's vision of the future, 97–102
search for common purpose, 90
seeking out of new symbols, 91
A Time for Action, 108
Trudeau's subsequent belief in one national community, 117
Freedom of information
absence from New Labour's first Queen's speech first Queen's Speech, 61
lack of interest under New Labour's modified stance on reform, 42
New Labour – May 1997 to November 1998, 67–8
New Labour – November 1998 to November 1999, 72–3
New Labour – November 1999 to June 2001, 75
policies under New Labour, 38
reform under first Blair administration, 2–3
Fundamental rights
see also **Indigenous peoples**
Canada
Charter of Rights and Freedoms, 3–4, 140–1
Trudeau's views on fundamental rights, 94
Canada and Australia compared, 217
public engagement in New Labour's reforms, 210
UK Labour Party's constitutional reform programme
Cook-Maclennan; talks with Liberal Democrats, 55
Labour's maximalism during 1987 Parliament, 28–30
Labour's policy-making in wake of 1992 defeat, 32–3
UK reform under Brown, 198–9
UK reform under coalition government, 200

H
'History wars', 2, 8, 183, 185–6, 201
House of Lords reform
early compromise, 3
Labour Party's constitutional reform programme
assessment of New Labour's first term, 77
Cook-Maclennan; talks with Liberal Democrats, 52–3, 55
manifesto of 2001, 78
New Labour government committees, 60
New Labour – May 1997 to November 1998, 64–5
New Labour – November 1998 to November 1999, 69–70
New Labour – November 1999 to June 2001, 75–6
New Labour's modified stance on reform, 43–4
New Labour's second term, 80
New Labour's third term – Blair's final years, 84–5
renewed programme audit in preparation for 1997 election, 56
Human rights
see also **Indigenous peoples**
Canada's Charter of Rights and Freedoms, 102
constitutional reform under first Blair administration, 2–3
impact of Brexit, 204
Labour Party's constitutional reform programme
assessment of New Labour reforms, 86
assessment of New Labour's first term, 77
Cook-Maclennan; talks with Liberal Democrats, 52–3
New Labour government committees, 60
New Labour – May 1997 to November 1998, 63–4, 68
New Labour's first Queen's speech first Queen's Speech, 60–1
New Labour's second term, 82–3
New Labour's third term – Blair's final years, 85
renewed programme audit in preparation for 1997 election, 56
Labour's policy-making in wake of 1992 defeat, 33
New Labour's modified stance on reform, 42–3
policies under New Labour, 36, 38
public engagement in New Labour's reforms, 210
public reaction to New Labour reforms, 212

UK reform under coalition government, 200–1
UK's search for a new nationalism, 220

I

Identity *see* **National identity**
Independence *see* **Australian republicanism; Patriation of Canadian constitution**
Indigenous peoples
Australia
Australian Republican Movement (ARM), 151, 180
Blainey's counter-attack, 185
criticisms of ALP, 176
Keating's Big Picture, 157
Mabo case, 185
national identity, 230
RAC's struggles, 182–3
rationale for choice of case studies, 4, 6, 8
tension in Howard's government, 184
Canada
Canadian Charter of Human Rights, 102
Charlottetown Accord, 142, 224
constitution signed on 12 April 1982, 148–9
demands for self-determination, 92
impact of oil-boom in Alberta, 89
impact of PQ's dramatic election victory 1976, 107–8
inherent right to self-government, 146
Joint Committee proposals, 136–7
liberal lobbying operation, 120, 127
oppression by early colonialists, 91
publication of *Time for Action*, 108
rejection of terms offered, 147
Trudeau's resistance to special status, 96–7
UK's continuing responsibilities, 139
preoccupation for reformists, 217–18
rationale for choice of case studies, 6
support for republicanism under Keating, 4

J

Joint Consultative Committee on Constitutional Reform (JCCCR), 65–6, 74
Judiciary
impact of Brexit, 204
Labour's maximalism during 1987 Parliament, 29
New Labour's second term
abolition of Lord Chancellor, 83
creation of a Supreme Court, 83–4
spats with Lord Chief Justice, 83
rationale for choice of case studies, 5–6
reform under first Blair administration, 3

K

Kilbrandon Commission, 25

L

Liberal democracies
commonalities of constitutional reform, 216
rationale for choice of case studies, 8–9
threat of populism, 208
Local government *see* **Decentralisation**

M

Multiculturalism
Australia
flashpoint in debate, 183–7, 220
Howard and the impact of his election victory, 167–8
Howard attempt to remake the Liberals, 167
Keating's vision of the future, 4, 157–8
Canada
Constitution signed on 12 april 1982, 148
elaborate national unity strategy, 97
language rights, 108, 127
need for 'founding' peoples to prosper, 100
Trudeau's commitment, 95
Trudeau's political and constitutional legacy, 149
global truths, 230
liberalism embraced by Canada and UK, 6
United Kingdom
Britain in the twenty-first century, 13–14
challenge posed by rapid immigration, 87
CRE group report, 206
debates on the future of Britain, 214–15
reason to stick together, 214
Myths and symbols *see* **National myths and symbols**

N

Nation states
defined, 9–11
Labour Party's constitutional reform programme, 34–5
Labour's ambiguous relationship, 1–2
National identity
Australia
attempts to refashion republicanism, 150

need to avoid identity politics and constitutional reform, 191–3
reasons for Australia's referendum No vote, 181–2
Canada
challenges to French and English colonialism, 90–1
fears of Anglo-Tories, 90
growing force of separatism, 90
inexorable lure of the US, 89–90
challenge to a coherent national identity from diversity, 22–3
conjuring up of new national vision, 14–15
debate over the nature of Britishness, 14
debates on the future of Britain, 212
future of constitutional reform, 229–31
hybrid representation, 230
impact of Brexit, 203–4
'lie that binds', 13–14
link with constitutional reform, 1–2, 15–21
nation as an imagined community, 15
rationale for choice of case studies, 6–8
re-engineering as part of reform
change to an unknowable goal, 227
disputes over characterisation, 227
nature of reformer's ambition, 227–8
preferred tool of reformers, 229
re-working of national myths, 228
retrospective rationalisation in the case of UK, 228–9
something that is experienced, 227
searching for patterns and common themes, 218–21
UK Labour Party's constitutional reform programme
approach to the nation state and national identity, 34–5
problems with social cohesion and racism, 86–7
UK reform under Brown
Brown's commitment to constitutional reform, 194–5
national debate about the nature of Britishness, 196–7
what might come next for the British constitution, 207–8
National myths and symbols
Australia
Keating's desire to modernise Australian identity, 191–3
war memorial, 12, 191–2
Canada
Charter of Rights and Freedoms, 89
language, 96
new symbols sought by Canadian federalists, 91
Trudeau's call for national symbols, 99
conjuring up of new national vision, 14–15
critical acceptance, 12–13
importance, 228
messages conveyed, 11
New Labour manifesto 1997, 57
significance, 11
social utility, 13
Nationalism
attempts to recover nation state, 1–2
Australian republicanism, 181
Canada
competition from federalism, 98
Trudeau's opposition to ethnic nationalism, 94–5
search for a new nationalism, 218–21
what might come next for the British constitution, 205–6
Nations
defined, 9–11
future of constitutional reform, 229–31
Pierre Trudeau's vision of the future, 97–101
rationale for choice of case studies, 6
reasons for Australia's referendum No vote, 180
UK debate about nature of Britishness, 196–7
what might come next for the British constitution, 206–7
Northern Ireland *see* **Devolution**

P
Proportional representation
early Labour support, 20
Labour Party's constitutional reform programme
assessment of New Labour's first term, 76
Cook-Maclennan; talks with Liberal Democrats, 53
Labour's maximalism during 1987 Parliament, 31
Labour's policy-making in wake of 1992 defeat, 33
manifesto of 2001, 78
New Labour – May 1997 to November 1998, 66, 66–7
New Labour – November 1998 to November 1999, 70–3, 73

New Labour – November 1999 to June 2001, 75
New Labour's modified stance on reform, 44
New Labour's second term, 79–80
New Labour's third term – Blair's final years, 84–5
renewed programme audit in preparation for 1997 election, 56
turning point in relations with the Liberal Democrats, 74–5
loss of Labour support after WW1, 25
New Labour's proposal for a single transferable Vote, 70
Power Inquiry 2006, 195
public reaction to New Labour reforms, 212
reform under first Blair administration, 2–3
Scottish Labour, 30
Social Democratic Party, 26
UK reform under Brown, 195
UK reform under coalition government, 200–1

R

Regional government *see* **Decentralisation**
Republicanism *see* **Australian republicanism**

S

Scotland *see* **Devolution**
Sovereignty *see* **Australian republicanism; Patriation of Canadian constitution**
Supreme Court
challenges to Canadian patriation, 127–9
reform under first Blair administration, 2–3
Symbols *see* **National myths and symbols**

U

United Kingdom
see also **Australian republicanism; Canada – patriation of the constitution**
constitutional reform under Brown
attempts to fuse reform with national renewal, 215
Bill of Rights and Responsibilities, 198–9
Brown's commitment to constitutional reform, 194–6
Constitutional Renewal Bill, 199
failed attempt, 199–200
national debate about the nature of Britishness, 196–7
constitutional reform under coalition government
Conservative concerns about devolution, 202–3
increased accent on Euro-scepticism in Conservative manifesto, 201–2
necessary compromise, 201
need to 'clean up Westminster', 200
debate over the nature of Britishness, 14
debates on the future of Britain
citizenship, 213
devolution, 212–13
importance of Irvine's lecture in 2000, 213–14
national identity, 212
need to work together, 214
rejection of liberal multiculturalism, 214–15
first Blair administration, 2–3
impact of Brexit
challenges to national identity, 203–4
New Labour's enduring constitutional settlement, 203
renewed Conservative disunity, 203
Labour Party's constitutional reform programme
approach to the nation state and national identity, 34–5
assessment of New Labour reforms, 86–7
assessment of New Labour's first term, 76–7
breaks from the past, 25–6
Cook-Maclennan; talks with Liberal Democrats, 49–56
election campaign 1997, 58–9
election success and into government, 59–62
failed attacks by Tory politicians, 24–5
lessons for reformers, 222–3
manifesto of 2001, 78–9
maximalism during 1987 Parliament, 28–32
New Labour – May 1997 to November 1998, 62–8
New Labour, New Danger campaign by Tories, 48–9
New Labour – November 1998 to November 1999, 68–73
New Labour – November 1999 to June 2001, 75–6
New Labour's modified stance on reform, 42–8
New Labour's second term, 79–84
New Labour's third term – Blair's final years, 84–6
origins of maximalist approach, 26–8
policies under New Labour, 35–41

policy-making in wake of 1992 defeat, 32–4
principal players, 41–2
renewed programme audit in preparation for 1997 election, 56–8
turning point in relations with the Liberal Democrats, 73–5
lessons for reformers
easier to mount a defence against than secure approval, 226
Labour Party's constitutional reform programme, 222–3
need for better preparation and popular engagement, 223–6
link between national identity and constitutional reform, 15, 21
nation as an imagined community, 15
public engagement in New Labour's reforms
Bill of Rights and Responsibilities, 210
devolution, 208–9
fundamental choice about the public's engagement, 210
Government reticence to generate public debate, 209
late attempts to develop its explanatory story, 209
public reaction to New Labour reforms, 211–12
rationale for choice as case study, 5–9
re-engineering of national identity, 228–9
searching for patterns and common themes
character and future of the nations, 217–18
impact of social change, 218
national identity, 217
search for a new nationalism, 218–21
what might come next for the British constitution
de-alignment and re-alignment of party loyalties, 205
effect of multiple nationalisms, 205–6
national identity, 207–8
need to codify constitution, 208

V

Voting reform *see* **Proportional representation**

W

Wales *see* **Devolution**

www.ingramcontent.com/pod-product-compliance
Ingram Content Group UK Ltd.
Pitfield, Milton Keynes, MK11 3LW, UK
UKHW020801290926
15470UKWH00003B/896

9 781509 928729